WAR TOURIST

MEMOIRS OF A FOREIGN CORRESPONDENT

HILARY BROWN

◆ FriesenPress

Suite 300 - 990 Fort St
Victoria, BC, V8V 3K2
Canada

www.friesenpress.com

Front Cover Photo
The Author and a unit of the Israeli Defense Force,
South Lebanon, 1982

Copyright © 2021 by Hilary Brown
First Edition — 2021

All rights reserved.

No part of this publication may be reproduced in any form, or by any means, electronic or mechanical, including photocopying, recording, or any information browsing, storage, or retrieval system, without permission in writing from FriesenPress.

ISBN
978-1-03-910415-0 (Hardcover)
978-1-03-910414-3 (Paperback)
978-1-03-910416-7 (eBook)

1. BIOGRAPHY & AUTOBIOGRAPHY, EDITORS, JOURNALISTS, PUBLISHERS

Distributed to the trade by The Ingram Book Company

"Foreign correspondents are like war tourists in flak jackets. They document human misery and then move on."

For the three most important men in my life:
John, Jonathan, and Jimmy.

"Most lives vanish. A person dies, and little by little all traces of that life disappear."

—Paul Auster, *The Brooklyn Follies*

Contents

Prologue: Just a Blonde — xi
1: Iran 1979: Close Call — 1
2: Small Town in Ontario — 7
3: Svengali — 12
4: The Great Canadian West — 17
5: London, The World — 20
6: Paris: The City of Light — 25
7: Montreal and Live Television — 32
8: New York, New York — 38
9: The Call of the Sea — 45
10: Love on the Open Atlantic — 50
11: Ottawa: TV News at Last — 58
12: Persepolis and the Himalayas — 67
13: Pakistan: Love and War — 75
14: A Short Goodbye — 84
15: A Long Engagement — 88
16: Our Life in Persia — 97
17: Persona Non Grata — 111
18: The Yom Kippur War — 127
19: The Best Job in the World — 139
20: Turkey, and the Invasion of Cyprus — 145
21: London, Cyprus, and the Occasional Hot Spot — 153
22: The Fall of Saigon — 159
23: The Vietnam Effect — 171
24: Alone Again — 182
25: Marriage, the Unspeakable Folly — 188

26: Paris Again	192
27: Dash to Africa	199
28: Israel, Jonathan, and the Best Years of our Lives	206
29: Washington, D.C.	215
30: New York Again	220
31: El Salvador: Slings and Arrows	226
32: Lebanon	230
33: Roman Holiday	234
34: Toronto: Anchorwoman, or Death by Hairspray	237
35: Fool's Paradise	253
36: Reversal of Fortune	267
37: The Wheel Turns	273
38: Bosnia: My Tenth War	285
39: Happy Again	296
40: "You Don't Really Know Me"	305
41: Two Genocides	311
42: The Very Worst … and the Very Best	321
43: Bhutan: The Country of Gross National Happiness	334
44: It Can't Get Better Than This	346
45: The Black Dog	354
46: All Roads Lead to Rome	373
47: The Greatest Gift of All	384
48: Iraq, and My Love is Gone	392
49: Regeneration	407
50: The Fountain of Youth is Love	419
Acknowledgements	440
Endnotes	441
Author Bio	448
Index	450

Prologue

JUST A BLONDE

Montreal, Quebec, in the late sixties, back in the Stone Age. I'm anchoring a truly terrible lunchtime TV show for the Canadian Broadcasting Corporation (CBC), mainly interviewing the sort of people who turn Javex bottles into piggy banks. I'm also co-hosting a current affairs program on CBC Radio, for which I'm actually required to use my brain, such as it is.

One of the program's regulars is a highbrow film and theatre critic—I'll call her Magda—whose breathless child-woman voice belies her colossal size and ego. We are not buddies. In fact, she rarely speaks to me.

That doesn't matter, since I spend most of my time dreaming of becoming a foreign correspondent. I want to get out of this safe little sinecure in Montreal and cover wars, revolution, general mayhem! But I can't get beyond the office of CBC TV's top news executive, where I'm subjected to a bad imitation of Humphrey Bogart.

"Aw sweetie, I couldn't put a dame like you in harm's way," he drawls, feet on desk, pulling on a cigarette. "If anything happened to you, my ass would be in a sling, ya know what I mean?" he goes on, blowing a cloud of smoke in my face.

Seven years later I'm in London, England, doing what I'd longed to do. I'm the first female foreign correspondent for ABC News, covering wars, revolution, and general mayhem. I'm in love, sharing a house in Regent's Park with a manly Englishman of rugged good looks, later described as "more John Wayne than Gregory Peck."[1]

Out of the blue I get a call from Magda, whom I still remember—probably because of the breathless voice and patronizing manner.

"I'm coming to London and I need to rent a room," she gushes. "I've heard you're living there now." Obviously, she wants to stay in my apartment—for free. Meaningful pause. "So tell me," she goes on, "what have you been doing?" implying that it was probably . . . not very much.

Perhaps because this pretentious woman had always made me feel stupid, I tell her who I'm working for, what my job is, all the big foreign stories I've covered: the Portuguese Revolution, the Turkish Invasion of Cyprus, the Fall of Saigon, and so on.

Another pause. Then the child-woman voice comes back.

"Funny," she says. "I always thought you were just a blonde."

1

IRAN 1979: CLOSE CALL

"Hilly, the place is on *fire* and the streets are full of raving lunatics baying for the blood of *all* Americans. It is absolute *madness* for you to go there!"

John was addressing me in his usual mild-mannered way as he cradled our new baby in his arms. Jonathan was four months old, and John was introducing our son to the music of Handel on the record player while he fed him.

"But I'm not an American, I'm *Canadian*. I just *work* for the Americans!" I cried, as if a mob of hysterical Iranian demonstrators could tell the difference.

"You think those crazies are going to politely ask you for your passport, then *cancel* their plans to tear you limb from delectable limb? How do you feel about the tooth fairy, for Chrissake?" John carefully removed the tip of the empty bottle from Jonnie's mouth.

The problem was, John almost always knew what he was talking about, so he was almost always right. And as far as he was concerned, even when he was wrong he was right. In the end he usually let me get my own way. In this case, I came very close to getting killed because of it.

We were in our charming rented house in Herzliya Pituach, north of Tel Aviv, close to the sea, and it was late November 1979. I was the Tel Aviv correspondent for a major American television network. John worked for the British Broadcasting Corporation (BBC). Three weeks before, on November 4, 1979, several hundred Iranian "students" had stormed the U.S. Embassy in Tehran and taken fifty-two American diplomats and military personnel hostage, parading them blindfolded before the TV cameras in a long, excruciating drama that would eventually cost U.S. President Jimmy Carter his re-election.

At first, the new Islamic fundamentalist regime of Ayatollah Khomeini kept most western journalists out of the country. But John had managed to get through. He'd lived and worked in Iran as the BBC's Tehran correspondent in 1972–73, in the bad old days of the Shah. I'd been living with him then, filing freelance radio and press reports, in those first two years of our long life together. John was eventually expelled from Iran for reporting about student unrest, the kind of news the Shah wanted suppressed.

For Khomeini's regime, however, John's expulsion was a distinction. So the first on-scene reports of the seizure of the U.S. Embassy in Tehran, on both British and American TV (NBC picked up his reports), were from my husband, the BBC correspondent John Bierman.

"Darling, I know you don't like to turn down any assignment, but I've *been* there," John said. "I wish you wouldn't go. We've got a baby now! What about Jonnie? It's a mob scene, and we've seen mobs before, remember?"

But as he spoke, he could see—we both could see—that he'd lost the argument. That I was already in that "don't-confuse-me-with-facts-my-mind-is-made-up" mode. I had just come back to work after four months of maternity leave. I was a new mother. But as a reporter I was desperate to prove myself again and get assigned to the biggest story in years.

By then the regime had lifted its ban on foreign journalists, having understood the enormous publicity value of non-stop coverage of its daily public humiliation of the Americans. The men and women of the international press pack were pouring in. The next day I got my gear together, embraced John and our beautiful baby, and flew to Tehran.

Most of the western media worked out of the former Intercontinental Hotel, whose urbane German manager appreciated the importance of alcohol for many reporters, before or after a deadline. Or both. Despite the fundamentalist ban on alcohol, he would arrange for wine and beer to be delivered from his locked storeroom to our workspace, on the condition that we hide the evidence. Within days every equipment case, duffel bag, and Travelpro in our edit suite was bulging with empty cans of Heineken and bottles of Chateau Musar. In the hotel dining room, journalists would make fun of the alcohol ban by "sending back" the water, saying loftily that it was corked.

The first few days were safe enough. We would go down to the gates of the U.S. Embassy for the daily anti-American, anti-Shah demonstrations. The ritualistic chant of "Bad! Bad! Amrika!" would go on for hours. It was always a huge, heaving crowd, demanding that the United States hand over the Shah, who had fled the country on January 16, 1979. After short stays in Egypt, Morocco, the Bahamas, and Mexico, His Imperial Majesty was receiving medical treatment for cancer in the States.

"Bad, bad Amrika! Death to the Carter. Death to the Shah!" the crowd cried, ad nauseam. At one point, the famous Irish correspondent Robert Fisk took it upon himself to correct the demonstrators' English. "No, no, *no*! A proper name does *not* require the definite article!" said Fisky, who wore glasses and always had an academic look about him. "It is 'Death to *Carter*. Death to *the* Shah.' Got that?"

It was a very big story in the United States, and the news shows would often take two or three reports from Iran every day. It was in the early days of tape (as opposed to film) and of transmission by satellite, which meant that you could tape a noon event in Tehran, for example, and transmit it to New York for broadcast at 7 a.m. Eastern. We found it kind of mind-blowing.

Anything, absolutely anything, that happened in the country was a possible news event for us. And that's how I came to be assigned to the northwestern city of Tabriz, to cover what at any other time would have been an obscure insurrection. I flew in with Brian Calvert, a British freelance cameraman, along with a soundman and translator, and we checked in to the best hotel in the town. "Okay, let's go out and commit television!" I said to my team, and we piled into our van to look for the action. We soon found it. An enormous crowd had surrounded the city's TV station, which had been taken over by the followers of a religious leader named Sayyid Mohammad Kazem Shariatmadari, a liberal who was against the involvement of clerics in government. We'd never heard of him, of course. "This looks like some kind of coup," we said to each other. "Let's check out the governor's house." We leapt back into the van and quickly located his mansion, mainly because it was surrounded by an even larger crowd. "I guess we better shoot some of this," I said to Brian. We jumped out of the van and I waded into the crowd, a few steps behind the boys.

I was wearing slacks and a knee-length trench coat but no head scarf. At that time, foreign women were not expected to cover their heads. Or so I thought. Within seconds, a screaming mob of men surrounded me, separated me from my team, and started to maul me. It felt as though every hand was either on, or inside, my body. I thought they were going to literally tear me apart. I was being swept farther and farther away from my crew, who were powerless to help. No one could have got me away from that hysterical rabble—not the police and not the army, if either had been there.

Apart from stark terror, what I felt was guilt. Guilt that I had utterly misread the situation and the mood of this crowd, that I hadn't listened to John, that I had completely let down my beautiful new baby within a few months of bringing him into the world. "My son, my son! How could I *do* this to you?" I cried out as the men pulled at my clothes and pawed every part of my anatomy.

But I did know a few words in Farsi. People in Iran are given to elaborate forms of expression when speaking to strangers and I knew some of these, having picked them up during our two years in Iran earlier in the decade. "Ha-hesh, miconam!" (*I beg you!*) "Hora befarmaid!" (*Please, sir!*) "Rorbun e shoma!" (*I am your sacrificial victim!*) I didn't know how to say "Let me go," but I knew the word for "out." "Biroon! Biroon!" I babbled, over and over again. Suddenly one of the men closest to me stepped *back* to let me go instead of leaning forward to grope me. And everyone else followed. It was a miracle. As quickly as they had surrounded me, one by one they all pulled back, and I got away.

The crew were already in the van, thinking quite rightly that it was the best place to be since there was no way on God's earth they could have rescued me. I scrambled into my seat in a state of shock. I'd been on many dangerous assignments, but I'd never been at the mercy of a fanatical all-male mob.

We decided to retreat to the hotel and shoot the rest of the action from the window as the horde surged past. The hotel was in a large garden, and the management had closed the wrought-iron gates in case the screaming, chanting rabble attacked the building as a symbol of western decadence. The situation was much too volatile. The crowds were completely out of control.

Still shaken, I wrote and recorded a script, leaving out any reference to my near-death experience. Brian fed the track to our workspace in Tehran, along with our videotape. Then we all had a stiff drink from our secret supply of booze.

Later that evening, a friend from the Associated Press (AP) contacted me, wanting to do a story about my experience—which by that time had spread like wildfire through the press corps. He had a "Network-News-Hen-Mauled-by-All-Male-Mob-in-Iran" angle in mind. I said absolutely not. He was annoyed, very annoyed.

I was afraid that if my masters in New York found out about the incident, they would never again assign me to a war or revolution or anything that carried any risk whatsoever.

So there was no story about me. The AP reporter never spoke to me again.

2

SMALL TOWN IN ONTARIO

Childhoods are boring if they're happy; and mine was mainly happy, with loving, civilized British parents, Jocelyn and Tony Brown, and two younger sisters, Virginia (Gingie), and Kathy. The first few years of my life were spent as a spoiled only child in Medicine Hat, Alberta. This was close to a military proving station called Suffield, where my father—an entomologist always known by his initials as Dr. A.W.A. Brown—was part of a high-powered, hush-hush team of British and Canadian scientists experimenting with germ warfare. It was 1943, and British Prime Minister Winston Churchill was worried that the Nazis were working on germs and disease as weapons of war. He wanted the same capability for the Allies, as a form of mutually assured destruction. Dad later received an MBE (Member of the Most Excellent Order of the British Empire) for his work.

After the Second World War, we moved east to the deeply conservative town of London, Ontario. Still in his early thirties, Dad became head of the Zoology Department at Western University, which was terrific . . . for him. Apart from lecturing on genetics and entomology, he had a well-equipped lab to carry out experiments in his special field, which was the control of insects that transmit disease to humans. He would work long hours, come home to supper with the family, and often go back to the lab in the evening.

"You're really a workaholic, aren't you, Dad?" I once asked, trying out a new word I'd just learned. "Well, Hil," he said, smiling down at me from his height of six-foot-four, "if you've lived through the Depression, you're so glad to have a job at all that you'll work all the hours God gives you."

In the summer, he worked as a consultant to foreign governments on what was called vector control, flying to Third World countries to direct eradication programs for malaria, dengue fever, and other forms of pestilence. In his field, he was quite famous.

But for my mother, it must have been pretty bleak, though she never complained. A sweet English rose of a lady, she had grown up in a lively, artistic household with five servants on an exquisite street of eighteenth-century houses called Church Row, in Hampstead, north London. *Not* London, Ontario. London, *the World*. For her marriage, in June 1938, she had a trousseau that included a "late-afternoon dress" and a full-length evening coat. But then she was whisked off for married life in Canada, otherwise known as The Frozen North, where she knew no one. She didn't see her own family again for ten years. Most of the clothes in her trousseau were never worn and ended up in her daughters' dress-up box.

My sisters and I went to public schools (not private), and for reasons best known to the Board of Education I was among a small group of so-called gifted children who at Grade 5 were streamed into a four-year program called The Advancement Classes. I had to ride four miles to school on my bicycle along a busy commercial road, and I was terrified that one of those huge noisy trucks would hit me and kill me. It gave me a phobia of cycling that lasted most of my life.

The Advancement Classes had just two teachers and my favourite was Miss Hooper, a tiny, bird-like creature with blue-rinsed hair. She was one of my early influences. She was full of aphorisms, such as "Always go the second mile" and "To thine own self be true." But the one that got me was "Dare to be a Daniel," an allusion to the biblical story of Daniel in the Lion's Den.

"Dare to be a Daniel, Hilary. D-a-a-re to be a Daniel!" she would cry in a quivering voice, wagging her finger and smiling up at me (at five-foot-ten I was already a giant). "Oh yes I will, Miss Hooper. I will!" I cried back, towering over her.

A puritanical, self-righteous, conformist atmosphere pervaded London, Ontario, in the fifties. John Kenneth Galbraith, the late economist, wrote about it in his book *The Scotch*. He grew up in Southwestern Ontario too, on a farm. His book is full of anecdotes about the priggishness of the people. He describes how he was once home alone when a girl from a neighbouring farm dropped by to visit his sisters. His sisters were out, and he fancied the girl. They walked out to a field, he writes, where a bull was servicing a cow.

"I think it would be fun to do that," he said.

"Well, it's your cow," she replied.[1]

Everybody in London went to church, and for a while my mother thought her children should go too. I remember being cornered after the Sunday service by a large Wagnerian lady with pursed lips: "We haven't seen your *father* come to church lately, have we, Hilary?" If only I'd been able to retort that "My father is a scientist and he doesn't do God." London, Ontario, was a very good place to grow up because you are very motivated . . . *to go somewhere else.*

Because of my height and my unusual name (in the fifties in Southwestern Ontario, the name 'Hilary' was seriously weird), I was often ridiculed in school. For a time I had only one friend, Noelle Grace, who grew up to become a revered pediatric surgeon. We are friends to this day. I was often the target of "anti-Hilary" campaigns by nasty little schoolmates with common little names like Linda-Lou or Bobby-Sue. But at some point I had a kind of epiphany and remember thinking, "You can treat me like this now, but when I grow up, I'm going to be somebody, somewhere. And you're going to be nobody, nowhere!

And then, lo! At the age of fifteen I found . . . freedom! Dad was given a two-year leave of absence from Western to join the World Health Organization in Geneva, Switzerland, working on its malaria program. By then he was a world expert on the Anopheles mosquito, which transmit malaria. That didn't stop us from getting eaten alive by the damn things up at our cottage in Muskoka, however.

Going from a small town in Ontario to an international European city was like going from night to day. My sisters and I went to a famous, fabulous school called Ecolint—the International School of Geneva. My classmates came from almost every country in the world. Conformism didn't exist. Dad loved his work, and Mum was thrilled to be back in Europe. We were all as happy as clams.

On every school holiday, Dad would pile us into our turquoise Chevrolet and drive to a new country. We drove all over western and southern Europe. I couldn't believe my eyes: the beauty, the variety, the culture, the people, the food . . . the adventure! At Christmas, Dad would take us skiing in Lech, Austria. At Easter, we'd travel to Italy or Spain, driving along the Costa Brava, at that time a pristine, empty coastline of jaw-dropping beauty. In the summers, we'd go on longer holidays, notably to the former Yugoslavia, as far as the beautiful walled town of Dubrovnik on the Adriatic Sea. This was along a cliffside coastal road that was still under construction. Overtaking another car was out of the question, and passing a vehicle coming the other way was a heart-stopping experience. I loved it! That was when I first learned that you never feel more alive . . . than when you think you may soon be dead.

We only survived because the road came to an abrupt end. We turned inland and later abandoned the car when the rear tires simply ran out of rubber. Fortunately this happened next to a small station, with a train pulling into the platform. Dad and Mum bundled us onto the train and, wild with excitement, we chugged through the mountains down to the "Jewel of the Adriatic." While we swam in its crystal waters, Dad found a garage, bought two tires, and drove back to the train station with the garage owner to retrieve our turquoise car. It was still there, untouched.

For all of us, the Geneva period was life-changing. It was as though Dad had taken us into our garden, pointed to the lawn and the flowers, and said, "You see this? This is *not* your backyard. *No!* The whole world is your backyard!" I was so grateful to him. And then I almost destroyed him—though by the grace of God, he never knew.

3

SVENGALI

On our return to London, Ontario, two years later, I went straight into university, going for a B.A. in Honours English and French at Western. Dad went back to head up the Zoology Department, Mum settled into her house and garden, and Gingie and Kathy returned to the local public school. For the first year all was happy and normal and we all lived together at home. I liked Western, which has a beautiful campus, and I had a good time there. I had a handsome boyfriend named Chuck Austin, who skied like an Olympian and who briefly loved me. I also had a few unconventional friends, notably an heiress named Suzy who later eloped with a Cuban and ended up as a Buddhist in the Gulf Islands of British Columbia, practising Urine Therapy. You don't want to know the details.

But I managed to lose Chuck to someone much nicer and prettier than I could ever be. In my second year, I made the fatal mistake of attending a lecture by the most charismatic professor on campus. Since he was a star in that tiny university world, his classes were always packed. He was tall and dark, with flashing black eyes, and his lectures were fascinating, laced with risqué jokes. I was as amused as the rest of the class. But unlike the other students, I was singled out by him in the hallway after the lecture. "You asked very intelligent questions," he said, fixing me with his gimlet eyes. "Would you like to meet later and discuss your ideas?"

At the age of eighteen, I didn't understand the subtext of this invitation. I thought he was actually interested in my *mind*. So I met him in some secret place, and he seduced me. I was a virgin. This was before the term '*abuse*' ever came into currency, though in retrospect I couldn't actually call it that. The man had me under a spell. He was more than twice my age and was a kind of Svengali. Wanting to know my every move, to see me every day or night, to have my complete, undivided attention and love. We would meet in fields or in the back of his car. He would organize clandestine trips—to the Shakespeare festival in Stratford, for example, where we would sit in separate seats but where I was supposed to gaze at him across a crowded lobby during intermission. He would get upset if I didn't gaze at him *all the time*. "How can you simply ignore me to look at the pictures on the wall? I want to look into your *eyes*! You are my *queen*!" et cetera, et cetera.

He was very, very intense. Unbearably so. From the beginning I was afraid, really afraid, of being found out, with all its implications not just for me but for my family. My father was teaching in the same university, after all. But I was hypnotized. Looking back, I wonder what the hell this man was *doing* with me. Yes, I was an adult . . . just. But still highly impressionable. I imagined that I was in love with him, and I suppose he was in love with me. Or at least infatuated, with a passionate nature. And in the end, pretty damn crazy.

After a few months he dreamed up a Big Trip for us. A Big Secret Trip. We would go to Boston together for a whole week, meeting at a bus station outside London where he would be waiting with his car.

I had a friend at Brandeis University, and I told my parents that she'd invited me down during the Spring Break. I could take the bus, I said. They bought the story without a murmur, being kind, generous parents who believed in giving their children lots of rope.

All went well until we came to Gloversville, a city in upstate New York. This man was not a very good driver—he was too busy telling me stories about his youth in Eastern Europe. As we approached the city's outskirts, he pulled into the passing lane to overtake a truck. He didn't notice that the truck driver had signalled that he was about to change into the passing lane too. As we overtook him, the truck driver turned, hit our rear bumper, and sent us spinning across the highway and into a ditch, where we rolled over.

The car was a write-off, yet incredibly we both crawled out of it with barely a scratch. Far from abandoning our trip, this man insisted that we press on to Boston by *bus* and live out this Dream Holiday. For me, it was now becoming a bit of a nightmare.

We returned to London by bus, separating at the same station where we'd met seven days before. Whatever slavish, puppy-love feelings I had for this man had evaporated, and all I wanted to do was remove myself from his orbit and get out of town before we were discovered in another insane escapade. I applied for an exchange scholarship to complete the last two years of my degree at the University of British Columbia (UBC) and flew to Vancouver for the first semester of 1960. To my surprise, the professor accepted my move, though he wrote to me almost every day. He said that if I would only agree to marry him, he would divorce his wife. I said I couldn't do that, and I felt very sorry for her. I think by then I realized that I wasn't the first female to fall under his spell—and I wouldn't be the last.

I was immensely relieved to get away from him, and I thought I'd escaped detection (I told absolutely nobody about this affair). A few months later, I returned to London during a school break to visit my family. A stranger came to the door (opened by my father) and identified himself as an insurance adjuster: "Just checking up on the details of an accident that your daughter Hilary Brown was involved in, driving with a man named Dr. X."

When I overheard this, my heart leapt into my mouth. But Dr. X—who sometimes had the mentality of a KGB agent—had worked out a story that we could tell should our accident ever come to light.

"Oh yes," I said quickly, speaking from our invisible playbook. "My bus had stopped for a tea break and I ran into Dr. X. in the restaurant. When we discovered that we were both going to Boston—he in his car and me by public transport—he suggested I accompany him. I decided not to tell you about the accident because I didn't want to worry you. I just carried on to Boston by bus and Dr. X stayed in Gloversville to deal with the car. I don't know what he did after that."

Both parents accepted this story. Was it because they were so naive (and they were, God bless them) that they were incapable of putting two and two together? Or did they suspect, and decide that they were absolutely *not* going to Think the Unthinkable? In any event, that was the last we heard from the insurance adjuster, and I never saw Dr. X again.

To this day I shudder to think what would have happened if our affair had become known. This was 1960. Dr. X would have been dismissed and run out of town. And my father—my clever, kind, indulgent, hard-working, distinguished father—would have suffered a terrible, irreparable disgrace. He might have lost his position too, or been transferred to some lesser institution. My mother would have been inconsolable.

But none of this happened. I was lucky, lucky, *lucky*. Lucky without deserving it. And as it turned out, I was lucky again, and again, and again in my long and mainly happy life.

4

THE GREAT CANADIAN WEST

At UBC, I quickly found another form of notoriety, but of the kind that amused Dad. He was unconventional and so was I. I continued with the third year of my Honours B.A. Program. I joined a lot of university clubs: the dramatic society, the school newspaper, the French cinema club, and on and on. I also joined the debating club. At least, I *think* that's what I did and that's what got me into trouble.

I was approached by two Bright Lights on campus and asked if I would like to take part in a debate between two men (themselves) and two women. The resolution: "Chastity is outmoded." The women would speak in the affirmative, the men would speak in the negative, and would I be the first speaker?

Well, *that* sounded like fun, I thought, stepping straight into the trap. The men were articulate, amusing types. I thought it would be an absolute gas, and so did my speaking partner, a nice girl called Judy who had been born and raised in Vancouver.

We worked hard on our arguments—and of course it wasn't that difficult to speak in favour of the resolution, even then, back in the Olden Days. The debate would be held in Brock Hall, which at that time was the largest venue at UBC. I expected that our audience would consist of debating club members and the odd anthropology professor, and that we'd be rattling around in an empty auditorium.

On the day of the debate, we walked into Brock Hall and climbed onto the stage. The auditorium was heaving. Several thousand screaming, chanting students packed the hall to the rafters, alternately booing and cheering as the women's team and the men's team were introduced. How on earth did they find out about this? But we were well prepared, and the size of the audience didn't scare us—it didn't scare me, anyway. I found it kind of exhilarating, especially when I pulled out one of my props: a copy of the *Kinsey Reports*, documenting the remarkably active sex lives of Americans. The crowd roared. Judy did well too, and the men were funny. I think one of them produced a replica eighteenth-century chastity belt, which he claimed was still widely used. Something like that. At the end of the debate, the audience voted on the winners. Judy and I won, hands down. We thought it was a great giggle and went back to class.

The next day all hell broke loose. Judy and I appeared on the front page of the *Vancouver Sun*, or maybe it was the *Vancouver Province*, or maybe both. The local press was Shocked and Appalled: "UBC Co-eds Advocate Free Love! Chastity is Outmoded!" in front-page splash headlines. The story was picked up by the Canadian Press wire service and went right across the country. We couldn't believe it. Why would the *local press* come to a silly little university debate? Who invited them anyway? Probably those two articulate, amusing men who got us involved in the first place.

We were not expelled. Not from the university. But I was thrown out of my studio apartment overlooking the bay by my hysterical Ukrainian landlady. She accused me of being a prostitute. "Dats vat all dose mens who come to see youse are *doing*!" she yelled, waving a copy of the newspaper, her flabby arms flapping. It wasn't that easy to find somewhere else to live, since every landlady in town seemed to have read about that damn debate. Judy was ostracized by her neighbours (she still lived with her parents). Neither of us realized just how prudish people were in Vancouver in 1960. Maybe as prudish as people in London, Ontario.

But the experience taught me that I really enjoyed writing and performing, especially in front of an audience. And while the notorious debate shocked the good people of Vancouver, it impressed my boyfriend at the time: a tall, good-looking, highly intelligent man named David Anderson who rowed for Canada in the 1960 Olympics (they won silver), became a superstar maverick MP and Cabinet minister in Jean Chrétien's Liberal government, and was eventually awarded the Order of Canada. He thought the debate was hilarious and kept bringing it up when he took me to Victoria to meet his terribly nice parents. He was a sailor and an outdoorsman too. Instead of chocolates or flowers, he would bring me enormous cuts of moose that he'd recently bagged on a hunting trip. And he was unconventional, one of the many reasons I liked him. I liked him even when he told me that my "best years would be my eighties," which I suppose was his idea of a compliment. Years later, I actually proposed to him, thinking he was just the kind of man I ought to marry. Fortunately he turned me down, in the nicest possible way. Quite right too. I would have ruined his career.

5

LONDON, THE WORLD

My second year at UBC (and the final year of my degree) was a little more serious. All Honours English students had to produce a ten-thousand-word thesis, which is like writing a novella. Chemical dependency got me through it. It was pretty easy to get hold of Benzedrine on campus, and that was the only way I could stay up for nights at a time to finish the wretched thing. My topic had something to do with the Romantic poet Percy Bysshe Shelley. At the time, as I popped the pills and burned the midnight oil, I thought it was a brilliant piece of work. At least I got my degree. Twelve years later my erudite husband read it and said he didn't understand a word. That's Benzedrine, baby.

That second year at UBC, David joined the Department of External Affairs, went to Hong Kong, and was out of my life for almost a decade. My new playmate was another tall, good-looking chap named Mike Jeffery, a young lawyer who lived in a coach house close to English Bay. We met in a restaurant—I worked as a waitress in the summers, to help pay for my tuition. We would often go swimming before breakfast or before bed. His parents had a spectacular house on the water in West Vancouver, which would be his one day.

We were in love, and Mike thought we should get married once I graduated. What a start in life that would be, right? Handsome lawyer husband, charming coach house, stunning cliffside residence to inherit . . . how could I say no?

It's not against the law to be stupid, so I said no. By then I'd decided I wanted to be a journalist, a broadcast journalist, on an *international* stage. Was I going to achieve that by leading an idyllic married life in one of the most spectacular cities in North America? *No!* So after graduation I took my meagre savings and flew to London, England, actually thinking that I could take that great city by storm. I was young and arrogant, as only the young and arrogant can be.

I got nowhere. Of course not. I had no qualifications. I had to take temporary jobs. I was reduced to demonstrating those awful painting-by-numbers sets. Not in a shop but in a shop *window*, dressed as Rembrandt. This was deeply embarrassing, even though I attracted quite a crowd.

By then I'd managed to get a bit of work as a freelance radio broadcaster. Among the many letters I sent out seeking employment was one to the BBC—*the* greatest broadcasting organization on earth. They replied with a list of upcoming positions. They have to do this, apparently, even though they generally know who they want to hire. The first position was floor manager, TV news. I wrote back asking for an interview, and they invited me to what they called a "Board." I had absolutely no idea what a floor manager *was*.

Picture a serious BBC type, face like a ploughed field, horn-rimmed glasses, staring across a large desk at a pudding-faced Ms. Brown, fresh out of university—university in *Canada*. You know, the former *colony*.

"Well, Miss Brown, can you first tell us what a microphone does?"

Silence. Ms. Brown thinks, '*What is this, a trick question?*'

"Umm. It . . . amplifies sound?"

She gets a withering look.

"No, Miss Brown, that is *not* the right answer. A microphone converts acoustic energy into electrical energy. I don't think you are really qualified for this job, are you?"

Ms. Brown looks tragic, and he feels sorry for her, in a patronizing sort of way.

"Why don't you go and see your *own* people, Miss Brown? At the *Canadian* Broadcasting Corporation? CBC is just across the road. I'm sure they would love to meet you."

To my surprise, they *were* very cordial at the CBC London bureau. Specifically, a man named Val Clery welcomed me into his office and described the various radio programs that were accepting freelance contributions. These were mainly daytime shows like *Trans-Canada Matinee*. Val suggested that I come back with a list of ideas for feature radio reports. A few days later I produced my list, he chose one or two ideas, gave me a short lesson on how to operate a tape recorder, and sent me off to gather my material. When I returned with my interviews, natural sound, and a script, Val looked it all over, made a few changes, and set me up with a technician to put the piece together.

I have the hand of *death* on any machine. I need only to pick up a tape recorder for it to fall apart in my hands. One of my first story ideas was about a young aristocrat named Charlotte Bingham, who had just published her autobiography, "Coronet Among the Weeds". It was a satire about life as a debutante in London, and I pitched it as a lifestyle piece: the mating rituals of the British upper class, et cetera, et cetera. CBC bought it.

I trotted off to Ms. Bingham's smart family house in Knightsbridge. She was charming and witty, and there was a spring in my step as I returned to CBC with my material. I hadn't checked the recording on location, but I checked it at the bureau, ready to select the quotes.

There was nothing on the tape. *Na-thing!* I obviously hadn't pressed the frigging Record button. No one was aware of this—yet. I picked up a phone behind a closed door and rang Charlotte Bingham. In a low voice I confessed my error. Could I possibly come back and re-record our interview?

"Oh you poor thing, of course you can! Come and have a bite of lunch with me. I'm having bacon on toast, would that be all right? In the meantime, I'll think up something even better to say." What a lovely, lovely girl! CBC was pleased with my story and aired it several times, which meant that I was paid a residual: the princely sum of $12, as I recall.

On the advice of my father (and at his expense), I had enrolled in a secretarial school that offered crash courses for university graduates like me. We both realized that the only way for a woman to get her foot in the journalism door in the early sixties was as a secretary. I did a three-month course in typing and shorthand and—bingo!—within a week I was hired as secretary to the editor of *Harper's Bazaar*. It was a temporary position. But I was convinced that I could make it permanent and that finally I would be In like Flynn.

The editor would dictate her correspondence to me and send me out on errands: taking the negatives to the photographer and plugging the parking meter. I could handle the photographer. But I couldn't read back my shorthand, and I would often plug the wrong meter. After a month, she let me go.

By this time, I'd been in London for almost a year. My only real friends were my beautiful, spirited aunt, Elisabeth Hunt, and my charismatic grandmother, Gerda Evill, whom I would visit once a week in her charming mews house in Hampstead. In the space of thirty days, I'd lost the job that I thought would be my ticket into journalism. I was shattered.

"If at first you don't succeed, try, try, try again" is how the saying goes. Well, up to a point. I've often found that when you try and try and are *still* stuck, you should *forget* it. Take another tack entirely. Or run away. And that's what I did.

6

PARIS: THE CITY OF LIGHT

During that rocky year in London, I had befriended a delightful French girl named Catherine de la Presle, who was visiting the city. She urged me to come and see her in Paris, anytime. "Whenever you like, Hil, you can stay with my family. We have a large apartment in the Seizième" (that's one of the chic quarters of Paris where the rich people live). So I called her. She could not have been more welcoming: "Come at once!"

Over a grand crème and hot croissant at the Café du Trocadéro, I gave her my sob story. "Je suis fichue, fichue, fichue," I wailed. "I'm finished!" The tears rolled down my face and ruined my mascara, which in Paris is simply *not* done.

"Mais non mais non mais non!" cried Catherine with a wave of her manicured hand. "You can come and work at my publishing company! The American editor needs an assistant. You would be perfect! I will take you there tomorrow."

The next morning we walked from her apartment in the Seizième to her office in the fashionable Huitieme, along the grand tree-lined Avenue Foch and through elegant little sidestreets to Editions des Deux Coqs d'Or (Two Golden Cockerels). It produced illustrated coffee-table books, in French and English, about wine and cheese and food and all the things that make life in France worth living. Cathe introduced me to the American editor, a personable chap named Alexandre Dorozynski. He offered me the job on the spot.

How lucky is *that*? I didn't have to take dictation in shorthand. Doro (his nickname) simply said, "Write to this man and tell him in a nice way that we're not interested in his manuscript." I would compose and type the letter myself, for his signature. *That* I could do. To hell with any shorthand. He was the nicest, most laidback boss imaginable. The office was small, and everyone was totally charming to me. Okay, it may have helped that I was tall, blond, and with a thirty-six-inch bustline. But none of the men hit on me. People would invite me to lunch and introduce me to their favourite bistro, their favourite dish, their favourite wine. I would stagger back, bump into office furniture, and eventually sober up to do my job again. It was heaven.

Within a couple of weeks, I got a call from CBC London (I'd given them my forwarding number in Paris), asking me if I'd like to cover the Paris Fashion Collections for *Trans-Canada Matinee*. "We know you worked for *Harper's Bazaar* so you're obviously a fashion expert, aren't you?" "Well yes, I suppose I am!" I replied, being extremely economical with the truth. So much for my abject failure as the editor's secretary. It's an ill wind, as they say.

So began my long and meaningful love affair with Paris. With the whole of France, for that matter. These were the happiest, most exciting years of my life so far. Other budding journalists may have been forced to cut their teeth in the backwoods of Oshkosh, Wisconsin, or Wawa, Ontario, but Mademoiselle Brown at the age of twenty-two was mincing around the loveliest city in the world, working for a

Franco-American publisher, and writing and recording feature radio reports for the Canadian Broadcasting Corporation. Within a year CBC asked me to join the staff in its spacious sunlit office near the Champs-Élysées. I was secretary and production assistant to the Paris correspondent, Stanley Burke. As with Doro at Deux Coqs d'Or, there was none of this business of taking dictation in my own indecipherable shorthand. Mais non mais non mais non! It was just: "Write to Monsieur Truc-Machin and tell him to fuck off, in the nicest possible way, and I'll sign it."

I was also available for any radio requests, and I continued to pitch my own ideas. France in general and Paris in particular provided a limitless source of feature stories, and on occasion I even got out of the country itself. One of my favourite assignments was a weekend in Amsterdam with the great Canadian jazz pianist Oscar Peterson and his trio (Ray Brown on double bass and Ed Thigpen on drums), who were touring Europe with Ella Fitzgerald. A colleague was filming a TV documentary and I tagged along to do radio. It was such a treat to hang out with these brilliant musicians, who were all perfect gentlemen. An interview with Ella was to be the highlight of my reportage. But when it came to it, just before her performance, she seemed to be in a trance and talked in monosyllables. "I just lo-o-ve music, any kind of music," she said, rocking back and forth with her eyes half closed. Then she went on stage, threw back her head, and out came the most perfect, most glorious sound on earth.

Stan helped me when he could, looking over my radio scripts and giving me ideas for better content. Within a year he was letting me do feature assignments for television news that he wasn't interested in himself. The camera crews helped me too, since I had absolutely no idea how to shoot a story or perform on camera. I couldn't believe it when my efforts at TV reporting actually made air.

All this was against the backdrop of this achingly beautiful French capital, known as the City of Light. At every turn of a cobbled street, there was another feast for the eyes: a tree-lined square, an exquisite fourteenth-century church, a crowded sidewalk café, a lively open-air market in the middle of a shaded avenue, spread out in a fabulous horizontal curtain of colour. The glamour and vitality of the city were electrifying.

Catherine took me under her wing completely. She introduced me to all her high-born girlfriends, who for some reason accepted me into their circle though we all knew I wasn't One of Them. They all came from families in the *Bottin Mondain*—France's answer to *Debrett's Peerage*—and would stage rotating supper parties known as "rallye diners" to expand their circle of suitable connections. Cathe and I would go together, since I was still living with her family.

"Un parfum! Il me faut un parfum!" (*Perfume! I must have some perfume!*) Cathe would cry as she rushed around the large, rambling apartment, putting her lovely self together for the next supper party. Each girl in turn would host a dinner, inviting all the other girls in the group, plus an equal number of eligible males. The male guests had to be different with each dinner party. The hard corps of females would remain the same. By the end of the season, each girl had met and scrutinized about seventy men. It was a marriage market, basically.

I was just "la Canadienne"—an amusing curiosity in this aristocratic mix, though I must say I wasn't all that impressed with the men. As far as I was concerned, they weren't good enough for my elegant, cultured friend Catherine, niece of Antoine de Saint-Exupéry (author of the famous novella *Le Petit Prince*). I remember being buttonholed by one of them and interrogated about my religious beliefs. When I stated that I didn't actually believe in God, he seized my arm and turned to the assembled company, crying, "Voici une fille qui ne croit à *rien!*" (*Here is a girl who doesn't believe in anything!*) This seemed a little intolerant in the country of Descartes and Voltaire.

In any event, I had a pretty good love life of my own, thank you very much, without any introductions to the Right People. And if you're wondering whether Frenchmen are good lovers, the answer is yes.

There was Gerard, a handsome architect whom I'd met at a party on the Left Bank and who would take me on long walks around the different quarters of Paris, pointing out this seventeenth-century square or that eighteenth-century library or the other historic bridge spanning the Seine. He loved his city and talked about it endlessly. We would often go on a midnight tour of Les Halles, the all-night wholesale fruit and vegetable market in the heart of Paris. We'd order onion soup, the favourite dish among the porters who worked there, and just watch the passing parade. (Les Halles was torn down in 1971 under President Pompidou and replaced by a grotesque museum and cultural centre known as the Beaubourg. It opened in 1977 and it looks like an oil refinery.) Gerard and I remained friends for years, and he would often regale me with stories of his conquests. "Les blondes, elles sont tres agréables, mais les brunes! Elles sautent en l'air!" I'm not going to translate that.

There was Etienne, a doctor, whom I'd met on a plane and who occasionally took me on his rounds in hospital. He wasn't handsome, but he was very suave, and dedicated to his patients, though he referred to them as "clients." He especially wanted me to see the clients who were in hospital with cirrhosis of the liver. They were all workmen with enormous bellies. "So, Gaston, how much wine do you drink a day, when you are on the job? Three or four bottles?" Etienne would say, patting his patient's colossal gut. "Oh no, doctor! Six or seven!" Gaston would reply, insulted that Etienne had underestimated his capacity for booze. This may explain why France then had one of the highest rates of alcoholism in Europe, maybe the world.

There was Bernard, a designer, whom I'd met on a chairlift in Val d'Isère. He was as suave as Etienne and as good-looking as Gerard. He was also a phenomenal cook. Many Frenchmen are. And I would say that *all* Frenchmen are absolutely obsessed with food. Obsessed with the correct composition of a meal, obsessed with a properly ripened cheese, obsessed with the right hors d'oeuvre before the right entrée, the right wine with the right "poulet roti à l'estragon," et cetera, et cetera. I would watch Bernard cook, but every time I tried to help he would just say, "Mais non mais non mais non!" and pour me another aperitif.

Some of my most delightful hours were spent with the Canadian painter Joe Plaskett, who lived with his partner, David Hill, in a sixteenth-century stone house on the Rue Pecquay, in Le Marais, a very old quarter on the right bank of the Seine. Joe was a sweet, gentle man, and he had invited me to his annual costume party.

"I have just the thing for you to wear!" said Cathe, and she produced a ravishing "Josephine" costume of cream-coloured chiffon shot with gold thread, and with the high-waisted, low-cut bodice that was fashionable in the time of Napoleon.

"I *must* paint you!" Joe cried as I made my way up the spiral stone staircase and into his large crowded living room. So it was that every Sunday for the rest of that winter I sat for Joe in this filmy, period garment, chatting dreamily with him as he worked.

His studio was full of gilded mirrors, on every wall, reflecting the pale winter light. He painted me seated on an antique chair, with my body slightly turned. "You have Boldini shoulders," he said, which is so much more original than saying you have eyes like limpid pools. (Boldini painted at in the late nineteenth century and specialized in portraits of fashionable women with sinuous shoulders. He was known as "the Master of Swish.") Joe gave me one of his mirrors as a present, to thank me for the sittings. And later my father bought the painting. After Dad's death, it came back to me. It's on the wall in my bedroom, a daily reminder of that magic time in Paris, when I was very young.

7

MONTREAL AND LIVE TELEVISION

After more than two years in Paris, I was sharing a sunlit apartment near the Rue de Grenelle in the 7th Arrondissement with a vivacious French girl named Catherine de la Faire. She was a perfect roommate, though she probably wouldn't say the same of me. On one occasion, I accidentally broke her treasured Baccarat crystal vase. On another, I cut into a large pâté de campagne that she had made for a special dinner. But she forgave me, and when she got engaged, she invited me to her spectacular wedding.

I had a terrific job at CBC, with terrific colleagues, though I was occasionally subjected to verbal abuse by Bernard Kaplan, a first-class journalist who never pulled his punches. "You're so wet behind the ears you're *dripping!*" he once shouted at me, reducing me to tears. He taught me a lot, however, and I liked him.

I had a red Volkswagen Beetle, a gift from my darling mother. I had a large circle of friends, and I felt completely at home in a city I loved. Then someone at the office told me there was a job opening at CBC Montreal. A television job. A daily *live* television job.

A local lunchtime TV show called *Calendar* was looking for a weather girl-cum-interviewer. This was daytime television, an hour a day, five days a week. It would be a step-up from freelance pieces on the radio, wouldn't it?

I wrote to the executive producer outlining my experience, such as it was, and my ambitions. I enclosed some samples of my work. He wrote back, said that my letter had "intrigued" him, and offered me the job.

So I packed up my clothes, Joe's mirror, and a few other French treasures; shipped my VW Bug; and left the City of Light with a long, tearful, backward glance. But this was a Good Career Move, I thought.

Calendar turned out to be a pretty awful program that mainly featured people with products to sell, such as Mikimoto pearls and leather handbags. "Always pay *something* for it" was the producer's one piece of advice. Advice I ignored,- I didn't think I should accept handouts, at all. *Calendar* included a self-help feature with a perky do-it-yourself type who did clever things like, you guessed it, turning Javex bottles into piggy banks. I shared the interview duties with three co-anchors. Since I was the only one who spoke French, I would often be assigned any interview with a French Canadian. Nationalism was already thriving among the artistic elite of Quebec. On one occasion, a Québécois playwright came on set but refused to answer any of my questions—presumably because I was a "misérable Anglo-Saxon." His mouth remained firmly shut, even when I addressed him in his own language. Unfortunately, I wasn't experienced enough to ask him politely, in his own language, why he couldn't just *grow up*.

Though the program was pretty cringe-making, it gave me confidence in front of a live TV camera. After a year, I was asked to go on staff as an announcer. It sounds incredibly quaint, but I was the first and the only female announcer on CBC at the time.

My job was to read (but not write) the news on television. I was only allowed to read the news after the late, late movie, which usually ended at about two in the morning. There was no actual studio for this performance. There was a room the size of a broom closet on the fifth floor with a desk, chair, and a slave camera fixed to the wall. The scripts would be sent up from the newsroom a couple of floors below. I would press a button that turned on the camera, and I was on the air.

The newscast always ended with a sports roundup, and one of the names that kept appearing was Sandy Koufax. All you sports buffs would know that he was a famous left-handed pitcher for the Brooklyn Dodgers. But I didn't know that. I didn't know a *thing* about sports. So I pronounced his name the way it was spelled: *Koo-fax*. Anyone interested in baseball knows that it's *Koh-fax*. But no one corrected me because no one was watching. It was two o'clock in the morning, after all.

No one was watching except the guy in the newsroom, three floors down, who wrote the scripts and sent them up to me. I didn't know him. I never *saw* him. Not, that is, until I happened to meet him at the bar of the Montreal Press Club. And God love him, he told me this story.

He said he saw me one morning in the elevator of the CBC building and thought, There's that dumb broad who reads the late-night news and can't pronounce the name of Sandy Koufax. I'll just clue her in, without any introductions. So he turned to me and said, "Sandy *Koh-fax*." I smiled and said, "Hilary Brown" and walked out of the elevator.

Fortunately, my job as the only female staff announcer on CBC meant that I could do more than mispronounce famous names in the middle of the night. I could also work on public affairs programs that required a host and interviewer, and I was soon assigned to a daily morning radio show called *CBM Magazine*. My co-host was a funny man named Pat McDougall, and it was a pretty civilized, informative program mainly because the producer was Gloria Bishop, an uber-efficient woman with a mind like a steel trap. I was terrified of Gloria ("That's *not* the right tack to take! You are *off topic!*" she would sometimes shout at me), though she later became one of my closest friends.

CBM Magazine was enhanced immensely by the fact that in 1967 Montreal hosted the wildly successful Expo 67, which included the greatest festival of the performing arts ever staged, anywhere. Over a period of two months in that extraordinary summer, the world's top musicians, dancers, singers, and actors all came to Montreal. An astonishing number were made available to us to interview: Arthur Rubinstein, Sir Laurence Olivier, Marlene Dietrich, Johnny Cash, Warren Beatty, Christopher Plummer, Sidney Poitier, and on and on. I'm not sure how good I was at this, since most of the time I was in awe of the person I was interviewing. The actors such as Olivier and Plummer were witty and courteous, almost courtly. Johnny Cash had an animal magnetism, and I'm not even a country-and-western fan. The rock star Frank Zappa (who was appearing with his band, The Mothers of Invention) attempted to put me at ease by suggesting that we conduct the interview *lying down*, and he promptly stretched out on the sofa. I stayed vertical.

My social life was pretty lively too, with lots of parties. At one of them I was introduced to Farley Mowat, the well-known wildlife writer who looked a bit like a leprechaun. Moments later he came up behind me and in one, deft move *bit* me on the bottom. This was his party piece apparently. I had the bruise for weeks.

In my first year in Montreal I ran around with a sensitive blond man named Neil Cole. He looked like a movie star and liked to recite poetry in a low voice that was pretty damn seductive. He was very attentive, until I fell for a German-born scientist in New York named Dr. Günter Blobel, who later won a Nobel Prize. That was the end of Neil.

Later I spent a lot of time with a producer at the National Film Board named Ian, except it was spelled Ioin because he was a Scot. He was artistic and well connected, but he was terribly uptight, perhaps because his father was a bishop. He complained about the effect my appearance had on his friends. "I walk into a room with you and hear the heads snap. What they're all thinking is: My God, Ioin, what did you do to get *that?*" He found this a burden. But I loved his company, and that of all his friends in the film and theatre world. Especially Mark Negin, the talented set designer who is still in my life.

Ioin and Mark introduced me to the voice coach Eleanor Stuart. She worked with a lot of actors and was the best in the business. I loved our afternoon sessions together and I think my broadcast style, such as it was, improved enormously under her tuition. Years later the documentary filmmaker John Zaritsky hired me to narrate one of his films, saying that my voice "combined warmth with authority." I hope you're impressed. I thank Eleanor for that.

Apart from the glittering lineup of international performing artists who came through Montreal that summer, we had our own homegrown celebrity, Leonard Cohen, who was then known as a poet and novelist. He was a pal—in spite of his doleful look, he was as friendly as a puppy. On one unforgettable evening, he came up to see me in my apartment, carrying a guitar. "I want to be a singer,"

Leonard announced in that deep, soulful voice of his. He pulled out his guitar and started to sing a song called "Suzanne by the River":

> "And you want to travel with her
> And you want to travel blind
> And you know that she will trust you
> For you've touched her perfect body with your mind."[1]

Beautiful lyrics, but that monotonous gravel voice! That dreary melody! I listened politely, thinking, *Leonard, stick to poetry! You'll never be a musician!* But I was much too nice to tell him so. As you can see, I had incredible insight.

In a way, Leonard might have shared this thought. "Only in Canada could somebody with a voice like mine win Vocalist of the Year," he said in his acceptance speech for his 1993 Juno Award, when he'd become one of the most successful poet-singers of all time.[2]

But knowing Leonard that special summer—when we were both so young and when he was only moderately famous—was such a treat. He was fun, and at the same time an intensely compassionate person. When you were with him, you felt you had his entire attention, that you were the most important person in the room. He once told a Norwegian radio interviewer that he "had a great appetite for the company of women, and for the sexual expression of friendship."[3] And that was true. Lucky me.

8

NEW YORK, NEW YORK

The greatest summer in the history of Montreal came with the bonus of a phenomenal news story. That was the visit of French President Charles de Gaulle and his unforgettable pronouncement from the balcony of l'hôtel de ville: "Vive le Québec!" (roar of the crowd) "Vive le Québec *libre!*"[1] (deafening roar). I can remember going into the CBC makeup room that day (which we shared with the French-speaking Radio-Canada) and spotting the Québécois reporter Gilles Loiselle, a chum from my CBC Paris days. "Gilles, can you *believe* what de Gaulle *said?*" I cried, thinking it was a total scandal. "Yes, it's fantastic!" Gilles cried back, his eyes shining. I suddenly understood what was meant by the term *two solitudes.*

Of course, de Gaulle had to cut his Canadian visit short. Canadian Prime Minister Lester Pearson said publicly that de Gaulle was no longer welcome. But the French president had done what he came to do. The following year, 1968, was another extraordinary year for news. The Prague Spring, the Soviet Invasion of Czechoslovakia, the Tet Offensive in Vietnam, the May riots in Paris, the assassination of Martin Luther King Jr. and later Robert Kennedy, and on and on. I was longing to get out of the genteel world of public affairs broadcasting and into *news*. In a profile about me in *The Globe and Mail* I even told the reporter that I wanted to be a foreign correspondent.² The reporter printed this ridiculous ambition. But it wasn't happening. The closest I got to any kind of war zone was during my over-the-top dinner parties in my large Montreal apartment, where I attempted to replicate almost every three-page recipe from *Mastering the Art of French Cooking* by Julia Child. My kitchen always looked like it had been hit by a bomb.

Occasionally I got away, at my own expense. I wangled a trip to Russia for the fiftieth anniversary of the Soviet Union (in 1967) thanks to my pal David Halton, who was then the CBC correspondent in Moscow. I stayed in his apartment in Kutuzovsky Prospekt (which was bugged, of course) and I filed reports for *CBM Magazine*. When I was in the apartment, I spent a lot of time taking phone messages for David from an endless succession of Russian women.

"No, Natasha, David's not in. You want to leave him a message? You want him to call you immediately? I'll tell him that." Click.

"Hello, Anastasia? No, he's *not*. No, I don't know where he is. Why don't you call back later?" Click.

"Hello, Irina?" "Hello, Natalia?" "Hello, hello hello?" It was non-*stop*. David wasn't married and so was a target for dozens of Russian women dying to marry a man from the West and get out of the Soviet Union. They were relentless. By the time his tour of duty ended in Moscow, one of them had managed to snare him. I saw them later in London, and although she was living with David in a huge house in Hampstead she was already complaining about life in a democracy. "Surely it's better than life in Russia?" I said. "Oh yes," she allowed, and then switched to French. "Mais il me manque, mon pays. La, au moins, je suis dans ma propre merde." (*I miss my country. There at least I'm in my own shit.*) Poor David.

I set up another freelance trip to Beirut (thanks to a friend at Air Canada) and did a feature report on its International Festival in the Roman ruins at Baalbek, where the Berlin Philharmonic was performing under Herbert von Karajan. I was desperate to get an interview with him and spent so much time following the all-male Philharmonic around that a local press report identified me as the only female member of the orchestra. The maestro finally gave me exactly three minutes of his time.

That was my first trip to the Middle East, which was then in a rare period of stability. I drove up to Damascus and discovered the wonders of the souk, staggering out of that great bazaar with a nineteenth-century gold-plated Ottoman Turkish belt that I found irresistible. I went to Jordan to see Petra, the "rose-red city, half as old as time," carved out of the pink rock two thousand years ago. A guide from the Ministry of Information organized a horse to take me into the ruins, and he was mortified when the beast kicked me. "The horse has been taken away, to be shot," he announced. I said the horse should live on, if only to kick another Canadian.

And to my surprise I was romanced by a high-flying businessman from New York named John Diebold, whom I'd met on the plane from Rome to Beirut. He'd written a book titled *Automation* and was credited with coining the word. His name is on ATM machines all over the world. He was on his way to Amman to receive an award from King Hussein. After a delightful dinner (we happened to be seated together in first class), this complete stranger insisted on escorting me off the aircraft in Beirut, folding me into his arms at passport control, and kissing me, on the lips. This is a thing you still can't do in public in the Middle East (outside of Israel). The next day he sent a telegram telling me to have dinner with him in Beirut on his way back from Amman. The man was a Don Juan and he completely turned my head, as Don Juans always do. As we said goodbye the next morning, he talked about how "we have the rest of our lives together." He was quite rich and quite famous. As it turned out, he toyed with my emotions for more than a year.

These mini-trips gave me a great taste for roaming the globe, and I was always able to sell radio reports or newspaper articles on a freelance basis. But I couldn't get a *job* doing that. "You can't parachute in, my dear," as one veteran CBC correspondent said to me in a patronizing way. So unlike David Halton, who was always a booster.

Then in 1969 I got a phone call from my friend Robin Green, who was the public affairs director of the Guggenheim Museum in New York.

"Hils, there's an opening down here for head of publicity. It's not a full-time job. But you could take it and use the extra time to go after the U.S. networks. Let's face it, the Canadians are never going to let a woman get into TV news. But the Americans would!"

Once again I was tempted to give up a plum job on the off-chance that I might get my heart's desire in the most competitive city on earth. So I gave up the plum job. Of course I did.

A few weeks later I was working in the dark, windowless offices of the Guggenheim Museum, aptly described by *Vogue* magazine as "Frank Lloyd Wright's Super Screw on Fifth Avenue." It was like being at the bottom of an empty well. The pay was so low (US$7,000 a year) that I couldn't afford to rent an apartment. I ended up babysitting the luxurious homes of the museum's many patrons. People were always happy to have a well-brought-up young lady occupy their residence while they were away, so obsessed were they about security.

The job turned out to be much more than part-time. With Robin's guidance I was propelled into the New York art scene and worked as publicist on all the museum's exhibitions and gala art openings. I met some of the great artists of the day—Roy Lichtenstein and Willem de Kooning—and some of the great collectors, notably Peggy Guggenheim. It was intoxicating.

A steady stream of celebrities would ask to be taken around the museum after hours, and it was often my job to look after them. Jackie Kennedy once came, dressed in a T-shirt and jeans. She chewed gum constantly and was painfully thin. But she didn't pull rank with me. "I *lo-o-v-e* this museum," she gushed in her surprisingly high-pitched voice.

Walter Matthau came with a film crew one day, to shoot a movie scene. He took one look at me and said, "With legs like yours, I could run the four-minute mile." I'm not sure this was a compliment. All I could think of to say in riposte was, "Thank you, Mr. Matthau. You *used* to be one of my favourite actors."

I even organized an exhibition myself—I got the eccentric Canadian filmmaker Norman McLaren (who drew images directly on film, in tiny, delicate scratches) to come to New York for a retrospective of his work, to be shown in the Guggenheim Auditorium. The New York cognoscenti loved it. They loved him! I set up a summer art program in the auditorium for Harlem kids, having convinced the director, Thomas Messer, that this would be good for the museum's image. The kids later staged an exhibition of their work that was covered by local TV and was a huge hit.

I also felt that this risky move to New York would bring me closer to Don Juan, and to the life that he said we were going to have together, eventually. He was stringing me along, mainly by sending enormous bouquets of flowers to the museum, addressed to me. But in a whole year I think I saw him once, for dinner. He took me to Lutèce (a top New York restaurant), followed by a nightcap in his sumptuous apartment overlooking the East River. At 6 a.m. the next day, I was hustled out the door and it was at that moment, I think, that I saw the light.

What I didn't understand at the time was the psychology of the character. Why does he tell you lies about "our future together," et cetera, et cetera? Is it to get you into bed? My generation (as opposed to his) grew up in the Golden Age of Sex: post-pill and pre-herpes and pre-AIDS. We didn't need professions of undying love or hints of marriage to jump into the sack. No, the Don Juan has to *possess* a person . . . body and *soul*. That is what drives him. And once he has both, he's not interested anymore. As it soon turned out, neither was I.

Six years later, after an article about me appeared in *Women's Wear Daily* (April 27, 1976), I got a letter from Don Juan, congratulating me on my high-profile job with ABC in London (by then I'd finally made it) and asking me if I could attend a black-tie dinner he was giving in the British capital. He dropped his usual handful of Names. The man was coming on to me all over again! Before I could think of a put-down, I got a long-distance call from his secretary, asking me if I would be attending The Dinner.

"I'm sorry, but I don't really know who this Diebold person is. I get quite a few letters like this. So no, I won't be attending," I said.I'll never know if she passed on the message to him, but I didn't hear from him again.

In any event, I had lots of friends in New York in the late sixties, including an executive at Warner Brothers named Ed Bleier who was a real *mensch*. He drove a Jaguar and had a fabulous apartment on Central Park East and a beautiful house in the Hamptons. He would take me to Studio 54 in Manhattan, and to Aspen for ski weekends. In his executive jet. We stayed in touch for years, and he eventually married a TV star from Brussels who was perfect for him.

I looked up Peter Jennings, the famous anchor at ABC News. I had met him in Canada through his sister Sarah, a chum from my Paris days. Peter took me to the ABC studios to watch him perform. That was his idea of a date. He was a very good performer: cocky, charming, informed, entertaining, and curious about everything. There was a boyish quality about him, which isn't surprising since he was so young. Fortunately, he didn't fancy me, so our first date . . . was our last. That gave us the freedom to become good friends. But back then, Peter couldn't help me get into ABC. Much later in life, he helped me enormously.

9

THE CALL OF THE SEA

The closest I got to any network was a freelance stint for the Public Broadcasting System (PBS), doing the occasional studio interview. During this period, the person who most impressed me was a British yachtsman named Robin Knox-Johnston. He'd just made history by sailing single-handed around the world, non-stop, without a landfall. The first man ever to do so. He said that his mother's only comment about this extraordinary achievement was that his voyage was "totally irresponsible." There is a type of Englishwoman who is impossible to impress, isn't there? But I thought, Sailing! That sounds so daring, so romantic!

Even with my work at PBS and the stipend from the museum, I was poor, *really* poor. I got a little work as a freelance chef, cooking and serving three-course dinners for up to twelve people in the privacy of the client's home. But it still didn't add up to much. After a year in New York, I had to admit that the networks weren't ready for me. I was stuck, again, though I loved the city.

To crawl back to Montreal with my tail between my legs just wasn't an option. I remember giving myself a pep talk: "Okay, Hils, you didn't get into the networks. You're still in your twenties. What else do you want to do in life?" A little voice in my head said, "Go sailing!"

"It's not what you know but who you know," as journalists say. A friend of a friend—I think his name was Schuyler—was about to sail in the Bermuda Race, the famous biennial race from Newport to the island of Bermuda, in the North Atlantic Ocean. Well-to-do yachtsmen from around the world compete in this prestigious event in their beautiful, expensive boats.

Yachtsmen are normally friendly types who don't stand on ceremony. When I called Schuyler, he couldn't have been more cordial. "You want to go sailing? Well, I could take you up to Newport this weekend and show you around, introduce you to a few people. I'll be racing myself, but I've got a little time. Why don't I pick you up after work on Friday?"

Done! How very kind! We had a comfortable drive from Manhattan to Rhode Island, and on arrival in Newport we went straight down to the piers. Dozens of sleek, ocean-racing yachts bobbed up and down in the water, their halyards going ping, ping, ping! against their masts in the brisk evening wind. Tanned young men with bodies like whipcord were crawling over the decks, getting the boats ready for the big race. These were the crew—extremely competent professional sailors who man and often maintain the yachts. The captains were the actual owners of the boats, usually rich businessmen. Schuyler seemed to know them all.

By this time, we were good mates. "Listen," he said, "if you really want to sail, why don't you try to get on the race yourself?"

"But I don't know *anything* about sailing," I stammered. "I just want to *learn* . . . at some point."

"Do you know how to cook?"

"Is the Pope Catholic?"

So we made a sign that read "Gourmet Sea-cook to Bermuda Available Here", pinned it onto my form-fitting T-shirt, and paraded up and down the piers.

"Hey, Preston!" Schuyler shouted at a distinguished middle-aged man in Bermuda shorts, standing at the helm of a colossal seventy-foot ketch. "Have you got a cook for the race? I got a gal here who studied at the Cordon Bleu in Paris!" (This was a complete fiction).

Preston declined, and so did a lot of other patrician-looking yachtsmen. But eventually a rather gloomy multimillionaire named Thor Ramsing, owner of a thirty-nine-foot sloop called *Solution*, said he'd take me on.

"Have you sailed before, Hilry?" he said, fixing me with his baleful blue eyes.

"Oh yes!" I cried, lying through my teeth.

"That's good," he intoned, "because our last girl fell and broke three ribs, first day at sea."

Very quickly I found out just how that could have happened. The galley on *Solution* was "forward," in the bow of the yacht (most galleys are midships), so when the yacht was underway the cook was bouncing around the galley like a ball in a tombola. In many yachts the cook is actually strapped in. *Solution* didn't have that feature.

The Bermuda Race is a "beat." The yachts are tacking into the wind for 635 nautical miles. They're also sailing through the Gulf Stream, which is turbulent and makes the yachts roll around even more. In five days at sea, I have never, ever, sustained so many bruises, up and down my legs, my arms, my back, my bottom. But I didn't break any ribs.

I turned out to be quite a good sea-cook, however, though it was damn difficult. I had a crew of nine men, with three watch changes, three meals a day, four men a sitting. (The navigator ate at his chart table.) The meals had to be *bang* on time. And they had to be . . . gourmet. That's what I'd advertised, right? I did sole amandine. I did jambon au madère. I did vitello tonnato, with my own mayonnaise and pureed tuna. I did . . . I did . . . I don't know what else I did, or *how* I did it.

The worst meal to prepare, bar none, was breakfast, which wasn't gourmet at all. It was the full-nine-yards English breakfast with eggs, bacon, and toast that I made on a terrible tent-like contraption balanced on top of the gas ring. I think I even did eggs to *order*: eggs over easy for the navigator, scrambled for the captain, poached for the first mate, and on and on. The stove itself was invented by the enemy. It first had to be primed with alcohol by pumping an incredibly stiff lever conveniently located at the base of the appliance. Impossible to push it in and out from a standing position. I eventually just sat down on the deck of the galley and pumped it with my foot. I was using muscles I didn't know I had.

But I loved it. The guys were all perfectly sweet to me. I even baked a cake when we crossed the finish line.

And after we tied up, it was Thor who took me along the piers, going from yacht to yacht, just as Schuyler had done in Newport. "Hey, Carter, what did you have to eat, first day at sea? A dog bowl? *We* had sole amandeen! [he meant *amandine*] Oh Burr! [he meant *au beurre*] Beat *that*!" he cried. "And come and meet our gour-may sea-cook, Hilry. She studied at the Cordon *Blue* in *Paris*!"

One hundred and forty-seven boats entered the Bermuda Race that year, 1970, which meant that hundreds of sailors were competing. Among them, I think, were just *two* women. One was a *real* sailor called Patty. And the other was Little Me. I wanted to spend the whole summer sailing on some yacht or other. And there in Bermuda, I had a lot of offers. I chose the best yacht, with the best-looking skipper, and so began one of the most exciting, most romantic summers of my life.

10

LOVE ON THE OPEN ATLANTIC

The yacht *Stormy* was a fifty-two-foot ketch with a clipper bow, moulded plywood hull, deep cockpit midships, and private captain's cabin, aft of the cockpit, with its own head (the nautical term for bathroom). It was designed by E.G. Van de Stadt and owned by a Dutch industrialist named C.B. Bruynzeel. C.B. captained his yacht in all the big ocean races.

The skipper of the yacht (that is, the professional sailor who delivers the boat from one race to the next) was a twenty-five-year-old, six-foot-four-inch blond Viking named Ted Sanford. He was from California.

Stormy was one beautiful boat, and Ted was one beautiful man. After Bermuda, his next assignment was to deliver the yacht to Cape Town, South Africa, for the inaugural Cape Town to Rio race in 1971. (*Stormy* came in third but in 1973 took first place, with Bruynzeel at the helm, age seventy-two and having had three heart attacks the previous year.[1])

The fastest route for this delivery, because of the prevailing trade winds and currents, was to cross the Atlantic three times. The boat was sailing east across the North Atlantic from Bermuda to the

Azores (off Portugal), west across the equator and into the South Atlantic from the Azores to Rio de Janeiro, and east again across the South Atlantic from Rio to Cape Town. Ted wanted a cook—a young female cook. It took me about thirty seconds to decide to sign on.

In the course of this extraordinary week, I was contacted by one of the many TV newsrooms I'd approached for a job. (Robin at the Guggenheim in New York knew how to reach me and had passed on their message.) This was CJOH-TV in Ottawa, and would I like to be their new parliamentary reporter? Would I fly up to Canada to talk about the position and we'll send you a ticket?

Ted and I agreed that whatever the outcome of that interview, we would meet on the island of São Miguel in the Azores in three weeks' time and I would join the yacht there. There was no *way* I was going to pass up this voyage, with this tanned *demigod*. As it turned out, the owner of CJOH, Stuart Griffiths, was a yachtsman himself. He even conducted our interview on his boat, then in dry-dock. I explained that I wanted to spend the summer sailing on *Stormy*, one of the better-known ocean-racing yachts on the circuit, and I would only be available for work in September. He understood completely.

I had just enough money to ship my few belongings from New York to Ottawa, pack a sea bag, and buy a ticket to the Azores. My flight would land in time to make my rendezvous with Ted on *Stormy*, with one day to spare. At least, that was the plan.

The Azores is an archipelago of nine volcanic islands in the North Atlantic and forms an autonomous region of Portugal. I was to meet the yacht on the island of São Miguel. Overseas flights all land at the international airport on the island of Terceira. Well, I thought, I can just take a commuter flight from Terceira to São Miguel, right? Wrong. So very wrong.

I land on Terceira to find that there are *no* commuter flights, at least not for a few days. "What about a *boat?*" I say, in mounting panic, at the airport's Information Desk.

"The next boat doesn't leave until the day after tomorrow, and it takes two days to get there," says the clerk impassively.

"Oh my *God!*" cries my inner voice. "I've missed the rendezvous! I have completely and utterly screwed up! I've missed my *whole summer of sailing*. With that *demigod!*" I'm on the verge of tears. No. By this time I *am* in tears. I am hysterical! There are no cellphones, no sat phones, no instant communications *at all*. Ted will just think that I've stood him up and sail on without me!

Once again this lucky star, which has been relentlessly pursuing me for most of my life, comes shining down. As I stand sobbing by the Information Desk, a dapper little man runs up, doffs his Panama hat, and takes a courtly bow.

"Excuse me, señora. I am Don Mighel-Octavio-Santa-Maria-de-Portovedo [or something like that] and you appear to be in distress. I am the mayor of Terceira and also the Pan Am representative on the island. Can I help you?"

Well, I just fall on him. From a great height, since he's barely five feet tall and I'm five-foot-ten without shoes.

"I'm-supposed-to-go-to-São-Miguel-tomorrow-to-meet-a-famous-yacht-called-*Stormy*-but-I-can't-get-there-because-there's-no-transport-and-I'm-going-to-miss-my-rendezvous-and-my-whole-summer-is-*ruined!*" I blurt out through my tears. God knows how he understood me.

"But that is not a problem!" says this adorable man. "The U.S. Air Force has a base on the island. I know the squadron leader, Captain

MacIlhenny, he is my personal friend. I'm sure he will fly you over. Come, I will introduce you."

We go to the other end of the airport and onto the U.S. base, where Captain MacIlhenny couldn't be nicer. "Sure, I can take you over there, Hilary. Sounds like you've got a great trip ahead of you. Care for a bite of lunch before we take off?"

I feel as though I've died and gone to heaven. We have a delightful lunch, a smooth flight to São Miguel, and the captain drops me off by military jeep at a boutique hotel overlooking the harbour.

I check in and go down to the water. There is *Stormy*, looking sleek and lovely but locked up. Well, I *am* a day early. I leave a note on the hatch.

Three hours later, as I take tea in the cozy hotel sitting room, a pageboy comes in and gestures behind him. Ted the demigod appears, tall and tanned, smiling down at me.

My heart skips a beat. I'm in love. Again.

Our course to Rio de Janeiro was via the island of Madeira, the Canary Islands, the Cape Verde Islands, and then across the South Atlantic, non-stop, to Rio. With those landfalls—and we would spend a few days in each one—this took pretty much the whole summer. I was to get off the yacht at Rio in early September, to go to my new TV job in Ottawa.

Initially we were five on the boat: Ted and I (in the captain's cabin); a young American couple, Terry and Tim (who slept in the main saloon); and Conrad, an experienced sailor who slept in the bow of the boat, known as the fo'c'sle. Ted wanted it to be a happy ship, but there was tension between him and Tim. With each landfall we would split up immediately and go our separate ways to explore ashore: Tim, Terry, and Conrad one way; Ted and I the other.

But once we weighed anchor and were underway, we quickly settled into a routine of watch changes and various chores, with Ted very much the captain and the rest of us as crew, obeying his orders. Voices were never raised. You can't afford arguments at sea because you know you all depend on each other to stay alive, out there on the wild and wasteful ocean. The boat is your only world as you move across the water, the sails billowing above you as you gaze at the rolling waves, the changing pattern of the clouds, or the setting sun as it slips into the sea.

Ted was a phenomenal sailor. He charted our course by celestial navigation, with a sextant, taking readings of the stars and the moon and the sun (this was well before the days of GPS). He called this a "cookbook science." "Anyone can do it," he said. I was in awe of this man: the way he handled the helm, trimmed the sails, constantly adjusting the point of sail to make the best possible time. How did he know how to *do* all this? He was only twenty-five! For the first time in my life I was in a kind of master–slave relationship. Not that he was abusive; it was just that he knew everything, and I knew *nothing*.

The only area in which I had any competence at all was the galley, and soon enough Terry and I became very competitive. We would take turns doing the meals, and we got more and more ambitious with each passing day. When we sailed into a new port and went ashore for provisions, we would each furtively seek out special ingredients for our next secret fabulous dish at sea. One of mine was Cherries Jubilee, which would have been a triumph if I hadn't brought it to the table just as the yacht lurched to starboard and the whole dish became a projectile. I didn't try that one again.

By the time we reached the Canaries, Ted decided that we really needed another hand on board. Conrad had to take his watch alone, and that wasn't fair. It wasn't even safe. You could fall asleep at the wheel without a partner to give you a kick or to spell you off. So Ted picked up a tattooed Spanish fisherman with the surprisingly top-drawer name of Julian. He looked desperate . . . the name of every woman he ever *had* was tattooed on his body. But Julian turned out to be an absolute darling and a genius at catching fish off the side. When you've been at sea for a couple of weeks and are down to canned or powdered food, a freshly caught fish, skinned and filleted by Julian and marinated by Chef Hilary, tasted better than anything you could ever eat in a Michelin two-star restaurant.

Only a few days out of the Cape Verde Islands, we hit the notorious Doldrums, an area just north of the equator where the winds drop to nothing. We were becalmed, and it was quite spooky. The sea was as flat as a millpond and finally Ted said we could swim off the yacht, provided we throw out some lines and that someone stay onboard. We lowered the ladder and jumped in. In a nanosecond the sea swell took us twenty feet away from the yacht. Then thirty feet. Then forty feet. It was very weird, and very frightening. We swam back immediately and scrambled onboard. There are stories about people who have gone swimming off their yacht in the middle of the ocean—without leaving someone on deck—and who then were lost at sea. Though when you think of it, how would anyone *know* this had happened? Perhaps by surmise, when the yacht was later found with no one onboard.

After a couple of days the wind finally picked up, and we were out of the Doldrums and on course to Rio. It was a perfect crossing, with fair winds all the way to the coast of Brazil. We had the spinnaker up—*Stormy* was made for downwind sailing—and it stayed up until we were going so fast that we were surfing, sailing on the crest of the waves. The spray from the bow was hitting the end of the main boom. We were logging 16 knots, and it was getting quite dangerous. In the middle of the night Ted called everyone up on deck to help pull the huge sail in. After two months on this superb yacht, you would think that I'd learned a lot about sailing, wouldn't you? Nah. I was pretty glib with the nautical lingo, but I couldn't even tie a bowline.

As we approached the famous harbour at Rio de Janeiro, a flotilla of boats came out to escort us into port. "Where you come from? What your names? How long you be sailing?" they shouted, smiling and waving. As I've said, *Stormy* was one beautiful boat, and she always drew a crowd.

We tied up at the exclusive Rio de Janeiro Yacht Club, in the shadow of Sugarloaf Mountain, after seventeen days on the open ocean. We were all deeply tanned and salty (to conserve freshwater we'd bathed in seawater and Fairy Liquid). The yacht club looked gorgeous. *But no one wanted to get off the boat!* Many sailors feel this after a long and successful crossing. You don't want to break the spell. And I, especially, didn't want to break the spell of this magical love affair at sea.

But we all needed a wash . . . badly. We eventually got off and that first shower was, for once, better than sex. Which is saying something, because sex at sea with Ted, in the completely private captain's cabin, was indescribable. So I won't…describe it.

I was due to start work at CJOH in Ottawa in early September, which gave us a few days together in Brazil before my flight to Canada. We sailed to the unspoiled Bay of Ilha Grande, south of Rio, after one of the members of the yacht club had invited us for a weekend cruise on his boat. He and his friends broke out the Johnnie

Walker Black Label at ten o'clock in the morning. They were legless by lunchtime and we ended up sailing the boat for them.

Saying goodbye to Ted at the Rio airport was pretty emotional for both of us. We just clung to each other, and we promised to meet in the course of the year, not really believing that this would ever happen.

11

OTTAWA: TV NEWS AT LAST

Say "Ottawa, Canada" to a sophisticated stranger and their response would probably be *"Bor-ring,"* right? Wrong, very wrong. As it happened, Ottawa in the fall of 1970 was suddenly in the middle of the most serious terrorist crisis in Canadian history. On October 5, two secret cells of the Front de Libération du Québec (FLQ) kidnapped British trade commissioner James Cross and Quebec Cabinet minister Pierre Laporte in Montreal. The FLQ demanded the release of twenty-three prisoners, half a million dollars, the broadcast of its manifesto, and safe passage for the kidnappers to Cuba or Algeria. The manifesto called for the independence of Quebec.

I had been on the job as a parliamentary reporter for about three weeks when this happened, so this put me on quite a steep learning curve. As I was to find out so many times in my career, you rely on the kindness of people with more experience and knowledge than you, and one of my better friends at this time was John Burns, then the Ottawa correspondent for *The Globe and Mail*. John later went to *The New York Times* and won two Pulitzer Prizes for his superb work in Bosnia and Afghanistan. He was constantly giving me tips, including a heads-up that the government of Pierre Elliott Trudeau was about to invoke the War Measures Act, granting sweeping powers of arrest and detention without charge.

On October 17, 1970, Pierre Laporte was found strangled in the trunk of an abandoned car outside Montreal. The Army took up positions on the city streets, the homes of almost five hundred citizens were raided without warrants, people were jailed without charge or bail, publications were censored. Though there were critics (notably René Lévesque, a separatist who later became premier of Quebec), the polls showed that the vast majority of Canadians (anglophone and francophone) supported the Act, which had never been imposed in peacetime. I spent most of my time interviewing Cabinet ministers and MPs outside the Parliament Buildings about the latest astonishing developments. But the best interview of all time was a doorstep scrum around Prime Minister Trudeau himself, when he was buttonholed by a pugnacious reporter named Tim Ralfe. Ralfe questioned the suspension of civil liberties.

"Yes, well there are a lot of bleeding hearts around who just don't like to see people with helmets and guns," the prime minister said. "All I can say is, go on and bleed, but it is more important to keep law and order in the society than to be worried about weak-kneed people who don't like the looks of—"

"At any cost?" Ralfe jumped in. "How far would you go with that? How far would you extend that?"

In his now famous riposte, Trudeau narrowed his eyes and said, "Well, just watch me."[1]

But there were negotiations with the kidnappers, and eventually, on December 4, 1970, James Cross was freed unharmed and his kidnappers flown to Cuba. Pierre Laporte's killers were later found in their subterranean hideout in rural Quebec, convicted of murder, and sentenced to life in prison. At the trial, their leader, Paul Rose, expressed no remorse and asserted that it was right to strangle a Cabinet minister to show they were "serious" about Quebec independence. They were paroled thirteen years later and allowed to return to peaceful civilian lives. All died natural deaths.

Six years later, the separatist René Lévesque became premier of Quebec. In 1980, he took the issue of Quebec independence to a referendum and lost, with 60 percent of the voters opposing his proposal that Quebec break away from the Canadian federation.

The October Crisis was a kind of baptism by fire for me, and I think I just about managed to stay whole. I think CJOH liked the fact that I was the only female TV reporter in the Press Gallery—in fact, apart from the veteran print reporter Marjorie Nicolson, I think I was the only female, period. I was not very glamorous, however. My biggest problem was my hair, badly damaged by the sun and the sea in my otherwise idyllic summer on the open Atlantic. I had quite a few Bad Hair Days, as my viewers kept pointing out in phone calls to the station. I also managed to distinguish myself by failing to correctly identify the location of a provincial leadership convention when broadcasting live from Toronto.

"This is Hilary Brown, CJOH, Madison Square Gardens," I said with a smug little smile, until the director screamed into my ear: "It's *Maple Leaf* Gardens, Hilary! You're about 400 miles out!" (Madison Square Gardens is in New York City.)

My mentor at CJOH was the news anchor Peter Reilly, a tough, completely professional newsman. I also owed a lot to my old B.C. boyfriend David Anderson. He had become a well-known Liberal MP, very plugged in, very outspoken and articulate. His riding was Victoria, and he was an environmentalist before anyone had even heard of the word. In Ottawa in 1970, there he was, ready to help me and take me out to dinner after the newscasts when he had time.

Remarkably, the quality of life in Ottawa was fantastic, mainly because I didn't *live* in Ottawa at all. I lived across the river in Old Chelsea, Quebec, a hamlet on the edge of a protected area of woodland and lakes, close to the Gatineau River. In a sense, I was returning to my roots since I'd lived there briefly as an infant with my mother while my father was away working on secret scientific projects related to the war. (Only later did we all move as a family to Medicine Hat). Mum didn't have a car and would go into Ottawa once a week, by train. She must have been very lonely.

Thirty years later there I was, back in Old Chelsea. It hadn't changed much. I lived on a farm. Okay, I was the only animal *on* it, and it was on three acres of land that required no maintenance whatsoever. At first the silence of the place, especially at night, was deafening. But very soon I became so addicted to its perfect peace and quiet that forever more I couldn't sleep with normal city sounds around me. This became a bit of a handicap later in life.

Through David's sister Fiona and her husband, Tom Hyslop, who lived nearby in Kingsmere, I hooked up with a whole circle of professional people who worked in town but lived in and loved the country. We could drive into the city in less than thirty minutes. We skied in the winter (cross-country and downhill) and played tennis, sailed, and swam in the summer. We had parties and picnics all the time. Some mornings I could even get in a few runs on the slopes at Camp Fortune before driving to Parliament Hill. How bad was *that?* Only occasionally in the winter was there so much snow that it reached the second floor of the house and I had to tunnel my way out of the front door.

Being one of only two women in the male-dominated press corps on Parliament Hill, it was inevitable, I guess, that I got roped into the annual Press Gallery Dinner. This is an evening of irreverent skits, staged by members of the press, satirizing members of the government. It's considered to be the best evening in Ottawa. People would work on their acts for months, often at the expense of their actual jobs. One day I was approached by one of the producers.

"Ah, Hilary, we wondered. Would you like to have a part in one of our skits for the Press Gallery Dinner this year?"

"I'd *love* to!" I gushed. I've always been a bit of a ham.

"Well, ah, we have developed an act that, ah, requires, ah, a strip-tease. Would you be willing to play *that* kind of part?"

That gave me pause. But not for long. I'd have done practically *anything* to be in their show.

"Okay. But I'll only strip down to a bikini."

"Ah, that's great, Hilary. We didn't want you to take *everything* off anyway."

There was a storyline for my act. I was Grace MacInnis, then the only female Member of Parliament (the NDP) and a very feisty lady who, in a desperate bid for the attention of the Minister of Consumer and Corporate Affairs (Ron Basford), takes off most of her clothes in the House of Commons. Of course, I threw myself into this routine, and did my own costumes and choreography. I started out in a frumpy dress, horn-rimmed glasses, orthopaedic shoes, and several strands of very long beads. I found that if you gave the beads a quick swing they would spiral around your body and land in a heap on the floor, which was quite effective. I went on from there . . . down to the proverbial bikini. Then I ran offstage, to what I hoped would be wild applause.

At the dress rehearsal, I was astonished to see that I actually had a live brass band playing raunchy music, really well.

The act got a lot of laughs. It was a hit. I know it was a hit because at the reception after the show Trudeau himself came up to me, adjusted the straps on my evening dress (by then I had obviously put my clothes back on), and murmured something like: "Where did you learn to do *that*? You were *so* professional." Grace MacInnis didn't mind the send-up one bit, and neither did Ron Basford.

I can't say I was remembered for a single TV report I did while at CJOH. But that striptease was impossible to live down, for years . . . even decades.

In 1973 in Tehran, at a Canada Day reception at the residence of the Canadian Ambassador, a bearded man scuttled over to me, tapped me on the shoulder, and said brightly, "I know you! When you were doing a striptease at the Press Gallery Dinner in Ottawa, I was playing the trumpet!" He was a geologist named Dickie Annels and was about to do a survey of the Elburz Mountains for the Government of Iran. We hit it off immediately, and I ended up joining one of his expeditions. (It was quite a challenge, as I later found out.)

In the mid-eighties, I literally ran into Trudeau in the remote Hunza Valley of Pakistan, in the Karakoram Mountains near the Chinese border. We were both guests of the Prince of Hunza. I was with a small group of journalists on a guided tour of the area, to see the work that the Aga Khan was doing for the local Ismaili Muslims. Trudeau was on his way to China.

As usual, his face was a mask, and he obviously didn't recognize me. "So what's your story?" he said when we were introduced. "Well, Prime Minister," I replied, "the last time we met I was taking off most of my clothes in the House of Commons." His eyes opened slightly. "Ah yes," he said with just a hint of a smile, "I remember you well."

In the course of my happy year in Ottawa I still kept in touch with my true love, Ted Sanford, who had left *Stormy* and was about to sign on as skipper of another yacht, *Baybea*, bound for the famous yacht regatta in Cowes, on the Isle of Wight in England. He flew up to see me on my farm in Old Chelsea and was quite impressed with the place. I took him to our family cottage in Muskoka and arranged a mini-trip in a canoe—the only vessel in which I had slightly more skill than he did, though he'd never admit that. We capsized within minutes.

Ted said he would be racing at Cowes in early August and then taking the yacht to Greece, making landfalls in France, Spain, and Portugal. We arranged to meet in Portugal in late August (when Parliament was still in recess), and I would sail with him for a couple of weeks. How divine.

Everything was going my way. Which, quite often, is the time when you are most likely to screw up. And that's precisely what I did.

I was friendly with a chap in the public relations department of Air Canada and when I mentioned to him, quite by chance, that I was going to be sailing on a yacht that would first be competing at Cowes, he said, "Why don't you go early and go to the regatta itself? I can get you a free seat on one of our flights to London. Then you just take a train and a ferry to the Isle of Wight."

This sounded like a great idea to me. I would *surprise* Ted and just turn up on the pier, the way I did when we first met. I set up a freelance print assignment on the race itself: the prime minister of Great Britain, Ted Heath, was competing on his yacht *Morning Cloud* and I pitched a story about him to *The Montreal Star*. I asked for a few days' vacation from CJOH, in addition to the two weeks I would be taking at the end of the month.

To any woman reading this, I offer this piece of advice: Never, *ever*, catch a man by surprise. When I finally found Ted on one of the crowded piers of Cowes (there are *hundreds* of yachts racing in that regatta), he was not pleased to see me. He was obviously busy ... with somebody else, and I could hardly blame him for that, given my various flings with David and John and one or two others.

We did spend a day and a night together. But it wasn't the same, and he didn't talk about our plan to meet on the yacht in Portugal later that month. I had broken the spell that we'd lived under for more than a year. When we parted, I knew with a sinking feeling that I would never see this beautiful man again.

But *The Montreal Star* ran my story about Ted Heath, and I contacted David, who I knew was sailing in the Bras d'Or Lake in Cape Breton, Nova Scotia, at that very moment. Would he like a first mate for a few days? I asked. He was obviously alone, and he thought it would be a great idea. So I flew to Halifax, took a bus to the port of Baddeck, and spent the rest of the week on David's twenty-four-foot yawl named *Firenze*, sailing around that lovely inland sea. Having turned down my proposal of marriage (on a ski trip to B.C. two years earlier), David by this time had basically become a friend-*boy* rather than a boy-*friend*—and I was forever grateful to him. I was quite crazy about Ted, that Viking, and my heart was broken.

I spent the rest of the summer in Ottawa nursing my broken heart. At least I had a job. Then once again, my lucky star came shining down on me.

The Shah of Iran was preparing an enormous party in the ruins of Persepolis, in southern Iran, to celebrate the so-called 2,500th anniversary of the Persian Empire. Heads of state from sixty countries were invited, including several dozen royals. On the guest list was the then Governor General of Canada, Roland Michener. His office contacted me. A small press corps would travel with him and they thought it would be good to have a lady journalist on board. Would I like to come?

12

PERSEPOLIS AND THE HIMALAYAS

The Shah of Iran's multimillion-dollar extravaganza in the Persian desert for two days in mid-October 1971 probably helped sow the seeds of his own overthrow eight years later by the Ayatollah Khomeini, who described the celebration as "the Devil's Festival." The international press described it as "the biggest party on earth."

To join the Governor General's travelling press corps, I had to take an unpaid leave of absence from CJOH. Of course, the station couldn't afford to send a crew and pay for TV coverage, so I set up another arrangement with *The Montreal Star*. With my usual overconfidence, I was sure that CJOH would keep my job open for me.

There were very few hotels in the southern city of Shiraz, next to the magnificent ruins of Persepolis and the site of the celebrations, so the members of the international press were all assigned rooms in the Shiraz University dorm. Two to a room. The authorities obviously didn't realize that "Hilary" is normally a woman's name, since my roommate turned out to be Michael Maclear, then a star CBC correspondent and later a famous documentary filmmaker. Mike and I became quite chummy.

The Iranian authorities had commissioned an enormous luxury campground in the desert outside Shiraz, next to the ruins that dated back to the fourth century BC. French architects, interior decorators, and couturiers were hired to design, build, and furnish fifty tent-like suites for the guests, all heads of state or royalty from around the world. The central banquet hall was more than 68 yards long and hung with 22 *miles* of silk. Fifty thousand songbirds were flown in from Europe to provide a morning chorus for the guests. The birds died—they couldn't take the blistering heat.

Except for the caviar, all the food was flown in from France. Maxim's, the famous restaurant in Paris, did the catering. There were two thousand bottles of fine wine and twenty-five hundred bottles of champagne. The dinner, described as the "longest and most lavish official banquet in history,"[1] consisted of quail's eggs, crayfish mousse, saddle of lamb, champagne sorbet, and peacocks' tails stuffed with foie gras. It took five and a half hours to consume.

After this colossal blowout, the guests were driven to the ruins of Persepolis to observe a sound and light show, glorifying Persian history and the twenty-five hundred so-called unbroken years of Persian monarchy. The press was finally allowed to cover this stage of the festivities (the tent city and banquet were out of bounds), and we lined up at the entrance to the ruins, under a starlit sky. By this time many of the guests were slightly the worse for wear. The King of Lesotho had to be carried in. Ethiopian Emperor Haile Selassie looked comatose. Princess Anne appeared to be cross about something (she reportedly said that she would "never again eat another peacock") though the Duke of Edinburgh was quite alert, and I can honestly say, he caught my eye. This is Really True. A French colleague nudged me and said, "Regardes! Le Duc te donne un clin d'oeil." (*The Duke winked at you.*)

The celebrations included an elaborate parade, carefully choreographed to show Persia's glorious history and the Shah's illustrious lineage as the legitimate successor to Cyrus the Great, founder of the Persian Empire in the fourth century BC. In fact, the Shah was the son of an ambitious peasant named Reza Khan who had joined the army, rose to the officer ranks, deposed the reigning Qajar Dynasty, and in 1925 proclaimed himself Shah. The parade was televised and broadcast around the world, although the entire event was completely closed to the Iranian public. The small international press corps was the only live audience. Iran was and still is a police state, and there was a security cordon of 40 miles around the site. Nothing would be allowed to spoil the glorification of Mohammad Reza Pahlavi, Shahanshah, King of Kings, Light of the Aryans, Shadow of the Almighty. The Empress, Farah Diba, later wrote in her memoirs that she was afraid there would be a wave of criticism about the extravagance of the affair: "What kind of monarchy is dressed by Lanvin and eats at Maxim's when its people still sometimes lack food and schools?"[2] But by then she was a widow living in permanent exile.

Once I'd filed my *Star* reports, I was free to . . . explore! Having got as far as Persia, I decided to go even farther east on my own, to India and Nepal. I flew to New Delhi, where I stayed with people I knew from the Ford Foundation. At one of their dinner parties I met a man who'd just returned from a trekking expedition in Nepal. He told me that it had cost practically nothing and that almost anyone in reasonable shape could hack it. The wife of the Canadian Ambassador, on the other hand, told me that I would probably get altitude sickness and this could be fatal. That was enough for me to buy a ticket for Kathmandu. I was still pining for Ted. I needed an adventure. Another adventure.

Kathmandu in 1971 was a small, picturesque mountain capital in the Himalayas. Its people left visitors alone, and the visitors seemed to be mainly mountaineers and the odd junkie. Pot and hash were legally sold in government shops. 'Best Government-inspected Hashish Sold Here' was a common sign. I had the name of a Sherpa guide, and I found him quite easily. He was about five feet tall and wreathed in smiles. I loved him immediately. He said his name was Lamalakbasherpa. I couldn't possibly remember that, so I called him Nijinsky because he stood with his toes out, in first position, like a ballet dancer. I told him I wanted to go to the foothills of Mount Everest, and he identified a region called the Helambu, about an eight-day march from Kathmandu. We would sleep in village huts on the way and would therefore only need to carry our food. *He* would carry our food. All I needed to carry was a small backpack with my sponge bag, a windbreaker, and a change of clothes.

Nijinsky took me to the central market, where we bought his carrying basket. This was an enormous wicker bin, about half his height, secured with a strap that went across his forehead. You paid your Sherpa a dollar a day, shared all your food with him, and at the end of your trek you gave him the basket. It seemed very reasonable to me.

We filled the basket with provisions, and Nijinsky hoisted the enormous unwieldy thing onto his tiny back. It must have weighed a hundred pounds. How could he possibly trek up the mountain with this? But he could. Sherpas are a famously tough breed of mountain people. After all, it was a Sherpa—Tenzing Norgay—who first conquered Mount Everest with the New Zealand mountaineer Edmund Hillary in 1953.

We walked for eight days, over a country of breathtaking beauty. We met local tribespeople, and a few trekkers, and at night would stay in a village, usually in the headman's house. I would bed down in a large communal room on the first floor of the house, with Nijinsky right beside me. We would pay a penny for a mat on the floor, another penny for an egg, and another penny for a cup of fresh milk, still steaming, hot from the cow.Or goat.

There were no roads in the mountains, so almost everything came in on a man's back. At that time, unlike today, anything that was discarded by trekkers would be snatched up and used somehow. Nothing was wasted. Cans of instant coffee would be converted into containers for staples such as sugar and salt. Even magazines would be taken apart and used as wallpaper. In one village house, I saw an entire article from *Cosmopolitan* magazine pasted across the wall. It was still readable too: "The Orgasm: what it is, and what it isn't." What the hell is a Cosmo Girl doing *here*? I thought.

At night, everyone would sit around the hearth to eat and then roll out their mats to sleep. Often they would pass around a bowl of "chang," a revolting yellow alcoholic mush, and drink from it in turn. "Chang chang!" they would cry before taking a sip. At this point I pictured myself as one of those intrepid English female explorers, born to enlighten the natives. I could possibly introduce a bit of variety into their diet, for example. I held up the three key ingredients of English custard—eggs, sugar, and milk (all of which were obtainable up there in the Himalayas and were part of my own stores)—and whipped up a smooth, creamy mixture over the fire. It was perfect, if I do say so myself. I tasted it, smacked my lips, then passed it around with a flourish, crying, "Custard custard!" I was convinced that everyone would love it and be eternally grateful to the Great White Woman from the West. No one would touch it. Not even Nijinsky.

We finally reached the Sherpa village of Tarkeyang, where normally Mount Everest was within sight. But the clouds had rolled in and I never did get my close-up view of the highest mountain in the world. Sitting in the warmth of the headman's house I stared at the white fog outside. His wife approached me, holding up two solid silver bangles. She clanked them together.

"Two hundred rupees," she said. These weren't just *any* silver bracelets. These were exquisitely crafted, matching solid-silver bangles, each in the shape of a serpent's head, with open mouths and eyes studded in turquoise and coral. They weighed about a quarter of a pound each. The Sherpa woman said that her grandmother had been given the bracelets as a reward by her husband, perhaps for the birth of a son, or something similar. Her grandmother must have been some chick. These bracelets were stunning.

But I didn't *have* 200 rupees (at the time $14). I only had $10. Things were so cheap that $10 was all I actually needed for an eight-day trip. I spent the rest of the afternoon haggling with her, and we eventually settled for $7, plus most of my clothes. Nijinsky thought I'd paid far too much and scolded me halfway down the mountain. At one point I lost sight of him, at a fork in the footpath, and in a panic thought that I had lost him for good. "Nijinsky?" I cried into the wilderness, which was useless because as far as he knows his name is Lamalakbasherpa. I eventually found him leaning against a rock.

So began my obsession with tribal jewellery, which I've been incapable of controlling to this day. The passion actually began in Damascus in 1968, got worse in Dubrovnik in 1969 and in Persia in 1971. (In Shiraz, I had picked up a massive silver link belt studded with agate and turquoise.) By the time I hit Nepal, it was a sickness. Part of the sickness is acquiring the jewellery in the country where it is made, preferably straight from the nomad. The other part is wearing the stuff, almost all the time.

After eight days of trekking with Nijinsky, I had lost ten pounds and was carrying almost nothing in my knapsack since I'd traded away most of my clothes . . . for tribal jewellery. We had eaten almost all the food in Nijinsky's basket, so his load was lighter too. We skipped down the mountain into Kathmandu, and I felt quite pleased with myself. I had also become extremely fond of Nijinsky. He was a perfect little person, and I was really sad to say goodbye. (I later wrote up our trip together in the form of a diary and submitted it to *The New York Times*, which ran it May 23, 1972, across the front page of its Travel and Resorts section.)

By this time I was down to my last few hundred dollars—there were no ATMs in those days, just cash and American Express Travellers Cheques. I had to make my way home to Canada. I got a ride on the cheapest transport available: the back of a Mack truck. A couple of Brits had installed a dozen upholstered seats in the rear of the truck, put a tarpaulin over it, and called it an "Overland Adventure Tour, from London to Kathmandu." They'd actually conned six couples into taking this excruciating tour, from west to east, which only proves that there's a sucker born every minute. The truck was going back to Britain empty. For $15, they said I was welcome to come along.

In my entire life, I have never, ever, been so dirty, or so uncomfortable. We bounced over the mountains from Kathmandu into India and across half the subcontinent, staying in dingy hotels or camping in malarial swamps. When we drove through Muslim villages, people threw stones at me because I was bareheaded, or because I was wearing jeans, or because I was blonde, or because I was a western woman, or all of the above. It was not a great way to see India.

But it was November 1971, and war was brewing between India and Pakistan. I had a fairly insane plan. I would get off the truck in Islamabad, the capital of Pakistan, and try to do freelance reports on the buildup to war. Maybe war would break out, and I would be there, on the spot! I had a tape recorder and a bit of money left. Youth and inexperience is a lethal combination. Who in the hell did I think I was, Martha Gellhorn?

We rumbled into Islamabad after dark, when the city was in a blackout. They took me to the Old Kamran, a very cheap hotel. I had become quite friendly with the two Brits driving the truck, and as I said goodbye, for one brief moment I thought, *What am I doing here?* Maybe I should stay on this terrible transport after all, all the way to London.

But I got off and groped my way into the Old Kamran. The next day, to paraphrase my Edwardian grandmother, I met my fate.

13

PAKISTAN: LOVE AND WAR

The Indo-Pak War of 1971 lasted for thirteen days and was one of the shortest wars in history, with the exception of the Arab–Israeli conflict of 1967. I had an extremely limited knowledge of the background to the war, or of Pakistan itself. But I did know that the country was divided into two states, West Pakistan and East Pakistan (formerly the state of Bengal under British rule), separated by a thousand miles of Indian territory.

The trouble had started in March 1971 when the secessionist leader of the Awami League in East Pakistan, Sheikh Mujibur Rahman, declared the Bengali right of independence. Within days the Pakistani Army, under the orders of President Yahya Khan, moved into East Pakistan and carried out a brutal crackdown, euphemistically known as Operation Searchlight. It was a campaign of murder, rape, and mass arrests that killed as many as three million Bengalis in a succession of massacres over a period of weeks. At an earlier press conference, in February, President Khan had reportedly said, "Kill three million of them, and the rest will eat out of our hands."[1] Ten million Bengalis poured into India, seeking refuge and placing a huge burden on the Indian economy. Indian Prime Minister Indira

Gandhi decided that it was cheaper to go to war with Pakistan than to shelter the Bengali masses indefinitely, ordering a massive mobilization of her armed forces. The war officially began on December 3, when Pakistan launched a series of pre-emptive air strikes on Indian airfields.

I had rattled into Islamabad five days earlier, having said a wistful goodbye to my friends on The Truck (they thought I was crazy). I called the one contact that I had in Islamabad—remarkably, the Old Kamran hotel had a working phone. He was an AP reporter named Arnold Zetlin, a very collegial guy who didn't think there was anything strange about being contacted by a Canadian wannabe foreign correspondent who had just arrived on the back of a truck. "Sure," Arnold said. "There's a press briefing tomorrow by the Pakistani military, I'll pick you up and take you there, okay?"

In Vietnam, these kinds of military briefings were known as the Five O'Clock Follies, but this was a start. The next day I showered and dressed in the only decent outfit I possessed: pale yellow silk pants and a matching blouse. Plus the tribal bangles from Nepal. I had lost even more weight on the bumpy ride across India (I lived on bread and tea since I can't stand spicy food), but I was tanned and fit and I guess I looked . . . quite good.

At the very least, I looked like a *Chick*, which became obvious at the end of the press conference. I was sitting at the back of the room with Arnold, and what I remember is a phalanx of male reporters advancing toward me, en masse. These were mainly randy, bored correspondents who had been in the country for days, waiting for war. A tanned, blue-eyed correspondent from the BBC was just one step ahead of the rest of them, and he was all over me like a *rash*. "Hi my name is John Bierman what's yours who are you working for did you just arrive where are you staying can I give you my background notes would you like to borrow my typewriter are you free for dinner what are you doing for *lunch?*"

At the time I remember thinking, *You're just too smooth, you're not going to get to first base with me*, even as I jumped at his offer of lunch, dinner, use of typewriter, background notes, everything. He was intelligent, well spoken, and well informed. Though at dinner, having given me a potted history of Indo-Pak relations, he turned and uttered that corny, time-honoured line: "Well, Hilary, tell me about yourself." Oh, *please*. This exchange was at the famous Flashman's Restaurant, and the only other patrons were Zulfiqar Ali Bhutto and his henchmen. (Bhutto, leader of the Pakistan Peoples Party, became president of Pakistan after the war.) Notwithstanding his hackneyed come-on line, John was a perfect gentleman. He took me back to my hotel in a tonga—a little horse-drawn carriage—kissed me on the cheek, and promised to collect me the next day, with his crew. They were going to cover a Bhutto rally in Lahore, and would I like to come along?

A mass rally of inflamed Pakistani men (there were never any women) is frightening, even when they're just listening to slogans and roaring approval at the rabble-rousing anti-Indian speeches. In the war fever of the time, the BBC was known as the "Bharat Broadcasting Corporation." In other words, pro-India. (*Bharat* is Sanskrit for India.) The BBC wasn't pro-India; it was just reporting inconvenient truths. John had buttonholed Bhutto before the rally, asking him if he could say a few words in English to the crowd at some point in his speech, and to just give his crew a signal beforehand. Bhutto—or "Boots" as he was known among members of the foreign press—said he would be delighted to do so. He was educated at Berkeley and Oxford, had his suits tailored in London, and spoke English beautifully.

Boots spoke in Urdu for about twenty minutes, whipping the crowd into a frenzy. John and his crew were at the side of the speakers' platform, with Little Me next to them recording the deafening sound on my tape recorder. Then Boots gave a little nod to John and switched to English.

"The British Broadcasting Corporation, the BBC, the *Bharat Broadcasting Corporation is here!*" Bhutto intoned, turning to John and his crew next to the stage.

"*Booooooooooo!*" roared the crowd.

"And the BBC says that India will *crush* Pakistan, into the *ground*." He pointed again to John and his crew.

"Oh *nooooooo!!!!*" the crowd thundered.

"But whatever the BBC says," Bhutto continued, "we will fight the Indians, and ... *drink their blood!*" The crowd roared even louder as he swept off the stage.

The mob then surged toward us, in a human tsunami. "*Get into the car!*" John yelled. We all piled in, locked the doors, and John told the driver to *drive*, not too fast, but *just drive*. "Do *not* stop! Don't stop for *anyone!*" We were surrounded within seconds by the shrieking rabble, banging on the doors of the car. By a miracle no one tried to smash a window and pull us out. They just shouted what I assumed were obscenities—it was all in Urdu, of course. Though one man spoke English. "*Back, Christian dogs!*" he cried, pounding the hood of our car with his fist. Later, back at the hotel bar, John said that he thought the insult was pretty funny. "I'm Jewish, actually."

But there's no question that if he hadn't got us away quickly, that hysterical mob would have pounded us to pieces. Thank you, Mr.

Bhutto. Six years later, he was overthrown in a military coup, imprisoned, and hanged by the new government of General Muhammad Zia-ul-Haq. In 1988, Bhutto's own daughter Benazir became prime minister and the first woman leader of a Muslim nation. Only to be assassinated in 2007 by Islamic fundamentalists in Rawalpindi on her return from self-imposed exile. Pakistan is a tough neighbourhood.

At the Five O'Clock Follies the next day, I caught the eye of one of the military briefers, the dashing Air Commodore Tahir Jan. He was flying to an airbase on the Indian border, he said. There was space on his plane, for me. As you can see, there was absolutely no disadvantage to being a female in a man's world. He didn't approach John, after all. Dressed in blue corduroy jeans, a long-sleeved shirt, and my Persian silver belt studded with agate and turquoise, I flew up to the base and, as if on cue, there was an air strike. Not very big, and not very accurate, but I got some natural sound on my little tape recorder and blundered my way through an on-scene report. After I remembered to change the batteries in my machine, that is. John and his crew turned up later, having travelled to the airbase by road. "So you beat me," he said. "Clever girl. Now show me your script."

This happened a lot in the two weeks that followed. John would vet my script, going through it with a blue pencil and editing it mercilessly. Take out *that*, add *this*, this is *wrong*, that's a good line, that's right but put it *this* way. *Scratch, scratch, scratch* went his blue pencil. "I'll make a journalist out of you *yet!*" he would say grimly, when there was very little left of my original report. I guess it said a lot for our relationship that I submitted to this without a murmur. He wasn't patronizing me. And what did I know anyway? He was a top BBC foreign correspondent with years of experience. I was just a raw, know-nothing reporter with blond hair and a body.

Two days later, on December 3, war was officially declared when the Pakistani Air Force carried out pre-emptive strikes on Indian airfields along the border. The Indians were ready for this. Even the Taj Mahal at Agra was camouflaged with twigs and branches so that its marble domes wouldn't gleam in the moonlight.

At this point, all the commercial airports in Pakistan were closed. The only way to get film out was over land. John promptly hired me to be what was then known in the business as a "Pigeon," and installed me in a comfortable room in his hotel. Just down the corridor . . . from his room. I would often visit him, for long periods of time. Such as all night. I would then hand-carry his film out of the country, via Peshawar, the Khyber Pass, through the Kabul Gorge, and up to Kabul, Afghanistan, where I would meet a BBC courier and transfer the film bag.

All this seems incredibly quaint now. But back then, in the Olden Days, there were no satellites, no uplinks, no portable satellite dishes to transmit material live from the battlefield. Your reports were on film or audio tape, they were put into an onion bag and driven out of the war zone. If you got your report on the air within twenty-four hours, you thought you were doing really well. And in that sense your Pigeon was critical.

I wasn't on a horse or a camel, of course. I had a driver, named Ashraf, who drove like a bat out of hell. I quickly realized that he was high on hash the whole time. As far as he was concerned, he wasn't going fast at all. On hash, a minute is an *hour*, right? The roads were atrocious—teeming with trucks, bullock carts, tongas, motorbikes, buses. Ashraf just slalomed through it all, at speed. Before we crossed the border into Afghanistan, he would stop in the smugglers' town of Landi Kotal, where you could get the very best drugs, and any kind of gun. Ashraf stocked up on hash. I limited myself to a leather ammunition belt, which I later wore to lunch with an astonished friend in a smart restaurant near Piccadilly Circus in London. I combined it with a red safari suit and knee-high Afghan carpet boots. At the time I thought this was cutting-edge fashion. I must have looked like Santa Claus.

Once out of the spectacular Khyber Pass, we would cross into Afghanistan and follow the Kabul gorge up into the city of Kabul. The road was not as crowded; the countryside was empty and beautiful in the pale yellow light. We would stop for Ashraf to say his prayers (as a good Muslim, he prayed five times a day, facing Mecca). That was when the Kochi nomads, camped under their black tents on the bare hillside, would run down the slopes to our car, pulling rings off their fingers and bracelets off their arms, asking outrageous prices for their tin and glass jewellery: $2 for a ring, and $5 for a pair of bangles. I bought it all. I wore it all.

In Kabul I would meet the BBC courier, Oggie Lomas, and he would get our film bag onto the next flight to London through his extensive contacts with the airlines and their pilots and crew. It had to be hand-carried all the way. I would put my own radio reports into the film bag, which the BBC would then send over to CBC in Portland Place. I recorded one of my earliest efforts in Landi Kotal so I could legitimately sign off as "Hilary Brown in the Khyber Pass." At least one person in the Ottawa Press Gallery caught this dispatch because he apparently said, "I just heard Hilary Brown in the Khyber Pass. Now I know what they're fighting about."

But the fighting was mainly in East Pakistan, not West Pakistan, though reporters in Dacca couldn't get their material out. Indira Gandhi had ordered a full-scale invasion of East Pakistan, and her army swiftly occupied Dacca and imposed a complete news blackout. The Pakistani Army capitulated in two weeks and India took more than ninety thousand prisoners, the largest POW capture since the Second World War. Almost no one was able to get film and photos of this past the Indian military. This led to one of the more famous cable exchanges between the BBC London newsroom and its correspondent in East Pakistan: "our troops in Westpak outshipping film via khyber pass," it said. "why you not do same?" The correspondent fired back: "please send one Khyber Pass."

That meant that what action there was in West Pakistan got lots of play, and Ashraf and I were going up and down the Khyber Pass like a yo-yo. CBC liked my reports and tripled my fee: from $25 a spot to the princely sum of $75. Sometimes when I came back down to Rawalpindi from Kabul after a run, I would find John waiting at the border. He would ride back with me, quoting Kipling and snaking his arm discreetly around my waist where no one could see. Public demonstrations of affection between a man and a woman were strictly forbidden, though no one had a problem when two *men* held hands in plain view. By this time I was completely disarmed by him. "You're the sort of girl I always wanted but never thought I'd find," he said to me after a long, lingering, secret embrace. The poor, deluded man. "I'm just your guy, never doubt it," he would go on, switching from the nineteenth-century poetry of Kipling to the twentieth-century language of lovers. I had a Tibetan prayer box, bought in Kathmandu, which I always wore around my neck for luck when I made the run up to Kabul and back. I'm superstitious. John would put little prayers into it, and I have them to this day. This was my favourite:

"The prayer
I make for you
Is simply this:
That you should have
What your heart
Most desires.

The prayer
I make for myself,
Is simpler.
That what your heart
Most desires
Should be me."[2]

We would drive back to the hotel, have drinks with the press corps at the bar, then dinner and even dancing . . . to the music of a terrible live band. We didn't care. We were in love. Though at the time I felt it was one of those Brief Encounters. It would end when the war ended and we would each go home, to our separate, far-flung lives, divided by an ocean and thousands of miles. And then I would never see him again.

Isn't it great, how wrong one can be?

14

A SHORT GOODBYE

The war ended in mid-December 1971 with a complete humiliating defeat for Pakistan, which lost half its population and a huge chunk of territory. The fall of East Pakistan shattered the prestige of the Pakistani military and decimated its air force and army. With the creation of the independent state of Bangladesh, Pakistan was no longer the largest Muslim country in the world.

Under Zulfiqar Ali Bhutto, now the post-war president, Pakistan started the clandestine development of nuclear weapons. Bhutto had famously vowed, "Even if we have to eat grass we will make nuclear bombs."[1] It was a crash program that produced a nuclear weapon in 1977. By then India had already carried out a surprise nuclear test, in 1974. As a result of the Indo-Pak War of 1971, the Global Nuclear Club expanded to seven: the U.S., Russia, China, the U.K., France, India, and Pakistan. North Korea later developed nuclear weapons in 2003 (probably with the help of the Pakistani nuclear physicist Abdul Qadeer Khan). This is not counting Israel, widely believed to have nuclear weapons, though its policy is never to acknowledge this.

Most of the press corps decamped to Kabul for a couple of nights before flying home, all of them relieved to be back with their families in time for Christmas. John and I had a few days to explore the city and gaze at its inhabitants. The men were in baggy cotton pyjamas known as *shalwar kameez*, worn with western jackets and enormous turbans. They had aquiline noses and long beards—sometimes died with henna, which is an alarming shade of orange. Most of the women were in *burqas*, the tent-like garments that covered the entire head and body. This medieval scene had the stunning backdrop of the Hindu Kush Mountains, and as we walked through the narrow unpaved streets we felt as though we'd gone back in time.

The BBC had issued me a ticket back to London on Iran Airlines. John and his crew were returning home a few days earlier, which gave me time to see a bit of Afghanistan. At least, that was my bright idea.

It was an emotional goodbye for John and me, especially as I honestly believed that I would never see him again. He had other ideas. "I just have this feeling about us, Hilly," he said as he folded me in his arms for what I thought was the last time.

My plan to see Afghanistan on my own was not a good plan at all. The few reporters left at the Intercon bar, namely the famous Murray Sayle of *The Sunday Times*, told me that I was out of my mind and rattled off a list of several western tourists who had met a grisly end while touring the country. Usually as victims of a religious Afghan who wished to become a "killer of infidels." For a fanatical Muslim, this is a glorious state of being that would send one straight to Paradise. Murray read aloud from what he claimed was a government guidebook to Afghanistan that said, "If you wake up and find an Afghan on one side, and a poisonous snake on the other, *kill the Afghan first*."

"Okay, Murray, you talked me out of it," I said. "I'll just change my Iran Air ticket to a ticket on Ariana Airlines and leave tomorrow."

I soon found out that Iran Air and Ariana Airlines didn't have that kind of arrangement—how on earth did I imagine they would? The Iran Air flight wasn't leaving for days. I had very little money, not enough to buy another ticket. I was stuck. I went back to the bar, looking for Murray or another western shoulder to cry on.

Murray is there, and without asking he orders me an enormous gin and tonic. "You look like you need this," he says in his Australian twang. I tell him my little story.

The great thing about propping up a bar is that you never know who might be propping it up with you. Next to Murray is a good-looking, clean-shaven chap who quickly introduces himself as a Canadian businessman. Name of Rick. Rick something or other. "You're Canadian too, eh?" Rick says.

"Yes, a Canadian in distress," I say, taking another gulp of my gin and tonic.

Rick has already overheard my tale of woe. "How much money do you need?" he asks.

The air ticket costs about $400.

"Do you happen to have a chequebook?" Rick asks. By a miracle, I *did* have my chequebook with me, in my room. Remember, this was long before ATMs.

"Yes. It's a *Canadian* dollar chequebook," I say.

"Write me an undated cheque, signed, for four hundred dollars," says Rick.

I retrieve my chequebook and return to the bar, where I sign a cheque without filling in the payee line. I hand it over to Rick.

"I'll see you in a couple of hours," he says.

I trust him. Of course I trust him. He is another Canadian. Anyway, I'm desperate.

An hour later Rick comes back and we retreat to a dark corner. He has a wad of bills the size of a brick. "Here's the Afghani equivalent of $400 Canadian. I've checked it, to make sure it isn't padded with fake currency in the middle. But check it again."

"How did you *do* this?" I ask. Rick tells me that he merely went to the money market, in the centre of town, which at the time was mainly run by Sikhs from India. In Kabul, a signed cheque on a western bank is as good as paper currency and is traded again and again. "Just don't cancel the cheque," he says. "You could end up dead."

Six months later, back in Canada, the cashed cheque came back to me with my regular monthly bank statement (in those days, banks returned your cheques once they were paid out). There was a jumble of signatures and the stamps of about a half-dozen banks on the back, from Geneva to London. It had obviously been traded several times within the Afghan diaspora in Europe—or at least I think that's what happened. I never saw Rick again. As I imagine, he is still doing "business" in some Third World country, probably for some intelligence agency. God bless him, wherever he is.

15

A LONG ENGAGEMENT

Thanks to Rick, I flew out of Afghanistan and joined Mum and Dad for Christmas—by then they'd retired to a pretty Swiss village called Genolier, overlooking Lake Geneva. I must have given John their phone number because on Boxing Day he phoned me: "Hilly, I can't live without you. My marriage has broken up. I want to come out and see you. *Now*."

Our conversation wasn't exactly private since my parents had only one phone, right in the middle of their living room. Of course I knew John was unhappily married, although when we were together he didn't talk about it. He wasn't the kind of man to disparage his wife or to complain that she "didn't understand" him. We agreed that we would take the train up to Zermatt, a beautiful ski village beneath the famous alpine peak, the Matterhorn.

We had dinner with Mum and Dad at their favourite restaurant, the Restaurant du Port in Nyon, with drinks first up at the house. John was very interested in all the framed family photos.

"What a remarkably *plain* child you were, darling," he said, picking up a picture of me at the age of two, standing in a puddle and clutching a bucket and spade. Tact was not his long suit. He'd once gazed at my size 11 feet in an intimate moment and said, "It's lucky for you I'm not a foot fetishist."

The next day we were on the train to Zermatt. "Do you ski?" I said brightly as we settled into our seats. "We can rent equipment and take a few runs." John said that he'd skied "a few times." We checked into a charming hotel and got kitted out with skis and boots and poles. John had no ski clothes—he was in a sheepskin coat and jeans.

It took him the entire afternoon to get down one run. He was covered in snow—on his hair, his eyebrows, all over his coat. He fell constantly and I hauled him up several times, only to see him fall over again and disappear under a cloud of snow. "You just go ahead and ski, Hilly. I'll get down this mountain eventually," he said through clenched teeth.

It says something about a man that he can take this kind of humiliation and yet, at the end of a *very* bad day, can shower, change, and be his debonair, witty, affectionate self over a candlelit dinner before taking his Tormentor to bed and being very, very nice to her.

He told me that he'd applied for an overseas posting with the BBC World Service in Tehran, and he would also cover news in Pakistan, Afghanistan, Iran, and Turkey. "It's a great patch, Hilly. We'd have so much fun exploring Central Asia and part of the subcontinent together. You could set up some strings with CBC and some Canadian papers. I'll help you."

By the time our weekend in Zermatt was over, he'd talked me into it. We agreed that I would fly to London with him for a few days, then return to Ottawa to my old job at CJOH. As soon as he got the results of his interview board at the BBC World Service, he would let me know. We would marry as soon as his divorce came through.

While in London I looked up Prue Emery, a friend from my Montreal days who had become the public relations director of the famous Savoy Hotel. She had carte blanche when it came to entertaining anyone at the bar and champagne was the tipple of choice, followed by a light lunch whipped up by the Savoy's famous Chef Trompetto. I told her my news: the Shah's birthday bash in the Persian desert, trekking up to the foothills of Mount Everest in Nepal, going up and down the Khyber Pass as a BBC Pigeon during the Indo-Pak War, and falling in love with the dashing BBC correspondent John Bierman.

"All that in *two months?* My God, what a story!" Prue said. "My friend Sue Arnold would love this for her 'Pendennis' column in *The Observer*." She seized the phone at the bar and called Sue.

Sue Arnold interviewed me the next day. She was half Burmese and exquisite, with a top-drawer English accent. Her article appeared (with photograph) on January 9, 1972, and I can still remember the opening sentences: "It's a relief to find one woman at least who says it's all for the asking. She is called Hilary Brown and she looks like Aphrodite and talks like Ernest Hemingway and not, as is unhappily sometimes the case with women journalists, the other way round."[1]

You won't be surprised to hear that Sue became my friend for *life*. Thirty years later I was able to even the score when I did a TV profile of her for ABC. By then she'd become clinically blind from a genetic condition called RP (retinitis pigmentosa). We filmed her riding horses in Richmond Park, cycling down the King's Road in Chelsea, and making crème brûlée for her husband's trendy restaurant, using a blowtorch. She was still working as a journalist. "Miss Arnold says she's not afraid of falling off her horse because she can't *see* that far down" was one of my lines, I think. Not as good as hers about me, of course.

A few days after my *Observer* interview, I flew back to Canada after a final romantic dinner with John. This time I knew I would see him again, though I didn't know exactly when. And so began the first of many separations that were typical of our long life together. It may be the reason we stayed together at all. Over the next few weeks we wrote letters to each other almost every day. "How lucky I was to find you," John wrote. "How clever I was not to let you drift out of my life," he added with his usual lack of modesty.[2]

I've kept all his letters from that time, for forty years, but only recently did I have the courage to take them out of their locked box and reread them, tears streaming down my face.

"I love you I love you I love you. However shall I get through the night without you in my arms?" "Dearest sweetest loveliest lady of my heart, how I adore you." "I believe in you, Hilly. You're honest and straight and true." "If I were to lose you now, I would look back in years to come with an unbearable sense of loss."[3]

In late January 1972, John was assigned to Ulster, or Northern Ireland, by BBC TV News for a regular tour of duty. Northern Ireland was then at the height of the British colonial war known as "The Troubles." At the request of the Ulster administration, the British Army had moved into Ulster in 1969 as a neutral force. Initially the soldiers were welcomed by the Catholics, who believed that they would protect them from the Protestant paramilitaries. They greeted them with cups of tea. But by 1972 the British were loathed by the Catholic minority, especially after internment without trial was introduced in August 1971.

On January 30, John got one of the biggest stories of his life as a TV reporter when he covered the infamous shootings in Londonderry that came to be known as "Bloody Sunday." British troops of the 1st Battalion, Parachute Regiment (known as One Para), opened fire on unarmed demonstrators taking part in a civil rights march. They killed thirteen people. It was the highest number of civilians killed in a single shooting incident in the whole history of the Troubles. Later at the inquest, the coroner, a retired British Army officer himself, reported that "the Army ran amok that day and shot without thinking what they were doing.... [I]t was sheer, unadulterated murder."[4]

John and his crew got the first and the only TV footage of the victims, notably the famous sequence showing a Catholic priest, Father Edward Daly, waving a blood-stained handkerchief as he and two others tried to carry a dying seventeen-year-old, Jackie Duddy, to safety. "It was outrageous! Disgraceful!" Father Daly said to John. "There was no provocation whatsoever!" Minutes later John buttonholed an officer of One Para to ask him why his men had opened fire on unarmed civilians. "They did not fire until they were fired upon," the officer drawled. "The Paras fired three rounds altogether."

"There are more than three dead already," John said pointedly.[5]

The attack came late in the afternoon, so close to John's deadline that he ended up voicing over his thirteen-minute report *without* a written script. The spectacular footage went straight from the "soup"—the film processing solution—and onto the airwaves, with John broadcasting his commentary *live* over the raw unedited pictures. It was one hell of a performance. Later the BBC transcribed what he'd said and had him re-record his commentary ... for submission to the Cannes TV Film Awards. He won.

The day after Bloody Sunday, the world's press descended on Northern Ireland, and naturally I wanted to be there. I had *not* managed to go back to my old job as parliamentary reporter for CJOH, after a three-month leave of absence. They had given my post to someone else, and what did I expect? So I was a freelancer again. At least I still had the farmhouse in Old Chelsea. John and I had a long talk on the phone, and to my surprise he didn't want me to come. "What's the matter, don't you think I can hack it?" I snapped. We hung up on each other, without our usual terms of endearment.

The next day John sent me a telegram (another quaint thing from the past): "YOU OVERSENSITIVE. ME OVERPROTECTIVE. WHEN YOU COMING TO BELFAST?"[6]

Bloody Sunday led to a surge of recruits to the Irish Republican Army (IRA). It was a highly volatile situation and John was just worried that I might get hurt. He *knew* the territory. He knew it so well that he'd just written a thriller set in Northern Ireland, as fiction on a factual framework. It was to be published that spring as *The Heart's Grown Brutal*, which is a line from the Irish poet W.B. Yeats: "We had fed the heart on fantasies, / The heart's grown brutal from the fare."[7]

John gave me some contacts and I did a radio documentary about the women of the IRA, focusing on one of the greatest viragos of them all, Máire Drumm. Máire gave a great imitation of a cozy, harmless housewife (she was then in her early fifties) and welcomed me into her home with coffee and cookies. In reality, she was a fierce, uncompromising Republican and vice-president of Sinn Féin (the political wing of the IRA). She was assassinated in 1976 by Ulster Protestant paramilitaries. She spoke beautifully and was the perfect subject for a radio profile. "Our steps must be onward," she said in her deep rich voice. "If we don't, the martyrs that died for you, for me, for this country, will haunt us forever."[8] What a quote. She used it a lot, I later learned.

For the end of my report I recorded an eight-year-old Catholic girl singing "The Men Behind the Wire," the Republican song of the moment, about the mass internment of Republican suspects by the British Army into Long Kesh Prison . . . behind the wire.

> "'Armoured cars and tanks and guns
> Came to take away our sons,'" went the little voice.
> "'But every man must stand behind
> The men behind the wire.'"[9]

John was actually impressed with my work, though he did *not* think it was a good idea for me to be wearing an expensive fur coat on the mean streets of Belfast. The radio documentary was broadcast on CBC.

After about a week together in Northern Ireland, John went back to London and I went back to Old Chelsea. We still had no idea whether he'd get the Tehran posting and, if so, when he would go. When *we* would go.

Absence makes the heart grow fonder, as the saying goes, and within a month he took some time off to come and see me in The Frozen North. In early March, *frozen* is exactly what Old Chelsea, Quebec, is. To welcome him, I thought it would be a great idea to have a cross-country ski party, through a woodland trail to a warming hut in the forest, where we'd have mulled wine and hot sausage rolls by the pot-bellied stove. This would be very special because it would be in the *moonlight*. Wasn't that romantic? I invited all my Gatineau friends, who naturally were very anxious to inspect Hilary's latest heartthrob. I also invited my beloved sister Gingie and her handsome boyfriend, Freddy Huber. They would drive down from Montreal.

Poor John! Another ski torture! We outfitted him in cross-country gear, clipped him into the skis, gave him a ten-minute primer in "langlauf," and set off along the narrow woodland trail, in the *dark*. John looked as though he was walking on eggs. He fell a lot. He swore a lot.

"Congratulations, Hils," I muttered to myself. "You've just screwed up another great relationship."

"It's not far now, darling!" I cried. I was also distressed that Gingie and Freddy wouldn't be with us after all because the ski rental shop had closed by the time they'd arrived from Montreal. Gingie had always been my Good Fairy, and I considered this a Bad Omen. Another Bad Omen.

Somehow, John made the 5 or 6 kilometres along the twisting forest track without breaking a bone or just kicking off his skis and refusing to go on. At last we came to the warming hut, which was like reaching the Promised Land.

Who should be there to greet us but . . . Gingie and Freddy. Having waved a sad goodbye to us at the start of the trek, they got into their car to drive home. Minutes later they picked up a couple of guys hitchhiking on the road. They told the boys their story—that they had missed a moonlight cross-country ski party because the rental shop was closed.

"We can help you out with *that*!" the boys said. "We work as trailblazers. We've got a whole hut full of equipment. Where's the party?"

This is what is known as serendipity. They took Gingie and Freddy to their storage hut, fitted them out with skis and boots and poles—even miner's headlamps—and then lead them, at speed, to the warming hut in the forest. Glasses in hand, they were all waiting for John and me. This was a very *Good* Omen.

We quickly poured about a pint of mulled wine into John. He felt *much* better. Everyone gathered round the pot-bellied stove and tucked into the hot sausage rolls—and lo! by the time we were ready to go back, the moon was up. It was shining down on us like a searchlight, high in the night sky. We skied home over a frozen lake, gliding along a flat surface at last and feeling absolutely no pain. John had survived Hilly's second Trial by Snow.

Gingie and Freddy stayed with us at the farmhouse after the ski party. The next morning they both said they'd dreamt about a baby girl. Seven and a half months later, their daughter, Karina, was born, six weeks premature. She was conceived on that magical night. I became her godmother and Karina grew up to be a beautiful, talented, courageous, resourceful, intelligent girl, a great reporter, and a very good mother herself.

And remarkably, Hilly's love affair with her dashing Englishman wasn't over after all.

16

OUR LIFE IN PERSIA

Looking back, it's hard to imagine a more exciting way to start a life together than in Persia in the early seventies. I know it's called Iran, but I prefer the more exotic, more musical name.

The BBC World Service assigned John to Tehran in early April 1972. I flew out to join him in early May. We could not marry, however. Once his wife, Alice, found out about me, she refused to give John the divorce that she said she always wanted. I took to calling John my "former fiancé."

It would be five years before we could tie the knot. "Marry in haste, repent at leisure" was not our experience.

We lived in Persia in the bad old days of the Shah, an autocrat and an absolute monarch who wished to westernize his country. Iran was a free-market economy based primarily on oil, and oil prices had quadrupled thanks to the OPEC cartel (the Organization of the Petroleum Exporting Countries). There was a rapidly emerging middle class. Women were unveiled and ostensibly liberated, people could drink wine and spirits in the restaurants, and males could consort openly with females. We were frequently invited to mixed dinner parties, in what appeared to be a very secular society. We had absolutely no inkling that within seven years, Iran would be taken over by Islamic fundamentalists and dragged back to the Middle Ages. We thought that if there was to be a revolution, it would come from the left, not the religious right. That's how much we knew.

We found a lovely place in the hills above Tehran, not far from the Saadabad Palace, where the Shah lived. It was at the end of a tree-lined lane with a high wall and a gate, and within its walls was a large pink villa overlooking a shaded garden and pool. One of our first visitors was a dung-seller, who arrived with a train of camels. Before I could stop him, his camels ambled into the courtyard, relieved themselves, and ambled out again, leaving enough fertilizer for the entire garden. For every garden on the lane.

I had a happy time furnishing the house with tribal rugs and saddlebags bought from a well-known carpet merchant called Bolour, who overcharged me, naturally. I had the furniture made to my design—all you could buy ready-made were outsize gilded chairs in the French provincial style that looked as though they belonged in an upmarket brothel.

For security reasons, we thought we should have a large dog, and we soon acquired an Alsatian puppy who we named Beowulf and who grew to the size of a small sheep. Fortunately, our maid Mooney was one of the few Iranians who was not afraid of dogs, and she was very good to him. She would say "Befarmaid" (*By your leave*) every time she opened the kitchen door to let him into the garden. We adored Mooney, even though she sometimes failed to meet expectations. When we had people to dinner and she would wait on table, she would come out of the kitchen with a cigarette hanging out of her mouth.

For a brief and glorious period, we had the extra security of two tall Bakhtiari tribesmen who lived on our roof. An eccentric British tribal expert had asked us to put them up, as a favour. They were magnificent men, extremely courteous, and they said I could accompany them on one of their tribal migrations, from summer to winter pastures. I got very excited about that.

As the first BBC correspondent to open a permanent bureau in Tehran, John had an entrée into the western diplomatic corps, and we quickly made friends among them, usually at the level of first or second secretary, such as Nick and Diana Browne of the British Embassy. (Years later Nick came back as British Ambassador to Tehran under the regime of Ayatollah Khomeini, received a knighthood, and then was forced to leave the foreign service early because he was struck down by Parkinson's disease.) Richard and Alison Broinowski of the Australian Embassy were great friends (Dick was an accomplished violinist and Alison became a diplomat herself). We were very close to David Housego of the *Financial Times*, and his wife, Jenny, who spoke Farsi and was a great expert on Persian carpets. We also had friends in the business world, notably Ian Brook, an engineer with Esso, and his spirited, multilingual wife, Frances. Frances was very talkative and was known as The Babbling Brook. She could pick up a language in weeks, mainly so she could keep on talking. Ian and Frances are great friends to this day. She now does private guided tours in England in Farsi, Thai, Italian, French, German, and occasionally English.

But when it came to making Iranian friends, it was quite different. Iran was and still is a police state, and the secret police, known as SAVAK, were everywhere, with a huge network of informers. We would invite Iranians to dinner and at first they would accept. Then a few days later they would ring up and cancel, making some excuse. For them it was simply too risky, too suspect, to go to the home of a foreign journalist. Someone would inform on you. That "someone" might even be at the same dinner. We soon realized that when you did make friends with an Iranian, and he came to your house, he was probably filing a report about you, your opinions, and your movements to SAVAK. Of course, our telephone was bugged so we had to be circumspect on the phone. SAVAK censored books and films; it even briefly confiscated some books that I'd brought into the country from my own collection: *Clementine in the Kitchen*, *Mastering the Art of French Cooking*, and an extremely rare limited edition of *Alice's Adventures in Wonderland*.

These were considered by SAVAK to be subversive. They were eventually returned, but the gold-embossed cover of *Alice in Wonderland* was marked in fountain pen across the top and with the indelible mark of a glass that the SAVAK agent had placed on it. I suppose I was lucky to get the books back at all. By that time, the Shah had taken to describing his country as "The Great Civilization."

There was one Iranian woman who befriended us almost immediately and frequently invited us to her comfortable family home. She was about my age, spoke fluent English, and was very westernized, having been to college in the United States. She was related to Amir-Abbas Hoveyda, an avuncular figure who was the longest-serving prime minister in the history of Iran. (After the revolution, he was imprisoned and later executed by the Islamist regime in April 1979.) On one occasion she proposed a short road trip into the countryside. Neither John nor I were very diplomatic (I'm still not), and we were probably a little too frank about the Shah and his "Great Civilization." She got an earful. Which was just what she was looking for, I suppose.

But I don't think we ever really understood just how all-pervasive and terrifying SAVAK was for ordinary Iranians. They lived in a perpetual state of fear and paranoia. Because there were so many informers, they knew they could be arrested at any moment, just for a single slip of the tongue or misplaced word. Then they could be carted off to jail, or just "disappeared." There was no free press or free speech. According to an Amnesty International report of the period, Iran had the highest rate of death penalties in the world and a record of torture that was "beyond belief."[1]

SAVAK agents could also operate as agents provocateurs. They would verbally attack the Shah or one of his policies, just to uncover a person who could be tricked into agreeing with them. Everyone was afraid of this. They trusted no one. To paraphrase the famous Polish journalist Ryszard Kapuściński (in his book *Shah of Shahs*): "Fear so debased people's thinking, they saw bravery in deceit, courage in collaboration."[2]

Journalistically, I managed to set up some "strings," as they are known in the business. I did radio reports for CBC and CBS—at last, I had got my toe, if not my foot, in the door of a big American network. CBS actually told me how to pronounce my own *name*. I had a pretty strong Canadian accent, with its hissing sibilants and elongated diphthongs. I said *"aboat"* instead of *"abowt"* and talked about *"shed*ules" instead of *"sked*ules." Very early on, after I'd filed another report to CBS, some editor in New York came on the line and said, "Hey, Hilary! Could you call yourself Hilary *Braown* and not ... whatever it is you call yourself." Playing back my reports from that period, I'm amazed that they put me on the air at all. I sounded like a hick from a small town in Ontario. Which, in a sense, is what I was.

I earned about $100 a month and most of that money went to pay our maid. John thought it was important that I should contribute to our household expenses. "You don't want to be a *Kept Woman*, do you?" John said. No, I didn't, but I didn't want to be an Impoverished Woman either. In the two years that we lived in Iran, I went through most of my modest savings. "For the dubious privilege," I used to say to John as I put my arms around him, "of sharing a life with *you*."

But shortly after I arrived in Tehran, I had one of the busiest work periods of our whole time there. And that was immediately followed by one of the most strenuous expeditions I have ever, ever undertaken. Looking back on it, I don't know how I survived.

The news story was U.S. President Richard Nixon's state visit to Iran in May 1972. By this time Iran had become the largest single buyer of American arms in the world. The trip marked the close relationship between the U.S. president and the Shah, who wanted Iran to become a member of the Club of Western Nations. In an interview with the distinguished Egyptian journalist Mohammed Heikal, the Shah even asserted that "in twenty years' time, we shall be ahead of the United States."[3] Nixon, for his part, had completely revised American thinking on Iran's regional role: his Middle Eastern policy was based on a militarily strong, pro-American Iran. In a public display of their friendship, the two men drove through the streets of Tehran in an open motorcade, in what must have been a nightmare for their security men.

I was doing radio spots for CBS News all day. Then when Nixon flew out of the country and the heat was off, I went home to get ready for a twenty-hour hike, starting in the *moonlight*, with *skis*, to the top of Mount Tochal, elevation 13,000 feet. Part of the Elburz mountain range, Mount Tochal looms over Tehran. I did not do this alone: I was invited on this hike by a crazy Englishman named John Malcolm. How on earth did Malcolm think I could actually *do* this? What the hell did John Bierman tell him about me, for God's sake? That I was some kind of mountaineer? I was a mountaineer like John Bierman was a downhill racer.

We set out at nine in the evening, with mules to carry our skis, boots, and provisions. An Austrian friend of Malcolm, equally crazy, came along with us. We walked up a trail in the foothills until the snow appeared. That was at about 2 a.m. At this point we had to abandon the mules, since they slip on snow. So we put on our ski boots and carried our skis and backpacks to the top of the mountain, which we reached at about ten in the morning. That's *thirteen* hours, walking straight up that frigging mountain. I remember looking up at the ridge on the horizon and thinking, *Okay. I just have to get to that ridge and then we're there*. But no! Another ridge, even higher, would come into view. The whole thing was insane.

When we reached the top (a shelf just below the summit), we put on our skis and skied down through the powder until the snow ran out. That took one hour. We hit the grass, took off our skis and walked, for another *five* hours, down to the nearest village. That was about 4 p.m. Finally Malcolm and his Austrian friend said we should stop under a tree to rest. I thought, *I'm just going to lie down on the grass for a moment and close my eyes*. I passed out. They could not wake me up. So they hired a donkey and flung me over its back, like a sack of flour. We were met in the next village by John; Malcolm's wife, Bini; and a few others who had formed a welcome party. I was comatose for my moment of triumph.

During our time in Iran, I made quite a few expeditions into the Elburz Mountains, sometimes with John and sometimes with friends when John was away. I also *walked* from Tehran to the Caspian Sea—a trek of eight days and a distance of 124 miles , as the crow flies—with my new geologist friend, Dickie Annels. (Yes, that's the little bearded chap who played the trumpet while I did a striptease at the Press Gallery Dinner in Ottawa in 1971.) My friend Suzy from Canada was visiting us at the time, so she came along too.

We crossed three mountain ranges, pitching our camp by ice-cold streams at the end of each day. The trail was breathtaking, with a constantly changing landscape, as we went up and down in altitude. What made it even more special was the performance of our handsome young muleteer. Every time we dropped down into another valley, he would throw back his head and sing, his rich tenor voice reverberating from peak to peak.

I completed this entire trek on foot, just like Dickie. Suzy, on the other hand, spent most of her time on the mule. She looked biblical.

John and I did a fantastic expedition into the fabled Valley of the Assassins, named after a fugitive called Hassan-i Sabbah who set up his headquarters there in the eleventh century. According to legend, he got the villagers high on hash to secure their devotion. Hassan's followers later fanned out all over Persia and the Levant, terrorizing their enemies. They became known as the "Hashishins." Hence the term "Assassins," don'tcha know.

All that was pretty evocative as we formed our little party and prepared to enter the famous valley. Our group consisted of John and me, Ian and Frances Brook, and Suzy. (She'd made a second trip to Iran. She was an heiress. She could afford it.) I had just read *The Valley of the Assassins and Other Persian Travels* by the famous British explorer Freya Stark. I saw myself as a younger, more attractive version of the writer, who was a bit of a bluestocking. We approached the valley through an opening in a high, sheer black rock, and then the trail descended into a lush green valley, full of fruit trees in blossom and with a river running through it. I was thinking, *This is it! We're going back in time! Very few westerners can have come this way! I'm an explorer, just like Freya, but younger, and more attractive!*

Dream on, Hils. I was yanked back to reality as we followed the bend in the river and came upon a group of English schoolboys on an Outward Bound trip. As it happened, they were from Wellington, a posh British boarding school where my great-uncle, Bobby Longden, was once headmaster. I did *not* care to share this remote and magical place with a bunch of spotty British teenagers, however. "Why can't you just *go away?*" I muttered. Fortunately, they soon broke camp and we ended up having the fabulous place to ourselves after all.

John and I would often go on overnight hikes into the Elburz, taking a little tent and a lot of black-market caviar. At that time in Iran you could get the top-quality "golden" caviar simply by picking up the phone, dialing a number, and saying, "Want caviar" (*Caviar micham* in Farsi).

"Balay balay," an urgent husky voice would say. "Cherad michay? Koja?" (*Yes, yes. How much? What address?*)

"Yek kilo. Bisto-yek kuche mehr." (*One kilo. Twenty-one Kuche Mehr.*)

"Chasm!" the voice would say (*Done!*), though it didn't usually mean that the job would, in fact, be done at all. For Iranians, the Word alone is often the Deed. But when it came to black-market caviar, the job was very much "done."

The phone would click, and within an hour a man in a suit would knock at the gate, carrying a briefcase. He would open his case to reveal little pots of top-quality caviar in neat rows. You could taste it if you wanted. You paid him cash and with a bow he would disappear. It was prime caviar and cost about $10 a pound. Caviar on the open market at the beginning of the millennium cost between $3,200 and $4,500 a pound.

It was one of the few services in the country that actually *worked*. The caviar was smuggled out of the government fisheries on the Caspian Sea and driven over the mountains to Tehran in a never-ending succession of clandestine transports. A small army of men in suits would take care of the distribution. The clientele came by word of mouth.

You can imagine the kind of luxurious mountain picnics we would have. We would carry white wine, bread, butter and lemons, choose a grassy spot by a mountain stream, chill the wine and the pot of caviar in the icy water, and have a feast. Sometimes we would carry champagne. We would celebrate in other ways too, until one of our friends—an old Persian hand—pointed out that we might not be alone. "There is *always* a pair of eyes," he said with a knowing smile.

If we camped overnight there was more than a single pair of eyes. We would walk to the outskirts of a village, and half the population would follow us to our campsite. These were children mainly, and football was the lingua franca. "Georgie Best!" one boy would shout. "Manchester United!" John would shout back. As night fell, our fans would go back to their village, only to reappear early in the morning. Very early.

"*Get! Up!*" said one, in a loud voice.

I opened one eye. "What time is it, John?"

"Five o'clock."

"*Five o'clock!*" I shouted and poked my head out of the tent. "It's *five o'clock in the morning!* Why don't you guys just *fuck off?*"

One of the boys looked at John, who now had his head out of the tent too.

"He . . . is *sad*," the boy said, pointing to me.

For the rest of our life together, John could defuse almost any argument between us by pointing at me and saying, "He . . . is *sad*."

Our adventures were not just limited to the great outdoors. We would plunge into the Grand Bazaar of Tehran to look at the extraordinary variety of goods that were still made by hand, on the spot. The tinsmiths, the coppersmiths, the silversmiths, all tap-tap-tapping away at intricate trays and bowls and jugs and jewellery.

Their hand-painted tiles were charming too, showing animated hunting scenes, or a man and a woman lounging under a tree, with a jug of wine and a distinct gleam in their eyes. And then there were the carpets, especially the flat-woven tribal kilims. They were works of art. I loved it all. I bought it all. I had a three-bedroom house to furnish.

It was just as well that we had three bedrooms because inevitably, within a few weeks of our arrival, John's mother, Bessie, descended on us for a "short visit." Without any hint of self-pity, John had told me about his childhood. His father, Richard, had deserted Bessie when she was pregnant, in the mistaken belief that she was carrying another man's child. Bessie ended up leaving their young son, John, with a succession of relatives in the working-class East End of London (where she grew up) while she lived it up in the West End.

John said that he couldn't remember having lived with his mother, ever. Bessie would occasionally sweep down to the East End and take him out for the day. Since he rarely saw her, he said he never developed any attachment to her. And he felt no love from the relatives who had agreed to house and feed him. "I didn't expect any affection, and I didn't feel sorry for myself," he told me. "I just thought that this was normal, this is the way life is." During the Second World War, John was among the one hundred thousand children who were evacuated from London in June 1940 and sent off to the country, to escape the Blitz. For many children, being separated from their families was a terrible trauma. He loved it. John's bleak childhood made him strong—the strongest man I have ever met.

He didn't meet his father, Richard, until he was twenty, while he was on leave from his compulsory military service with the Royal Marines. He decided to trace him. He knew that Dick Bierman had an antique store in Soho, and he had only to ask around before he found him. He walked into the shop and saw a bearded man in his mid-forties, sitting at the back. The man looked up, smiled at John, and said quietly, "Hello, son."

John kept in touch with his father for years after this encounter, until Dick Bierman's death in 1964. John named his first-born son after him.

It wasn't until his mother had reached a certain age that she turned her attention to her only child, by then a successful journalist. Bessie would then say helpful things like "I saw you on television last night. You didn't look well."

After Bessie's visit to Tehran (she spent quite a lot of time criticizing my clothes, usually in front of guests), we had John's three children, two of whom came to stay for good since they no longer wished to live with their mother, Alice. Alice was going through what the psychiatrists call Crazy Time, sending poison-pen letters to us and sometimes to her own children.

By the end of the summer, Katie, age seventeen, had come out to Tehran, followed by Richard, age eleven and then known by his nursery name, Bong. John's second child Alison, age fifteen, flew out for a visit. She went back to England to live with an older friend, who later married her (the first of her three husbands). I took on a new role: that of Wicked Stepmother.

In truth, John's children were warm and affectionate with me, when they could have resented me bitterly as a homewrecker and turned against me. The girls both said they were glad that their father had found someone who really made him happy. Katie soon found a job as a live-in nanny with an American family in Tehran. Bong enrolled in an international school and followed me around like a puppy. When he first arrived, he was as white as a sheet, talked nonstop, and hugged John incessantly. He seemed disturbed. I felt sorry for him and tried to be a good pal, teaching him to ski at a resort in the Elburz, taking him to karate class, and going on hikes with him.

He also learned to ride. We took him to a beautiful farm called Norouzabad outside Tehran, owned and operated by Louise Firouz, an American horse breeder who was married to an Iranian. Louise discovered the tiny Caspian horse (only four feet high) from a herd that was running wild in the foothills of the Elburz Mountains. She took a number of them back to Norouzabad and started to breed them, later presenting the Duke of Edinburgh with a pair. She was very hospitable and would invite Bong to stay at Norouzabad, which she had turned into an equestrian academy.

Within a few months there was colour in Bong's cheeks and no more anxiety in his eyes—even when Alice phoned to ask him if he would like to "live with his father forever and never see Mummy again." John, of course, didn't believe that a child should be cut off from his mother. He was later awarded custody of Bong after Alice said she couldn't, or wouldn't, care for him anymore.

About the same time, John started getting the reviews of *The Heart's Grown Brutal*, the thriller he'd tossed off in a white heat in the space of two months. "Dammit, if Freddy Forsyth can do it, I can!" he'd said as he pounded away on his typewriter. (John knew Forsyth when Freddy was also a BBC reporter, and before he'd published the best-selling *Day of the Jackal*. At the time, Freddy didn't command that much respect in the BBC newsroom. After he'd published *Day of the Jackal*, the attitude changed completely.) John had to publish his book under a nom de plume (David Brewster) since he was a BBC staff correspondent. One of the reviews compared his work to that of Graham Greene, which John thought was hilarious. My all-time favourite photo of him is on the terrace of our house in the hills above Tehran, grinning from ear to ear, eating caviar and surrounded by the rave reviews on the table in front of him.

Several years later, when I was earning real money, I had *The Heart's Grown Brutal* handbound for him, with his own name (not the nom de plume) in gold lettering on the spine. By then he'd published a half-dozen books, which all received the same treatment from me, bound in deep red or green leather, with gold lettering. It became known as "The John Bierman Oeuvre, or Egg."

17

PERSONA NON GRATA

Though John and I were now a family, with his son and our dog and a maid, we still managed to travel together around his "patch," leaving Richard and Beowulf with our wonderful friends the Brooks. We went often to Pakistan, and Afghanistan, and Turkey, to cover breaking news stories, or to do feature stories, or both.

In Afghanistan, we saw the last Royal *buzkashi* ever played in the country. This was before the coup d'état in July 1973 that overthrew the king and established a republic. The Royal Buzkashi took place annually in the capital of Kabul, in front of the monarch, King Mohammed Zahir Shah, and his invited guests. The players, called *Chapandazes*, came mainly from the north and were the bravest, fiercest, most murderous horsemen in Central Asia. Buzkashi is one of the wildest, most spectacular, most dangerous games ever played, anywhere. It's performed on horseback and is similar to polo, except that instead of a ball, the decapitated corpse of a goat is in play, stuffed with sand and weighing about a hundred pounds. The object of the game is to pick up the goat from a mounted position and carry it, at a gallop, to the nearest goalpost, which can be anywhere from 100 yards to several miles away. This is difficult, especially when you have a dozen screaming horsemen trying to get the goat away from you, lashing and slashing at you with whips and knives, respectively. The rules are definitely according to Genghis Khan and not the Marquess of Queensberry.

The court of Genghis Khan, the famous Mongol emperor, is where buzkashi is said to have originated. His horsemen played it with the corpses of their enemies, after they'd been beheaded. Yes, I know: lovely people. But on that field in Kabul in 1972, in front of the king of Afghanistan and his guests, and with the horsemen dressed in high leather boots and silk dressing gowns, gripping their whips and knives with their *teeth*, we felt quite transported, right back to the twelfth century. People *died* playing this game. People died just *watching* it, since the horsemen would on occasion gallop straight into the crowd.

Less lethal was a romantic weekend in Bamiyan, north of Kabul, famous for its two colossal stone statues of Buddha carved into the cliffs above the valley. We stayed in the only comfortable hotel in the area, which consisted of a main dining hall and a collection of dome-shaped yurts, each furnished, heated, and equipped with its own bathroom. It was quite wonderful to spend the day scrambling up and down these sixth century statues, 181 and 125 feet high, and then return to the kind of dwelling that was used by Central Asian nomads for hundreds of years. The Buddhas were blown up by Taliban fanatics in 2001 because they were pre-Islamic monuments and therefore sacrilegious. UNESCO has declared the whole Bamiyan Valley a World Heritage Site in Danger, and experts say the statues can never be rebuilt. That makes my memory of our weekend in Bamiyan even more special.

While John was covering a political story in the capital of Pakistan, I went off on my own and walked into Kafiristan, in the foothills of the Hindu Kush Mountains, on the border with Afghanistan. This region had been made famous by Rudyard Kipling in his story "The Man Who Would Be King." (Much later it became a movie, starring Michael Caine and the late Sean Connery.) Kafiristan wasn't that easy to get to, however, and I couldn't have done it without the help of Air Commodore Tahir Jan of the Pakistan Air Force. He'd remained a friend after the war and he introduced me to the district officer in Chitral, who set me up with one of his guides. Kafiristan is so named because the people are *Kafirs*, or "unbelievers." Not Muslims, but pagans, whose religion seems to consist mainly of ancestor worship. The people were said to be descended from a deserting legion of Alexander the Great—many have green eyes, and pale skins. The women wear long dark robes and elaborate headdresses made of cowrie shells.

Kafiristan consisted of not one but three mountain valleys and the first was called Bumboret, accessible only on foot. Following my guide, I hauled myself up and down the trail, and after a march of two or three hours, we dropped down into a wide, open valley with a river tumbling through it. There were mulberry trees along the river, and beneath them women had spread out lengths of cloth to catch the berries. It was a beautiful sight. I felt I'd stepped back in time! *I am probably one of the first western women ever to set foot in this hidden valley, this Shangri-La,* I said to myself.

Once again, my grand illusion was shattered by the appearance of a small group of . . . yes . . . *western* persons. Not a group of British schoolboys. It was worse. This time it was a film crew from the National Film Board (NFB) of Canada. Good grief. The four-man team didn't seem especially enchanted to see me either, even though I was careful not to get into their damn shot. We barely exchanged a word as we passed each other on the narrow path. I'm not even sure I told them we were compatriots.

But once the NFB left the valley, I had it all to myself. The women stopped gathering mulberries and surrounded me, playing with my blond hair and trying on my tribal jewellery. (For this trek I had limited myself to my Nepalese silver bangles and my Tibetan prayer box.) Taking my hands, they led me into their village, a cluster of flat-roofed, single-storey wooden houses scattered up and down the hillside, away from the river. They showed me the segregation hut, where girls and women were isolated when in labour. And they showed me the simple wooden coffins, all above ground, where the remains of their ancestors were kept. My guide translated for the women, and we understood each other perfectly.

The Kafirs practise a form of animism and have festivals to celebrate the riches of their three fertile valleys. The women aren't veiled, and even divorce is permitted. I mean, a woman can divorce a *man*. If she wants to change husbands, her new spouse must pay double what her old spouse paid to marry her. Therefore, if Husband Number One paid one cow, then Husband Number Two must pay two cows . . . to Husband Number One. Elopement is apparently quite common among the Kafirs. It would be, wouldn't it, given the expense of marriage.

The Kafirs sang and danced for me, and I got it all on my little tape recorder. Then came the moment of truth, where I really *did* feel that I was one of the few western women ever to venture into this secret place. They started to show me their various ailments, using hand gestures to ask me if I had any medicine to help them. I always travel with a few pills (Aspirin, Imodium, and so on) and I gave them what I had. The real challenge came from a young man who hobbled in with a filthy bandage around his leg. With a graphic swipe of his arm he indicated that he'd cut his ankle while chopping wood. At least I thought that's what he meant. He obviously expected me to examine his wound and make it better.

Good lord, do you think he cut through to the bone? I was thinking, in mounting panic. *Maybe* gangrene *has set in! I've gotta bluff my way through this, there's no telling what they might do if I don't make him* seem *to be better.*

Mercifully, I didn't smell any infection as I started to peel back the disgusting rags wrapped around his leg. The whole village was watching. But as I exposed the leg itself, what I found was a clean wound, and quite a lot of chicken shit. Literally. That's what he'd used to treat his wound and as far as I could see, it worked a treat. So I cleaned up his leg, applied a bit of iodine, and wrapped a nice fresh bandage around it.

He was so grateful that he presented me with a beautiful wooden footstool that he had made himself. It was held together with leather thongs—not a nail in sight. I felt a complete fraud, but I graciously accepted his gift. I would have insulted him had I refused, right? I carried that stool for the rest of the trek. I carried it all the way home too, and from one home and one country to another throughout my nomadic life.

I stayed in Kafiristan for a couple of days, and at night my guide took me to the home of the local prince, which was close to the river. Like some of the Kafirs, he had converted to Islam and for my stay I was required to go into *purdah*, secluded in the women's quarters. The women taught me how to enhance my eyes with kohl, the ancient cosmetic made of charcoal and used to underline the eyes. It had an effect: within a few hours the prince announced that he would like to marry me. For one split second I was actually tempted. I mean, what a story.

Incredibly, I was able to place little feature radio reports about my esoteric travels with CBS News, and I would sell the odd print feature, with photos, to *The Montreal Star* and other publications. I rarely did any hard news reporting during our time in Persia because the stories simply weren't there. It was too far off the beaten track. I began to feel that I would never become a foreign correspondent, not a real one. The consolation prize was trekking into the remote and fabulous corners of Central Asia.

Although we didn't realize it, our unmarried status in Tehran shocked the Persians. On one occasion, British Ambassador Sir Peter Ramsbotham invited us for drinks in the beautiful summer residence of the British Embassy for the sole purpose, it seemed, of telling John he should make an honest woman of me. "For appearances' sake, you two might at least *pretend* that you've tied the knot. . . . It would be quite a good idea, wouldn't it?" et cetera, et cetera. He also suggested that John should perhaps write some "positive pieces" about the country. From this we understood that the Shah and his court had been complaining to Sir Peter about the BBC's reports of unrest in the universities and elsewhere. John's reports were not just broadcast by the World Service in English, they were also translated into Farsi and broadcast straight back to Iran by the BBC Persian Service, in programs that could be picked up by any Persian with a transistor radio. Ambassadors have always believed that the Press is a menace to Diplomacy.

I suppose that it was inevitable that the Shah would finally stamp his royal foot and say, "Get this BBC man out of here." It happened in October 1973. The press officer of the British Embassy called with the urgent message that John should come and see him immediately. John had just returned from a tiring assignment in Pakistan. "Can't it wait until tomorrow?" John snapped. "No, you must come right now." He returned about an hour later looking shell-shocked.

"Hilly, I've been declared persona non grata. We have to leave the country in three days."

"*Three days?* How can we possibly *do* that? What happens to Bong? Beowulf? All our things?"

"The Shah wants me out. Doesn't like my reports. And especially he didn't like the BBC *Panorama* documentary on Iran that was broadcast a few days ago."

The news of John's expulsion spread like wildfire through the international community and also among Iranians. Hate mail was pushed through the front gate. But we also had a steady stream of friends and acquaintances dropping by to commiserate. The American chargé d'affaires came around with a bottle of whiskey. Nick Browne of the British Embassy dropped by, though we didn't see Ambassador Ramsbotham ever again. Jenny and David Housego brought over a three-course dinner, which we ate on the floor, Persian-style, since someone had already bought our marble dining table. Haleh Esfandiari and her husband, Shaul Bakhash, both academics, courageously invited us to dinner, though they were Iranian. (She was half Austrian, and he was born in Iraq). The Canadian Ambassador invited us to his residence for drinks. His houseguest at the time happened to be Lesley Blanch, author of the best-selling book *The Wilder Shores of Love*. She floated down the staircase in a chiffon gown, clasped my two hands, and said breathlessly, "You look *just* like Ursula Andress." Another friend for life.

Fortunately, the three-day deadline was extended to a week, and somehow we managed to pack up the house and find a home for Beowulf. The Brooks cabled from England (they'd gone home a few months before): "We can take richard until the dust settles." John's expulsion had been reported in the British papers. It was as though the Brooks had read our half-crazed minds. We put Bong on a plane the next day. And that was a blessing because on the fourth day of that terrible week, the Egyptian Army crossed the Suez Canal into the Israeli-occupied Sinai Peninsula, and the Yom Kippur War began.

But every cloud has a silver lining. And in this case, the silver lining turned out to be pure gold.

Author aged 1. Old Chelsea, Quebec. Her first standup to camera.

My British parents, Jocelyn and Tony Brown, at the start of their new life together in Canada, in the Gatineau, Quebec, 1939.

My youngest sister Kathy, with her daughter Emily, Primrose Hill, London 1974.

Montreal, 1967. The author, dreaming of becoming a foreign correspondent, and getting nowhere.

With Air Commodore Tahir Jan of the Pakistan Air Force, who flew me to the front in the Indo-Pakistan war, December 1971. I'm already wearing a massive tribal belt into a war zone.

John and I on a hike in the Elburz Mountains of Persia, 1972. A rare moment of respite away from the BBC in Tehran. One of our greatest pleasures.

My all-time favourite picture of John, in our house in the hills above Tehran, 1972, eating caviar and reading the rave reviews of his first book.

On the aircraft carrier USS Hancock South China Sea, after the fall of Saigon. Interviewing one of the US servicemen who helped evacuate 6800 people from the city in less than 24 hours, without a single loss of civilian life (photo courtesy ABC News).

Newport Bridge, Saigon, April 1975, the day before the Fall of Saigon. Covering a firefight between the Viet Cong and the Army of South Vietnam. My standup had to be done lying down (courtesy ABC News).

"The Unspeakable Folly", Cyprus, August 22, 1976. The groom in a safari suit, the bride wearing yet another tribal belt, clutching flowers picked from the garden.

Jonathan and I, getting to know each other.

Israel, 1978. My favourite publicity shot, mainly because I never, EVER looked this good (photo courtesy Sami Ben Gad).

Calypso Cottage, Cyprus. Every room has a view, including the bathroom.

Ho Chi Minh City, April 27, 1995. ABC sent me back to cover the twentieth anniversary of the Fall of Saigon. Ironically, Vietnam's communist leaders had turned to the free market as the only way out of their country's poverty (photo courtesy ABC News).

With my younger sister Gingie, in Stowe, Vermont, 2012. Gingie is five years younger than I am, but I keep claiming that she's my twin.

My niece and god-child Karina Huber. Like me, she became a TV reporter. But much more beautiful, and unlike her aunt, highly skilled, technically.

18

THE YOM KIPPUR WAR

The news that the Egyptian Army had crossed the Suez Canal on October 6, 1973, and rolled, virtually unopposed, into the Israeli-occupied Sinai Peninsula took almost everyone by surprise, notably the Israelis. At the same time, the Syrian Army came very close to reoccupying the Golan Heights (seized by Israel in the Six-Day War of 1967). "They caught us with our pants down,"[1] as one Israeli army officer said. The coordinated Arab attacks were timed to start on the Day of Atonement, Yom Kippur, the holiest day in the Jewish calendar, when many soldiers and airmen were away from their posts. Though Israel pushed back the Egyptian and Syrian forces within a few days, the failure of Israeli intelligence to foresee the Arab campaign was later the subject of a formal inquiry in Israel. And though the Arab armies were defeated, the war brought Egyptian President Anwar Sadat enormous prestige.

After the Six-Day War in 1967, Israel occupied territory four times its original size. It captured the Sinai Peninsula and the Gaza Strip from Egypt, East Jerusalem and the West Bank from Jordan, and much of the Golan Heights from Syria. When Sadat became president of Egypt in 1970, he determined that the Arab countries could not carry on an endless crusade against Israel. In 1972, he expelled twenty thousand Soviet advisers from Egypt and opened diplomatic relations with Washington. His daring secret plan was to make a surprise attack on Israel, and then negotiate for peace. That eventually came to pass in September 1978 with the Camp David Accords, signed by Sadat, Israeli Prime Minister Menachem Begin, and U.S. President Jimmy Carter. It was the first peace agreement ever between Israel and an Arab neighbour. I ended up covering that historic moment, though of course I couldn't know this at the time.

In Tehran, John and I were still doing our fairly frantic last-minute packing. It is quite a challenge to close down a furnished three-bedroom house, with a large dog and a twelve-year-old child, in less than a week. And then to scramble on a major news story. The BBC wanted John to go to Egypt and cover the war from there. I'd been planning to go on a migration with the Bakhtiari tribe—I'd made the arrangements weeks before, with those two gorgeous Bakhtiari tribesmen who had briefly lived on our roof.

John and I went out to our favourite local restaurant for a final chelo kebab together. I was in a fairly confused state, which I thought was perfectly normal under the circumstances. Should I stay behind in Iran and go on this migration? After all, I hadn't been expelled from the country. It was John who was persona non grata.

He gave me a long, hard look with his compelling ice-blue eyes.

"Hilly, you keep talking about how you want to be a foreign correspondent. If that's what you really want, you should *not* be running after some obscure Persian tribe on their annual bloody migration. You should get your royal ass to Israel. There's a war on, or hadn't you noticed?"

John could be quite acerbic.

"You mean, you think I could pick up some freelance work there?"

"If you don't, you shouldn't be in the business, honey-bunch. This is one huge story. Just *go*."

The next day I booked a flight, packed my tape recorder plus some samples of my work, along with the usual twenty pounds of tribal jewellery and a few changes of clothes. I wasn't coming back, after all. Mooney came with a little van and took our leftover furniture, bedding, glasses, and dishes. John packed all his gear for Cairo, and we left for the airport together, with barely a backward glance at the lovely Persian house where we'd spent so many happy days and nights together. We assumed we would meet again when the war was over. But when would that be, and where?

I landed in Tel Aviv a few hours later and very quickly found out that the Park Hotel, on the seafront, was offering a special rate for the press: $36 a night, including breakfast. Incredibly, they had a room—even though the country was swarming with foreign journalists. I immediately called the CBS radio assignment desk, told them where I was, and do they need me? By then they mainly knew who I was from all those funny feature reports I'd filed from Iran and other parts of Central Asia.

"Nah, Hilary, we're pretty well set up. We've got a whole team in Israel already."

My heart sank. Bloody hell, I'd come all this way and my number-one string didn't need me. What about CBC? They were always on a tight budget, maybe they could use an extra body. I contacted their radio news desk. Well yes, they could take some on-scene reports. They had a radio man in Jerusalem, pulling together all the strands of the story, but they didn't have anyone in the field. They switched me to the accounts department, and someone with a Scottish name said he'd authorize a hotel for me for four nights.

Four nights? You think the war will be over by then? I was thinking to myself. But I'm in no position to argue. A freelancer never is.

At the press centre I met a lot of journalists I had known in Islamabad in the Indo-Pak War of 1971, and a quite a few let me hitch a ride in their transport to the front, either down to the Sinai or up to the Golan Heights. I got interviews and ambient sound and did on-scene reports. CBC Radio used almost everything I filed.

I met some interesting people. My pal from Montreal, Leonard Cohen, was on the scene as some kind of observer—he wasn't yet a world-famous poet-singer and was able to move around without being mobbed. We had dinner together and caught up on each other's news. And Group Captain Peter Townsend, a former Royal Air Force flying ace, was often seen propping up the bar with the international press corps. He was the royal equerry whom Princess Margaret famously wanted to marry, remember? He was in the country doing a feature story on the Israeli Air Force for one of the British Sunday papers. Because of his military background, and possibly because of his royal connections, he had unusual access to that elite and secretive force. Peter (as he insisted we call him) was extremely charming and utterly discreet—not a word about what he called "the Margaret Thing."

But something much more wonderful happened. I ran into Lou Cioffi, ABC's Paris-based correspondent, whom I'd last seen in Pakistan. He was his usual urbane, friendly self.

"Hey babe, you know that ABC is looking for a female foreign correspondent? It's all the heat they've been getting from the Women's Liberation Movement. The Suits have decided they hafta show that

ABC supports feminism. You should apply! You're a femme if ever there was one!"

"Wha? Looking *for* a female? You think *me*?" I was so incredulous I couldn't get out a grammatical sentence.

Lou told me who I should apply to, and I sat down that very night and wrote a letter, enclosing a couple of samples of my work. In spite of the war, the postal service was still operating in Israel; and back in the Stone Age, one still wrote letters. Lou also gave me the name of the ABC bureau chief in London—George Watson—and told me to contact him at the end of the war. ABC's first female foreign correspondent would be based in London.

In spite of the initial Egyptian gains and Israel's lack of preparedness, within a few days the Israeli Defense Forces (IDF) were fully mobilized and pushed back the Egyptian and Syrian armies, in some of the greatest tank battles ever seen since the Second World War. Casualties were high, on all sides. The Israelis lost between twenty-six hundred and twenty-eight hundred men. There were an estimated twenty thousand Egyptian dead, and about thirty-five hundred Syrian fatalities.

Journalists were also among the casualties. Notably Nicholas Tomalin, who was killed by a Syrian wire-guided missile on the Golan Heights. Tomalin was a great British reporter who never pulled his punches. He once wrote that the only qualities essential for real success in journalism are "rat-like cunning, a plausible manner, and a little literary ability."[2] This should be taught in all journalism schools.

The Egyptians were forced to retreat back across the Suez Canal. The Syrian Army was driven out of the Israeli-occupied Golan Heights, and the Israelis took even more Syrian territory on the

Heights themselves. On October 25, 1973, a United Nations–brokered ceasefire was signed between Egypt and Israel.

I had what I thought was a pretty productive couple of weeks, filing my little on-scene radio reports to CBC from the Sinai Peninsula and the Golan Heights. CBC thanked me, paying me $25 a spot. I later submitted my hotel bill for the whole fourteen days. It was rejected. "We only authorized four nights, Hilary" was the prim response. So I actually ended up *paying* for the honour of working for CBC Radio during the Arab–Israeli War of October 1973. Years later, at a dinner party in Toronto (I was by then anchoring the six o'clock news on CBC), I found myself sitting next to a neat little man with a Scottish name who turned to me with a smug smile and said, "I was the man who rejected your claim for hotel expenses during the Yom Kippur War."

"Oh yes, Mr. McTwerp. Is that what you do to feel truly alive?"

No, I didn't say that. But I wish I had.

I flew to London soon after the ceasefire agreement. John was already there, talking to his masters at the BBC World Service about his immediate future. Having been expelled from Iran, the question was where he should now be based, to continue covering his patch, which included Pakistan, Afghanistan, and Turkey. We fell into each other's arms, and I told him about the ABC search for a female foreign correspondent. Neither of us thought I had a hope in hell of getting the job.

Within a couple of days the World Service determined that John Bierman should rebase in Turkey. They wanted him to go to Istanbul as soon as possible. They weren't being unreasonable.

In the meantime, I made an appointment to see George Watson at the ABC London bureau. I fully expected him to look at my flimsy résumé and politely show me the door. Then I would follow John, wherever he was assigned. Whither thou goest, I will go.

John was due to leave the following morning. We went out for a farewell dinner, one of the many farewell dinners in our life together. He became very serious.

"Listen, Hilly. You've got to think very carefully about my next assignment, and about your own life and career. It's obvious now that Alice won't give me a divorce. I can't marry you, and I really can't go on being your 'former fiancé.' I desperately want you to be with me in Turkey, darling, but I can't promise that you'll get anything more than the odd freelance assignment. So you've got to think about yourself, and *your* future. If you want to build a career in the news business, you're not going to get very far as my camp follower."

I was stunned. This man, whom I had lived with and loved for two years, wasn't trying to get rid of me. He was being the Complete Gentleman. Telling me not to have any false hopes about marriage, making me think very hard about my options in life.

We were staying in a friend's apartment and we just clung to each other for our last night together. Neither of us slept very much. I knew what my answer had to be. In the morning, I told this manly man, my lover and my best friend, that I would not follow him to his new posting. I would try to make my way on my own. I kissed him, and hugged him, shaking with sobs. He was crying too. I thought it would be our last embrace. I stumbled out the door.

I remember being in a state of shock as I stumbled to the home of my beloved Aunt Elisabeth, who lived in a large flat on Cadogan Square in Knightsbridge. I felt that the ground was sinking beneath my feet. I was truly devastated, both at the enormity of my decision and the prospect of life without John. I really loved this man, in a way

I had never loved any man before. It's a cliché, but John was my rock. And now I had decided to let him go.

Aunt Elisabeth was immensely sympathetic. She'd met John several times, and she liked him enormously. But she was practical.

"Right, Hilly. You've made your decision. You must think about your next step. When is your appointment with ABC and what are you going to wear?" Aunt Elisabeth was also very chic. My wardrobe consisted of several pairs of jeans and an impressive collection of tribal jewellery, and that was *it*. She lent me a tailored jacket that she thought worked well with my best denim pants.

To my surprise, George Watson was happy to see me that very day, and he couldn't have been more cordial. He suggested that I do a TV report as a trial assignment. At the time, London was in a fever of excitement over the imminent wedding of Princess Anne to Captain Mark Phillips, the first time in two hundred years that a member of the British Royal Family was to marry a commoner.

"Why don't you do a report on Mark Phillips's hometown?" George said. Or village, as it happened. He lived in one of those quaint English hamlets with low stone walls, half-timbered houses, and men and women on horseback clip-clopping down every lane.

What a *gift*! How could you miss with an assignment like that? Especially as George gave me his top cameraman, Jim Godfrey, and his delightful soundman, Robin Springate. I felt immediately that they were on my side.

We drove down to the Cotswolds, and the village was everything a pretty English village should be. Though it was early November, the sun was actually shining. We spotted a girl on horseback and I rushed up for a quick sound bite, microphone in hand. "What do you think of a boy from the village marrying a *princess*?"

She could barely hold back her tears . . . obviously Captain Phillips was the local heart throb. "I'm very happy for them," she blurted out with a little sob, and then cantered off. Perfect sound bite! Perfect shot! Then we went to the Phillipses' house itself, thinking that we'd just get an exterior of the place. But what the hell, let's knock on the door and ask for an interview. Captain Phillips's father appeared, was utterly charming with me, and asked us to set up our camera on the lawn. The crafty old publicity hound. Five minutes later he came out, along with his wife, who would like to be interviewed too, thank you very much.

My report really wrote itself, and with Jim's beautiful visuals it made a very nice piece, if I do say so myself. George said so too. The show producers in New York even said they would like to put the piece on the air.

Then I waited, for days. For weeks. I waited until the Royal Wedding itself, on November 14, 1973, when I did freelance on-scene reports for ABC Radio News. But I had no answer from the ABC brass in New York about the position of first female foreign correspondent. My fallback was to return to Canada and try to get a job back at CJOH-TV. I was running out of money. I couldn't batten on Aunt Elisabeth forever. I missed John, terribly. From Turkey, he'd sent me a message that if, by any remote chance, I did get the ABC job, which was to be based in London, he would leave the World Service and get himself reassigned to London, to work for BBC TV News. Then we could be together again.

In desperation, toward the end of November I decided that I would spend my last few hundred dollars to fly myself to New York and try to get some face time with the ABC brass. Then they might, they *just might*, hire me. I bought a one-way ticket. If I succeeded,

ABC would fly me back to London, wouldn't they? If I failed, I would go to Ottawa, probably by bus.

I arrived in New York on the last Thursday of November. Which, I suddenly realized, is Thanksgiving. *Nobody* in the United States of America is in their office on Thanksgiving. No one is in their office for *four days*! No one is at home either; at least not anyone I knew in New York, though I made a half-dozen calls. I checked into the YWCA, thinking that my terrible timing was a *very* bad omen. Apart from that, I had barely enough money to last the weekend.

The next day I made a second call to my friend Alexandra Anderson. There had been no answer when I rang the day of my arrival, and answering machines (let alone voicemail) didn't exist in the Olden Days. Ally picked up the phone.

"*Where* are you?" she said in her breathless, husky voice. "You're staying at the YMCA? For God's sake, pack your bag and come over here right now!"

Ally lived with her then husband, Kelly (a stockbroker), and their two small children in a huge apartment on East 72nd Street. She was an art critic and journalist, knew everybody in New York, and was one of the friendliest, warmest, least stuck-up people I'd ever met. We'd been pals since my days as Head of Publicity at the Guggenheim Museum in 1969. We spent the rest of the Thanksgiving weekend together, and I was eternally grateful to her for taking me in.

On the Monday morning, I telephoned ABC and managed to get an appointment that day with Nick Archer, manager of TV News. He was an Italian American who had standardized his name, but he had Latin charm and an electric smile. You may not believe me, but there was absolutely *no* casting couch in his office. He said that everyone had seen and liked my audition report and my sample tapes.

"You are *impressed*! My God!" I didn't say this out loud, of course. I was both shocked and excited. I really, really wanted that job.

What I did say, with my heart in my mouth, was: "Do you think you could take me on for a trial period, say two or three months, no obligation?" At that point I remember thinking, *I can't leave this office without* talking *this lovely man into hiring me.*

Mr. Archer said he thought that could work, and that he'd like me to start, in London, in two weeks' time. Would I be able to get my affairs in order by then? Would I like an advance of, say, $1,000 to cover my expenses? The ABC travel department would give me a ticket.

Would I like an advance of a thousand *dollars?* I don't think I'd ever handled that much money, at one time, in my whole life! He arranged for me to come back the next day for a tour of the New York bureau, to meet the executive producer, foreign editor, evening news anchor, radio editors, and so on. We exchanged a few more pleasantries, he shook my hand, and I floated out of his office. Someone from accounts gave me ten crisp hundred-dollar bills, and I continued to float on out the door, onto West 66th Street.

Twenty minutes later I was back at Ally's apartment.

"*Well?* What happened? *Don't* be discouraged if they were noncommittal," Ally said, always positive but at the same time realistic. She'd held my hand through all my attempts to get into the networks four years before.

"Well, I *think* I got the job. They gave me a thousand-dollar advance on expenses and are going to fly me back to London in about ten days."

"They gave you a thousand dollars and you're not sure you got the *job?* For God's sake, Hils, get real! *Of course* you got the job!" Ally cried, giving me a huge hug. In those days, $1,000 really was a lot of money.

I spent the first $25 on a bottle of champagne for my hostess, which we demolished that evening. Then I flew to Ann Arbor, Michigan, where my parents were based temporarily (Dad was on a two-year teaching fellowship at the University of Michigan). We celebrated my thirty-third birthday and my amazing new job. Mum and Dad promptly went out and bought their very first TV set, so they could see my reports on television. The funny old things.

Then I sent a cable to John in Turkey: "landed ABC job. when you coming to London to join me?"

I had been struck by lightning; there was no other way of putting it. Except to say that impossible dreams . . . can sometimes come true.

19

THE BEST JOB IN THE WORLD

The next few years were the happiest, most exciting, most fulfilling that I had ever known. From the outset, ABC treated me like a professional, in spite of my inexperience. It was a relatively young network, compared with CBS and NBC, but it was already known as the "best shop in the business." In New York, I was given a tour of the bureau and introduced to all the key people. At the time, they were taking in a piece from Peter Jennings, then based in Beirut. After the feed, they patched me through to him, knowing that we already knew each other.

"Mabrouk!" said Peter when told of my new position. I actually knew that *mabrouk* is Arabic for "congratulations." So I cleverly responded with "Chukran!" which is Arabic for "thank you." Even after he became uber-famous, Peter helped me during all my years at ABC. One of his greatest qualities was his loyalty to old friends. His fame never went to his head.

I was also introduced to the anchorman of the *Evening News*, Harry Reasoner. A man seldom known for his charm.

"Harry, this is Hilary Brown. She'll be working in London as our new foreign correspondent."

I extended my hand. It was left hanging in the air.

"*Working* in London, you say? We have correspondents *in* London. We don't have any who are actually *working* there," he retorted.

I had no idea how to respond so I just murmured something about "how much I admire your work, Mr. Reasoner" and backed away. Eighteen months later, after I'd covered the Portuguese Revolution, the Turkish Invasion of Cyprus, and the Fall of Saigon, I did a feature piece on Royal Ascot, with the irresistible theme of the British upper class at play. Hats are required for the ladies at Ascot, and so I wore an enormous wide-brimmed confection for my closing piece to camera. I felt quite pleased with myself. Reasoner paused for a moment after my report and said, "Well, usually we have a rule against funny hats. But I guess we'll make an exception for that one."

After that, I kind of liked him.

Just to get my feet wet, ABC had me do a few reports out of New York before they flew me to London. Nick Archer said that I could take a week off at Christmas and start work on the first week of January 1974.

I flew to Istanbul to spend Christmas with John. What a turnaround from our parting in London only two months before! When I truly thought I would never see him again. He was living in a hotel on the Bosphorus, which was a pretty romantic spot for a lovers' reunion. But this was Christmas, and this particular lover has a *thing* about that time of year. Turkey, a mainly Muslim country, is not the place to get into the Yuletide spirit, especially since in 1973 the Christian Christmas coincided with the Muslim feast of Bayram. That's when the faithful slaughter sheep, goats, and even camels and the streets run red with their blood.

"John, get me out of this place *now*! We can't celebrate Christmas in a bloody butcher's shop."

"Well, *where?*" John cried. "I can't stop a custom that's been going on for hundreds of years!" Then he brightened. "I know. We could go to Cyprus. That's a Christian country. And it's only a forty-minute flight from Istanbul!"

And so began another great love affair, this time with the then bucolic, pastoral, unspoiled island of Cyprus, in the Eastern Mediterranean. In late 1973, Cyprus was not yet a tourist destination. We stayed at the Ledra Palace Hotel in Nicosia, and Silly Hilly had her Christmas dinner, by candlelight and with all the trimmings. (Cyprus is actually Orthodox Christian, but because of its history as a British colony, it observes the Roman Christian calendar too.) By Boxing Day, I'd decided that we *had to* have a home on the island, overlooking the sea. A home we can call our own and where we can always meet, come what may. We had exactly three days to find this, maybe four, before I was to fly back to London.

We drove over the coastal mountain range to the charming port of Kyrenia, on the north coast, in the shadow of the famous ruined Crusader castles, and then up to Bellapais, where British author Lawrence Durrell once had a house. He wrote about it in his book *Bitter Lemons*.

"We could follow in Durrell's footsteps!" cried Ms. Brown, sipping coffee in the main square of the village, beneath the famous Tree of Idleness.

One look at the real estate prices and we quickly understood that Kyrenia was way beyond our means. Okay, what about the west coast? The next day we drove to the seaside town of Paphos and contacted the one real estate broker in town, an elderly man named Joseph Charalambous. He drove us into the hills to a tiny village called Tala. It was then a cluster of stone houses beneath a lovely

Byzantine monastery called Agios Neophytos, known for its medieval cave paintings. (As we later learned, it was also known for one of its lascivious priests, who couldn't keep his hands off any female visitor, of whatever age, or species.)

The land just fell away from this hilltop village, sweeping down to the sea through olive groves and vineyards. The views were stunning. Joseph showed us a one-room stone farmhouse and barn in a state of collapse. They were on two terraces of land, planted with carob and almond trees, with an unblemished view of the coastline. The sea sparkled in the middle distance, a twenty-minute drive away. It was heart-stoppingly beautiful. This was the Mediterranean retreat we were looking for! Never mind that it was basically uninhabitable.

Joseph quoted a price of 2,000 Cypriot pounds, which was about $10,000. We bought it on the spot, though we had only enough money for the deposit. But then, oh joy! My beloved father said he would send us the balance—his gift to me, he said, for my exciting new job with ABC.

John and I parted once again. He flew back to Istanbul, and I flew to London. But he would join me later in the year, when he would rebase to BBC TV News. We would be together again.

All of this was one hell of a way to start 1974. The bureau chief at ABC London, George Watson, became my mentor and a lifelong friend. Forty years later, he sent me a copy of his memoir, where he described me as "the beautiful and intrepid Hilary Brown." He signed it, with this inscription:

> "You were, and are, the most intelligent and glamorous woman I've known in my career. And putting gender distinctions aside, you are simply tops in our field. And a great friend. Love, George."[1]

Gosh, George! Good thing I didn't know that back then. I would have become impossible.

There were two cameramen—Jim Godfrey and Peter MacIntyr—and two soundmen, Robin Springate and Patrick Etcheverry, an enormous Frenchman. (Actually, he was Basque, which is apparently different.) I adored them all. After a few assignments together, they were like brothers to me. There was a radio reporter, Jerry King, a Canadian from southwestern Ontario, just like me. He soon became a full-time TV correspondent for the network. He was openly gay; and considering the social attitudes of the day, his success was a real achievement. The bureau was small then, small and perfectly formed. Less than fifteen people, and we were like a family. If the president of ABC News, Elmer Lower, came to town, he would take everybody out to dinner.

One of my first big stories was the Portuguese Revolution, which ended more than forty years of authoritarian rule under the Estado Novo regime, founded by the dictator António de Oliveira Salazar in 1932. (Salazar died in 1970, but his repressive regime continued.) It had been the longest-lived autocracy in Western Europe and was overthrown in a coup d'état in April 1974 by low-ranking army officers. At first, ABC was reluctant to send me into a possibly dangerous situation, but of course I protested, saying that I should be allowed to risk my life right along with the boys.

As it turned out, the Portuguese Revolution was almost completely bloodless. The old regime killed just four people before it surrendered. Later there was a handful of deaths, all accidental. It became known as the Carnation Revolution. No shots were fired, and when the people took to the streets to celebrate, they would place a carnation in the barrel of every soldier's gun. They would occasionally embrace them. There were no reprisals, no mass imprisonments, no murderous settling of scores. People just demonstrated, ad nauseam, day and night, rejoicing in their newfound political freedom. They were extremely polite with the international press, delighted that their revolution was getting so much coverage. If there was even the slightest scuffle, they would apologize profusely. On one occasion I was accidentally hit on the forehead with a small rock. The blow drew a trickle of blood. A half-dozen Portuguese men rushed to my aid, shouting, "Hoshpital! Hoshpital!" They were quite disappointed when my head stopped bleeding, which was almost immediately.

At the time, we were only reporting for one TV program, the *ABC Evening News*, and for ABC Radio News. There was no morning show, and no *Nightline*. And no satellite communications. After you'd shot your story and written and recorded your narrative track, you'd ship the film by air to London, where it would be edited or shipped on to New York. You and your team could then go out to a civilized dinner, usually with other journalists, who are the best company in the world. Or if you were a packrat like me, you might possibly slip into the famous Fábrica Sant'Anna ceramic shop in Lisbon to buy several substantial items of beautiful hand-painted pottery. I came back from this assignment with three large ceramic lamps, a pair of candelabras, and a fountain, quickly establishing my reputation as ABC's leading Stuff Queen.

20

TURKEY, AND THE INVASION OF CYPRUS

A couple of weeks before my Portuguese assignment, I had flown out to southern Turkey with Jim and Robin to interview two young American girls who'd been sentenced to death for drug smuggling. The girls—Joanne McDaniel from Oregon and Katherine Zenz from Wisconsin—were on their first trip overseas and had been talked into driving a Volkswagen van from Lebanon to Turkey by another American, twenty-two-year-old Robert Hubbard. The girls were in their late twenties. At the border of Syria and Turkey, near the Turkish town of Antakya, they were stopped by customs officers, who dismantled the van and found 396 pounds of hashish stashed in the bulkheads, under the seats, and in the upholstery. They were arrested on the spot and promptly put on trial. Hubbard pleaded guilty and testified that the girls knew nothing about the drugs. The judge discounted this and gave all three the death sentence.

In a magnanimous gesture, their sentences were commuted to life in December 1973. In March 1974, the girls were being held in a crowded jail in the port town of Mersin, with little hope of an early release. The Turkish government took a tough line on drugs, making no distinction between hard and soft narcotics.

But thanks to the influence of our Istanbul stringer, Metin Munir, the Turkish authorities gave us access to the American girls, allowing us to record a televised interview with them. (Metin later became one of the leading columnists in Turkey.) The interview was in the presence of the prison warden, in his office. We could not go into the girls' cell or show the conditions of their imprisonment. But I was amazed that we were able to meet them at all.

Call me naive, but I believed their story. I saw them as inexperienced, innocent young women on their first trip abroad who simply got taken. They didn't weep, and they described the jail conditions as "adequate." They wouldn't dare say otherwise. They said they were allowed to cook their own food from the prison stores. They insisted that they hadn't been abused by their jailors in any way. But they both looked traumatized, and my heart went out to them. I wore jeans, not wanting to play Lady Muck in some smart designer suit. After the interview, one of the girls admired a tribal bracelet I was wearing. I immediately pulled it off my wrist and gave it to her, glad that I could cheer her up in some way. ABC loved our report.

Over the years there was hope that the girls would be released on a general amnesty. But this never happened. Their case was not helped by the 1978 film *Midnight Express*, based on the true story of another American, Billy Hayes, who was also incarcerated on drug charges in a Turkish jail. (He later escaped.) Turkey took exception to its shocking prison scenes and considered the film to be an insult to the nation.

By 1980 the girls were being held in a guarded dormitory with forty Turkish women and some children, with no heat or electric light. They suffered bouts of depression, which was hardly surprising. Suddenly, without warning, in February 1981 they were extradited to the United States, along with Robert Hubbard and another American prisoner. They were held in a secret location and paroled almost immediately. By then they were in their mid-thirties, and the bloom on their once youthful faces had turned to chalk. I have no idea what happened to them, but I hope they were able to make up for all those lost years behind bars, so far from home.

In the late spring of 1974, John left his post with the World Service and came back to BBC TV News in London. Back to me. We had another joyful reunion, and set up a new home in a tiny mews house behind 14 Hanover Terrace. Our landlady was the actress Marion Topolski, ex-wife of the famous artist Feliks Topolski. (Their son, Daniel, was an old friend. He was known as "the man who slept with ten thousand women"—a rumour that was probably started by Daniel himself.)

The little house was filled with Topolski drawings and overlooked a tangled garden, which we shared with Marion. She occupied the grand house and would often invite us to dinner. I loved the place and its position next to Regent's Park, the loveliest in London. When I was in town, I would walk through the park to the office, rain or shine, and it made my heart sing.

In mid-July, John was suddenly sent to Cyprus. The president of the island, Archbishop Makarios, had been overthrown in a coup d'état by right-wing Greek extremists. He'd fled the Presidential Palace, allegedly disguised as a woman. The coup leaders, backed by the military junta in Greece, wanted *enosis*, or "union with Greece." Cyprus had gained independence from Britain in 1960 but had gone through years of communal strife between the Turkish Cypriot minority (about 18 percent of the population) and the Greek Cypriot majority. In 1964, a United Nations (UN) peacekeeping force was sent in to help restore law and order and to protect the Turkish villages that were dotted around the island like currants in a bun. The Turkish Cypriots saw the coup as a mortal danger to their community, and they were probably right.

I kissed John goodbye and the next day got myself tarted up for the Royal Garden Party in the grounds of Buckingham Palace. For some reason I was one of the hundreds of foreign residents of Britain who'd received an invitation that year. I wore a silk suit, high heels, the obligatory hat, and most of my heirloom jewellery: a garnet-and-pearl necklace, *circa* 1820, with matching earrings and ring. I looked pretty posh, I modestly thought. I was really looking forward to dropping a curtsy to the Queen, without toppling over.

Inevitably, the office paged me just as I was about to pass through the palace gates. The message was: "Call immediately, you have to catch a plane to Cyprus, NOW." In the meantime, our office manager, Liz Debenham, had rushed to our mews house, packed a bag for me, and hand-carried it to the British Airways check-in desk at Heathrow Airport. So ABC's first female foreign correspondent flew into a war zone in a silk suit, high heels, and dripping in heirloom jewellery.

The world's press had by this time converged on the capital of Nicosia, most of them staying at the Ledra Palace Hotel, close to the walls of the old town. It was full, but that wasn't a problem for me. I could share a room with the BBC correspondent, John Bierman. He updated me on the latest developments. Among other things.

This time my cameraman was Rupen Vosgimorukian, who had flown in from Beirut. We decided to go into the Turkish quarter of Nicosia and try to get an interview with the Turkish Cypriot leader,

Rauf Denktash. As it turned out, that wasn't difficult. The coup leaders had installed a notorious Greek extremist named Nikos Sampson as their new president, and the Turkish Cypriots were terrified that they would be massacred. Sampson had once boasted that he'd murdered more than fifteen English policemen and civilians—he'd been a leading member of the guerilla organization EOKA (*Ethniki Organosis Kyprion Agoniston*) during its colonial war against the British. After independence he campaigned for union with Greece. In inter-ethnic clashes that broke out in 1964, he led a militia group that attacked Turkish Cypriots, bulldozing their houses and possibly worse.

Denktash would talk to anybody, and he was easy to interview since he spoke fluent English. A bit too fluent—it was hard to shut him up. He had no idea how to talk in sound bites, which is an essential requirement of American television. You have to say what's important in fifteen seconds, max. Denktash preferred to give you the whole history of Cyprus. We did a walking shot on the street outside his residence, though I towered over him. He said the coup was illegal and the Turkish Cypriot minority couldn't possibly accept "the so-called President Sampson," whom he described as a thug. At the time, I don't think I fully understood the implication of his remarks.

Within twenty-four hours, I understood all too well. That night, after we'd tracked and shipped our report, dined, drank, and gone to bed, John's BBC colleague Mike Sullivan burst into our room.

"The shit's hit the fan!" Mike shouted. "The Turkish Army has landed on the north coast, about six miles west of Kyrenia. It's an invasion!"

John jumped out of bed, pulled on some clothes, and disappeared. He woke up his crew and headed straight for the north coast. I didn't seem him again for several days. I later learned that he'd got through to the coastal mountain range above Kyrenia, to a place called Cyclos, where he and his crew had a bird's-eye view of the beach landing zone and filmed it all. That was the good news. The bad news was that he couldn't get the film out for two days because of the fighting.

My stroke of luck was to come upon an abandoned UN jeep, left by soldiers of the Austrian UN contingent in Nicosia. They had been considerate enough to leave the keys. So Rupen and I hopped in and were able to roar around at will, crossing the Green Line between Greek and Turkish sectors with impunity. Or so I thought. We would gather material on one side of the line, then drive back and transfer it to our fixer/shipper on the other side.

By this time, the shots were flying thick and fast between the Greek Cypriot National Guard and the Turkish Cypriot militia. Some of the Guardsmen were holed up on the roof of our hotel, the Ledra Palace, home of the international press corps. I was zipping back and forth across the Green Line, gathering my material, until a famous Israeli military correspondent, Ron Ben-Yishai, put his hand on my shoulder and said, in his seductive Israeli accent: "Heelary, don't *do* that. They aren't shooting at each other anymore. They are shooting at *you!*" Ron was a colonel in the reserve of the Israeli Defense Forces, and he knew what he was talking about. Unlike me. People used to say that "Hilary Brown doesn't know the meaning of fear." That's true. It was one of the many words I didn't know the meaning of.

We often gave a lift to the famous war photographer Catherine Leroy, a tiny French girl who was even crazier than I was. She'd gone to Vietnam at the age of twenty-one and quickly made her name. She was a trained skydiver and would parachute into battle with airborne troops. Cathe and I would meet up in a succession of trouble spots and she became a great friend, though she was often in our shot when we were filming the action, always a few steps ahead of us, snapping away at her award-winning photos.

My second stroke of luck was to rescue my heirloom jewellery from the hotel safe. The staff had fled in a panic at the news of an invasion, but somehow I'd found the pass key, opened up the safe, and got my baubles out. I thought they would be safer in my bra, which, as everyone knows, is where I always keep money and valuables. I keep everything in there but the kitchen sink.

The Turkish Army eventually occupied one-third of the entire island. They bombed selected targets from the air, notably a military barracks near the Athalassa Forest, outside Nicosia. On at least one occasion they used napalm. We filmed the victims in hospital, and I was actually able to talk to one of them in English. He was an officer, and his skin had turned black. It was a shocking sight. I can't imagine that he survived such burns. I think our report had quite an impact because the CBS producer, Dan Bloom, reportedly walked around asking "how ABC could put out such a tasteless piece." That meant that we'd beat them that night. The three American networks—CBS, ABC, and NBC—were very competitive.

Though they fought bravely, the Greek Cypriots didn't have a chance. They were hopelessly outgunned and outmanned, and of course didn't have an air force. The military junta in Greece, which had planned the coup, did nothing to help the Cypriots, and was itself overthrown on July 24, 1974, four days after the Turkish invasion.

The coup, which lasted just eight days, was a disaster for the Greek Cypriots. The *enosis* fanatics had basically handed Cyprus to Turkey on a silver platter, though you couldn't actually say this in Cyprus without being lynched. One-third of the entire Greek Cypriot population—those people living in the north of the island—fled into makeshift refugee camps in the south. The Turkish Cypriots were later moved from their towns and villages in the south . . . into the north, installing themselves in Greek Cypriot homes and protected by an occupation force of forty thousand Turkish troops. Turkey controlled more than 30 percent of the island, which until then had been mainly inhabited and owned by Greek Cypriots. It was a kind of ethnic cleansing, before the term came into general use. The British, as one of the three guarantor powers of independent Cyprus, facilitated the transfer, using troops from the sovereign British bases of Episkopi, Akrotiri, and Dhekelia. Makarios returned as president of a divided island. It has remained divided to this day, though there is now free movement across the border.

John and I spent most of the summer of 1974 covering all this. At the time we had great sympathy for those Greek Cypriots in the north, who had lost everything. They wouldn't have access to their homes again for thirty years, when a UN reunification plan was put to a referendum in 2004. It was known as the Annan Plan, named after the then Secretary-General Kofi Annan, and was mainly written by an old school friend of mine from Geneva named Álvaro de Soto. But that's another story.

21

LONDON, CYPRUS, AND THE OCCASIONAL HOT SPOT

After the world had lost interest in the Turkish invasion of Cyprus, I asked ABC for a few days off and John and I drove back to our little dream home in the west of the island.

It was a ruin, basically. We decided to make the one-room farmhouse habitable, adding a galley kitchen and a bathroom, and installing plumbing and electricity. In the post-war economic slump on the island, I think we were the only source of foreign exchange for the entire village. Our neighbour Nicolas Achilleas did everything for us in a matter of days, demanding 70 Cypriot pounds (about $350) for his labour, plus materials.

"I am builder!" he cried, immensely proud of his work. He was also quite proprietorial. Whenever we came back from an afternoon by the sea, we would find his entire family seated under the walnut tree, on *our* terrace. "Sit down!" Nicolas would say to us, with a magnanimous sweep of his hand.

I liked Nicolas, but there are limits.

"Nicolas! This is *our* house, and you are our *neighbours*! *Not* the other way around, for Chrissake!" I shouted. "Now do you *mind*, I would like to change in the privacy of my own bedroom!" I stalked past him and into our tiny house, furnished with an antique Cypriot four-poster bed and very little else.

"*He . . . is sad,*" said John, pointing at me. We both cracked up.

On many occasions we would return from a day out to find Nicolas's daughter and granddaughter doing their washing in our sink—to keep their own water bills down. This kind of economy measure was quite common among Mediterranean peasants, we later learned. Just like the habit of tossing their rubbish onto their neighbour's property rather than taking it to the local dump. John had another talk with Nicolas about that, and his family cut back on their washing. Or at least they cut back when we weren't in residence. We didn't really begrudge them that much. Especially after Nicolas came to us one morning and said:

"Cunt Stiffen."

"*What?*" John and I said, of one voice.

"Cunt Stiffen."

It took a few minutes for us to figure out that he was talking about *Cat Stevens*, the British pop star. His father, Stavros Georgiou, was a Cypriot who came from our village, Tala. Everyone was very proud of Cat Stevens. I'm not sure they were that keen when he became a Muslim and took the name of Yusuf Islam. We all preferred Cunt Stiffen.

We called our cottage Calypso, named after the Greek goddess who tempted Odysseus after the fall of Troy. We loved our Mediterranean retreat, and it loved us back. It had that special quality of *baraka*, which means "blessed, and conferring blessing on all who live within." For more than thirty years it was our refuge and a very happy place.

Every time we returned, we would look at each other and say, "Ah, here we are, this is where we ought to be."

In that first, fantastic year with ABC, I was sent to Israel to cover the war of attrition between Israel and Syria on the Golan Heights, before the disengagement-of-forces agreement in June 1974, brokered by the then U.S. Secretary of State Henry Kissinger. It was a pretty low-level war, though there were some casualties.

It was during this period that we produced that rare thing in foreign news reporting: a Happy Story. The disengagement agreement included a provision for the return of POWs. I was working with a brilliant Israeli cameraman named Meir Grego. Grego had a million contacts, and one of them was a Yemeni Jewish family whose son, an officer, was among the prisoners. I think his name was Boaz. We showed the extended family at home, getting ready for his return. They had this family likeness—they were all white of teeth, tanned of skin, and clear of eye. A really beautiful family.

We went with them to the airport to greet the returning POWs. The authorities had set up barriers between the runway and a section of tarmac, where the families were told to wait for the arrival of the plane. There was another section for the press. The idea was that the POWs would disembark from the plane and walk in an orderly fashion across the tarmac to the family section. Then there would be a reunion, and the press would film it all, right? Wrong. So very wrong.

We set up our camera and trained it on our family. They were wild with excitement; they could barely contain themselves behind their barrier. The plane landed, but there was some delay in getting the mobile stairs to the doors of the plane. The returning prisoners couldn't wait—these were highly trained young men, without an ounce of spare flesh on their muscle-bound bodies. They broke open the emergency doors, spilled out onto the wings of the plane, and rappelled or jumped down to the ground. At the same time, the families pushed over their barriers and surged onto the runway.

Grego got all of this, but we lost our family! They had disappeared in the hopeless jumble of people running to embrace their loved ones.

Then I spotted Boaz, *our* prisoner of war. I spotted him because of this family likeness: he was white of teeth, tanned of skin, clear of eye. He was unmistakable.

"Grego! That's him!" I shouted. Grego swung his camera around just in time to see our boy, arms outstretched. And then to see his entire family jump on him, one after the other. Grego did a beautiful pan shot that went round and round the whole magic circle of mother, father, son, sisters, and brothers. It was the moment they'd all been waiting for. And that's what I wrote in my narrative track, pausing to bring up the natural sound of laughter and tears.

We followed the family back to their home in Tel Aviv. The whole street was filled with cheering people waiting to welcome their neighbourhood hero. He was hoisted up onto someone's shoulders. An open bottle of champagne was thrust into his hand. I asked that hackneyed question:

"Boaz! How do you feel?"

He took a long swig from the bottle and wiped the foam from his mouth. Then, in perfect English and with a huge smile, he said:

"I feel *extra-ordinarily* fine!"

Back in the edit room, we had very little time to put our report together. But our editor, Bob Goldman, was fast and very talented.

"This is one hell of a spot," he said as he worked away on his Steenbeck, cutting and sealing the beautiful images together.

Normally the average report runs about 1 minute, 50 seconds; 2 minutes tops. But our producer, Bill Milldyke, had seen our pictures and had negotiated 2 minutes, 30 seconds. Practically a documentary.

"Hilary's piece runs 2.45," he said to New York. "She's fat, but she's good."

It is rare that a report comes together exactly as you want it. But this one did. I still remember our closing image, and my last line. Grego had caught Boaz laughing and talking inside his family home, as his mother draped her arms around him, kissing his forehead.

Over this we ran my sign-off, in voice-over. I still remember it: "In wartime, the return of prisoners is the only moment of pure joy that can be shared by both sides. Hilary Brown, ABC News, Tel Aviv."[1]

We fed the piece. There were no dry eyes in the control room.

Back in London, our domestic life ticked over happily in the little mews house. Bong, age thirteen, was enrolled in a progressive boarding school called Dartington Hall, in a beautiful part of Devon. (The school later closed down in 1987 after the headmaster and his wife became just a little too progressive.) On school breaks Bong would stay with us, sleeping on a divan in the tiny living room. It wasn't ideal, but his mother, Alice (who was still living alone in the spacious "matrimonial home"), refused to see him. I felt sorry for her, but only in my mature moments. She was now completely estranged from two of her three children.

It was around this time that the new president of ABC News, Bill Sheehan, came to London and in accordance with company practice took everybody out to dinner. He then had one-on-one meetings with each of us. He was incredibly complimentary about my work. "You haven't done a bad spot," he said. "We'd like you to come back to the States so we can put you on the air all the time."

I was immensely flattered, but not the least bit interested in going to the States. I had my dream job as a foreign correspondent, something I'd always wanted. Why would I want to change that? And I would have to leave John, who was everything to me. I thanked Mr. Sheehan, saying that I was supremely happy in London, working with people I loved, and please can I stay exactly where I am?

22

THE FALL OF SAIGON

In December 1975, ABC transferred Peter Jennings from Beirut to London, where he became chief international correspondent. I was very much the junior correspondent. We didn't see a lot of each other because we both travelled so much on different assignments. But when we were both in town, we got along very well. And I was pals with his Lebanese wife, Annie, with whom I spoke French most of the time. I used to call her "ma petite casserole." I still do.

My crews—Peter MacIntyr and Robin Springate—had talked me into buying a second-hand E-type Jaguar, which broke down pretty much every day. At that time gas-guzzling luxury cars were being sold for a pittance, and the crews thought I should have this kind of status symbol. "You deserve it, Hils," they said, appealing to my worst instincts. It became known as "The Silver Canoe." On the rare occasions that it was actually running, it was not so much a car as a low-flying plane. I had it for a year, which in many ways was the most stressful year of my life. When I was lucky, the garage let me have it on the weekends. Peter was a merciless tease about this. He called it "the jalopy," and every time I had trouble with it, he would lean out his office window and say, "Hey, Hils! I can give you fifty bucks for it and take it off your hands." That kind of thing.

In the spring of 1975, the North Vietnamese Army (NVA) began its final offensive in a campaign to occupy South Vietnam and its capital, Saigon, and to at last reunify the whole country, North and South, under Communist rule. The architect of the campaign, General Vo Nguyen Giap, later said that he thought the offensive could take two years. It took six weeks. In the South, the ARVN (the Army of the Republic of Vietnam) simply disintegrated. After the Paris Peace Accords in 1973, the Americans had withdrawn all combat forces from South Vietnam, leaving the ARVN to fight the NVA and the Viet Cong on its own. The ARVN had been a rich man's army. Without American support, it had to do much more, with much less. President Nguyen Van Thieu had staked the survival of South Vietnam on U.S. President Richard Nixon's personal pledge that any North Vietnamese aggression would be met with American air power. Then Nixon resigned in August 1974 and that promise was forgotten.

Once the Spring Offensive started in March 1975, all the networks beefed up their bureaus and increased their coverage. This was obviously the End Game, the last stage of the thirty-year war, though no one knew how long that stage would last. I was desperate to go to Vietnam, so I kept volunteering. Other correspondents would be sent instead, such as Ken Kashiwahara, who was assigned from the U.S., and the veteran correspondent Jim Bennett, who had more experience in Vietnam than almost anybody at any network. Finally, the assignment editor gave in to my constant agitation and in late March sent me to Saigon.

At this stage in my career, I had less than two years' experience as a network foreign news correspondent. I was to have almost thirty more years, covering wars, revolutions, and general mayhem around the world. But Vietnam seems to be the story that I was most associated with, though I knew practically nothing about its long and terrible history. I knew the death toll: 58,000 American troops, almost a quarter-million South Vietnamese troops, 1.1 million North Vietnamese and Viet Cong communist fighters, and 2 million civilians. That's the sort of information you can get out of the file that you read on the plane (though the North Vietnamese didn't release their final casualty figures until 1995). But I had no experience of the war itself. When I arrived in Saigon I was, as Bernie Kaplan might have said, "so wet behind the ears I was dripping." This was in sharp and embarrassing contrast to the correspondents working for the rival networks: Bob Simon, Dick Threlkeld, and Ed Bradley at CBS; Jim Laurie and George Lewis at NBC. But the ABC bureau had Jim Bennett. I did whatever he told me to do.

And I was lucky enough to be working with Asian crews who knew the area intimately. I had Yasutsune "Tony" Hirashiki, who'd turned up at the ABC Saigon bureau in 1966 from Japan, speaking no English and politely requesting to become a cameraman. And Joe Lee from South Korea. Both were among the best, most experienced, most courageous combat cameramen in the region. They'd recently flown in from Phnom Penh, having been ordered out of the city for their own safety in advance of the Khmer Rouge takeover. Later, just before and during the Fall of Saigon, I worked with the Fox brothers (Barry and Peter) from Northern Ireland. They were Jewish, though the running joke about them was always: "Yes, but are they Catholic Jews or Protestant Jews?"

I arrived in Saigon about two weeks after the massive attack by the North Vietnamese Army on the Central Highlands. The NVA outnumbered the ARVN troops by six to one, and the Communist forces overran Ban Me Thuot in just two days. Four hundred thousand ARVN soldiers and their families took flight. Thousands were killed, not just by NVA shells, but run over by their own retreating tanks, or trampled to death by other terrified refugees. Reporters called it "The Convoy of Tears."

The North Vietnamese forces then just rolled southward along the coast, taking one city after another. By the end of the month, they had reached the coastal town of Da Nang, which was in chaos. The road was littered with boots and uniforms, abandoned by retreating ARVN troops. South Vietnamese marines fought for places on an overcrowded ship going south. In Nha Trang, desperate Vietnamese civilians mobbed a U.S. transport plane, climbing onto the wings, forcing their way into the still-open hatch, sometimes throwing their infant children before them in scenes of pure panic. Cam Ranh Bay in early April became a huge depot for tens of thousands of refugees from Da Nang. ARVN soldiers had been abandoned by their officers, who escaped by plane and helicopter to Saigon. The soldiers were left behind with their families, all starving and dying of thirst. In the space of three weeks, eight provinces in South Vietnam had fallen to the Communist forces. More than a million people were displaced and homeless. The refugee problem was enormous.

My first story was from the southern port of Vung Tau, which was already filling up with refugees. Three weeks later it would be shelled by the NVA, and thousands of civilians would crowd onto any kind of vessel and sail out to the South China Sea in a desperate bid to be rescued by the Americans and taken onto ships of the Seventh Fleet.

Sixty thousand were picked up, but thousands more were left drifting helplessly on the water, many of them lost forever.

But in early April, the refugees may have thought they were still relatively safe in the port city. There was an uneasy atmosphere of calm—the calm before the storm. We showed the conditions of the displaced people and interviewed American medics who were running clinics for the most vulnerable: women and children and the elderly.

Having just got off a thirteen-hour flight, I was feeling a little vulnerable myself. We were working in blistering heat—it was 100° Fahrenheit and very humid. As I started my first interview, standing up outside one of the clinics, the medic suddenly stretched out his arm and said, "Hilary, you're not well."

What the hell is he talking about? I thought. The next moment I fainted, into his arms basically. When I regained consciousness minutes later, I felt a complete fool and made Tony promise he would start a new roll of film. There should be no record of this humiliation. I could hear the conversation back in New York: "Yeah, we finally agree to send Brown to Vietnam and she passed out the first day."

"Change the film and throw the old roll away, Tony! *Promise!*" I said in a low voice, trying to sound as though I was back in control.

"Yes, I promise, Hilary-san!" said Tony, a huge grin on his face.

Saigon itself still had a deceptive air of normalcy about it, though the black market for dollars had gone through the roof. People were desperate for hard currency to bribe their way onto a plane, a boat, anything to get them out of the country. The shops were open, the restaurants were busy, and the bar girls were doing a brisk trade. They were breathtakingly beautiful, with waist-length dark hair and long, filmy tunics flowing over their slim, graceful bodies. Remarkably, one could still dine extremely well. My first meal in Saigon was in a smart restaurant run by a Corsican, who served me an exquisite soufflé au Grand Marnier for dessert. One felt the French influence, though the French had abandoned Vietnam after their infamous defeat at Dien Bien Phu in 1954. The favourite meeting spot was the Continental Hotel, where journalists would drink and place bets on the time it would take for the North Vietnamese Army to occupy Saigon. By this time, the NVA was within 100 miles of the capital. But I can't remember that anyone predicted that the Fall of Saigon would come quite as quickly as it did.

By early April, the U.S. Embassy was making arrangements to evacuate all Americans still in Saigon, along with the estimated two hundred thousand South Vietnamese who had worked for the Americans. Most were being flown out of Tan Son Nhut airbase on fixed-wing transports to Guam and the Philippines. Incredibly, the American Ambassador, Graham Martin, was still insisting that there could be some kind of negotiated settlement with the North Vietnamese, and a coalition government could be formed. Phil Caputo, an American journalist and former serviceman who later became a best-selling author with his powerful book *A Rumor of War*, called it "the Great American Delusion Machine."[1] Embassy staffers were secretly getting their "friendly" Vietnamese employees and friends out on evacuation flights as fast as they could, behind the ambassador's back.

ABC had flown in Kevin Delaney to look after all our long-time Vietnamese staffers and contract employees and see that they got out with their families. Kevin had done several tours of duty as a producer in the Saigon bureau. I did a profile of a freelance Vietnamese translator and his family, a man who'd worked occasionally for ABC but not enough to qualify for Kevin's evacuation program. At considerable risk he showed his face, and his family, and described the work he'd done for the Americans over the years. He was desperate to get his wife and children out. He was terrified that they would all be killed by the Viet Cong and the NVA. There were thousands of south Vietnamese families like this one. Their mounting hysteria wasn't helped by the statement of U.S. Defense Secretary James Schlesinger, who'd predicted that tens of thousands of South Vietnamese would be butchered in Saigon if the Communists took over.

But even with the steady stream of Americans and friendly Vietnamese fleeing Saigon every day, I still thought that my assignment in Vietnam would go on for weeks. That's how much I knew.

On April 10, the NVA attacked Xuan Loc, just 48 miles north of Saigon. This time, the South Vietnamese Army fought back, and fought bravely, for twelve days. The ARVN finally surrendered on April 21, leaving Highway One open and undefended, all the way to Saigon.

I went up Highway One with the Fox brothers to film the huge, moving mass of refugees pouring down the road. We saw whole families on a single bicycle, with their belongings. The old and infirm were being pushed in their wheelchairs, piled high with bags and bedding and supplies. Many people were on foot, carrying their children on their backs or their shoulders or in their arms. They weren't shouting or crying—they were beyond tears. There was stark, wordless terror on their faces.

Barry filmed these apocalyptic scenes, and I did a stand-up on the highway with the mass of people behind me. Then we saw black smoke billowing up over the skyline of Saigon. Our driver, Mr. Dang, said he knew where the smoke was coming from and we raced back toward the capital. He took us to Newport Bridge, on the outskirts of the city, spanning the Saigon River and serving as a main artery into the city from the north. There was a lively firefight going on between a Viet Cong (VC) unit on one side of the bridge and ARVN forces on the other side. The South Vietnamese had air cover, and their helicopter gunships were flying close and low, firing down on the VC. This was the closest the fighting had ever come to Saigon since the Tet Offensive of 1968. I said exactly that in my stand-up. Except I did my stand-up . . . lying down. Barry and I had both agreed that it would be safer that way. To stand at our full height seemed an easy way to get caught in the crossfire.

But we needed to get to the other side of the bridge, to get to the car and, basically get the hell out of there. It seemed a good place *not* to be. I stayed close to the ground and *rolled* across the bridge. Barry was rolling too, with his camera, and so the images we shipped out to Hong Kong that night (our reports were cut in Hong Kong or Bangkok and transmitted to New York) included a sequence of Brown, flat on the tarmac, performing a slow and tortuous spin across the bridge. Our producer in Hong Kong, Betsy Aaron, put the sequence in the cut spot. Hokey as it must have been, New York loved it. As it turned out, that was the last report I filed from Saigon. The North Vietnamese were at the gates of the city.

At 4 a.m. the next day, the NVA shelled Tan Son Nhut airbase, killing two marines. These were the last American soldiers to be killed in Vietnam. A few hours later, U.S. President Gerald Ford gave orders for the evacuation by helicopter of the estimated two thousand Americans still in Vietnam. Eighty-one choppers from a fleet of thirty American warships in the South China Sea started to fly in to designated pickup points around the city, mainly the DAO (Defense

Attaché's Office) compound at the airport and the roof of the U.S. Embassy. The signal for the evacuation was a recording of "White Christmas"—a grotesque and incongruous soundtrack for the scenes of pure pandemonium around the city. Panic-stricken Vietnamese were running in all directions, in wild, purposeless movement, like so much debris beneath the blades of a chopper on takeoff. A huge crowd mobbed the U.S. Commissary, stripping it bare within minutes. I was robbed of $2,000, taken from my room *while I was in it* having a shower. I normally kept the money in my bra. Inevitably, the story later became "Hilary Brown had $2,000 stolen from her bra, while she was wearing it."

Very soon the airport pickup point became too dangerous, and the choppers were landing on the roof and in the courtyard of the American Embassy and on the roof of the Pittman Building nearby. A huge, hysterical mob surrounded the Embassy compound and pressed against the gates, which were manned by a handful of marines, armed only with rifles. The marines would haul up the "round eyes" and help them over the wall. They would kick back any Vietnamese. I saw a man scale the wall with a baby in his arms, and then try to throw the child over the wall to safety. It was a terrible scene. Many of these people had worked for the Americans for years and had put their faith in them. They were convinced that with the Communist takeover, there would be merciless retribution, a bloodbath. They were desperate to get out.

I was yanked up the 10-foot wall by a burly marine who looked completely shattered, almost shell-shocked. He wasn't trained to kick civilians in the ribs, or to smash them with the butt of his rifle. As I dropped down to the other side, the first thing I saw was an Embassy staffer hurling millions of dollars into a burning oil drum. It was the Embassy contingency fund.

"What are you *doing?*" I shouted. "You're *burning money!*"

"Whaddaya want us to do, leave it to the VC?" the staffer shouted back as she flung another hundred thousand onto the flames.

It was obvious that America's final hour in Vietnam was not its finest, and everyone knew that, and felt that. There was a great sense of shame among Americans, who now speak openly about it. I was already feeling guilty myself. My Vietnamese translator, who at great risk had allowed me to film his family, had turned up at the Caravelle Hotel that morning while we assembled at our pickup point. He was there with his wife and children and he begged me to help them all get away. There was a marine guard at the front of the bus, and I knew he wouldn't let any Vietnamese on board. Certainly not a family of five. And if he did, how would I get them on a helicopter? I told him I couldn't help him. I will never forget the look of despair on his face, and it haunted me for years. Until I found a way to atone for my sin.

Compounding my sense of guilt was the fact that I was leaving the city myself. I had volunteered to stay in Saigon after the evacuation and cover the Communist takeover. I had an Irish crew, the Fox brothers, and I was not an American, so I should be safe, shouldn't I? John had heard about this and was not happy at all. In one of our rare phone calls, he had tried to talk me out of it. This was just after the fall of Phnom Penh on April 17, when the entire population of the city was driven out into the countryside. There was also a rumour that those foreign journalists who had stayed in the city had all been executed.

"Hilly, this is crazy. You don't have to *do* this," John said with mounting urgency on a bad phone connection to London. "The North Vietnamese won't give a damn that you're Canadian. You're *working* for the Americans, that's what matters. America is The Enemy. You don't know *what* they'll do."

I was still planning to stay, however. The Fox brothers were willing. Then a few friends in the press corps heard about this and started to work on me. "You're out of your *mind*, Hilary," said Henry Champ of CTV News, a Canadian himself. "The commies don't know there's any *difference* between a Canadian and a Yank. If you're lucky, they'll arrest you and hold you for months, maybe years. Or they'll just shoot you."

"You would be a bit vulnerable, my dear," a British colleague weighed in, with classic British understatement. "I mean, you're not exactly easy to miss. And your press card says you are the *American Broadcasting Company*. Not worth the risk, I'd say."

All this was going on against the background of an entire city in meltdown. Suddenly our producer Kevin Delaney came up to me, grabbed my tote bag, and said, "Hilary, you've got to *leave*." He then boarded the bus, with my tote bag, and the bus took off, leaving me without my possessions. Including my passport.

Any good journalist will tell you that the one unbreakable rule when on assignment in a foreign country is *always* have your passport *on your person*. That kind of did it. If I stayed, I would have nothing to prove that I *was* Canadian, assuming that this would help me. I wouldn't have anything to prove who I was, period. So I left Saigon, along with the thousands of South Vietnamese and Americans who were choppered out of the city in those final, frantic hours. We were on one of the last flights, after dark, and we could see the tracers of enemy fire as we flew over the city.

We landed on the USS *Hancock*, part of the Seventh Fleet in the South China Sea, 40 miles off the coast of Vietnam. Hundreds of

South Vietnamese were crowded into the hold of the ship. In the skies above the carrier, ARVN helicopters carrying South Vietnamese officers would circle and then land, without clearance, one after the other. The pilots would just touch down on the deck and unload themselves and their families. Any chopper that landed on the deck would be stripped immediately by U.S. servicemen, who would take out the instruments and anything else that could be cannibalized and then push the carcass into the sea. They had to keep the deck of the carrier clear, there was simply no room for all those aircraft. It was an extraordinary sight, and a metaphor for the war itself. Such a waste, of blood and treasure.

In the space of nineteen hours, the American military evacuated thirteen hundred Americans and fifty-five hundred South Vietnamese without a single loss of civilian life. Two pilots died when their chopper crashed into the sea as they approached a carrier. It was the largest helicopter evacuation in history. I did a stand-up on the deck, as another helicopter was pushed overboard. I was wearing my silver Nepalese prayer box, with John's prayers inside, for luck. Kind of over-the- top, I guess, but nobody noticed.

"This seems to be the last chapter in the history of American involvement in Vietnam. It's also been the largest single movement of people in the history of America itself."

"Hilary Brown, ABC News, on the attack aircraft carrier USS *Hancock*, in the South China Sea."[2]

That was my last stand-up about the war in Vietnam. I didn't know then that it would later appear in the classic motion picture *The Deer Hunter*. And that this would be what Andy Warhol might have called my fifteen seconds of fame. Except I had seventeen seconds. And I would return to a very different Vietnam exactly twenty years later.

23

THE VIETNAM EFFECT

We were in the South China Sea for a couple of days and we did a few reports with the U.S. Marine Corps pilots who had run that extraordinary evacuation. One of the airmen who had ditched into the sea told me they had "sustained fuel starvation." It took me a few seconds to understand this meant they ran out of gas. I was reunited with my tote bag and my passport when Kevin Delaney turned up on the same aircraft carrier. Journalists were playing poker with South Vietnamese currency, now worthless. There was theft on board—some of the photographers' equipment went missing and there was little doubt that some of the refugees were taking advantage of the chaos. There were a few bar girls on board, but they were turning an honest dollar.

When our carrier put into Subic Bay in the Philippines, an ABC team was there to meet us. Joe Lee was the cameraman and he was weeping with joy. He gave me a huge hug. He'd heard the predictions of a bloodbath in Saigon and feared the worst. Joe later lost a leg in action but kept on working in the TV business, which he loved.

My orders were to fly to New York, via Hong Kong, to do post-Vietnam interviews on the morning show and other programs. Since each journalist was allowed only one tote bag on the helicopter evacuation, I had almost no clothes—just a grubby safari suit and a spare pair of slacks. But I had a night and a day in Hong Kong, maybe I could pick up something there? Impossible. At six feet in shoes, there was nothing for me off any rack, so I consoled myself with a trip to the Peking China Department Store, which sold mainly gold and jade jewellery at astonishing prices. Astonishing, as in low. I bought a small gold watch, the first I'd ever possessed. As it turned out, I possessed it for exactly forty-eight hours.

ABC had me booked into The Pierre hotel on Central Park East and set up a couple of appearances on the morning show *AM America*, along with lunch with the brass. On *AM America*, they first interviewed me about the Fall of Saigon, then welcomed another guest onto the set, a best-selling author named Richard Condon (*The Manchurian Candidate*, *Prizzi's Honor*, and many other books, most of which became major motion pictures). This was my cue to interview Condon about his latest book, which of course I hadn't read. But I knew him, having done a TV profile of him in his home in Rossenarra, Ireland. He had been exceptionally warm, and later wrote me into one of his books, *The Abandoned Woman*. I was "Lady Hilary Brown, the Canadian Beauty." He even sent me a certificate making me a member of Book Actors' Equity, with a covering note: "Richard Condon says, Support the Active Verb!"

So as you can imagine, the morning TV appearances went quite well, though I was still wearing my Vietnam gear and must have looked pretty scruffy. Never mind—I had sent out my one change of clothes to be express-cleaned and I rushed back to The Pierre to change before the next set of interviews. I found the bag of cleaning all right, but no sign of the new gold watch that I'd hidden in the mini-fridge. There had been no time to put it in the hotel safe and no one was taking that risk anyway, since The Pierre had just had a well-publicized heist of its safe-deposit boxes. When I tried to report the disappearance, the hotel manager looked up and without making eye contact said, "Don't bother me. I've had a bad day too." Fabulous hotel.

But Richard Condon sent me a huge bunch of flowers, like the Hollywood press agent he once was before he started writing bestselling novels. "I can't help it, babe, it's a reflex action!" he said.

A few weeks later ABC sent out a note to all the staff who had covered the Fall of Saigon and offered them a week's holiday, for two, all expenses paid, to a place of their choosing, anywhere in the world. John and I immediately decided to go to Cyprus, to our little one-room stone farmhouse overlooking the sea. The folks in the ABC travel department in New York couldn't believe this.

"Hilary, you can stay *anywhere*! Anywhere in the *world*! Five-star hotel, all the amenities, are you *sure* you want to check into a *one-room farmhouse?*"

There were no tourists, of course, and the island was in a deep post-war recession. But the sun was shining, the wildflowers were still in bloom, the sea was exquisite, and it was where we wanted to be. We swam in all our favourite places, the secret little bays in the shade of ancient pine trees, or the empty sandy beaches with family-run tavernas serving the catch of the day. It was still an unspoiled, pastoral Mediterranean landscape and we had it all to ourselves.

This was when we decided to renovate the stone barn next to our farmhouse, where our neighbour Nicolas secretly corralled his goats at night. We pretended we didn't know this. (Never pick a fight with your neighbours in Cyprus: you will always lose.) We wanted a sitting room with a fireplace, a dining room, a well-equipped kitchen, a large bedroom and en-suite bathroom. We would basically triple the habitable size of our property. We got an architect from Nicosia named Theo Lambrides, who loved traditional stone buildings. He basically said, "Leave it to me," and in six months, in our absence, we had a beautiful new space with white interior walls, exposed beams, exterior and interior arches, floor-to-ceiling sliding doors connecting to a large outside veranda, and a paved Mediterranean garden beyond, planted with clouds of bougainvillea and plumbago and jasmine. We wanted a seamless connection between the indoors and the outdoors, and Theo gave us exactly that. The sunlight poured into the rooms, which we furnished with Cyprus antiques, carved wedding chests, and more wrought-iron four-poster beds.

Theo built a stone wall connecting the renovated barn to the original one-room farmhouse, and set an arched entrance into it, so it brought the two buildings together nicely. We installed my Portuguese tile fountain opposite the entrance. That's the fountain I'd bought at the Fábrica Sant'Anna ceramic shop in Lisbon during the Portuguese Revolution. I *knew* I would find a place for it, some day! The whole renovation cost $12,000. This time, we could afford it.

Over the years we kept adding on to the cottage. We built a second-storey bedroom, with windows on three sides and an even more phenomenal view. Theo put in a 33-foot tile pool that cantilevered over the lower terrace. The sight lines were perfect. Once you slipped into the water, you looked over fields below, straight out to sea. We had many happy hours swimming in that pool with Jonnie when he was a little boy. And with a succession of friends who came to stay. *Baraka!*

It was at some point during this period that the president of ABC News, Bill Sheehan, called to ask me if I would come back to the States and co-anchor the morning news program, *AM America*. For the second time, Mr. Sheehan was asking me to move to the States for a high-profile role. Peter Jennings was now the anchor, having been transferred from London. But I was blissfully happy where I was, covering foreign news with crews I loved and coming home to a man I adored. Why would I want to throw that away? I didn't have a New York agent to tell me that I should jump at the chance and that am I crazy or *what?* I didn't have any idea of the impact of live daily television, or of TV celebrity, or anything. I said no thank you. This was on a conference call with a number of executives, one of whom paused and said, "Hilary, we don't think you have *any idea* what you're turning down." That's perfectly true. But as I've demonstrated, it's not against the law to be stupid. As it happened, *AM America* was short-lived and Peter came back to the London bureau. If I had taken the co-anchor job, I assume they would have sent me back to London too.

Having splashed out on a major renovation of our Cyprus cottage, John and I decided we should get on the London property ladder, so we bought a two-storey apartment in a nineteenth-century house in Primrose Hill, for £20,000. Property in Central London was affordable then, and so was antique furniture. I bought Regency and Georgian pieces, including a set of sabre-legged chairs that I constantly tripped over and an elegant eighteenth-century wing chair that was impossible to sit in for more than fifteen minutes. But what the hell, it looked good. It was sad to leave our little mews house, but here at least we had a spare room for Bong on his school breaks, and I could still walk through the glorious Regent's Park to the office.

In the fall of 1975, ABC sent me to Iran to do a series of pieces on the Shah's so-called "Great Civilization." This was his ambitious plan to broaden the industrial base of the economy beyond oil, which brought huge revenues since the Organization of Petroleum Exporting Countries (OPEC) had agreed to quadruple oil prices. Much of the revenue was spent on arms—Iran was still the biggest buyer of U.S. arms in the world.

ABC thought that because I'd lived in Iran I'd be the person for this assignment, which began with an interview with the Shah, in the Saadabad Palace, in the hills above Tehran. The palace was about a mile away from the lovely shaded villa that John and I had lived in. We set up our camera in one of the gold-encrusted reception rooms, furnished with two gilded French provincial chairs. The chairs were the same size. I had expected that the Shahanshah of Iran, King of Kings and Light of the Aryans, would be perched on some sort of throne. As I recall, the interview went something like this:

The Shah enters the room, shakes my hand, and sits down quietly while my soundman Patrick Etcheverry attaches the Lavalier mic to him. There are no courtiers in attendance, just a couple of men in ill-fitting suits. I assume they are his bodyguards.

I go through the obvious softball questions about the economy, his ambitions to turn Iran into a great bridge nation with a diversified economy, et cetera et cetera.

"My, Miss Brown, you seem to be well informed," says the Shah, with a courtly smile.

This is Ms. Brown's cue to start on the less convenient questions about the stories of human rights abuses in Iran that are now leaking out, reported by Amnesty International, Human Rights Watch, and other organizations. The Shah has to know about these abuses, since nothing is done without his orders. At least, that's what we think. On the other hand, his secret service, SAVAK, might have become a law unto itself. The Shah had surrounded himself with sycophants who tell him what he wants to hear. A slippery slope, as he later found out.

"There have been a number of reports of the arrest of dissidents who have criticized you or your policies." I say. "Some have simply disappeared. Is it your policy to arrest and detain without trial any Iranian who questions your regime?"

The Shah stiffens in his seat and starts to tremble slightly.

"What kind of question is this! I am the Monarch!"

"But, Your Imperial Majesty, no one else will answer these questions. You say you want your country to become a member of the Club of Western Nations. These are questions that are being asked about Iran, in the West. It's my duty to ask them," I answer. My cameraman Jim Godfrey starts to cough.

"I am not obliged to comment on this. How dare you ask me such questions!" the Shah says, still trembling.

"But, Your Imperial Majesty, I see that only last month Mike Wallace of CBS *60 Minutes* was asking you questions along similar lines."

"Mike Wallace was a baby next to you!" the Shah replies.

"Your Imperial Majesty," I say, "that is a very great compliment."

The Shah then carefully removes his microphone, stands up, and stalks out.

We sit in silence, waiting for the guards to remove us physically from the palace and take us directly to Evin Prison. Both Jim and Patrick give me dark looks. "You've really dropped us in the shit, Hils. How are we gonna get out of this one?"

But no! Nothing happens! The guards remain in the room. I don't think they spoke English or had any idea that ABC News had just insulted His Imperial Majesty, the Shahanshah, King of Kings, Light of the Aryans.

"Okay, might as well do the reverse questions," we say to each other. That is when the cameraman films the interviewer, instead of the interviewee, and the interviewer re-asks the questions. It's then spliced together, to make it appear that the interview has been shot with two cameras instead of just one. It's pretty outmoded now but was a common practice then.

We shoot our reverse questions, in the presence of the guards, and then pack up our gear and leave the palace. The next day we are told that all our requests for access at various sites—army bases, oil installations, and so on—are approved. Go figure.

In the meantime, the Shah's information minister at court, a Mr. Kambiz Yazdanpanah, called to say he would like to take me out to lunch. Having survived the royal rage, I got very cocky and decided I would find out what the real story was behind the expulsion of John Bierman, the BBC Tehran correspondent, only two years ago, along with his household. Which included me.

Of course, Yazdanpanah knew exactly who I was. I was the girlfriend of John Bierman who ended up leaving the country with one week's notice. I knew that he knew. And he knew that I knew that he knew. We were both aware of the reality of the situation, but in Iran it's very bad form to acknowledge that.

"Well," I say, as the waiters brought out the dessert, "you have certainly seen a lot of western journalists come and go in the past couple of years, haven't you?"

"Oh yes, the whole world wants to come to Iran," says Yazdanpanah, stroking his tie. "They want to see the achievements of the Great Civilization, brought about by His Majesty the Shah."

"Didn't the Shah expel one of those western journalists? The BBC correspondent in Tehran? What was his name . . . John Bierman, wasn't it?" I say.

"Oh yes," says Yazdanpanah, "that was unfortunate, but imperative. Bierman told lies. And of course, he was an alcoholic."

"Is that so?" I reply. "I must say, I've never heard that John was a drunk. He has a very good reputation as a first-class reporter."

"Oh yes," says Yazdanpanah. "He drank. He had a nice girlfriend and of course she had to leave in a hurry too. We were sorry about that."

"Oh really?" I say. "Maybe she was happy to get out of the country." Both of us knew, of course, that we were both talking about *me*.

"Perhaps," says Yazdanpanah smoothly. "But she would be welcome to come back to Iran anytime."

After this surreal lunch, I ceased to worry about our safety in Iran. Weirdly, ABC suddenly decided that we should cut short our assignment and go home. We left the next day. Who knows—perhaps His Imperial Majesty, the Shahanshah, Light of Aryans, might have changed his mind about me.

In the meantime, things were not going well for John at the BBC. Having been one of their top TV reporters, he'd managed to get himself grounded after he made the mistake of pointing out the shortcomings of the BBC's coverage of the Turkish invasion of Cyprus, in writing. John was always a hopeless politician. He never pulled his punches. His memo highlighted the incompetence of certain executives, men who actually held John's fate in their hands. So you can imagine what happened to him. He was essentially Un-personed—not given any meaningful assignments at all. This ate away at him, he couldn't sleep, he had no idea how to make things right again. He was only forty-seven. It didn't help that my career was going gangbusters.

Finally, in the winter of 1976, the BBC made him an offer. In partnership with the news agency Reuters and *The Guardian* newspaper, they would set him up as a super stringer in Cyprus, based in the capital of Nicosia. Eighteen months after the Turkish invasion, Cyprus was still A Story, especially in the British media. He would be busy again, and he would make a good living. He would have our cottage as a weekend retreat. "They're throwing me a lifeline, Hilly," he said. "I have to take it." I realized with a sinking heart that he was leaving me.

It was more than a sinking heart. It was a visceral, overwhelming feeling of loss, like losing a limb. John was my rock, I depended on him for everything. How to handle a story, how to research and write a script, what to *think*. We had lots of friends, and we were living in one of the great cities of the world. I had a job I loved and was living with a man I adored. But I was about to lose him, probably forever.

The BBC wanted John to start as soon as possible, and as the time for his departure drew closer, I would cling to him at night, holding him tight, as though I could somehow keep the imprint of his long, tanned body on mine. John made no attempt to talk me into joining him in Cyprus. We had been together in London for almost two years, in what had been a charmed life. Now it was over.

The day he left, he wouldn't let me take him to the airport. It would have been too painful, for both of us. I just stood on the street and gave him a last, lingering embrace before he got into the taxi and sped off. Then I walked back into the house, weeping.

As I crossed the threshold into the kitchen, the roof fell in. I mean, literally. A heavy Tiffany-glass chandelier suddenly came down with a crash, and within seconds a fine film of dust had settled on everything in the room, including the entire contents of all the cupboards and drawers. As a parting gift, John had installed the chandelier over our kitchen table. Unfortunately, he had screwed it into a lathe instead of a beam, and the weight of the light brought the whole ceiling down. It took a week to clean up.

24

ALONE AGAIN

I was lucky that I still had a dream job, with a bureau that was like a family. We not only worked together, we would meet socially and have dinner in each other's houses. With John gone, my crews thought that I should get myself into circulation right away, so I would feel a little less lonely. They had already talked me into buying that second-hand E-type Jaguar, which certainly did a lot for my image, though very little for my nerves. For one insane period, the boys even persuaded me to buy a Harley-Davidson motorbike, "so we could go on road trips together." Yeah, right. I took one trial run around West London and was so terrified I never got on the bike again.

For another split second I took up riding after Jim Godfrey and I did a story about the Hunt Saboteurs Association—the people who campaigned against the ancient British sport of fox hunting because they felt it was cruel to the fox. We made contact with the Tickham Hunt, in Kent, and were immediately invited down for their next meet, given complete access to the Master of the Hounds and everyone else. I dressed up in a pair of riding boots, jodhpurs, a black blazer, a silk stock and pin, and a riding hat. Jim said he wanted to bite my neck.

We shot the story, interviewing the Tickham Field as they gathered round for the traditional stirrup cup, and the Hunt Saboteurs as they shouted in protest. It was a beautiful day, and I did my stand-up sitting down . . . on a horse actually, lent to me by one of the riders. The Saboteurs were surprisingly prudish, as it turned out.

"Do you know what these people do *after* the hunt?" one of the demonstrators asked me.

"No, but you're going to tell me," I answered.

"They have *sex!*"

Well, shock horror! Years later, in 2004, the Saboteurs actually managed to have fox hunting banned by an Act of Parliament. Hunters on horseback could no longer track, chase, and kill the fox with hounds. Most Hunts around the United Kingdom could only pursue the smell of a fox, galloping after a scented rag dragged across the countryside.

But the members of the Tickham Hunt were frightfully friendly to me and invited me to come back and hunt with them. "But I don't know how to ride," I said. "Oh, that doesn't matter! We can teach you in a couple of days!" they said. "Anyway, we've seen you on a horse, when you did your piece to the camera. You've got a very good seat." In the parlance of the horsey set, this does *not* mean that you've got a great ass.

Have you ever noticed how people who are themselves proficient at a certain sport, usually a dangerous one, always assume that *anyone* can pick it up? All you need is a couple of lessons, right? That's what these terribly nice people were like. And fool that I was, I believed them. I made a date to come back for my "lesson." I thought, with John gone from my life, I needed a new interest.

I drove down to Kent, dressed in the full riding gear, and they brought out an absolutely enormous horse. It took me three or four attempts just to get onto the beast. Fortunately we were in an enclosed space, or manège; otherwise, the horse probably would have bolted, recognizing that he had a completely terrified rider on his back.

I'm not sure what that first lesson would have involved, or whether I would have survived it at all, because within minutes my pager went off. The office wanted me to go back to London immediately to cover a breaking news story. I clambered off the stallion, made my apologies, and rushed back to the city. That story probably saved me from a fate worse than death.

Before he left, John had encouraged me to try for an interview with the British prime minister, Harold Wilson. "This would be good for your network, and for you, honey-bunch," he said, and he saw the perfect angle.

"The Brits are very upset with the amount of support that NORAID, the Irish Northern Aid Committee, is getting from Americans. It's supposed to be a charitable organization, but basically the money goes to the IRA, which is a terrorist organization as far as Her Majesty's government is concerned. You should approach the Prime Minister's Office and ask for an interview *specifically* on that subject."

I ran this past ABC and they were all for it, so we put in our request. We got an answer within days, along with a date for the interview at Number 10.

Harold Wilson had been Labour prime minister of Great Britain from 1964 to 1970. He'd become prime minister again in 1974, when the Labour Party defeated the Conservatives under Edward Heath. He was later falsely accused by the chief of CIA Counterintelligence,

James Jesus Angleton, of being a "Soviet agent." Angleton's claim was never proven. Wilson was educated in a Yorkshire grammar school and got into Oxford on his own merit. He never lost his Yorkshire accent and he was never at a loss for words. On occasion he could resort to force when dealing with reporters. When the famous John Simpson of the BBC dared to ask him, in 1970, if he was thinking of calling an election, Wilson punched him in the stomach. (Simpson wasn't famous then: it was his first day as a news reporter.) In 1974, Wilson had tried to resolve the conflict in Northern Ireland between the Catholic Nationalists and the Protestant Unionists, without success.

In March 1976, we set up our cameras in one of the side rooms at Number 10 Downing Street. We were shocked when the prime minister came in. He barely made eye contact, with any of us, and was surprisingly unkempt, with dandruff all over his jacket. I didn't dare mention this to his handlers. The prime minister knew what our line of questioning was to be—the ground rules were that we were to focus only on NORAID. But as I went through the interview, the PM kept turning to cue cards that he held in his hands. This was a man who normally could speak for hours without a note. Now he needed cue cards to answer a simple question for which he'd received advance notice. We finished the interview quickly and the prime minister shuffled out, without a word.

Within a few weeks Wilson stunned the nation when he announced his resignation. No reason was given, though there was a lot of speculation again about the unsubstantiated rumours that he was a Soviet "agent of influence." Several years later it was revealed that Harold Wilson had Alzheimer's disease. This was clearly the reason he'd resigned without warning. That explained his strange performance during our interview.

After John left for Cyprus, I took up briefly with a good-looking, hard-drinking Australian columnist inevitably called Bruce. My crews egged me on. He was fun, but he was a terrible binge-drinker and I realized that I couldn't possibly have a real relationship with this guy. I just ended up missing John even more.

But Bruce was friendly with the famous author John le Carré, whom I was dying to meet. Le Carré had invited us both to his spectacular cliffside home in Cornwall for a weekend. I could certainly put up with Bruce until that came to pass.

We drove down in the E-type Jaguar, and for once the Car from Hell made the seven-hour journey without breaking down. John le Carré's real name is David Cornwell, and he lived with his second wife, Jane, and young son, Nicholas, in a row of converted stone cottages on a cliff near Land's End. After he'd bought the cottages, David said he was astonished to find that there was a mile of Cornish coastline thrown in. Their house was fantastic, filled with antique furniture, crystal, and china. David loved beautiful things. Plush oriental carpets on the floors made it very cozy, and the casement windows opened onto a wild Celtic sea, crashing onto an empty shore.

The Cornwells were immensely cordial and didn't stand on ceremony. David had us in stitches within minutes with his merciless impersonations of various people in public life. Jane was remarkably open about how and when she'd met David. ("He was heavily married," she said to me after a few drinks.) She showed what David called her "ball-breaking patience" with their precocious son, then about four, though he thought he was thirty. The Cornwells seemed to have a very good working relationship: David wrote his novels by hand, often standing up; and Jane would type up the manuscript as his pages came through.(She later described herself as 'a service industry.') David's friend John Miller, a well-known landscape painter, came over for dinner with his partner, Michael Truscott, and we had one of the most delightful evenings I have ever spent, anywhere. In fact, the whole weekend was delightful, from beginning to end. Bruce behaved himself and was almost as funny as David. We walked for miles along the twisting coastal paths, through dense groves of deep blue hydrangea. We explored the nearby port of Penzance. We went to Miller's studio at Sancreed House, where I bought a large oil painting of Venice in winter. It has since had pride of place in a dozen houses in a half-dozen countries. The Cornwells were perfect hosts, with a way of making you feel that you were their new best friends. As it happened, they did remain friends, for years, and so did John Miller, whom I adored.

On the third and last day of our visit, the office contacted me to say that I should fly directly to Belfast in the morning. Bruce had to drive the E-Type back to London. I came down from the Cornish clouds with a thud. While in Belfast, I got a surprise call from Cyprus. It was John, with some shocking news.

25

MARRIAGE, THE UNSPEAKABLE FOLLY

John's call started with a long list of things he wanted me to bring out to Cyprus for our vacation together that summer. In spite of my brief attempt to be a bachelorette again, I missed him terribly and basically couldn't give him up, even though we didn't live together anymore. We still jointly owned the Cyprus cottage, though I had sole possession of the London apartment. He listed books and beach-tennis equipment. Then he paused.

"One more thing. Shall we get married?"

"Wha-wha-what are you talking about? You are already married. Alice won't give you a divorce."

"After five years' separation, divorce becomes automatic. She can't stop it anymore."

I was in Belfast, remember? It was then one of the darkest, most depressing places on earth. Catholic and Protestant paramilitaries knocking each other off, bombing public places, each side convinced it was in the right, with religion sanctifying the violence on both sides.

John got me in a weak moment. I said yes. When I returned to London, I wondered what in God's name I'd done, agreeing to marry a man I couldn't actually live with. Unless I was ready to give up the job of my dreams and I wasn't that crazy.

John saw it slightly differently. He called his friend Nick Ludington of the Associated Press and said, "Nick, I just wanted you to know that I am about to commit the unspeakable folly of marrying Hilary."

We were now up against a deadline. We had two weeks, basically, to arrange the wedding. For my wedding dress, I bought a blouse made from antique lace and a full-length Fortuny-style ivory skirt. I would wear this with heirloom jewellery and my gold filigree belt from Dubrovnik.

More important was the service itself. Having abandoned the Church of England as an adolescent, I suddenly felt the need for a religious ritual to sanctify this act of Unspeakable Folly. I phone John and explain this.

"You mean, you want a *church service?*" says John. "I, ah, I don't really know if the C of E even allows divorced people to remarry. Especially in the time we've got. But I do know one person who might be able to help," he adds brightly, ever the resourceful journalist who has never missed a deadline. Our wedding was in ten days' time.

Two days later, John calls me back. "Darling, we can be married in St. Anthony's in Paphos, a Byzantine chapel that was given to the Anglican community of Cyprus. It seats about thirty people."

How did he pull this one off? Only a few weeks earlier he'd been having a quiet drink at a well-known watering hole in Nicosia. He starts chatting with a chap at the bar, and they have a civilized exchange of views on the issues of the day, over several glasses of beer. Finally, John extends his hand and introduces himself.

"I'm John Bierman, the BBC and Reuters."

"How do you do. I'm the Bishop of Cyprus and the Gulf," replies the stranger.

"Oh fuck off, of course you're not," says John with his usual impeccable manners.

"No, I really am! Look! Here's my ring!" and the bishop extends his hand with its ring of office. He obviously isn't wearing his clerical collar.

"Well I'm damned! You certainly fooled me. Forgive me if I showed any disrespect," says John.

"No, not at all. Here's my card. If ever you need anything, do give me a call."

John puts the card away and fortunately doesn't lose it. Because only a few weeks later, he is calling the bishop in a panic about his imminent nuptials and the wishes of his betrothed, a lapsed member of the Church of England. Thanks to his drinking buddy, John is given a special emergency dispensation to be married in an Anglican Church, though he is a divorced man. He didn't tell the bishop he's also Jewish. That might have been a bridge too far.

And so it came to pass, on August 22, 1976. First with a civil ceremony in the Paphos Town Hall, where we took our vows in a second-storey room with the windows thrown open. This was compulsory. According to an enlightened Cyprus custom, bride and groom are each permitted to make a last-minute escape from matrimony by jumping out of a window, separately or together.

Later at the Church of St. Anthony, a British curate took the service, attended by my sweet sister Gingie, who flew in from Canada; two of John's three children (Richard and Katie); my best friend from school in Geneva (Sally Widnell and her family, including my goddaughter Katherine Widnell); and about twenty assorted journalists. Frances

Brook came out from England and played a shaky "Wedding March" on the little keyboard that was used in the absence of an organ. No one wore a tie, not even the groom, who was in a white safari suit. The reception was on the terrace of Calypso Cottage, with the Mediterranean sparkling below us. The caterers couldn't believe the amount of champagne that was consumed. That was pretty normal back then, when journalists got together. Now, as the great Australian journalist Tony Clifton once said, "Give them a bottle of Barolo and it takes them a week to get through it."

To my undying shame, my parents were not invited. We didn't even tell them about the wedding until it was too late. That's because we couldn't tell John's mother, Bessie, either. She would have insisted on coming and would have been like the Bad Fairy, criticizing my dress and the tiny chapel and the reception in our rustic cottage. She would have jinxed the whole marriage. Therefore, no parents on either side.

But Mum and Dad took it in stride, and I think they forgave me. We later invited them to stay for two weeks at our expense in what Mum said was the best holiday she had ever had. The day before the wedding, I phoned them in Switzerland. Mum answered.

"Mum, I'm getting married."

"Oh that's nice, dear. Who are you marrying?"

"I'm marrying John, of course. Who else?"

"Does that mean you'll be going to Cyprus to live with him?"

"No, I'll be staying in London."

"Then will John be going back to London to live with you?"

"No. We won't actually be living together after the wedding."

My darling mother then uttered one of the few worldly-wise, sophisticated remarks I had ever heard come out of her mouth.

"That's nice, dear. I know you'll have a very happy marriage."

26

PARIS AGAIN

Both Gingie and Frances stayed on in Cyprus after our Unspeakable Folly and joined us for part of our honeymoon. We picnicked and swam in our usual hidden coves along the coast, ate in our favourite waterside tavernas, hiked along the seaside cliffs, and explored some of the Greco-Roman ruins on the island. After three weeks we all went back to our respective homes, leaving John alone with his work for the BBC, Reuters, and *The Guardian*. He was busy; and when he was busy, he was happy; and when he was happy, I was happy.

Within weeks of my return to London, ABC asked me if I would like to become the chief correspondent in Paris. This was not quite as grand as it sounds, since there was a total of two correspondents in the entire bureau. But it was a beautiful bureau, in a beautiful city, and I accepted immediately. I would replace Lou Cioffi, the man who'd helped me get my job with ABC in the first place and therefore my number-one guru. (Lou was taking the UN post in New York.) I ended up selling the Primrose Hill apartment, which was a mistake. Never sell well-located property in a capital city unless you are absolutely destitute.

The ABC Paris bureau in the fall of 1976 was in an elegant converted apartment on the top two floors of a handsome building in the 16th Arrondisement, one block from the Place Victor Hugo. My office was about 20 feet long, with a large antique desk and tall French windows opening onto a large balcony. If you leaned on the wrought-iron railing, you had the unmistakable profile of the Eiffel Tower behind you, in the distance. A perfect stand-up location. And all you needed to do was take three giant steps from your desk and ask your cameraman to start rolling.

I was thrilled to be back in my favourite city, with a wonderful team of people to work with. My cameraman was Nicolas Gedrinsky, a great bear of a man whose family had fled from Russia to Paris during the 1917 Revolution. He was six-foot-four and a terrific extrovert, full of stories that were about 50 percent true. He was wonderful on the road. Patrick Etcheverry had been transferred from London as his soundman. Patrick was also six-foot-four. When the three of us worked together, we had a combined height of about 20 feet. That could intimidate people. Which was useful.

The bureau ran like clockwork thanks to its chic and highly effective manager, Renate Gozlan. Because the office had a working kitchen, Renate set up a system of optional office lunches, prepared by our Portuguese cleaning lady, Bianca. You would sign up for lunch by mid-morning, pay 6 francs, Bianca would go to the shops, and by one o'clock she had a three-course meal ready for all those who'd made a booking. It was always a good lunch at a reasonable price, and great for office morale. Great, that is, until some American journalist reported that "The ABC Paris bureau has its own cook." The brass in New York got very upset and the whole delightful custom came to an end.

The second correspondent was Jack Smith, son of Howard K. Smith, former anchor of the *ABC Evening News*. Jack was a Rhodes Scholar. He'd also served in Vietnam, in combat, and almost died when his unit was ambushed by the Viet Cong. He survived because he was buried under the bodies of his dead comrades. Jack was obsessed with rock climbing, and his office was full of crampons and spikes and ropes and all the paraphernalia of that insane sport. When under pressure, he would often climb the walls, literally.

We ended up renting apartments on the same narrow street on the Left Bank, near the Île Saint-Louise. His flat was on one side of the street, and mine was directly opposite. Had I ever needed a cup of sugar, he could have just put his hand out and passed it over. Jack and I remained friends for life.

Bernard Kaplan, whom I had known when I was working at CBC in Paris, was also in the bureau as a tenant. The space was so large and rambling that we could rent out an office to Bernie, who worked freelance for a number of clients. By this time, I think he had some respect for me as a television reporter. "Hilary, you are at your apogee," he intoned, after he had consumed a few glasses of wine.

And as it happened, my best friend from my days in Paris in the sixties, Catherine de la Presle, was living on the same street as the ABC bureau, with her husband, Olivier. She was now Madame de Monicault. By then she had four children, with another on the way. I would often go down the street to join them for lunch. On one such occasion, Cathe discreetly went into labour. "Olivier, I think you should take me to the clinic," she said evenly as Olivier flapped around her. "But, Hil, you must stay for the mousse au chocolat," she cried as she sailed out the door, ever the Perfect Hostess. Her fifth child, Priscille, was born two hours later.

With my best friend down the street, Jack as my so-called junior correspondent, great crews, and an extremely friendly bureau, I felt very much at home in Paris. It helped that I liked the French and spoke the language, and of course loved the country. But I missed John. In the first year of our marriage, we saw each other only six times, when he would fly to Paris for a long weekend. Paris was a travelling bureau and I travelled all the time. On Valentine's Day, I sent him a funny greeting by telex, then the fastest written form of communication. He answered immediately in telex-ese:

"TKS YR COMIC VALENTINE
SENT TO ME BY TELEX LINE
ST.VAL EYEM SURE WD LIKE TO KNOW
THE SPEED SUCH MSGES CAN GO
BUT TKS AND BI AND GA AND MOM
CD ONLY TURN A TELEX ON
EYED LIKE A GADGET TT WD SPEED
THE THINGS TT LOVERS REALLY NEED."[1]

One of my wilder assignments during this period was to Zaire, formerly known as the Belgian Congo, to cover a rebellion in the southern province of Shaba. The rebels were Congolese veterans of the civil war in Angola who'd crossed into Shaba from Angola unopposed in March 1977. Incredibly, they invaded on bicycles. Known as the FLNC (Front de Libération Nationale Congolaise), the rebels made swift progress because of the ineptitude of the Zaire Army (the FAZ, or Forces Armées Zaïroises), and because they had the sympathy of the local population. The FAZ terrorized the people, and more than fifty thousand fled to Angola and Zambia. The rebels set up their headquarters in a village near the mining town of Kolwezi.

The rebellion was the greatest threat to the presidency of Mobutu Sese Seko since he'd first seized power in 1965 and began to siphon billions from government coffers. Mobutu cut all air and road access to Shaba, prevented the local press from reporting the story at all, and banned all foreign journalists from the area.

All, that is, except Nicolas, Patrick, and me. We had an insane plan for getting down to Kolwezi. Our lunatic idea was to stow away on one of the military transport planes carrying arms from the capital of Kinshasa to Shaba. We went to one of the local markets, where you could actually buy military fatigues, including caps and boots. In the middle of the night we dressed up in our camouflage gear, loaded up our equipment, and drove to the military airport. Incredibly, we were waved through. We stopped close to the runway where several transport planes were parked. I don't know how we decided which plane to board—did we just go "eeny, meany, miny, moe"?

In any event, we grabbed our gear, dismissed our driver, walked purposefully toward the chosen aircraft, and climbed in. No one, but *no one* stopped us. Was it because of our combined height of 20 feet? Nicolas gave the pilot a salute, though the pilot didn't seem to be that interested. In fact, he looked as though he was on some kind of weed. We strapped ourselves into the bucket seats and looked around for the cargo. It seemed to consist of nothing but oil drums, which was pretty ominous. Presumably, they contained oil, as in gasoline. Within half an hour, the plane took off.

A few hours later, we were in the forbidden town of Kolwezi, at an airport that was crawling with military traffic. Nicolas shot everything that moved, I did a script and a stand-up (massive military buildup, Mobutu facing greatest threat to his presidency, et cetera, et cetera), we packaged up our report in an onion bag and found someone who was going back to Kinshasa on an empty transport, and who would hand-carry our film to our producer at the Intercontinental Hotel. It must have been an aid worker because the film was actually delivered and our report got on the air.

We checked in to a Belgian-run motel and operated unhindered in Kolwezi for about a week. We even went into the bush on a so-called punitive raid with a unit of Moroccan troops. I wore my tribal belt from Damascus over my military fatigues. Just to distinguish myself from the combatants, you understand. About fifteen hundred Moroccan soldiers had been flown into the area on French transport planes to help the inept Zaire Army. Many Central African soldiers refused to fight because they hadn't been paid. There was very little fighting anyway. In the two days we spent with the Moroccan troops, we didn't hear a single shot fired in anger. An expat Belgian engineer said this wasn't surprising. "What can you expect? If the rebels get too close, many Zairean soldiers will just run away. One bang and off they go."

By this time, there was a CBS team in Kolwezi and we were both staying in the same motel, spying on each other. The CBS correspondent was Robin Wright, who later had a successful career as an academic and analyst. She disarmed me with her flattery, saying that her masters in New York told her to "Copy Hilary Brown. She's tough, competitive, and good." Yeah, right. It became impossible to go anywhere without being followed by Robin and her team. After a week in Kolwezi, New York ordered us back to Kinshasa. Mobutu had thrown about seven foreign journalists in jail by then, including one reporter who'd only been in the country for twenty-four hours.

But for some reason we didn't end up in the slammer and instead were granted an interview with the president on our return to the capital. It was in his palace, where we were shown into an empty room with one large chair—for President Mobutu himself. I had to conduct the interview on my knees.

The rebellion ended in May when the rebels withdrew to Angola. We had rebased to Paris long before that. Mobutu accused the Soviet Union and Cuba of sponsoring the rebels, saying he would continue his battle against Soviet influence in Africa. He ended up getting loans from the International Monetary Fund and the World Bank. In spite of the dismal performance of his army, the rebellion turned out to be a public relations triumph for one of the greatest kleptocrats on the continent.

The next year, the rebels returned to Shaba Province. This time, they massacred eighty unarmed Europeans and two hundred African civilians in Kolwezi. The French Foreign Legion drove out the rebels in a seven-day battle and airlifted more than two thousand Europeans out of the country. But by then I was in a completely different part of the world. Thank God.

My enduring memory of Zaire was not so much our life-threatening plot to stow away on a military transport plane. It was the large sign on the lawn next to the swimming pool at the Intercontinental Hotel in Kinshasa, where the foreign press corps stayed. In very big letters, it said:

"IT IS FORBIDDEN TO PICNIC ON THE GRASS, PISS IN THE POOL, OR COME WITH ANIMALS."[2]

The sign was later stolen by a *New York Times* correspondent who was a good friend and who at great personal risk, managed to smuggle it out of the country. I asked him to leave it to me in his will.

27

DASH TO AFRICA

If you are based in the Paris bureau of an American network, unfortunately you spend very little time doing stories in Paris or in France itself. France was much too stable. We were always pitching feature ideas that would keep us in the country, and sometimes New York let us go down one of those beautiful, tree-lined French country roads in search of a colourful "good news" story. Such as a report on cognac, and the Cognac region of France, for example. The French were very upset that producers of brandy in other parts of the world had the nerve to call their product "cognac." Only brandy produced in the Cognac region of France could take that venerable name. Naturellement.

The producers of a fine cognac called Prince Hubert de Polignac showed us incredible hospitality and gave us total access, insisting that we sample their best vintages. Nicolas and Patrick were in their element. I, on the other hand, was basically legless after two or three sips.

We did another feature story in Paris itself about the thirtieth anniversary of the New Look, the revolutionary post-war change in fashion launched by Christian Dior in 1947. The New Look was a tight waist and a very full long skirt, using yards of fabric. It replaced the drab narrow silhouette of the war years, when everything, including cloth, was so scarce.

We arranged to shoot in the workrooms of the famous couture house on the Avenue Montaigne, asking if by any chance we could film one of their clients being fitted for a dress.

"Mais bien sur! On peut arranger ça!" says the public relations officer. I am amazed, but *télévision Américaine* seemed to be a magic word. Two words, actually. Within a day the Dior salon calls back and says that one of their best clients, the Vicomtesse de Ribes, would be happy to be filmed. Jacqueline de Ribes is in *all* the fashion magazines.

I arrive with Patrick and Nicolas at the Dior Salon in plenty of time. The Vicomtesse is already there, in the cabine, or fitting room. She had stripped down and is in a loose cotton garment with very little underneath. In a couture house, the dress is cut on the client's living body, starting with a pattern drawn and cut in cotton, then transferred to expensive fabric. This way, the garment will fit perfectly. A couture dress takes hours to make and prices start at about $10,000, for a day dress. An evening gown can cost hundreds of thousands of dollars, depending on the beadwork.

I want to do the interview with the Vicomtesse while the cutters are actually working on her. This means that we have to use a Lavalier mic, passing it underneath her cotton garment and clipping it onto the neckline so the wire won't show. Patrick is not only tall but has a trim beard and a full head of hair. He is really quite dashing. He also speaks beautiful French. He bows slightly, holding the mic as if it were an exotic flower.

"Alors si son altesse la Vicomtesse veut bien mettre le micro elle même, par dessous sa robe . . . ?" he murmurs. (*Would the Vicomtesse care to put the microphone on, under her dress?*)

"Mais non mais non mais non!" the Vicomtesse cries, raising her arms with a little laugh and wriggling slightly. "Mettez-le vous même!" (*Put it on yourself!*) So with great delicacy, Patrick gives another bow, slips the mic under the hem of the lady's garment, passes it up to her aristocratic neck, and clips it on. She gives us a terrific interview.

But my favourite feature story during this period was back in Africa, in the tiny West African country of The Gambia. One Friday in late January 1977, as we were all getting ready to enjoy a rare, quiet weekend in the City of Light, Renate came rushing into my office. "New York wants you and the crew to go to The Gambia *right now*! They want a piece on Alex Haley's ancestral home! You're booked on a flight to Dakar in four hours!" She produced a huge cash advance. That was a sign that New York *really* wanted this story. Where's The Gambia? Who is Alex Haley?

Very quickly we learned that Alex Haley was the African American author of a best-selling book titled *Roots*. He describes his enslaved ancestor, Kunta Kinte, and how he, Haley, traced his roots back to The Gambia in West Africa. The book had just been made into an eight-part TV miniseries airing on ABC. At the time, it received the highest ratings in American television history. ABC had a huge hit on its hands, and the news division wanted a story, *now*. I took off on Friday afternoon from Paris with Nicolas and Patrick. New York wanted our report for Monday night's show.

We land in Dakar, Senegal, late that night and rent a car first thing in the morning. A Peugeot. This is an inspired choice, as we later find out. We drive at top speed to the border of The Gambia, which remarkably doesn't have any visa requirements for French and Canadian passport holders. Once inside the country, we have to find Alex Haley's "ancestral home," as New York had put it. We have absolutely no idea where that is. We don't even have a name. As it happens, there's an election going on. The Gambia, which basically consists of the two banks of the Gambia River, is a former British colony and a multi-party democracy. There are campaign posters everywhere, and even the odd party rally in the capital of Banjul. We jump out of the car and start rolling. "We're gonna need B-roll!" I cry (that's TV jargon for generic background visuals). Wherever we stop, we ask in mounting desperation if anyone has heard of Alex Haley or Kunta Kinte and do they know where his family lives. It's now Saturday afternoon and we only have until Sunday evening. How can we possibly find this place?

This is Africa, baby. The bush telegraph is still one of the principal means of communication, and The Gambia is the smallest country on the continent. In the eighteenth century, it played a key part in the slave trade, and the people here seem to be aware of their frightful history. An estimated three million people were captured as slaves from this region.

One after the other, people tell us, Oh yes, it's outside the city limits, on the other side of the river, turn right at the market, et cetera, et cetera. Eventually we end up on a dirt road, driving straight into the jungle. By now we have the *name* of the village (Juffure). It's not so much a road as a dirt track, and it seems to get more and more narrow as we go deeper into the jungle. A jungle full of ominous jungle noises. By this time it's late afternoon. We *have* to get our material before nightfall.

Suddenly the track leads into a clearing, with a cluster of mud huts. Women are pounding away at some kind of nut. Half-naked children are running around. An elderly man in a full-length robe is moving across the clearing.

Can this be the place? We are now right on deadline. We've got to get our material and our interviews and go. I rush up to the man and start stammering in pidgin English.

"We ABC Television! We lookin' for Alex Haley! He big writer, from America! Very famous! His family, they come from here? You know him?"

The man turns to me, smiles, and replies in perfect Oxford English:

"Oh yes, I know Alex. Awfully nice chap. Came here looking for his roots. Funny thing to do. But he seemed sincere."

Hallelujah! Talk about Reporter's Luck! This gentleman is a product of the British colonial educational system! A *perfect* product! We interview him, of course. Nicolas shoots the village scene, we get lots of B-roll of the kids playing, the women pounding nuts, and so on. I do a piece to camera and we start to drive back, in the failing evening light. This time we're not only faced with the terrible dirt track and the all-pervasive jungle, but a jungle *fire*. Nicolas puts his foot on the accelerator and just powers through it. I told you the Peugeot was an inspired choice.

We get back across the border into Senegal on Sunday and are able to hand-carry the film back to Paris ourselves, in plenty of time for the Monday deadline. New York loved the piece. We loved it too.

In June that year, ABC asked me to co-anchor the Queen's Silver Jubilee celebrations in London with Peter Jennings. Any royal assignment is an absolute treat. The BBC coverage of the procession to St. Paul's Cathedral (to which we all had access) was flawless. We had to study all the London landmarks along the route—Peter and I walked the route together before the Big Day. We had to be able to identify the different royal carriages, apart from all the members of the extended royal family, and the Great and the Good of British society. Peter had an incredible head for detail and, of course, acted me right off the set. I remember having asked Howard K. Smith, the venerable anchorman, how to handle the assignment and he said, "Don't be afraid to keep your mouth shut and let the pictures tell the story." By that standard, I suppose I can claim that I did quite well.

But through all this busy, happy period, I really longed for John. Seeing each other every other month, for a long weekend, just wasn't enough. We were supposed to be married, after all. Yes, absence makes the heart grow fonder, but it also makes it ache with loneliness. Especially when John would send me beautiful love letters, often ending with poems that he knew from memory. One of my favourites was this sixteenth-century anonymous lament about a soldier, far from his sweetheart.

> "Oh western wind, when wilt thou blow,
> And the small rain down doth rain.
> Christ, if my love were in my arms,
> And I in my bed again."[1]

John was my rock, and without him I just didn't feel grounded. Eventually, that set me up for a major career move.

In 1977, ABC named Roone Arledge, then head of ABC Sports, to be president of ABC News. Arledge was a brilliant producer and executive, and he saw Peter Jennings as ABC's Big Star.

Peter started covering stories absolutely everywhere—not just in Europe, but in Africa, the Middle East, and India. It was known as the Jennings Flying Circus. He would even cover stories that other correspondents had been working on. And that's what happened to me when I was preparing to go on the air with a hostage crisis in Paris. I'd been working following the story all day. At the last minute,

Peter flew in from London and just took it over. It was as though he'd said, "Here, Hils, hold my trench coat, I can handle this." Dammit all, I was the Paris correspondent. I was the *senior* Paris correspondent! I got very cross and threw my toys out of my playpen.

This happened to coincide with an overture from NBC News. They wanted to know if I would be interested in becoming their correspondent in Tel Aviv. Tel Aviv was a forty-minute flight from Cyprus. Forty minutes from John.

I was so upset about being big-footed by Peter, and so excited about being closer to John, that I told ABC I wanted out of my contract. I had a long, emotional talk with Bill Sheehan, the man who'd been so kind to me, who'd always supported me and offered me big jobs in the States that I kept turning down. (Bill was made senior vice-president after Arledge took over his job, staying on with the network for two more years.)

I finally got an agent, Richard Leibner ("You're the woman offered a co-anchor job and you *vacillated?* I'd love to represent you!"), and he negotiated the deal. Leibner got me a four-year contract with a 30 percent increase in salary and a starting date that gave me lots of time to pack up my things in Paris. John came over to help me. The ABC Paris bureau gave me a set of copper cooking pots as a goodbye present. It was a very tearful farewell. I loved ABC. It was my family.

I moved to Tel Aviv about a month later, in November 1977, and that coincided with one of the biggest stories to hit the Middle East: the surprise visit to Jerusalem by Egyptian President Anwar Sadat, and the historic Egyptian–Israeli peace agreement that eventually followed. John got transferred to Tel Aviv by the BBC eight months later, two years after our wedding day. That's when we discovered that living together ... didn't ruin our marriage.

28

ISRAEL, JONATHAN, AND THE BEST YEARS OF OUR LIVES

Enough books have been written by enough people about the history and politics of the Middle East: the world doesn't need my half-baked views. Though, of course, I acquired a lot of them. I will only say that the two years I lived and worked in Israel as a foreign correspondent for an American television network were among the best, most interesting, most exhausting, most infuriating, and most rewarding of my life.

The "story" was huge, fantastic, and demanding. It started with Sadat's surprise trip to Jerusalem—the first ever by an Arab leader—his historic meeting with the right-wing Israeli Prime Minister Menachem Begin; the early, optimistic beginnings of a Mid-East peace process; the first Israeli invasion of Lebanon (following the first and one of the worst Palestinian terror attacks in the heart of Israel); and the Camp David peace accords in September 1978. America's interest in the story was insatiable. It was as though we correspondents were on a local beat, rather than a foreign tour of duty. New York wanted a report on everything, and on every nuance of everything. It was one of those foreign postings where the home desk was more interested in the story than the foreign reporters themselves. Usually it's the other way round.

My personal life was also wonderful. I rented a spectacular house on a cliff overlooking the Mediterranean in the sought-after suburb of Herzliya Pituach, just north of Tel Aviv. The day after I moved in, I was promptly befriended by my next-door neighbour, Ziona Leshem, and her handsome husband, Avraham. She was an architect living in her own iconic house—a concrete dome, rather like a yurt. It was in all the architecture books. I quickly made other Israeli friends too, along with some delightful members of the diplomatic corps, notably the U.K. Chargé d'Affaires, Mike Newington, and his wife, Nina. I met them through David Cornwell (a.k.a. John Le Carré) when David came to Israel to research a book (*The Little Drummer Girl*, I think). The Newingtons gave a dinner party for him and he took me along as his date. David loved women, and I was no exception.

It impressed me that in spite of his fame, he rejected all the glittering prizes. 'I don't want to be a Loser in a dinner jacket and I don't want to be a Winner in a dinner jacket.' he would say. He always refused to be included in the Queen's Birthday Honours List, though he did once accept an invitation to lunch at Buckingham Palace. He admitted that he was completely smitten by Her Majesty, and it might have been mutual. 'I did notice a rather wistful look in her eyes,' he said, with a knowing smile.

In the summer of 1978 another dream came true. The BBC transferred John to Israel. We were under the same roof again, and we threw a big party to celebrate. Catherine Leroy, (the famous war photographer) came out to stay with her boyfriend Bernard Estrade, a top reporter for Agence France Presse, and she took pictures, as she always did. Except that this time it was a different kind of battlefield.

One guest got so tight she fell down the stairs and cracked her skull. A minor injury, as it turned out, but there was quite a lot of blood.

John had a term contract with BBC TV, which allowed him to also freelance for *The Boston Globe*—an arrangement set up by our good friend David Greenway. And by the end of our time in Israel, John had discovered an extraordinary, untold human rights story that he first made into an hour-long documentary for the BBC program *Man Alive*. He then produced a book on the subject, which became a best-seller: *Righteous Gentile: The Story of Raoul Wallenberg, Missing Hero of the Holocaust*. Wallenberg was a Swedish diplomat who was dispatched to Budapest in mid-1944 by the War Refugees Board and who is credited with saving up to one hundred thousand Hungarian Jews from the Nazi extermination camps. Though Germany was losing the war, Hungary's Jews were being rounded up by Adolf Eichmann and put into transports to be gassed or turned into soap. Wallenberg issued fake Swedish identity cards called "Schutz Passes" to as many Jews as he could. At the end of the war, he was arrested by the Russians and disappeared into the Gulag, though there were sightings of him years later.

Righteous Gentile was the start of John's successful career as a biographer, even as he continued to practise journalism. . He subsequently wrote and published seven first-class works of historical popular biography (two with fellow journalist Colin Smith). "Working, in the sense of writing books, I shall do until I drop, because it's my life," he once said in an interview (*The Daily Telegraph Weekend Magazine*.[1)] Years after the publication of his Wallenberg book, he was asked to write the inscription for the statue of Wallenberg in Great Cumberland Place in London (unveiled by the Queen). These were his well-chosen words:

"The 20th century spawned two of history's vilest tyrannies. Raoul Wallenberg outwitted the first, but was swallowed up by the second. His triumph over Nazi genocide reminds us that the courageous and committed individual can prevail against even the cruellest state machine. The fate of the six million Jews he was unable to rescue reminds us of the evil to which racist ideas can drive whole nations. Finally, his imprisonment reminds us not only of Soviet brutality but also of the ignorance and indifference, which led the free world to abandon him. We must never forget his lesson."[2]

Very, very powerful, though John's name couldn't be on this inscription. "Dammit all!" he once said, "These are the most enduring words I've ever written, and there's no byline!"

There was just one problem with our idyllic new life in Israel. The bureau chief at NBC Tel Aviv, a former UPI (United Press International) reporter named Tom Cheatham, was not happy with his new correspondent. Initially he was afraid that I would be spending too much time visiting my husband in Cyprus and would therefore be out of position in a country where the news just never stopped.

During the next two years, Tom and I rarely exchanged more than a few words each day. But we were actually a good team. He knew the region well, and he had good contacts. I respected his judgment, most of the time. In any event, New York liked our work, and we had terrific camera crews. A wild twenty-eight-year-old named Yossi Greenberg was my favourite. He was quick, never missed a shot, and produced beautiful pictures. We were competitive too. We were up against Bob Simon of CBS and his producer Joel Bernstein, and Joel himself told me they used to worry that I might beat them on a story.

Worry about *me*? Joel and his wife, Toby, a talented artist, became our best pals; and long after our days in Israel were over, we would meet up again and again in other parts of the world.

In early 1979, my relationship with Tom seemed to take a definite turn for the better. That was when I had to confess to him, and to my masters at NBC in New York, that I was expecting a baby. This somehow humanized me in his eyes. Or maybe he thought I would just have to stop work. Maybe for good.

In the seventies, it was much more difficult for a woman in a high-profile job to get pregnant and still keep her job. That was how I saw it, anyway. I was afraid that if I were to start a family, they would fire me. "See what happens when you give a dame a man's job? She starts having children, and she can't work anymore." That's how I imagined the conversation in the executive suite in New York.

Then two things happened. Lesley Stahl of CBS had a baby, and that certainly didn't blight her career. And I got a letter from my great friend Krystyne Griffin in Toronto. We are the same age, and she had a highly successful career in fashion and merchandising.

"Great news!" she wrote in her large, sloping hand. "We are having a spring child!"

Dammit, I thought, if Krystyne can, and if Lesley can . . . so can I!

Without consulting John, I stopped practising birth control and we conceived within a month. When I finally told my husband about my condition, he was Shocked, Shocked and Appalled. "But, Hilly, you know what they say about older parents. They have *puny children*." That's how much he knew. Our baby was almost ten pounds at birth.

Everyone at NBC was very kind and supportive. The brass in New York actually asked me how much maternity leave I would like, and when did I think I could come back to work? Another person in Human Resources phoned to remind me that I was entitled to a complete reimbursement of all my hospital expenses. Yossi and the other cameramen shot me in close-up for all my stand-ups. I must have looked all right—John came home one day saying he had been accosted by a Jewish American lady at some event who'd narrowed her eyes, poked at his chest, and said, "I seen your wife on television. She's not chopped liver."

I worked until my eighth month, the absolute limit for air travel. And the absolute limit for anyone at NBC who was willing to work with me. They were all terrified that I would go into labour while chasing a story. I became quite large.

We decided to have the baby in England. I first flew to France to visit Catherine de Monicault—she was expecting her sixth child at pretty much the same time, and I stayed in their sixteenth-century château in Normandy. My bedroom, in a far-flung tower, was about 500 yards from the nearest bathroom, which for a person in my condition was a little tricky. My other Catherine took pictures of me on the Pont des Arts in Paris, on a wide-angle lens. I spanned the entire width of the Seine.

I then took a ferry across the Channel to Sussex. The Newingtons had offered us their lovely house in exchange for the use of our car in Israel, which was a pretty lopsided swap, in our favour. Their house was charming, with a beautiful garden. Nina connected me with a disarmingly frank gynecologist named Douglas Kerr, attached to a hospital in nearby Cuckfield.

"You could drive a London bus through those hips," Dr. Kerr said after our first consultation. My hips are actually quite trim, thank you very much. But gynecologists are often like this. Dr. Goss, the Israeli doctor who looked after me through my pregnancy, gave me a letter for Dr. Kerr with this opening sentence: "Hilary Brown Bierman is an elderly primigravida with an unusual gait and stance." *Elderly??* I was thirty-eight, for God's sake. "*Unusual* gait and stance?" Yeah, well, that might be true.

Jonathan Anthony David Bierman was born on August 18, 1979, with John beside me, at the north end, wiping a tear from his eye. In all my thirty-eight years, in my exciting happy lucky life, I had never known such a joyful moment. It didn't matter that Dr. Kerr was wearing a butcher's apron for the delivery. Our baby was on his way after lunch and was born just before dinner. He came out all long and slippery and absolutely perfect. He weighed nine pounds, nine ounces, and later grew to a height of six-foot-eight. So older parents produce *puny children*, is that what you said, John? We named him after his father; his grandfather Tony Brown; and David Cornwell, (a.k.a. John le Carré), who had accepted my cheeky request to be Jonnie's godfather. During his first few months, Jonnie was known as the Little Colonel because he looked like one of those gentlemen in a London Club who spends his whole time drinking, sleeping, or complaining about the service. John's son Richard came to the hospital to take pictures. Richard was then working in London as a photographer's assistant. (He later won the Vogue Young Photographer of the Year Award.)

We flew to Switzerland a week later, to introduce the Little Colonel to his grandparents Jocelyn and Tony. They were pretty pleased to inspect a male descendant. Two weeks later we took him into the NBC office in Tel Aviv. "That is a *really* good-looking baby!" Tom Cheatham exclaimed. I guess he expected that a child of mine would have horns coming out of his head. Bob Simon was more direct. He called Jonnie "the Thug."

The rest of our time in Israel went swimmingly. While in England I'd found a nanny from Cumbria named Mary Milne and she flew out to Tel Aviv with us. She might as well have been called Mary Poppins. She had the Little Colonel sleeping through the night within a week.

Mary not only handled our baby with complete authority, but she looked after John and me too, cooking and cleaning for us, and always with a smile on her face. That smile may have been because she had met Musa, a clever, good-looking Palestinian who was doing very well as a handyman for the rich Israeli households in the district. He came to repair our garden wall, clapped eyes on our Mary, and was smitten. On Mary's days off, Musa would sweep her off in his pickup truck and take her down to his family home in Gaza for the weekend. In the heady, early days of the peace process, that kind of mobility was possible.

It was a pretty perfect existence, for all of us. I took four months' maternity leave at our cottage in Cyprus before going back to work in Israel. Our great friends Rod and Maggie Tyler came out to stay with us for a couple of weeks, in the first of many visits. (Their daughter, Rachel, was born six months later.) Rod was the features editor of *News of the World* and he gleefully took pictures of me nursing Jonathan. "This will be great splashed across our Men's Section," he said with a cackle.

My near-fatal assignment in Iran during the revolution came a few weeks later. Having survived that attack by an all-male mob in Tabriz, I returned to Tehran and did quite a few reports, which my masters in New York seemed to like. I know, at least, that my husband liked them. Having tried to stop me from going to Iran in the first place, he looked at my show-reel of stories, paused, and then said, "Hilly, you're a Rolls-Royce of a reporter." I said, "Darling, that's one of the most romantic things you have ever said to me."

About a month later, the executives in New York offered me a job as Pentagon correspondent in Washington. I thought I should take it. I thought I *had* to take it. I'd refused ABC's big offers to go back to the States, and that was a very big mistake. I wouldn't make that mistake again. So I accepted.

Error compounds error. Tom gave me a great going-away party, and the office presented me with a beautiful silver bracelet, which I wore constantly. In my farewell speech, I quoted the actor George Sanders and the comment he allegedly made before he became the third husband of Zsa Zsa Gabor (she had a total of nine): "I know I can do it, but the question is, can I make it interesting."[3] Haw haw haw.

John was dead against the move, and so was my agent Richard Leibner. If only I'd listened to them.

29

WASHINGTON, D.C.

"Jesus Christ, Hilary, you can't take the Pentagon beat!" Leibner had shouted down the phone. "It'll take you two weeks to find the ladies' washroom!" Twenty-five thousand people worked in this colossal building. My "office" was shared with two veteran correspondents at ABC and CBS —Jack McWethy and Ike Pappas, respectively—and we were separated only by a paper-thin wall. If you wanted to have a private phone conversation, you had to crawl under the desk, or talk in code. Jack and Ike were talking in code all the time, or murmuring to their contacts, while I twisted in the wind, wondering how I was going to get scooped ... again.

My predecessor had left NBC without leaving me a single note, contact, or file. I had virtually no contacts myself, though the deputy director of one of the intelligence agencies took pity on me and used to tell me things at six o'clock in the morning (by phone, thank God). I could get those kinds of tips into a report for the *Today* show, but never on the *NBC Nightly News* because I couldn't get anyone else to corroborate the information. The terribly nice editor of *Aviation Week* tried to help me. "We're going to make you into the best female correspondent the Pentagon never had!" he said. That'll be the day. I knew the New York Times columnist Bill Safire (he was a pal of my old boyfriend Ed Bleier), and he tried to help me too.

But basically I was completely lost in that awful place, and McWethy and Pappas wiped the floor with me. Most of the other Pentagon correspondents regarded me with a combination of pity and contempt. Apart from the military's failed attempt to rescue the American hostages in Iran in April 1980, one of the more important stories out of the Pentagon that year was the false report of an abortive nuclear strike by Russia on the United States, due to a faulty early warning system called Wimex. It was so serious that B-52 bombers were scrambled into the air with their payload of air-launched nuclear weapons. At the Pentagon briefing that day, I asked the spokesman how close we were to World War Three. That certainly would be the question on the minds of our viewers, I thought. For the rest of my benighted time at the Pentagon, I was addressed by the veteran Pentagon reporter Fred Hoffman as "Miss World War Three." This was not a term of endearment.

John's view was that I had been fatally mis-cast by the corporate geniuses. "NBC thought that because you were a good foreign correspondent, you'd be gangbusters at the Pentagon. You made the mistake of proving them wrong."

Our Washington period wasn't all bad. John's book *Righteous Gentile* was published the day that Raoul Wallenberg was made an honorary American citizen, in a special ceremony at the White House, to which John was invited. His dedication in the book read simply:

> "For Jonathan,
> so that when he is old enough to understand
> he should know the best—
> and the worst."[1]

John's BBC *Man Alive* documentary was broadcast on PBS around the same time, and we had a terrific pre-broadcast party in our home, with the documentary set up to run simultaneously on several TV screens around the house. John got a front-page rave review in the influential *New York Times Book Review* and in a half-dozen other mainstream newspapers. He was interviewed on the *Today show*. *Righteous Gentile* was also a Book of the Month Club choice. Which was all great publicity for the book. Unfortunately, Viking Penguin was unable to get the books into the bookstores to take advantage of this publicity. This happens to authors all the time. It was still a best-seller.

We had a pretty colonial house and garden on 49th Street in the fashionable Foxhall Road area. This was a house that I had actually bought in *one day* while covering the Camp David talks in 1978. In Washington, D.C., real estate agents can convey property, eliminating the need for lawyers. The bank gave me a mortgage on the spot. Both the estate agent and the bank officer were women.

Washington itself is a beautiful city, and easy to live in, if you are relatively well off. That's apart from the stifling heat of summer, worse than anything I had known anywhere, including Vietnam. But we had a great social life. There were some terrific people at NBC who were kind to me. We also had friends from our days on the road overseas—a lot of foreign correspondents end up in Washington. And we made new friends. Carl Bernstein and his mistress Margaret Jay (later Baroness Jay) often came to dinner. She was then the wife of the British Ambassador to Washington, Peter Jay, who was having an affair with his nanny at the time. Carl was estranged from his wife, Nora Ephron, the brilliant screenwriter (her masterpiece was *When Harry Met Sally ...*). The chattering classes had a field day with that scandal. And there was the cabaret singer Karen Akers, known in the business as a "chantoozie" (after the French term *chanteuse*). She was, and still is, a talented, sensitive, stunning woman and I am so proud of our friendship. (In the movie *Heartburn*, based on Nora Ephron's memoir, Karen played the part of Margaret Jay.) Another new chum was the gifted psychotherapist Jerilyn Ross. She treated people with phobias, including famous people such as Aretha Franklin—and was famous herself, having won recognition of phobias as a behavioural disorder. She appeared often on *The Oprah Winfrey Show* and had a phone-in radio program of her own. I did a profile of her for the *Today* show, and we hit it off immediately. My phobia was the Pentagon, but she couldn't help me with that.

And we had our dear little blue-eyed boy, Jonathan, a constant joy for both of us. Our house had a small garden full of azaleas and dogwood trees and this is where he took his first steps, laughing and gurgling with pleasure at his newfound mobility. I lived for the magic moment each day when I would come home and take him in my arms.

After about nine months at the Pentagon, I was taken off my prestigious terrible beat and put on general assignment. A major demotion, of course. But I was still on good terms with the folks at ABC. I missed them. I had missed them from the moment I first left them, three and a half years before. Incredibly, they said they wanted me back.

Leibner then went after NBC, telling them they'd mishandled me. "I want this act *cleaned up*," he apparently said to them. He got them to pay me to the end of my four-year contract (which was up that September) but release me from work. That meant I had five months off, *paid*. At the end of my last day at NBC, I met Jerilyn and two other friends and we drove into West Virginia, to go white-water rafting down the Cheat River. It was a wonderful weekend that washed away all the professional misery of the previous year.

Then John and Jonnie and I went to Cyprus for four idyllic months, with our new nanny, Amanda Spencer. Mary had to go back to England because her mother was gravely ill. Mandy was just as efficient as Mary, and we loved her just as much. I went back to ABC in the fall of 1981. Back to my family.

30

NEW YORK AGAIN

It was great to be back at ABC, where I belonged. They wanted me to cover foreign stories mainly, which was what I think I did best. The bad news was that the news director, Bob Murphy, wanted me to work out of New York, not Washington. We had to give up our house in Washington and buy another home in New York, at a time of record-high interest rates (about 18 percent). Now that we were four (John, me, Jonnie, and Mandy), we required a four-bedroom residence and that meant buying something in the suburbs. New York City was much too expensive. We ended up in a nineteenth-century clapboard farmhouse on four acres of land outside the village of Chappaqua. When he learned to talk, Jonnie called it "My White House." Chappaqua was an attractive but rather soulless place with good public schools. It was a one-hour drive into the office in the city, and even longer by train. The commute was an absolute killer. John and I had never earned so much money and had so little disposable income.

But there was a silver lining. One morning while John was waiting for the train (I was on assignment), he was accosted by the proverbial funny little man with staring eyes. "I know you!" he said, stabbing at

John's jacket. "You're John Bierman and you wrote the book about Raoul Wallenberg! I know another incredible Holocaust story and *you* are the person to write it!"

John had done quite a few TV appearances while promoting his book on Wallenberg, including a half-hour on ABC's *Nightline*. (I did the set-up piece: the only time John and I appeared together on network television.) This man had recognized him from the *Nightline* appearance. John was itching to write another biography and was always on the lookout for another good subject. Instead of giving this man the brush off, John took his name and phone number.

Out of this chance encounter at a Westchester train station, John produced his second Holocaust book, *Odyssey*. This was the true story of a group of Jews from Bratislava, capital of the Nazi puppet state of Slovakia. In May 1940, they managed to escape Nazi persecution by crowding aboard a decrepit paddle steamer, captained by a one-legged Russian morphine addict, and sailing down the Danube into the Black Sea, the Aegean Sea, and finally into the Mediterranean to Palestine. That was their crazy plan. There were 514 of them, including women and a few children. They thought their flight to freedom would take a month. It took four years.

The boat, called the *Pentcho*, ran aground on an uninhabited Greek island, broke up, and eventually sank, but not before the refugees had salvaged enough supplies and equipment to survive. They were eventually picked up by the Italian Navy and detained in a makeshift camp on the island of Rhodes and later in a larger camp in Calabria. But they were treated humanely. The Italians refused to turn their Jewish prisoners over to their Axis allies, the Germans, so they could be transported to a concentration camp to be gassed or worked to death.

"Despite the anti-semitic laws foisted on them by Mussolini, the Italian people, with few exceptions, never allowed themselves to be infected by the virus of racialism that ran through Europe before and after World War II,"[1] John wrote. The *Pentcho* prisoners were all in good condition when they were liberated after the Allied invasion of Italy. In June 1944, they finally reached Palestine.

John was able to substantiate their incredible story and, by a stroke of luck and timing, to meet many of the survivors, all in one place. They were having a reunion in Israel, where most of them still lived. Though they were then in their sixties, they had documents and very clear memories of their great escape from the Nazi Holocaust. Because of the success of *Righteous Gentile*, there was a lot of interest in the book and John's agent, Gloria Loomis, ended up having an auction for the rights. Simon & Schuster bought it.

While John was happily researching and writing his *Odyssey* book, I was on the foreign news beat, covering wars. Some of them were completely inaccessible, such as the U.S. invasion of the Caribbean island of Grenada following a Marxist coup in October 1983. Journalists were only admitted after the American military had secured the island with seven thousand troops. The press pack included gonzo journalist Hunter S. Thompson (best known for his novel *Fear and Loathing in Las Vegas*), who to my surprise turned out to be very courtly. At least with me.

Even more inaccessible was the Falklands War in 1982. The military regime in Argentina, under General Leopoldo Galtieri, invaded and occupied the Falkland Islands in April 1982. The islands were known to the Argentines as the Malvinas, but since 1892 had been a British colony, occupied by about two thousand British sheep farmers. U.K. Prime Minister Margaret Thatcher saw this as a chance to save her sinking popularity ratings and to prove that Britain shall never again appease a dictator, as Neville Chamberlain had done in 1938. She assembled a huge naval task force to sail 7,800 miles across the South Atlantic and liberate the islands, which it did, on June 14, 1982—though British journalists and naval officers alike all agree it was "a close-run thing." It made the careers of people like Max Hastings, who was embedded with the British Navy along with a select British press corps and was among the first ashore with the British commandos. Max was later given a knighthood and became a respected historian. (The BBC produced a documentary about his career, which he showed to his children, perhaps hoping to impress them. Anyone who has children knows this can be a challenge. Max told me over dinner one evening that he played the doc for his kids and after about ten minutes they said, "Can we go now, Daddy?")

For North American journalists, the Falklands War was a dud. With one exception (an NBC reporter was flown out to the island for a few hours), none of us could get anywhere near the Malvinas. I thought I had a chance since I was good friends with Federico del Campo, the Argentine deputy foreign minister, whom I had known in Israel. I thought he would have some influence. Silly me. Argentina was a military dictatorship. The civilian ministries had no influence whatsoever.

I got as far as the main air force base at Comodoro Rividavia, in Patagonia, about 100 miles south of Buenos Aires, where the Argentine Air Force, equipped with French Exocet missiles, was running highly effective bombing runs over the British task force. The air force allowed us to interview their pilots, who all had Brylcreemed hair, wore white silk scarves, and spoke English with posh British accents. I thought I was on the set of a movie. A World War Two movie, about the Battle of Britain. Later even the British acknowledged that in contrast to the army and navy, the Argentine Air Force was very professional.

Apart from that story, I was stuck in Buenos Aires trying to read between the lines of military press releases. Or interviewing the Mothers of the Plaza de Mayo, extremely brave ladies who demonstrated every week, demanding to know what had happened to their sons and fathers and brothers and husbands who'd been arrested by the military regime and were never seen again. Known as *Los Desaparecidos* ("The Disappeared"), an estimated thirty thousand people were arrested and murdered between 1976 and 1983 by the military government and right-wing death squads. The military described this as a "crackdown on terrorists," though most of their victims were unarmed civilians—students, journalists, artists, trade unionists—anyone suspected of left-wing views. Victims were executed en masse or incredibly, thrown alive out of planes into the Atlantic Ocean

After the war, the British reoccupied the Falkland Islands and established a large garrison, the military junta collapsed, and Argentina became a democracy for the first time, under the democratically elected president Raúl Alfonsín. In an inquiry years later, we learned that the Malvinas had been invaded by untrained, underfed conscripts who were abandoned by their Argentinian officers once the British task force got within a few hundred miles of the islands.

Unlike the Falklands War in South America, there was another war going on in Central America that one could get very close to indeed. Far too close. That was the civil war in El Salvador, between left-wing guerillas and the U.S.-backed right-wing government forces. Much of the fighting was urban guerilla warfare, in the crowded towns and cities. There were massacres of civilians on both sides. You did not want to annoy either a heavily armed government soldier, a heavily armed civilian vigilante, or a heavily armed guerilla fighter. All the networks had trouble getting correspondents and crews to volunteer for El Salvador; and if they did volunteer, they would insist on a firm date *out*.

Around the time that El Salvador was the conflict du jour, I was in the charming Italian town of Verona. In 1981 it was the home of General James Dozier, an American major general assigned to NATO. Then he was kidnapped (on December 17) by the Italian Red Brigades, a Marxist terror group.

Encouraged by the Rome correspondent Bill Blakemore, I did a piece in January 1982 on the investigation by the Italian police: who they had talked to, what ground they had covered, et cetera, et cetera. Dozier had been held for more than five weeks. My producer did a first-class job of putting the piece together, the gist of which was that the Italians hadn't done very much. ABC loved it. The day after it aired, an Italian SWAT team found General Dozier, alive. The *Washington Journalism Review* gave me the "Nobody's Perfect" Award. I accepted graciously and immediately volunteered to go to El Salvador.

31

EL SALVADOR: SLINGS AND ARROWS

Trying to cover an urban civil war for television was dangerous, and not just because I had absolutely no experience in that kind of conflict, which in El Salvador lasted from 1980 to 1992. The front line keeps changing. You don't know where the rebels are—and they can be anywhere. This situation makes it very easy for journalists to get caught in crossfire. That is what happened to the British reporter David Blundy, of the *Sunday Correspondent,* when he was in El Salvador in 1989. He died of his wounds as a result. His last words were "Get me out of here."[1]

Getting caught in the crossfire is your one of your greatest fears when you attempt to cover an urban gunfight between rebels and government troops. But it's important to do a piece to camera to show that your network is actually on the scene. In El Salvador, as in Vietnam, a stand-up was often done lying down. In one take.

Another great risk was in the countryside, crossing the no man's land between areas under government control and those held by rebels. Journalists often did this, to meet and talk with the rebels. But it could be dangerous if you were caught by government soldiers, or by the armed "vigilantes" who usually drove around in the back of a pickup truck. During my assignment in the country, a team of Dutch journalists made an assignation with a group of rebels and were ambushed and killed by the notorious Treasury Police, in a hail of machine-gun fire.

My rendezvous with the rebels took place a few days before that atrocity. From one of the NGOs (non-governmental organizations) operating in the country, we got wind of a massacre, allegedly by government troops, in a village 40 miles south of the capital of San Salvador. We thought we were slightly ahead of the press pack—the country was stiff with journalists at the time—and rushed out to find the village. I was working with an experienced Mexican crew often used by ABC in Central America.

We reached the side road leading to the village and found a handful of journalists but, to my relief, no TV crews. These journalists had heard about the massacre too, but they were hesitating because they thought it was too dangerous to go down the road and into a possible ambush. I looked at my crew.

"It's your call, guys," I said. "You know this place and I don't."

They thought we could go. So we set off on foot, leaving the other journalists behind.

Or so we thought. After a few minutes' walk a voice behind us called out, "Wait for me!" It was a female journalist who at the time was filing clever little columns about the international press corps in El Salvador for the "Style" section of her newspaper. She wanted to walk in with us, and against our better judgment we allowed this. We could hardly stop her.

After about a mile we came into a clearing, and suddenly two or three armed rebels rose up out of the long grass. Wild-eyed, they pointed their guns at us. The crew identified themselves, and me, and stated our mission. The rebels then relaxed and said they would take us to their leader (yes, people actually *say* that).

We met outside the village, had a chat in Spanish, and for reasons I didn't fully understand agreed to return the next day. Then we started the walk back, through the no man's land.

We set a pretty brisk pace, all of us aware of a possible ambush by government troops or vigilantes. All of us except, it seemed, Ms. Tagalong. She was unable to keep up the pace, and we had to stop several times for her to sit and catch her breath. The crew was worried. They said that she was overweight and not in good shape and was holding us back, which was dangerous.

As we rounded a bend in the road, a pickup truck came into view, with four or five armed men in the back. I thought, *This is it. They're vigilantes. We've had it.*

To our immense relief, they were merely bringing supplies to the rebels. After a few more rest stops for Ms. Tagalong, we eventually made it back to the main road and then to the capital. At the hotel where most of the press were staying, we arranged to return at an appointed time the following morning.

Later that evening, the Mexican crew took our bureau chief aside and said they weren't happy about going back into the bush to meet the rebels with a woman. Especially two women. They thought it was too risky, they said, since one of the women was not very fit and couldn't walk any distance at speed. She didn't even work for ABC, they said.

Then our orders changed for the following day. ABC wanted me to stay in the capital to do a short status report and a two-way live debrief with the Sunday morning show. So I couldn't return to the rebel camp anyway. This development made it easier to tell

Ms. Tagalong that she couldn't accompany our crew. They would go in alone.

I found her in the hotel bar and told her about the situation. Her response was clear enough. "Fuck you, sister!" she said, taking another swig of her drink. I think I might've suggested that she do the same. I returned to our workspace, thinking that I should have known better than to pick up a hitchhiker.

Several months later, a journalism magazine published an issue devoted to "Women in War." Ms. Tagalong was on the cover, and inside was her first-person piece about working in El Salvador. She was very impressed with herself. She included a paragraph about meeting the rebels with an ABC crew and its correspondent, Hilary Brown, writing that Brown didn't go back to the area the second day as arranged. According to Ms. Tagalong, Brown preferred to leave the reporting to her cameramen.

I have many faults, but not even my enemies would say that cowardice is one of them. With the exception, it seems, of Ms. Tagalong, ace war reporter. This wretched flabby woman could actually have got us all killed. I thought I should have at least sent a letter to the editor of the magazine, setting out my own recollection of events. But ABC's public relations officer didn't think the article was worth getting upset about, having little respect for the publication. Or Ms. Tagalong.

Then an Israeli diplomat was shot in London, and Israel launched an invasion of South Lebanon. I had to jump on a plane to cover that war—my ninth, I believe.

32

LEBANON

In spite of all the optimism and euphoria after the Camp David peace accords (signed in Washington in September 1978), the Mid-East conflict did not come to an end. But at least Egypt was out of the equation. Anwar Sadat, whose vision and courage had made the peace accord possible, was assassinated by Islamic extremists in 1981, gunned down while he reviewed a military parade outside Cairo. ABC cameraman Fabrice Moussus got the only footage of this attack, which was promptly lifted and broadcast, without attribution, by all the other networks as it was put out on the satellite.

In June 1982, the Israeli ambassador to the United Kingdom, Shlomo Argov, was shot in London. Although Argov survived, this attempt became a *casus belli* for Israel to again invade Lebanon. Israel immediately blamed the Palestine Liberation Organization (PLO). The PLO had become a "state within a state" in Lebanon, frequently attacking Israeli border settlements and causing civilian casualties. The Israeli defense minister, Ariel Sharon, wanted to crush the PLO and its leader, Yasser Arafat, once and for all.

On June 6, the Israel Defense Forces (IDF) rolled across the border into South Lebanon, in force. Much of the world's press was up in the Israeli border town of Metulla, trying to get in too. That included me and my cameraman Brian Kelley. I'd heard that CBS had managed to get into Lebanon. I just *had* to get in too.

The best time to attempt this, I thought, was very early in the morning, before dawn, when a person's resistance is at its lowest ebb. "The hour of the wolf," John used to call it. The border guards would be half asleep at that time, I thought. I knew about a small crossing point on the crest of a hill. The road paralleled the actual border, so you could see the checkpoint from a distance, approach it at speed, and do a sharp right turn into Lebanon.

We crept into our car at about 3:30 a.m. and slipped out of Metulla, driving toward the checkpoint. I could see the Israeli guard post on the left side of the road, a few yards away from the barrier, which made it ideal. But our Israeli driver didn't think so, and he stopped the car, refusing to go on. Obsessed with getting into Lebanon, I insisted on taking the wheel myself. As we approached the checkpoint, I put my foot on the gas, roared past the guard, did a sharp right turn, knocked the low metal barrier aside, and sped into South Lebanon. Normally you can expect the guards to shoot at your wheels, but that was a chance I had to take. This time, I think the guards were too surprised, or too sleepy, to react. Brian and the driver were absolutely silent through this escapade, but they did a lot of hyper-ventilating. Obviously they thought they were in the hands of a complete Crazy Woman.

We managed to stay in South Lebanon for three days, documenting the death and devastation wrought by the IDF and shipping our material back across the border. Brian Kelley is a great cameraman and we had strong pictures. I can't remember how we smuggled our film out, but I do remember the herogram we later got from Bill

Lord, then the executive producer of ABC's *Nightline*. "Outstanding" was the operative word.

Eventually we were stopped by an Israeli colonel, who ordered us back to Israel and threatened to arrest me if he caught me in Lebanon again. I said, "Colonel, if we can film the arrest and my imprisonment, it's a deal."

The Israeli invasion of Lebanon of June 1982 (which Israel called Operation Peace for Galilee) left a trail of destruction through South Lebanon. The Israelis laid siege to Beirut and reduced much of the city to a field of ruins. Lebanon estimated that between fifteen thousand and twenty thousand people were killed, mainly civilians. The operation ended when Yasser Arafat and his PLO fighters were forced to leave Beirut, under the protection of international peacekeepers and the U.S. Special Envoy Philip Habib. They relocated their headquarters to Tripoli.

In September 1982, the Palestinian refugee camps of Sabra and Shatila were attacked by a Christian right-wing militia known as the Phalange. It was a massacre. In the space of two days, with the occupying Israeli Army looking on, a force of four hundred men murdered as many as thirty-five hundred Palestinian civilians, mainly women, children, and old men. The Israelis reportedly stationed troops outside the camp, trapping the people inside, and fired illuminating flares at night so the Phalange could track down their victims.

In 1983, the Kahan Commission in Israel found that Israeli military personnel in Lebanon had failed to stop the massacre and stated that Israel was indirectly responsible for the atrocity. Israeli Defense Minister Ariel Sharon was found to be personally responsible for "ignoring the danger of bloodshed and revenge."[1] He was forced to resign.

Israel withdrew from most of Lebanon in 1985 but continued to control a 12-mile strip of territory along the Israeli–Lebanese border. This so-called security zone soon became infiltrated by the Hezbollah, a Lebanese Islamic fundamentalist movement armed by Iran and Syria, which forced a complete Israeli withdrawal from Lebanon in 2000.

It was at some point during the 1982 war that an Israeli journalist, whom I will call Schlomo, decided to attack me personally in one of his columns. Israeli television was routinely picking up American television reports, from both sides of the conflict, and broadcasting them without commentary. Schlomo saw one of my reports—about the destruction of South Lebanon by the IDF—and then he saw a report from my ABC colleague based in Beirut, Chris Harper. In his stand-up, Chris said that the IDF attacks on South Lebanon "are being described *here in Beirut* [my italics] as Israel's Final Solution to the Palestinian problem."

The so-called columnist turned this into a story about "ABC's Hilary Brown, a tall, blond, assertive woman who describes Operation Peace for Galilee as 'Israel's Final Solution' to the Palestinian problem."[2] He didn't call me a neo-Nazi, or an anti-Semite, but he implied that I was, and then put highly loaded words into my mouth, words that I never uttered. And never *would* utter.

This time, I did write a letter to the editor of the newspaper asking for a retraction. It wasn't even acknowledged. Once again, the ABC public relations officer told me I should let it go. But it was a cheap, calculated libel. I hope that Schlomo burns in hell.

33

ROMAN HOLIDAY

Sometime in the spring of 1983, ABC News Director Bob Murphy asked me if I would be interested in the Rome bureau. The Rome correspondent, Bill Blakemore, was returning to the United States in the summer.

They might as well have asked me if I would care to win the lottery. Of *course* I would! Jonnie was then three years old, with blond hair and dark blue eyes. He was a very beautiful child. The Italians would adore him. John loved hot, sunny countries. He'd always said he was a palm-tree man. We could both see that we would have a long and meaningful love affair with Italy and the Italians, possibly for life.

This was still in the heyday of the U.S. networks, with relocation plans that allowed the employee and spouse to survey their new posting twice before actually taking up residence. Leaving Jonnie with Mandy, John and I flew to Rome, checked into the Hassler Hotel at the top of the Spanish Steps, and looked at schools and housing. We wanted to live in the historical centre of the Eternal City, where everything would be within walking distance. How about a penthouse apartment in Trastevere with a rooftop terrace and clouds of potted bougainvillea? The Italians would shake their heads, smile, and say,

"E difficile. *Molto* difficile. Ma non impossibile!" I loved that positive approach, even if they were lying. We would then show pictures of our little blond boy. "O que bello bambino!" They weren't lying there.

Our trip coincided with the auction of John's book *Odyssey*. I had never seen John so happy, stretched out on the silk brocade sofa in our hotel room, listening to his agent's account of the proceedings, holding the antique phone to his ear, astonished at the amounts that rival publishers were bidding. It all seemed too good to be true. And it was.

We flew back to New York and started to plan for the big move. John gave up his string with *The Boston Globe*, we put the house on the market, started selling off appliances, making arrangements for the movers. Mandy would be coming too, of course. ABC wanted me to start in Rome in the fall and we had to be ready. We were all very excited about our Italian adventure.

In my long and lucky life, I have found that any misfortune that ever befell me was usually my fault. Either I miscalculated, or misspoke, or was just stupid. This time, I don't think I was responsible for the blow that came down on us. About three weeks before we were due to leave for Rome, my agent called. Leibner never beat around the bush.

"Hilary, you're screwed. You're not going to Rome," he said without any preliminaries. "Arledge has cancelled all relocation plans. You were on the express train to Rome, so you're the first victim." Something like that.

Roone Arledge, president of ABC News, had been out of the office for weeks. The rumour was that he'd gone into a depression after the breakup of his marriage. Now he was back at work, reviewing decisions that had been made in his absence, and cancelling at least one of them: Brown's relocation to Rome.

Bob Murphy said the relocation was postponed, not cancelled. In the meantime, I was in a weird kind of limbo, the coulda been, woulda been, shoulda been Rome correspondent, still in New York and without much of a role. That is not a good position to be in. Fortunately, our house in Chappaqua had not yet sold, so we weren't homeless. Jonnie could go back to his nursery school. Mandy was still happy to stay with us, running all our lives. But John had given up *The Boston Globe* and someone else was already occupying his old office. He was in limbo too.

I spent the better part of the next year trying to become what I called the "compassion correspondent," doing stories about courageous children with disabilities, or the homeless, or one-pound premature babies, et cetera, et cetera. I was also still on the roster for foreign news stories.

John stayed at home and in a matter of months knocked out a book about Italy and the Jews during the war—how most Italians simply refused to collaborate with the Nazis in their campaign of anti-semitism. In *Odyssey*, John had singled out this quality in the Italians: "Not only did they refuse to go along with their ally, Hitler, and his plans for solving the 'Jewish question' by extermination, they actively opposed those plans at all levels and in all areas of Europe where they held sway as an occupying power."[1] This manuscript was a spinoff from his *Odyssey* book, using material he'd gathered but couldn't use. He couldn't get a publisher. "Italian Americans don't read books," was the verdict of his agent Gloria Loomis, who was of Italian descent herself. Then one day I got a phone call. From Canada. It would change all our lives.

34

TORONTO: ANCHORWOMAN, OR DEATH BY HAIRSPRAY

The phone call happened while I was sitting in my windowless office at ABC, writing a pitch for another feature story and still mourning the loss of the Rome posting.

"Hi, Hilary, this is Cynthia Kinch, at CBC in Toronto. I produce the local supper-hour show here. Our executive producer, Howard Bernstein, wants to know if you'd be interested in an anchor job. He wants someone with overseas experience and has admired your work for years."

Anchoring the six o'clock news for the premier Canadian news network in the biggest city in the country? That was certainly worth talking about. It wasn't just that I was in a kind of limbo at ABC at that moment. I was also painfully aware that when I did go off on foreign assignments, I could sometimes be away for weeks. I barely saw John and our beautiful little boy, who by now was walking and talking and full of affection and funny expressions. He asked for "mluk" instead of milk and was always losing his "siplers" instead of slippers. Those terms and others became a permanent part our lexicon. I calculated that in the past year, not counting holidays, I'd been away from home for more than 70 percent of the time. When I came back from an assignment, John would meet me at the airport with our son on his shoulders, laughing and gurgling and squealing with recognition and delight. I would usually just burst into tears ... tears of joy at seeing my precious family again.

That wouldn't happen if you were sitting in an anchor chair, would it? You would come home every night, read your child a story, and tuck him into bed. You and your husband would have breakfast with your son the next morning and watch him trotting off to kindergarten. Your husband could be working happily on another book. So I said I would indeed be interested to talk to Mr. Bernstein, if he'd like to send me a ticket to Toronto. Then I phoned my agent.

"Aw, Hilary," Leibner said, "you don't want to go up to *Canada*! You'll freeze your *ass* off! CBC won't be able to pay you real money—they haven't got any. And if you go, you'll never, ever work for the American networks again."

Right, I thought. *If they make me an offer, I better not ask you to negotiate for me. You'll scare the hell out of them.* I went to see George Watson, my mentor and friend since ABC had hired me in London in 1973 as their first female foreign correspondent. He was then an executive at ABC in New York. His face lit up when I told him the news.

"Hils, that sounds terrific! That could be just right for you, at this stage in your life!" By this time George and his wife, Ellen, had a son named George Henry, who was only a few months younger than Jonnie. George knew all about the joys of parenthood. (Years later, in two separate tragedies, he and Ellen lost their two children but somehow found the courage to go on living.) I talked to Jack Smith, my "junior" correspondent in Paris who'd since been transferred to

Washington. Jack had a shrewd eye for the Judicious Career Move. As a Rhodes Scholar, he normally talked at great if not interminable length on most subjects. This time he uttered just two words: "Take it."

And John, my loyal long-suffering husband, had an open mind. He'd worked in Quebec City and Winnipeg years ago as a young reporter. He knew Canada was frozen solid for six months of the year. And he was a palm-tree man. But he was supportive. At this stage in *his* life, all he really wanted to do was write more biographies, and he could do that anywhere.

So by the time I flew up to Toronto to see Bernstein and other CBC executives, I had pretty much made up my mind. I was very interested, to the extent that I was blind to most of its drawbacks.

Along with Howard Bernstein, I talked to Joan Donaldson, the head of regional TV programming. They were very complimentary about my work with ABC. With me, flattery will get you absolutely everywhere. (Joan was a lovely, talented woman who in 1990 was hit by a cyclist in Montreal, went into a coma for two years, was permanently brain damaged, and died fifteen years later . . . a truly terrible fate.)

In 1984, CBC in Toronto operated out of a hopeless jumble of run-down buildings spread over several blocks, between Church and Jarvis Streets in the heart of the city. The CBLT newsroom was a semi-slum on two floors above a convenience store called Mac's Milk, equipped with antiquated wooden desks, post-war typewriters, and a cheap carpet with every conceivable stain on it. The actual studio was two blocks away, on Jarvis Street, and featured stacked glass blocks under the anchor desk and on the wall behind it. It was known as "The Toilet Bowl."

To get on the air, the anchors, show producer, and director had to run, on deadline and clutching about sixty loose pages of script, from the newsroom, across an intersection, up a side street, and into the Jarvis Street building, where the studio was located. For at least six months of the year this involved a mad dash through sleet and snow, frequently pushing startled pedestrians aside, shouting, "Out of our way! We have to make air!"

But at the time I was unaware of this, mainly because Howard kept me well away from the newsroom and the studio, confining our negotiations to Joan Donaldson's executive suite and a smart restaurant in Toronto's trendy Yorkville district. CBC made me the best offer it could manage—which was $125,000 a year. It was less than my earnings as a network correspondent at ABC, but there were perks: a dress allowance of $25,000 and ten weeks annual paid leave. Ten whole weeks! As well as anchoring five nights a week, I would do my own long-form feature reports for the show. I accepted the offer and started about a month later. I was forty-three. I later learned that a CBC Radio executive, Vince Carlin, referred to me as "a million-dollar baby in a five-and-ten-cent store."

For the first year and a half I worked with a co-anchor, a veteran newsman named Fraser Kelly. I found him perfectly congenial, but he left the show in 1986 to start his own consulting firm and I continued as solo anchor. At the time, I think I was one of the few females in North America hosting a live local news show on her own. (They had auditioned a couple of possible replacements for Kelly, but Howard said I "blew them off the set." No, I didn't. I just kicked the chair out from under them.) In the second and third segments of the show, I was joined on set by the entertainment editor, Beth Harrington, a gorgeous woman from Newfoundland, and a very original sports editor named Bruce Dowbiggin. I liked them both very much, and I thought we made a good team.

The studio lighting was diabolical, mainly because the lights themselves had been in use since the fifties. However good your makeup was (the CBC makeup artists were very professional), once on set you looked like an old-age pensioner suffering from some weird flesh-eating disease. I know this because complete strangers used to stop me in the street to tell me "how much better I looked in real life." They'd tell me all sorts of things, not necessarily complimentary. In the U.S., local TV anchors are treated like celebrities. In Canada, they are treated with about as much respect as an unwanted relative who keeps turning up at family gatherings, uninvited and inappropriately dressed.

I would go into a grocery store and some woman I had never seen before would tap me on the shoulder, fix me with a disapproving look, and say, "That red satin blouse looked ridiculous." Then walk away. At social occasions, people (usually women) would push their way across the crowded room to tell me that "the lighting on your show is brutal, Hilary. You look *terrible* on set." Thank you so much. I think I already knew that.

There were some talented young reporters in our newsroom, many of whom later went on to network jobs. Jonathan Mann went to CNN, Susan Ormiston and Paul Hunter became top network reporters at CBC, Steve Paikin ended up with his own nightly program on TVOntario, plus an Order of Canada and seven published books under his belt. That's just to name a few. We had some good editors and cameramen. Good writers, such as Peter McCluskey and Cheryl Hawkes. And good producers, especially Edith Champagne, whom I worked with on most of my stories and who was an absolute diamond.

So we had some first-class reports on the show, which ran for an hour each night. But there weren't enough editors and edit suites and there was always a panic for the reporters to make their deadline. When that happened, which was often, the anchor would have to jump from page one to, say, page fifteen with very little notice. That's because the first three reports on the lineup weren't ready yet. The anchor would only find this out when the director, who was in the control room, would suddenly shout into her earpiece:

"The lead story's not ready yet neither are the next two items go to page *fifteen!*" This would be about ten seconds to airtime. So it would be: (smile pasted on anchor's face)

"Good evening, I'm Hilary Brown and tonight we have a shocking story about medical malpractice in a small-town nursing home . . ." (pause for three seconds while anchor attempts to shuffle script to page fifteen)

"And . . . we will bring you that report . . . later in the program. In the meantime . . . here's the latest news from Toronto police headquarters." Then read page fifteen. Assuming that you've found it.

At the same time the auto-cue operator would be spinning forward to page fifteen. But not always. Some nights the auto-cue machine would malfunction and spin *backwards*, leaving me staring at a blank screen. I would often end up looking into the camera and saying, "We like to remind our viewers that this program . . . is not rehearsed."

There was the odd, awful occasion when the anchor herself didn't make her slot. Every afternoon before the show my hair was done by my stylist, Lyle Isset. He was temperamental but very good. One day I was studying madly for a couple of live interviews, with my head over my work while Lyle brushed and fluffed away. I was so preoccupied with my notes that I didn't notice he'd cut off my hair. Completely off. I looked up in horror.

"Lyle! What have you *done?*" I cried.

"Oh I can't *ever* seem to please you, can I?" Lyle snapped, and flounced out of the salon. A reporter in the newsroom took my place that night, and that was the start of *her* brilliant career. I had to wear a wig for several months before my hair grew back. (Lyle went to the U.S. soon after this incident, and I forgave him. Thousands wouldn't.)

The local press did the odd story about me, and the *TV Times* put me on its cover, with the caption "Ms. Brown . . . settles down." That was okay, but I was wearing a ruffled silk blouse, heirloom jewellery, and my hair was like a helmet. What was I *thinking?* I looked more like a Rosedale matron than a globetrotting reporter.

CBC created some fairly cringe-making publicity drives about me too. Such as the infamous "Solid Brown" campaign that ran on the side of Toronto buses. The posters were about ten feet long, with a huge head-and-shoulders picture of me. SOLID BROWN appeared in enormous letters next to my head, and below: "Newshour with Hilary Brown, Weeknights at 6 pm." At the annual Christmas party, there is always a gag reel of all the bloopers committed through the year. That year, they showed the poster, and then did man-in-the-street interviews, asking people what "Solid Brown" meant to them. Everyone said, "Shit."

Of course, I had my own technical problems, for which I became well known. My life has always been a losing battle with hostile inanimate objects. I had great difficulty in making the transition to computers, preferring to pound away on an ancient typewriter. People were very patient with me, in a way I didn't deserve. God knows I wasn't always patient with others, or even myself. I had a thing about accuracy, and grammar. When I was unhappy about something, I wasn't exactly subtle about it. Long after I left the show, I still felt guilty about this. Then Howard sent me an email that surprised and touched me, after a small reunion at Steve Paikin's house:

> "Let me make it as clear as I can: we joke about the small things like the infrequent fights with the technology. But I have never regretted hiring you. You brought a wealth of experience and professionalism to our little newsroom that I could never have instilled myself. Whether you knew it or not, we were all in awe of your tremendous talents. Together we were able to get the highest ratings CBLT ever achieved. I am proud of that. I hope you are too.
>
> You should also know that whenever Steve, Bruce, Peter McCluskey, Beth and I have got together we always remember the great times we had with you and we still talk about what a terrific journalist you are. You are only remembered in the best possible way.
>
> Howard
> December 30, 2011"[1]

Of course, I have had this printed and framed and put in a prominent place in my living room, where it is noticed by no one.

In fact, it was Howard who was the terrific journalist. He produced a remarkable documentary called *Runaways* about the thousands of underage victims of domestic violence in Canada who run away from their abusive homes and end up living on the street or working in the sex trade. He deployed dozens of cameras, producers, and reporters across the country, each following a teenage runaway through a twenty-four-hour period and documenting in real time how they survived. He asked me to anchor the production and do a couple of cut spots, which were inserted along with others throughout the narrative. It was a powerful piece of work and won a Gemini Award. I was proud to be part of it.

There were other stories during those early years on the show that I was quite pleased with too. Such as the use of cattle prods on patients with mental illness in a southwestern Ontario hospital. Appalling, isn't it? Bad, very bad! Except that I ended up believing that it wasn't that bad at all.

I had spotted a small notice in the *Toronto Star* about "experimental treatment of severely disabled mental patients in a western Ontario hospital . . . involving electric cattle prods."[2] Up went my reporter's antennae. Good god! What a story!

I call the hospital, expecting to be brushed off. On the contrary, they put me straight through to the doctor who is carrying out the treatment, an affable man named Dr. Barrera. He says, Oh yes, he's treating a small group of violent, self-harming patients who hit others and mutilate themselves, and have been institutionalized for years. He has been allowed to use cattle prods as a form of aversion therapy, and he's getting wonderful results, he says.

"Can we come and film this treatment?" I ask, thinking there's not a hope in hell that they'll let our cameras in to actually *show* this.

"Yes, absolutely!" says Dr. Barrera. "We only require that you have the parents' consent. The patients are all under eighteen."

He's treating children?? This is incredible! I got the parents' consent very quickly, and some even agreed to come to the hospital to be interviewed with their child. Edith Champagne and I set up a date, and we're shown into the ward by the doctor himself, with our cameraman ready to roll. All the patients are wearing hockey helmets. That's to protect them . . . from themselves. He removes the helmet of one girl to show what he called her "cauliflower ears," completely deformed from years of self-abuse.

"We monitor the patients closely," says Dr. Barrera, "and when one of them acts out, we move in with the cattle prod. It's a mild electric shock. It's not harmful, but it's unpleasant. They associate their self-harming act with the unpleasant electric shock. And they don't do it again. Or they don't do it . . . quite as often."

We record all this with the doctor. Then suddenly one of the patients, a twelve-year-old boy, starts throwing himself against the wall and hitting himself repeatedly. The staff immediately move in on the boy, force him into a corner, and apply the cattle prod. *Zap!* He stops, right away. Our cameraman gets all this. It's pretty riveting footage.

Then I ask if they'll use the cattle prod on *me*, so I can report just how unpleasant it really is. They are happy to oblige. *Zap!* I think I let out a little shriek. It wasn't exactly painful, but it was unpleasant. We then interview the parents. They all say that this is the only treatment that has helped their child, and that now, at last, they can have a relationship with them. They think Dr. Barrera has worked miracles.

All this made quite a strong report that ran about six minutes, which is a long time in television. I did a live interview in studio with the provincial minister of health, talking about the ethics of this kind of treatment. Initially I thought I was going to be doing an exposé of a scandalous, secret practice in an Ontario hospital. I ended up with a compelling picture of an extreme, experimental program that was actually helping a small group of young people. Things aren't always black or white. There is a lot of grey.

Our personal life during these Toronto years was pretty terrific. I saw my little Beamish Boy every single day. I watched him run through the lane to school in the morning, and I read him bedtime stories at night. When I wasn't at home in the early evening, he could see *me* on the TV set, so he knew I was still there.

Our nanny Mandy was with us for the first year in Toronto, looking after all three of us. I missed her terribly when she left. Mandy was replaced by Anne Millar, a pretty blonde from Scotland—small and perfectly formed. She practised judo and would give Jonnie a fireman's carry up the stairs, though at the age of six he was already more than half her height. Mandy had gone back to England and Anne eventually went home to Scotland. We are still in touch with them. They are like family.

We had a wonderful circle of friends, who remain friends to this day. Who said "You can't go home again"? It was Thomas Wolfe, that's who. Some of these friends evolved from family connections that went back decades. Lindsay Dale-Harris and Rupert Field-Marsham, for example, often invited us to their lovely house in the hills north of Toronto. Her father had been my father's best friend when they were fraternity brothers (Kappa Alpha) at the University of Toronto. Her grandfather was Leslie Howard, the matinee idol, and Lindsay had inherited his good looks. She ran her own company, was a fantastic cook, and a master gardener. Staying with them in their sprawling property north-west of Toronto was like a weekend in an English country house. Their youngest son, Jake, was Jonnie's age and they played together. Quite nicely, most of the time.

There was Noelle Grace, my old schoolfriend who became a pediatric surgeon and lived with her developer husband, Mori Shohet, in a beautiful house on the Don River, in north Toronto. We would sometimes go up there and swim in their pool overlooking the river, while Jonnie attempted to play with their high-achieving daughters (the younger girl, Tegan, later won a Rhodes Scholarship to Oxford). "She thinks she's so smart," Jonnie would mutter as we drove home.

Krystyne and Scott Griffin were also great friends. I had known Krystyne since 1967 when she was a protocol officer at Expo in Montreal. The Griffins would often invite us to their big log cottage on Balsam Lake. It had an airstrip for Scott's single-engine Cessna, known as *Charlie Foxtrot*. Scott would often take me up for a flight and suddenly throw up his hands and tell me to take over the controls. There were always lots of children at the lake for Jonnie to play with. Being a Griffin family compound, it was very competitive. Scott and his brother Tim would organize the Annual Summer Griffin Games, which would often end in tears. Among the guests, I mean. Griffins don't cry.

John and I bought and completely renovated a nineteenth-century house on a ravine garden in central Toronto. It was the first townhouse ever built in Toronto, circa 1880. It was only 16 feet wide, but 50 feet deep, with high ceilings and a magnificent central staircase. We took the house down to the studs and rebuilt the interior using an Italian master carpenter named Michelangelo. Our architect was Christopher Erikson, nephew of the famous architect Arthur Erikson. Christopher opened up the south side of the house and put high French windows on every floor, facing the ravine garden, which was illuminated.

I loved that house. Like our cottage in Cyprus, it had *baraka*. With its rooms of smoky blue and pale yellow, it lifted my spirits every time I crossed the threshold.

It was perfect for parties, and we had the odd illustrious guest. Such as Patrick Macnee, the British actor (he achieved fame, and fortune, with the TV series *The Avengers*), who came to Toronto for a long-running play and became a great friend. David Cornwell (a.k.a. John le Carré) came through town to promoting his latest book. We threw a big party for him too. He gave his godson Jonnie extravagant presents, and for me, a dozen eighteenth-century champagne glasses that have since seen an awful lot of action.

In the winter we would have the fire going in the sitting room, and in the summer we would spill out onto the lower deck in the garden, under our big walnut tree. Though we had a dining room on the main floor, we ended up having most of our dinner parties downstairs in the big kitchen, on an antique trestle table. That instantly broke the ice. And that also helped when disaster would inevitably strike. Such as the time when Rafiki, our cocker spaniel, came bounding into the house after a brief but spectacular encounter with a skunk. The smell was indescribable. But the guests, unlike their hostess, knew immediately what to do. *"Get tomato juice! Get a whole crate!"* they all cried. Someone ran off to the convenience store, and fifteen minutes later Rafiki was immersed in a huge tub of tomato cocktail. The smell was gone! It was a terrific evening.

Not long after I'd started my anchor job at CBC, John was approached by *Maclean's* magazine. Would he be interested in a position as foreign editor? *Maclean's* was described as "Canada's Weekly Newsmagazine." It was also described as "The Bland leading the Bland." But the job turned out to be perfect for John. On most days, his work was finished by lunchtime, and then he would go to the John Robarts Library to research whatever book he was working on.

His routine was to go into *Maclean's* at 10 a.m., smile at the pretty girls and address them by some politically incorrect epithet such as "sweetie pie" or "honey-bunch," call his contacts around the world, and commission whatever stories he thought would make the magazine that week. After lunch, he would spend several hours in the library, come home to dinner with Jonnie and me, maybe go to a movie or the theatre with friends, retire around 11 p.m. Snap awake at 3 a.m. and start writing, creatively writing, at the rate of sixty words a minute. I would hear him tap-tap-tapping away in his study, his large, beautiful hands flying across the keyboard, writing, without a pause, until about 6 a.m. He would come back to bed, snooze until 8 a.m., rise and have breakfast with Jonnie and me, go to *Maclean's* at 10 a.m., smile at the pretty girls, et cetera. And that is how my brilliant husband was able to research and write a first-class work of popular historical biography in eighteen months. He published two books in those Toronto years. He wrote like an angel. He had no idea how special he was.

John used to say that "history is biography." In early 1985, he got interested in the character of Louis Napoleon (nephew of the famous Bonaparte), an adventurer and compulsive Don Juan who got himself elected president of France in 1848. Within three years, he staged a coup d'état and became Emperor. His reign was known as the Second Empire and was one of the most glittering and licentious epochs in French history. As John saw it, it also marked the beginning of modern politics, in its use of the campaign tour and the calculated leak.

Among Louis Napoleon's many mistresses was the English courtesan Harriet Howard, who helped finance his first, failed attempt at the throne of France. At first, John wanted to write a book about her. But his agent, Gloria Loomis, said he should do a much bigger book, about Louis Napoleon himself. John dedicated the book to Gloria, "who convinced me that a cat, may indeed, look at a king."

Napoleon III and His Carnival Empire was published by St. Martin's Press in 1988. A wonderful book, it got good reviews. John had the gift of writing about historical characters the way a journalist would write about a contemporary newsmaker, using direct quotes when he could find them. Our friends Jean and Jeremy Riley gave him an elegant dinner in their pretty house to celebrate. Guests were invited to contribute a limerick to honour the author. Mine was the best, if I do say myself. I wrote:

> "An author who sought new direction
> Found a tart with a royal connection
> He said a book about that
> Simply couldn't fall flat
> Since the King's reign was one long erection."[3]

Looking back on those first few years in Toronto, our life was pretty damn good. As my friend Annie Garrels of NPR said, "You've got it made, Hils. *Don't* knock it." We spent our summer holidays in our stone farmhouse in the Mediterranean. Unlike cottage country in Canada, there is no weather lottery in Cyprus, and very few insects. We had winter holidays either skiing in Europe or sailing in the Caribbean. With my ten weeks paid leave, I could do this and still have time for a foreign assignment somewhere, reporting for CBC and sometimes writing for the *Toronto Star*. Such as a ten-day stint in Jerusalem at the start of the first Palestinian Intifada. Or my trip to the Karakoram Mountains of north Pakistan, where I found myself standing next to Prime Minister Pierre Trudeau in the palace of the Prince of Hunza. I did a radio documentary for CBC about this stunning region, and a full-page feature for the *Star*.

Jonnie was happy in primary school, John was happy writing biographies, I was happy anchoring the six o'clock news, which was getting good ratings. We were all happy in our lovely house on a ravine garden, being looked after beautifully by our pretty Scottish nanny. We got away from the atrocious Canadian winter more often than most people. Everything was coming up roses.

But as my godmother Natalie Lieberman used to say, "If everything's going right, something's wrong."

35

FOOL'S PARADISE

One morning as I was working away in my scruffy little office above Mac's Milk, one of the CBC publicity officers knocked on my door. She was very excited. *The Globe and Mail* wanted to do a story about me! They wanted to spend the whole day with me! *The Globe and Mail* (sometimes known as the Mop and Pail) is Canada's national newspaper. Until then, only the *Toronto Star* had shown an interest in me. Its features editor, Ellie Tesher, had written a thousand-word puff piece about me when I first arrived on the Toronto scene. "Brown, on screen, is polished and professional. But in person, she is a powerhouse," she wrote. "A striking blonde at 5'10" with long arms that fling out for emphasis and knock things off shelves."[1] Ellie became another friend for life, naturally.

I had a funny feeling about the *Globe*. Why would it want to do a story about a local anchor, even if she did have a background in network news? It's true, I did anchor *The National* (the CBC network news show) on the weekends, on occasion. But print people *hate* television people. They think we're overpaid and underqualified. I said I didn't really want to do it. But the powers-that-be weighed in and said it would be great for the profile of our show.

The *Globe* reporter had an unusual double-barrelled name (Haslett Cuff) and he did indeed follow me around all day. He saw our scruffy newsroom, the mad dash across two blocks from newsroom to studio. As the day wore on, I started to feel a bit more positive. I thought that he would write about how under-resourced we were. How hard everyone worked, how much pressure there was. I even thought we might end up with an increase in our operating budget.

The story didn't run for several weeks, and in the meantime we left for our summer holiday in Cyprus. No one at CBC contacted me about the piece while we were away. Possibly because they were too embarrassed. Or maybe because some were pleased to see me taken down. But our nanny kept the article. It was a full-page spread, with pictures. "It's not very nice," Anne said in her genteel Highland accent.

No, it was not very nice. It was pure vitriol, it seemed to me, with an opening sentence that I can still remember: "Hilary Brown has a network-size ego and a notoriously bad temper for which she offers no apologies." Haslett Cuff wrote, and continued, in a statement of pure fiction: "On one occasion, it is said, she threw an expensive microphone on the floor and stomped on it." Then he quotes me, out of context. "'I think that if you don't have a temper about something you are missing a gland,' says Brown."[2] He went on to describe my clothes—I was wearing a jumpsuit cinched with what he called an "ammunition belt" (it was that damn tribal belt from Syria again). He wrote that before the show, I consumed a glass of champagne and orange juice at the hair salon, implying that I routinely fortified myself with alcohol before going on the air. The truth was that it was my hairdresser's birthday, and it would have been churlish to decline a drink to her health. He may have said something about my salary and mentioned that I drove a BMW while my husband drove an

MG, that we lived in a four-storey house on a ravine garden and that our summer cottage was in the Mediterranean. In other words, that I'm spoiled, spoiled, spoiled. He quoted some professor of TV journalism at Carlton University, who said: "I have a grudging respect for her. She's gone farther than a lot of people, with no greater talent."[3] The only positive sentence in the entire piece was that I had "a sense of humour," citing my satirical striptease at the Press Gallery Dinner in Ottawa in 1971. And that since I'd joined CBC's *Newshour* two years ago, "ratings have increased by 50 percent."

I was shattered, which only shows how thin my skin was. This was a hatchet job, it seemed to me, an unwarranted personal attack. Why did they pick on *me*? John was away somewhere, doing research on a book. I was so upset that I took to my bed, and stayed there, for several days. Not very professional, was it? I just could not bring myself to go into the newsroom and go on the air. All this poison had to have come from somewhere. Presumably, that was from my own workplace.

Then I got a call from Barbara Frum, host of *The Journal* and a television icon. We had become friends, from the long talks we used to have in her dressing room, close to my studio. Barbara said I was taking the whole thing too seriously, that bad press comes with the territory, that it wasn't that bad anyway, et cetera, et cetera. I wasn't convinced, but it helped enormously to hear her calm contralto voice in my ear, and to know that she was in my corner. Howard persuaded me to get back into harness. We wrote a letter to the editor of the *Globe* and got several high-profile colleagues (including an American network executive) to do the same. Most said that I had been a role model for years, and why did Canadians want to attack a woman who had been a trailblazer for others? Maybe I was overreacting. Peter

Jennings sent me a note saying he thought the article was wonderful. "I'm thrilled to see you are doing so well," he wrote, "but I must tell you there are still a few of us old crocks around here who miss you."[4]

Several years later, Haslett Cuff seemed to have changed his mind about me. He reviewed an hour-long live program we did out of the newly built SkyDome and described me as "the best reporter to anchor a news program in this country."[5] I considered sending him a bottle of whiskey, with a note saying, "Thanks for the review, Mr. Haslett Cuff. Where did I go wrong?"

After the *Globe* piece, I informed the publicity department that I would not do any more print interviews, ever. But I felt less confident and more paranoid. The truth is, I admired the kids in the newsroom who toiled away in such squalid conditions, at the same time raising their young families, constantly juggling work and home duties. It was all right for me—I could afford home help. I appreciated the pressures they were under.

We were now in the middle of the AIDS epidemic and were doing a lot of pieces around that subject. Edith and I profiled people with AIDS and did a sort of "show and tell" piece, setting out the do's and don'ts of getting infected, with me waving latex condoms in front of the camera. We got quite a few letters saying, "Thank God, someone is giving us the facts about this disease." At least they didn't say, "Who does Brown think she is now, a frigging doctor?"

In the summer of 1988, the marathon swimmer Vicki Keith was swimming across all the Great Lakes. She was doing this for charity, and I thought she wasn't getting the attention that she deserved. I decided to do a profile of Ms. Keith, and that we would follow her in a boat for one of her lake crossings. Then I got the bright idea that I should plunge into the water and swim along with her for a few yards, doing an interview as we swam along, side by side.

Edith was my producer, with cameraman Chuck Tuzi. The waters of Lake Ontario were green, opaque, and deeply unpleasant. I was in a track suit, with my bathing suit underneath. Vicki was powering through the water in her butterfly stroke, a few metres away, with her chase boat close behind.

"Okay, Chuck," I said, through gritted teeth that had already started to chatter. "This is going to be one take, and one take only. Are you ready? I mean, *really* ready?" I was beginning to regret my bright idea, of showing what a good swimmer I thought I was.

He nodded. I whipped off my track suit and plunged in.

Christ, it was cold! And I couldn't *see* through that green muck (I dive with my eyes open). Somehow I surfaced, and swam toward Vicki, in the crawl. I think I was able to remain parallel with her for about two seconds. With one stroke she just surged forward and steamed ahead of me. So much for my water-borne interview. Edith couldn't stop laughing.

For the Christmas gag reel that year, they ran the Brown/Keith swim sequence, in slow motion, with the theme song from *Chariots of Fire* as soundtrack. It was very funny. I guess a few people still liked me.

Sometime in the late eighties Howard Bernstein left our show as executive producer, replaced by a large Ukrainian Canadian from Winnipeg named Slawko Klymkiw (rhymes with Dim View). He had energy and flair, and he did a very good imitation of a Really Nice Guy. He certainly fooled me. After he took over, I went around saying what a great new leader we had, much as I missed my rabbi, Howard Bernstein. Slawko, in contrast, went around saying that he was "stuck" with an anchor (me) who had a three-year, no-cut contract (meaning I couldn't be fired within the three-year period). Even though the show that she anchored was high in the ratings. And obviously I had a no-cut contract. Did he think I should work from month to month? I didn't know I was being bad-mouthed until a producer warned me about him. "Don't trust Slawko too much," she said. I ignored her advice and gave him my total loyalty.

We did some good programs. A series called *Toronto the Dark Side*, for example, looking at the problems of crime and homelessness and addiction in the city once known as Toronto the Good. I started doing reports on books and authors, interviewing the steady stream of international writers who came through Toronto. I would fill out these reports with archive material from the CBC Library, and often shoot the interview in our house, with our wall of bookshelves in the background.

One author I could not interview, however, was my own husband. Conflict of interest, you understand. After the publication of *Napoleon III and His Carnival Empire,* John got interested in Henry Morton Stanley, the journalist and African explorer who became famous when he tracked down the missing missionary, David Livingstone, on the shores of Lake Tanganyika in 1871. He achieved immortality with his classic greeting "Dr. Livingstone, I presume?" Stanley later led two expeditions of far greater scope and scientific importance. He found the source of the Nile, charted the great Congo River, and discovered the Mountains of the Moon in Uganda. He also built roads in the Congo Free State (now Zaire) for his patron, King Leopold II of Belgium. He survived malaria, a litany of tropical diseases, and cannibals.

It was not just Stanley's expeditions that interested John. It was his complex character and background. Born illegitimate, raised in a workhouse in Wales, he fled to America, fought on both sides in the civil war, became a newspaperman, then a foreign correspondent, and then the most celebrated explorer of his age. But he never overcame the trauma of his miserable early years. Here is how John described him in his opening chapter:

> "Abandonment, rejection, betrayal. These were the themes that haunted the inner life of the swaggering, assertive little man known as Henry Morton Stanley. Evasion, suppression, falsification. These were the defenses he threw up to protect a deeply wounded personality which never recovered from the savaging it received in childhood. . . . By his own account, at the age of forty-four he said that he had 'not found one man—and I have travelled over 400,000 miles of this globe—who did not venture to say something unkind the minute I turned my back to him.'"[6]

John researched and wrote a magnificent four-hundred-page biography of Stanley called *Dark Safari: The Life Behind the Legend of Henry Morton Stanley*, published by Knopf in 1990. Our friend David Cornwell gave him a terrific endorsement for the book jacket:

> "Absorbing, entertaining, enlightening and admirably presented, *Dark Safari* evokes place, period and story with great skill, and leads us deftly to the heart of Henry Stanley's own darkness.—John le Carré"[7]

The critics loved *Dark Safari*, except for *The New York Review of Books*, which assigned a spiteful British academic named Tim Jeal to review it, knowing that Jeal himself was writing his own unreadable biography of Stanley. So naturally he panned John's work. But none of this hurt sales, and *Dark Safari* was made a Book-of-the-Month Club alternate choice. All of John's books received that distinction. "So why aren'tcha rich, ya bum?" I used to say to him.

I coasted along in my fool's paradise under Slawko's leadership for a couple of years. He made a point of submitting the good reports that came out of the newsroom for awards, always attaching his name as executive producer to the reporter's work. As he was entitled to do, of course. He framed the awards for display in the newsroom. He brought in two male colleagues from Winnipeg as his senior producers. I referred to this troika as "the all-male decision-making body." Basically, women got the show on the air: we had a female show producer, a female director and assistant director, and a female anchor. Many of the reporters were female, and so were the production assistants. In fairness, all the cameramen and editors were male. But without the women, there would have been no show.

At some point in this period I got a letter from a group calling itself The Mountain Fund to Save the Vietnamese Boat People. I used to get quite a lot of letters and phone calls asking me to support this or that charity. (After I'd appeared on camera wearing a brooch in the shape of a snake, a viewer phoned to ask if I would like to join the Adopt-a-Reptile Society. He was serious. I fostered a lizard.)

But this letter stopped me in my tracks. Vietnam! The Fall of Saigon! My translator, who begged me to take his family out of the city and onto a U.S. aircraft carrier! How I had told him I couldn't help him! How I had never really forgotten him! How I had never forgiven myself for leaving him behind! This could be my chance to atone for that sin!

I contacted the Mountain Fund immediately. The organizer was a city alderman from Hamilton, John Smith, and his wife, Judy. They had been horrified by the TV images of the hundreds of thousands of South Vietnamese who crowded into flimsy, leaking boats in a desperate bid to escape the oppressive Communist rule in the years that followed the Fall of Saigon. Those who survived the sea ended up in camps in Hong Kong and countries in Southeast Asia—the countries of so-called First Asylum. Most were stuck there for years because no country would take them.

The Smiths set up a fund to privately sponsor as many Vietnamese boat people as they could to Canada, as legal immigrants. What they needed were Canadians willing to sign on as sponsors. I signed up immediately. I wanted to sponsor a *whole family*, just like the family I'd left behind in Saigon. Then I started thinking like a TV reporter. Why couldn't I do a documentary about this? About the whole process of getting a Vietnamese family into Canada, starting with my own background as a reporter in Vietnam all those years ago.

I talked to Slawko about my idea. His eyes narrowed and he allowed that yeah, it could be an interesting documentary. You would need money, you would have to go to Hong Kong with a cameraman and producer, et cetera, et cetera. He would see if he could get some interest in a project like that. Slawko lived on the phone, schmoozing and wheeling and dealing. He was very good at it.

I couldn't wait. I decided to make a start on the doc, at my own expense. I set up a series of interviews with the British authorities in Hong Kong (this was before the handover to Beijing), got permission to visit the Vietnamese camps around the territory, got the Mountain Fund's list of Vietnamese candidates for possible sponsorship to Canada, took a two-week vacation, and flew to Hong Kong.

The British administration in Hong Kong was highly efficient. The day after my arrival I was taken to a couple of camps and introduced to the refugees on my Mountain Fund list. They took me to a camp at Kaitak International Airport, where Vietnamese boat people were living in unbelievable squalor. I met the Dam family—four people living in a collection of cardboard boxes. Immediately I associated them with the family I'd left behind in Saigon in 1975. This would be the family I would sponsor, all four of them! I especially identified with one of them, who was about eleven and reminded me of my translator's child. I got very excited.

By this time, I was blurting out my story to my British government escort. "Actually, there is a refugee here in one of the camps who worked as a translator in Saigon, I've heard of him," the official said. "Can I see him?" I cried. The British authorities located the refugee and set up a meeting in the camp. I got hold of a freelance cameraman, Eric Thirer (an old friend), so I could videotape our interview.

The "translator" turned out to be the former editor of a Saigon newspaper, and he looked like Ho Chi Minh. He had stayed behind in Saigon after the Communist takeover and was quickly arrested and sent to a "re-education" camp. He was held there for years. "Is this the sort of thing that might have happened to my translator?" I asked. "Oh yes," he said. "He would have suffered the same fate as me." My heart sank.

I left Hong Kong with this precious interview plus footage of the camp, a file on the Dam family, and a list of my British government contacts. On the way home I met John and Jonnie in Bangkok: we did a fabulous elephant safari in the north of the country, and a holiday with our good friends the Brooks on the Gulf of Thailand (they had been posted there). The Hong Kong trip hadn't cost me that much, since I stayed in a two-star hotel and took meals at the Foreign Correspondents' Club. I'd made a good start.

Not long after my return, Slawko said he'd managed to squeeze $30,000 out of CBC. He gave me a first-class documentary producer, John Scully, and Peter Zim, one of the best cameramen in our newsroom. Peter was a great shooter, and he was fast. We were a good team.

On our first day, we shot my opening stand-up on a ferry between Hong Kong and the island of Lantau—the very ferry I'd taken years before after the Fall of Saigon, in April 1975. As I said in my stand-up, I'd been lifted off the roof of the American Embassy to the U.S. Seventh Fleet in the South China Sea, landed in the Philippines, and taken a plane to Hong Kong for a twenty-four-hour stopover, to decompress, before flying to New York.

"Foreign reporters are like war tourists in flak jackets, documenting human misery," I said on the deck of the ferry, with the shoreline of Hong Kong sliding past me. I described how Saigon in April 1975 was another just war zone for me. How it was my job to report on the sufferings of others, and then move on. How it was my job . . . not to feel.

"What I didn't know," I continued, "is that I would end up with the kind of emotional baggage a reporter doesn't usually carry. And with a conscience that has remained not clear, but clouded, to this day."[8]

We then filmed the Dam family inside their cardboard boxes at Kaitak airport. We filmed the young boy, Tan Tung, at the school that the British authorities provided for the boat people, though Vietnam was not their war and they had no obligation to do so. We filmed other boat people, in other camps, where they had been waiting for as long, or even longer, than the Dam family. Seven years. Ten years.

Fourteen years. We interviewed non-governmental aid agencies working as advocates for the boat people. "Think of what you've been doing for the last ten years of your life," they said. "Then think of the boat people, sitting and rotting in their camps, with nothing to do except wait, and hope against hope for an end to their misery."[9]

Then we showed the fast-track for rich Hong Kong Chinese, wanting to emigrate to Canada as an insurance policy against the 1997 handover of the territory to the government in Beijing. Scully found a self-made millionairess named Sandy Koo who'd pledged to invest $250,000 in a business in Canada. She had an immigration visa for herself and her family in a matter of months. Great sequences of Sandy in a trendy restaurant with her family.

We shot a group of refugee families who had finally got clearance to go to Canada, boarding the transports to take them to the airport, and then to faraway places with strange-sounding names . . . like Winnipeg, and Etobicoke, and Mississauga. And we shot inside the Canadian High Commission, showing row upon row of files, interviewing a consular officer about the Dam family's prospects. She told me that their case was slowly making its way through the system. Not very encouraging.

We interviewed an Australian author who said that the only real future for the boat people, after years of incarceration abroad, was back in their own country. We showed a small group boarding a plane for Ho Chi Minh City—they'd been paid $200 each to go home.

We even filmed a boat full of new refugees from Saigon as they landed just outside the city, thanks to a tip from the British authorities. The boat people were traumatized, seeming not to fully understand that they would be put into a camp immediately, and be stuck there, probably for years.

We did all this and more in a week. Scully had me do all the stand-ups on the last day, in various spectacular locations around the city. The last one was at sunset, by the water:

"I've now accepted that the only hope for most boat people now is back in Vietnam. But a reformed Vietnam, that's part of the international community. I live in hope that my family will make it out on that plane to Canada, putting past miseries behind."

"And I also pray for the forgiveness of the family I left behind in Saigon, fifteen years ago."[10]

I think I did that in one take, and my words came straight from the heart.

The script for my first-person documentary, which I called "A Reporter's Atonement," kind of wrote itself. ABC gave me permission to use sequences from my Vietnam reports from their archive. And Mike Maclear, my one-time roommate in Iran and producer of the famous documentary *Vietnam: The Ten Thousand Day War*, gave us a sequence showing me outside the walls of the U.S. Embassy on the day Saigon fell.

Our doc was broadcast in the spring of 1990. The publicity department called it "Searching the Past." Whatever the hell that means. What's wrong with "Reporter's Atonement"? But nothing could diminish the fact that, one year to the day of that broadcast, my Vietnamese family landed at Pearson Airport in Toronto. I was there to meet them, with a huge bunch of flowers, ready to burst into song. Friends said I looked like Snow White and the Seven Dwarfs.

Years later I got in contact with the Dams. Though the matriarch had died, the youngest, Huyen Dam, was working on a doctorate in psychology at McMaster University. How about that? We had an emotional meeting together in Hamilton, holding hands.

I was proud of that documentary, on several levels. Not just that it was well shot and edited and produced. But that it was a personal story, that it revealed a lot about a foreign correspondent's own feelings of compassion and guilt. Even though my job was *not* to feel, only to report and move on, like the war tourist I am. My doc was based on one of the great news stories of the decade, and it actually helped a few victims of war.

Our work was nominated for a Gemini, with Slawko's name as executive producer, of course. It did not win. I think we got an award from the Houston Film Festival. A few months later, Slawko took me off the show.

36

REVERSAL OF FORTUNE

I say that Slawko took me off the air, but he didn't actually fire me. It was more Byzantine. He manoeuvred me into a resignation, in a brilliant master stroke. Here's how he did it.

About ten months before the end of my contract, he set up a meeting between me and the head of CBLT. Slawko "accompanied" me to the meeting, as though he was my guru. The CBLT executive is all smiles.

"Your contract is coming up and we feel that you can do two things. You can either go on anchoring. Or you can do more documentaries. Like that fantastic doc on the Vietnamese boat people. We've talked to the network program executives, and they think they can make time for twelve half-hour documentaries a year from you."

That sounded very appealing, which is exactly how they wanted it to sound. There was no mention of salary, but I understood that my remuneration wouldn't change. So of course I said I would rather do documentaries than continue presenting the six o'clock news, after more than six years in the anchor chair. I should go and talk to the executives.

What a nice meeting. I went home that night and told John. "They really seem to care about me after all," I remember saying. That's how deluded I was.

I went to see the network executives and they were very cordial. But they made it clear that my salary would be about half of my earnings as an anchor.

By this time John and I had made the fateful decision to send our dear little boy to boarding school. He had been spoiled by three adoring adults for his entire young life. We felt that he should learn to get along with his contemporaries by actually living with them. So at the age of eleven, we sent him to Ridley College in St. Catharines, all three of us in tears. This was one of the greatest regrets of my life. No parent should ever be separated from a young child unless there is absolutely no alternative. We didn't have to do this.

But we were stuck with that decision, and its expense. There was no way I could afford to take a 50 percent cut in salary. I had another meeting with Slawko and the head of CBLT. I said that while the idea of doing documentaries was very appealing, I couldn't afford the cut in salary. So I would like to continue anchoring, thank you very much.

"The anchor option is not there anymore, not beyond the end of your current contract, in a few months' time," says the CBLT bureaucrat.

I'm stunned.

"The show has just had the highest Nielson ratings in the station's history. But you want me off the air by the spring, is that right?" I say.

"We'd like to you stay on until the spring sweeps," he says. (A "sweeps" period is a time when TV channels try to attract a larger audience with special programming, to get more advertising revenue.) So presumably they think I'm still capable of helping their ratings.

I stagger out of the meeting, with Slawko alleging that he doesn't understand what's going on. I arrange another appointment with the network executives. I'm just going to have to take a 50 percent pay cut and do the documentaries.

In a brief meeting, it's made clear that the documentary option isn't there anymore either. "We just can't give you that amount of airtime," they say. Something like that.

Slawko says that he thinks it's "just about money." I'm earning too much, he asserts, and they can't afford me as anchor anymore. Though I later learned that he'd been trying to get a correspondent named Keith Morrison, who had a perfectly good network job with NBC News in Los Angeles, to come back to Toronto and anchor the CBC local news. Morrison never came, and if he had, I doubt that he would have accepted less money than I was getting.

So that is how Slawko Klymkiw and his CBC colleagues lowered the axe on me. They manoeuvred me into saying that I didn't want to anchor anymore. This would have been their argument had I gone to law over their treatment of me. I considered suing for unfair dismissal, claiming both sexism and ageism. But my lawyer, who was a very smart lady, advised against it. She thought we could lose because CBC was still willing to pay me a base salary of $40,000 (minus the big contracted amount for anchoring), for which I could "train" young reporters, staying off the air myself. She thought that CBC could play very dirty indeed, and we already had a taste of that.

My only option was to go to the press, but I didn't like my chances there, after the hatchet job by *The Globe and Mail* six years earlier. The *Toronto Star* might have gone to bat for me, but by this time I was so demoralized that I didn't want to admit that I'd been shafted. It was too humiliating. I didn't even tell my friends, though in the end, everyone knew that I'd been beaten up.

All of this played out in slow motion during one of the most extraordinary periods *ever* for foreign news. In 1989 we saw the collapse of communism in Eastern Europe, the fall of the Berlin Wall, the Velvet Revolution in Czechoslovakia, the Romanian revolution and the execution of Ceaușescu, and on and on. I was dying to cover just *one* of those fantastic stories. The night the Berlin Wall came down, which was right on our airtime, our show was pre-empted, without notice, by live coverage of some obscure Federal–Provincial Conference, produced by CBC Special Events, which has a mandate for this kind of lunacy. For once, Slawko and I saw eye to eye. We were both outraged.

I know that at least one viewer felt my pain. A man stopped me in the street one day and started shaking my hand up and down, saying, "You're Hilary Brown and you've reported from all over the world and CBC won't let you cover any of these incredible stories overseas and it's *not fair!*" It was like meeting my alter ego.

My one confidante was Marjorie Blackburn, mother of Suzy the heiress. "Hilly, you are a magnificent woman! Don't let *anybody* make you feel otherwise," she said in a shaking voice. She was dying of emphysema.

My other soulmate was John, and he was very angry. Angry and decisive.

"Hilly, we're going to go back on the road together. We can base ourselves in Cyprus and freelance. We both have the contacts to do this. I can't stand *Maclean's*. I'm sixty-five and I'm not going to give them one more year of my life. You'll work to the end of your contract. Jonnie will finish his year at Ridley. And then we'll get out of this bloody awful place."

I didn't think Toronto was a bloody awful place. I loved my friends, I loved our house, I loved the city. I loved the life the three of us had enjoyed there for all those years. But I felt humiliated and betrayed by Slawko and the CBC. At fifty, I thought that I was still at the top of my game. I didn't see why I should be suddenly taken off the air, never again to tell news stories for television.

For the next few months my story was that John and I had decided to go abroad again, to show the world to our young son "while we still can." I worked until the end of my contract. I did a documentary on penny-stock fraud with Diane Francis and it got one of the highest ratings ever recorded on CBLT. So to paraphrase Michelle Obama, 'when they go low, we go high.' . I made it very easy for the CBC, and that was like casting pearls before swine. Slawko gave the *Toronto Star* his most disingenuous quote: "Hilary's leaving on an enormous high. We'll miss her."[1] Yeah right. My quote would have been: "I don't want to give a cool appraisal of Slawko Klymkiw. I'd just like to boil him in oil."

Packing up our beautiful house was heartbreaking. Seeing it turn into an empty shell, where once it had been so full of life and laughter, was awful. By now our friends understood why we were really leaving, and they were all there for us. Ellie Tesher and Diane Francis gave us a party in Ellie's garden. The artist Charles Pachter, a good friend, did a beautiful portrait of Jonnie, then age eleven. Steve Paikin, Beth Harrington, Susan Papp, and my other newsroom favourites gave me a dinner, where I pretended that I had a secret job offer that I could not yet reveal. Barbara Frum called, saying, "There will be an Outpouring." In truth, I did get some touching letters from viewers.

One of my favourites was from a Ms. J. Flood, who wrote: "There isn't another journalist with quite the same down-to-earth and believable quality that you display night after night before the camera."[2] Anna Maria Tremonti wrote to say that my work "has been the stuff of legend.... You are one of those rare reporters who manages to reach through the screen, grab the viewer by the neck and say 'look at this.'"[3] (AMT was a foreign correspondent who then became a radio star, hosting the prestigious daily network show *The Current*.)

Slawko insisted on throwing a farewell party for me, where I was given an out-of-date computer as a going-away present. It was at the Bamboo Club, but just for half the evening. Complete strangers started coming into the room at about nine o'clock, literally pushing me aside to get at the bar.

We left Toronto for Cyprus in the late summer of 1991, and it took me a year to recover. That's when I found that sometimes a kick in the teeth ... is just the kick you need.

37

THE WHEEL TURNS

We rented a large sunlit apartment overlooking the Athalassa Forest in Nicosia, Cyprus, registered Jonnie in an English school nearby, and set up a company called MMP, for Mixed Media Partners. I wanted to call it NSD, for Never Say Die. Jonnie quickly adjusted to his new school. Rafiki loved the forest and went for walks there every day with John or me. John started writing a column for the *National Post*, a gig that Diane Francis set up for him (she was the Editor).

I got a couple of assignments to fill in for the regular CBC correspondent in Jerusalem. Before I left, CBC *The National* had tossed me a bone in the form of a $10,000 retainer. CBC Radio did the same thing. I did the odd assignment for National Public Radio (NPR) in Jerusalem and in Kuwait. But in that first year, I earned about 10 percent of what I made as an anchor in Toronto.

My one treat was the 1992 Winter Games in Albertville, France. I had applied for press accreditation from Canada almost a year before. To my surprise, the press card arrived, though I was no longer employed by CBC. I flew myself to Albertville and covered the Games for CBC Radio as a features contributor. A pathetic role, you may say, but hey, any port in a storm. Anyway, I loved it. I managed to do one TV report for some show in which I slalomed down the piste after my sign-off. The mountains were magnificent, the weather was glorious, and incredibly I didn't fall flat on my face. The CBC Sports people were nice to me. One of the top CBC executives, Ivan Fecan, turned up, put his arms around me, and said, "I don't know why Slawko let you go. You were terrific!" You don't say.

Though we didn't have much money, we could still afford holidays in the region. We took a cruise down the Nile from Luxor to Aswan, going ashore each day to explore the magnificent Egyptian temples and tombs along the river. I wanted Jonnie to see the wonders of the world. He may not have been quite ready for this, however. His comment after our first day at Luxor was "I'm tired of tombs."

We went to the famous ruins at Petra, in Jordan. We took a boat across the Gulf of Aqaba to the Sinai Peninsula and to Sharm el-Sheikh, for some of the best skin and scuba diving in the world. John and I had gone diving there while based in Tel Aviv, when the Sinai was still occupied by Israel. Now it was under Egyptian sovereignty and the authorities seemed to be doing a good job of protecting the extraordinary coral reefs.

And for my fiftieth birthday, John took me on a surprise sailing cruise around St. Martin, in the Caribbean. The winds were so strong that the only sheltered anchorage was in a bay colonized by nudists. Incredibly, my birthday dinner was in a restaurant where we were the only people with clothes on.

So, Life After Television wasn't all bad—it never is. And then suddenly, the wheel of fortune turned.

Just before Christmas 1992, the Israeli government under Prime Minister Yitzhak Rabin rounded up four hundred fundamentalists from the Gaza Strip and expelled them to Lebanon, thinking that the Lebanese would simply absorb them into South Beirut. The expulsion followed the murder of an Israeli border police officer, and Israel accused the four hundred of supporting Islamic activism. But Lebanon refused to let the Palestinians into the country and instead kept them in the mountainous no man's land between Israel and South Lebanon. The men were stuck in an uncomfortable tented camp on a hillside.

This happened to be a very slow news period, around the world. So I tried the Impossible. I called John Arrowsmith at ABC, an old pal who had always encouraged me to keep in touch. "I'm Canadian and I can get you a good Australian cameraman here in Cyprus. Do you want us to go in?" At the time there was a State Department Advisory forbidding all Americans to travel to Lebanon. More than one hundred Americans and western Europeans were currently being held hostage in the country by the Hezbollah, the Iranian-backed Islamic militants.

Arrowsmith called back in a couple of hours. "Can you go in tomorrow?"

I went in to Lebanon with a terrific cameraman named Scott Hillier, an Australian based in Cyprus who could edit as well as shoot. We picked up a translator and car in Beirut, drove into the Beqaa Valley, and set up headquarters in a hotel that looked as though it had been built by the Mafia. For the next couple of weeks we went in and out of the fundamentalists' mountain camp, filing report after report that, strangely, kept making air. We even did a long piece for ABC's *Nightline*. When Scott had to leave for another assignment, he was replaced by Bartley Price, another Antipodean. They are a great breed. Many of the fundamentalists spoke English, though the interviews were rather strange. Because I was female, they were not allowed to actually look at me. My interviewees would piously avert their gaze while I was talking to them, delivering their answers to the mountaintop.

It was grand to be working for ABC again, if only as a freelancer on a one-off assignment. They thanked me for my work. They praised me for my work! Our next holiday was to be in France, meeting Gingie and Karina, in Courchevel for a week's skiing (yeah, I know, we had a lot of holidays). Jonnie (now age thirteen) and I flew together to Paris and took the train up to a delightful little hotel on the slopes called the Kilimanjaro, recommended by my old CBS rival, Bob Simon. I was really looking forward to a rendezvous with my beloved sister and niece. But a little voice told me to let ABC know my whereabouts—just in case.

The weather was perfect, the snow was like champagne powder, and we had two wonderful days together, skiing back to the Kilimanjaro at the end of the day.

"Madame, vous avez un coup de fil de New York," the proprietress tells me as we come in and pull off our boots. "On vous demande de rappeller le plus tôt possible."

I look at Gingie. "That's ABC, Ginge. They may want me to work for them again."

Gingie looks back at me. "Do it, Hil! We can have a ski holiday anytime. This is more important. I'll look after Jonnie and get him back to Cyprus."

So I call New York. "Hilary, we've got a problem with our team going into Bosnia. The correspondent can't make it. Can you take his place? You would need to get to Split on the Adriatic Coast as soon as possible."

You know my answer.

Jonathan in a much better frame of mind, on his first birthday. Another all-time favourite picture, taken by war photographer, Catherine Leroy.

John, Jonathan and I in the garden of our cottage in Cyprus.

Iran, 1973. The author, riding into the remote Valley of the Assassins. She fell off the mule moments later.

With the Israeli Defense Forces, invading South Lebanon in 1982.

Jonathan, age 10, with his godfather John Le Carré at the Griffins' family compound on Balsam Lake, Ontario.

With Pierre Elliott Trudeau in the remote Hunza Valley of Pakistan, 1986. A chance encounter, when we were both guests of the Prince of Hunza. I'm wearing another, colossal tribal belt.

Bosnia, 1994, during the siege of Sarajevo. The longest siege of a capital city in the history of modern warfare, lasting 1421 days, and killing 11,541 civilians (photo courtesy ABC News).

Christmas 1992 in No Man's Land, on the Israeli-Lebanese border, after Israel expelled 400 Islamic Fundamentalists from Gaza. They were camped on a windswept mountainside for weeks (photo courtesy ABC News).

*CBC's infamous, **Solid Brown** campaign, featured on Toronto's buses. For the gag-reel that year, my newsroom did street interviews asking people what 'Solid Brown' meant to them. Most said 's+#t', and quite right too (photo courtesy Canadian Broadcasting Corporation).*

Disco Bay, Greenland, 1995. With my favourite producer, Clark Bentson, on a ridiculous Christmas story about a Santa Claus Summit. A break from the war zones.

Bhutan, 1996 with actress Joanna Lumley. We were the only two TV crews operating in the country at the time. She was a lot of fun.

Bandiagara Escarpment, Mali, 1995, where the Dogon people live. Their exquisite carvings have been snapped up by European collectors, in a great loss for the country's cultural heritage.

With our Security Detail in Kandahar, Afghanistan, 2002. We took them out to the desert for target practice, but they couldn't shoot straight.

With one of my favourite cameramen, Bartley Price, Iraq, 2006, on the banks of the Tigris River. Bartley is an Antipodean, a great breed.

Cyprus, August 22, 2005. Our anniversary lunch and as it turned out, our last photograph together, after 33 years.

Baghdad, Iraq, 2006. ABC put me back to work after John's death and it was my salvation (photo courtesy ABC News).

British Columbia, Canada, 2010. Jonnie on the ferry between Victoria and Vancouver, his new home.

With Jimmy in Devon, England, 2012. Falling in love again, never wanted to.

With Jimmy in Segeste, Sicily, 2012, on the first of many bike trips. Somehow I completely forgot about my cycling phobia.

38

BOSNIA: MY TENTH WAR

The war in Bosnia had been going on since the spring of 1992. In a referendum on February 29, 1992, Bosnia and Herzegovina voted for independence from the former federation of Yugoslavia. Their independence was recognized by the United States and the European Union on April 7. By then, the war had already started.

On April 6, Serb forces (the Army of Republika Srpska) began shelling the capital of Sarajevo from the surrounding hills, cutting off all water, electricity, heating, food, and medical supplies. Unless they could bribe their way out, the inhabitants of Sarajevo were trapped inside the city. The Serbs dominated the JNA, the army of the former Yugoslavia, and they had all the weapons. The Bosnian government had no arms to speak of, and it begged the United Nations to help protect its people. Beyond sending in aid, the UN refused. The siege of Sarajevo went on for almost four years (1,421 days) and killed 11,541 civilians, including more than 1,500 children. The inhabitants of Sarajevo were reduced to a state of medieval deprivation, subjected to daily, continuous bombardment from Serb forces. It was the longest siege of a capital city in the history of modern warfare—longer than the siege of Leningrad (900 days; from September 8, 1941, to January 27, 1944).

By the winter of 1993, the Serbs had started their loathsome campaign of ethnic cleansing in Eastern Bosnia, making the region "pure for Serbs" by attacking villages and putting their unarmed Bosnian Muslim inhabitants to flight, burning and raping and killing. The irony was that Serbs, Bosnians, and Croats were all Southern Slavs and ethnically the same. What divided them was religion. The Serbs were Orthodox Christians, the Bosnians were Muslim, and the Croats were Catholic. At this point in the war, the Bosnians were streaming westward in a human tide of misery, taking refuge where they could. Others were thrown into concentration camps. The first TV pictures of these emaciated prisoners shocked the world, though not enough for the western nations to intervene.

My assignment was to get up to the northern Bosnian town of Tuzla, in the middle of winter, travelling with a crew and a satellite dish so that we could broadcast directly from the region and cover the story of the Serb advance, feeding material from Srebrenica and other places of refuge in territory still held by the Bosnians. We were a team of seven, in a strange convoy of vehicles. We had a Bedford truck with all the satellite gear, driven by our engineer, Ken Suckling, along with our translator, Elvis. We had an armoured Land Rover, driven by our logistics man, David Mills, and occupied by an ABC staff producer, Marcus Wilford, and me. And we had a Russian-made Lada, a kind of mini Land Rover that was incredibly good on snow-covered roads. The Lada was driven by our freelance Australian camera crew, Niki Millard and Matt Logan.

Armed with walkie-talkies to communicate with one another, we carried all our supplies, including food, gas, generators, satellite phones, bedding, camera gear, and a large supply of tapes. Our mission was to take our dish from Split, on the Adriatic Coast, over the Bosnian mountains to Tuzla. It helped that I had come directly from a French ski resort, with a complete wardrobe of ski clothes. It was very, very cold.

Tuzla was only 220 miles from Split and on paved roads it was about a five-and-a-half-hour drive. But the highway frequently came under shellfire and was much too dangerous. So we had to take the back roads, which turned out to be little more than logging trails covered in snow. The trip took four days.

The roads weren't ploughed, of course, so we had no idea where the shoulder was, and where the ditch began. Sometimes the road simply fell away on one side into a steep ravine. Throughout the journey we kept passing the wrecks of other trucks, and even UN armoured personnel carriers, that had gone over the side.

On Day One, Ken Suckling, our engineer at the wheel of the Bedford, suddenly came onto the two-way radio.

"I'm outa control I'm outa control! Get outa my way! I'm outa control!" he shouted as the truck, loaded with satellite gear, went into a skid and thundered down the mountain track. We thought it would be certain death for Ken and Elvis. We thought it could be certain death for our camera crew too. Niki and Matt were in front of the Bedford in the little Lada, listening to a Presley tape at full volume.

"Suddenly all we could see in the rear-view mirror were the whites of Ken's eyes," Niki said later. They shot forward in the Lada to get out of the way. Somehow Ken managed to turn the Bedford into the skid and shudder to a stop at the bottom of the hill. From that point on, we hooked the steel cable on the front of the Land Rover onto the rear bumper of the truck, to control its speed. That worked well until we hit a flat, wooded stretch of road beside a river. Then we were just tethered together like pack animals.

In the late afternoon of Day Two, the Land Rover broke down, in bone-chilling cold. Each one of us silently calculated the odds of survival if we didn't get the thing going within a few hours. We figured we would either freeze to death in an attempt to walk through deep snow to the nearest village. Or we would freeze to death huddled together in our little convoy. Fortunately, Ken and the logistics man, David Mills, were former servicemen in the British Army, and they got the Land Rover going again. As night fell, we rumbled into what David called a Significant Village and I absolutely insisted that we stop for the night, inside someone's house. It says a lot for the innate hospitality of the Bosnian Muslims that the first door we knocked on was thrown open with a smile and all seven of us were shoehorned into a warm, cozy dwelling filled with the smell of freshly baked bread. A young housewife, dressed in the traditional Bosnian pantaloons, offered us cups of tea to share with her family, along with slab after slab of hot unleavened bread, fresh from her oven. I called her the Woman of the Year. We gave her money, of course, and some of our food supplies. I often wondered how she and her family survived that terrible war, which took 200,000 lives and displaced 2.2 million people. It was the most destructive conflict in Europe since the Second World War.

On Day Three, under clear blue skies and in achingly beautiful mountain country, the Land Rover, which was top-heavy with its armour plating, suddenly slithered off the trail and into the ditch. Then it went into an awful, unforgettable, slow-motion roll. David was at the wheel, I was in the passenger seat, and Marcus was in the back. Somehow the distribution of our weight in the vehicle stopped us just as we were about to flip over.

Though suspended in mid-air, we somehow managed to crawl out through the passenger door. David pulled out the steel cable, wrapped it around a tree, hooked it back onto the Land Rover, and crawled back into the vehicle, *winching* the thing out of the snow-covered ditch and onto the road again.

By comparison, Day Four was uneventful. Nothing worse than a major snowstorm. But by a miracle, we ran into a Dutch UN engineering platoon assigned to clear the road. We promptly attached ourselves to this awesomely efficient unit. If any vehicle was blocking the road, the soldiers either towed it out of the way or pushed it over the side into the ravine, having first invited its occupants to get out. If a ditch made the road impassable, they would cut down several trees and build a bridge over it. The platoon spent the night in an abandoned school and we dossed down with them.

In the morning the platoon escorted us into Tuzla along the final stretch: 20 miles of paved road known as "Bomb Alley" because it was within range of Serb guns. At this point we put on our bullet-proof vests, said a collective prayer, and took it at speed. We said an emotional goodbye to our tall, strapping Dutch engineers. I may have kissed one or two of them, on the lips.

It is rare that reporters do stories about how they actually carry out their jobs. But at Peter Jennings's encouragement, my first report from Bosnia on *ABC World News Tonight* was about that atrocious trip and how we got through it.

I spent about two weeks in Tuzla, mainly doing stories about the Bosnian refugees who were staggering into the city and taking shelter in a UN-controlled refugee camp inside a stadium. ABC's big story at that time had come out of one of the enclaves in eastern Bosnia not yet occupied by the Serbs. They had a freelance reporter named Tony Birtley who was operating in the area and was smuggling out his reports, until he was shot in the leg and was medevacked out.

I was then sent to the besieged capital of Sarajevo, which by then was a field of ruins, under constant shelling by the Serb army in the hills above the city. Since the Serbs had cut off all the utilities, people had to go out every day and stand in water lines, or bread lines, or food lines, to be targeted and shelled again. No place was safe in the city, not a hospital, not a mosque, not a house or an apartment building. You could be hit anytime, and not just by shells, but by snipers, who of course took aim at their targets and knew exactly who they were about to kill. A woman, a child, an old man. The snipers were crack shots: it was said that one of them had won an Olympic medal in the Winter Games in 1984, which by a cruel irony had taken place ... in Sarajevo.

It was difficult to get permission to go to the front line, which ran through the centre of the city, from the Old City to the new suburbs to the west. Anyway, it was too dangerous. It ran parallel to the main avenue between the Holiday Inn and the TV station, which quickly became known among journalists as Snipers' Alley. Anyone using Snipers' Alley was in the sights of Serb sharpshooters. An ABC producer, David Kaplan, died there in 1992, shot in the back. He was in a 'soft-skinned' vehicle, without armour plating. Kaplan was the first American journalist to be killed in Sarajevo, though at least thirty journalists of other nationalities were known to have already died in the first four months of the war. More journalists died in Bosnia than any other conflict since the Second World War.

CNN camerawoman Margaret Moth was shot in the face by a Serb sniper while driving along the same lethal avenue. It shattered her jaw, but she survived, and returned to work six months later, saying that she was coming back 'to look for her missing teeth.' Her injuries disfigured her beautiful face and she was unable to speak clearly ever again. Very quickly the major networks and news organizations provided their people with armoured vehicles, and bulletproof vests and helmets, for the life-threatening drive between the TV station and the Holiday Inn, where most of the journalists stayed. A few refused to wear the vests, out of solidarity with the people of Sarajevo, who had no protection at all. A French journalist named Paul Marchand used to drive around in a Volkswagen, without armour plating, and with a sign that said "Don't waste your bullets. I am immortal."[1] Inevitably his car was hit but Paul survived, proving his point I suppose.

On average, the Serbs fired 330 shells a *day* into Sarajevo. On one terrible day in July 1993, they fired almost 4,000. There were very few ambulances to rush the wounded to hospital, and no one, except the journalists, carried first-aid kits with bomb dressings to staunch the bleeding. Wounded, broken people were dragged into the nearest car and often just stuffed into the trunk. The hospitals themselves usually had no electricity, or medicine or anaesthetic. What lifesaving machines they had were often operated with a foot pump. They were chronically understaffed because many of the doctors and nurses had second jobs, usually as translators, to earn some money. They were also understaffed because the doctors and nurses kept getting killed themselves.

When I arrived, after almost a year of the siege, the people of Sarajevo still couldn't believe what was happening to them. They still thought that the so-called advanced western nations would intervene and stop the Serbs and their barbaric campaign. After all, western leaders could see what was happening to a defenceless people, in Europe, every single day on their TV sets. Most of the journalists believed this too, or at least they believed that the west *should* intervene.

We thought that our daily reports of the carnage would change things and get the siege lifted. We were quickly described with a sneer by the then British foreign secretary, Douglas Hurd, as members of the "Something-Must-Be-Done Club." The favourite quote in Whitehall was that of Prussian leader Otto von Bismarck a century earlier: "[The Balkans are] not worth the healthy bones of a single Pomeranian Grenadier."[2] Lord David Owen, the British mediator in the Balkans, was only slightly more diplomatic when he told the people that they shouldn't get their hopes up. "Don't dream dreams," he said to the Bosnians as they battled mass murderers, rapists, and thieves, licensed to commit war crimes by their nationalist Serb leaders. "Don't, don't, don't live under this dream that the west is going to come and sort this problem out."[3]

I was appalled by the barbarity of the siege, and at the same time deeply impressed by the courage of the inhabitants of Sarajevo, who were determined that they wouldn't be brutalized... by this brutality. I wanted to document their suffering, their fortitude, their dignity, their determination to preserve what they could of their previous, civilized lives. We did a story on the Sarajevo String Quartet, which kept meeting every month to give concerts of chamber music. Except that the players kept changing, as yet another musician was killed. This was not long after the famous cellist of Sarajevo, Vedran Smailović, started performing on the bombed-out streets, playing Albinoni's *Adagio in G Minor* in an open act of resistance against the

Serb snipers and bombers in the hills. Incredibly, Smailović survived the war, though he could easily have been taken out by a sniper.

A group of artists staged an exhibition of their sculptures and paintings, which they were still somehow able to produce. One of the painters, Planinka Mikulić, became a friend. Like most of the women in Sarajevo, Planinka took great trouble with her appearance. She applied makeup carefully (luxuries like cosmetics would be smuggled in). She dressed as well as she could. A few months after we'd met, I was able to help her father—who had been the prime minister of Yugoslavia during the 1984 Olympics—get out of Sarajevo for cancer treatment in Geneva. I contacted the former head of the International Olympic Committee, Juan Antonio Samaranch, in Switzerland and told him what had happened to his old friend Premier Mikulić. To his credit, Samaranch acted immediately and within a couple of days got Premier Mikulić onto a Red Cross flight out of the city. I later visited Mr. Mikulić in hospital in Lausanne and he pressed an Olympic watch into my hands. His eyes were full of tears.

I also managed to get a young Olympic hopeful out of the city, to realize his dream of competing in the two-man bobsled race in the next Winter Games in Lillehammer, Norway. (His partner was already out of Sarajevo.) At six-foot-three, Igor Boras used to practise in the bombed-out shell of the Supreme Court building. He could jump up the stairs three steps at a time, on *one foot*. That was our opening sequence. Then we cut to a soundbite, with Igor talking in near-perfect English. "I can run on the streets or I can run in the building. I prefer to run here, not in the open, where grenades can . . . kill me"[4] We showed how Igor lived, how he scavenged for food, and so on. Our report made quite an impact, and viewers called in offering money and other assistance. We managed to smuggle him out on a UN relief flight, and he was able to compete in Lillehammer in 1994. He never returned to Sarajevo, later settling in the United States. I was very touched when I received a letter from him, thanking me for my help. "I've got married with a special American girl," he wrote. "This spring we are expecting a baby boy. Love, Igor."[5]

Most people were trapped in the city. Before the Bosnians built a tunnel under the airport, in the summer of 1993, the only way out was to make a run for it, across the front line, bribing the right commanders on the other side. That's what two star-crossed lovers, Boško (Brckić) and Admira (Ismić), tried to do in May 1993. He was a non-nationalist Serb, and she was a Muslim. They knew that, as people in a mixed relationship, they had even less chance of survival than most couples. On May 19, they crept out of a trench on the Bosnian side of the line and made a dash for it. They were gunned down immediately. They had bribed the wrong people and were betrayed. Admira crawled over to her lover, put her arm over him, and died. He was already dead. Their bodies lay there for days, until Reuters reporter Kurt Schork (who was later killed in Sierra Leone) and BBC correspondent Jeremy Bowen found out about them and told their story. It was picked up by news organizations around the world, and the young lovers inevitably became known as Sarajevo's Romeo and Juliet. Modern guidebooks to post-war Sarajevo now recommend a stop at what they call the Romeo and Juliet Bridge. My friend John Zaritsky made a moving documentary about them.

I found my own Romeo and Juliet in Sarajevo, but they survived. At least, I think they did. Like Boško and Admira, he was a Serb, she was a Muslim. He hated the Serb nationalist leaders who had broken up the former Yugoslavia and turned it into a killing field. They had been lovers before the siege. They were walking together in Sarajevo, on their way to a bread line, when they were hit by a shell. The same shell. She lost her leg, he had shrapnel all over his body. They were taken to the same hospital, and after emergency treatment, they asked if they could be married and stay in the same room. They didn't know how long either of them would live. He was very handsome, and she was absolutely beautiful. We started the story with a medium shot of the pair sitting in the hospital cafeteria. Then we pulled out into a wide shot, to show her crutches, and what was left of her amputated leg. She was smiling at him. It was another moving example of the courage of a people under siege and, corny as it sounds, of the power of love.

After about six weeks in Bosnia, ABC pulled me out and sent in a replacement. I had loved my assignment, but it was wonderful to be back with John and Jonnie in our spacious apartment in Nicosia overlooking the green expanse of the Athalassa Forest. We had only managed a few short conversations on the satellite phone, and I missed them. Within an hour of my return, the phone rang. It was Ned Warwick, the bureau manager of ABC in London.

"Great job in Bosnia, Hilary!" he said. "We'd like to offer you a contract."

For the second time in eleven years, ABC takes me back.

39

HAPPY AGAIN

I'll never forget the huge smile on John's face when I told him the news. He threw his arms around me, and Jonnie was quite impressed too, though he was worried that I might be away from home too much.

But ABC offered me an ideal contract. We agreed on a guaranteed minimum of one hundred days, for a three-year period, renewable. I always ended up working more than the guaranteed minimum. I would be paid on a generous per diem basis, without deductions for pension contribution, health plan, and so on. That meant that my gross was my net. And ABC didn't have to cover those pension and health benefits itself, as it did for salaried employees. It was a marriage made in heaven, and ABC treated me like a queen. They liked my work, and they thought I was still good on television. Unlike Slawko at CBC. I was fifty-two years old.

Suddenly I was earning more than I'd ever taken home as a TV anchor in Toronto. I made my own pension arrangements, and John and I had private family medical insurance. I still had a happy home life with John and Jonnie and our little spaniel, Rafiki. Basically, I could sit by our pool at Calypso Cottage and wait for the phone to ring. When I was on the road, I had all the benefits of a salaried correspondent and was covered by ABC's accident insurance. I told ABC that I wanted to be off the clock on my son's school holidays, and they accepted that.

I spent much of the time in that first contract in Bosnia. The war went on until 1995, when it ended with the Dayton Peace Accord, negotiated mainly by U.S. Assistant Secretary of State Richard Holbrooke, who had a reputation for toughness. (I'd met Holbrooke in 1980 when we were both on an official trip to China with the then U.S. Defense Secretary Harold Browne. Dick was a lot of fun—the antithesis of the stuffy State Department mandarin.) In 1995, Holbrooke described the fate of the Bosnian Muslims as "the greatest failure of the West since the 1930s."[1]

In many of the conflicts I've covered, I've had the same mixed emotions of excitement and fear. But also of guilt. That I'm just a war tourist in a flak jacket, documenting human misery, and then moving on. Jeremy Bowen, one of the best war reporters in the business, once wrote that "For us to have a good day, someone else has to have a bad day, or the last day of their lives."[2]

That happened all the time in Bosnia. Here's just one example. A Serb shell hits an apartment building near the TV building where we work. We race over to the bombsite, which is still a smouldering pile of rubble. No one inside has survived. A woman is standing outside what remains of the building, in a state of shock. Her name is Samira. Like many of the educated inhabitants of the city, she speaks good English. She tells us that, until an hour ago, she had lived in one of the apartments with her family. She'd gone out to try to find bread. In a low voice, she names those who died.

"I lost my mother, my father, my uncle, my sister, my nephew, and my niece. I don't know what to do." She speaks softly, in a monotone.

We take her in our armoured Land Rover to the home of one of her friends, who she says will put her up, if only for a few days. We give her money and food, everything that we can spare. It makes a short but powerful piece for ABC's morning show, *Good Morning America*.

It was shocking, though there were no upsetting images of broken bodies. We wouldn't have been allowed to show that on American television anyway. We had a strong report about the nightmare that ordinary people were living in a city under siege. I got a herogram for my work that day. Samira lost her entire family, in the worst day of her life.

I felt guilt of another kind when I found myself shaking the hand of Radovan Karadžić, president of the self-declared Bosnian Republic of Srpska, a psychiatrist and the mastermind of the siege of Sarajevo and the whole hateful criminal policy of ethnic cleansing. He operated out of a scruffy little mountain town called Pale, above Sarajevo. We drove up there to interview him, and he immediately extended his hand. I had to take it. I wouldn't have got the interview otherwise, would I? Then Karadžić was cut short in mid-sentence by his infamous daughter Sonja, an enormous, aggressive woman whom he'd named as his "press secretary." She was outraged that I hadn't gone through *her* office for permission to interview her father, ordering us to leave. We'd already got what we wanted, which was his preposterous assertion that the shells that were raining down on Sarajevo, at an average rate of 330 a day, were actually launched by the Bosnian Muslims themselves to "gain international sympathy." "Nothing to do with my Serb soldiers in the hills,"[3] Karadžić claimed, in a bold-faced lie.

Karadžić was later convicted of genocide, war crimes, and crimes against humanity at the International Criminal Court in The Hague.

But it took more than twenty years to bring him to justice. He was finally arrested in July 2008 in Belgrade, where he had been hiding, in plain sight, under an assumed name (Dr. Dabic) and posing as a doctor of alternative medicine. He even made TV appearances as a "new age" guru, with long hair and a beard, though there was a multimillion-dollar price on his head and a warrant for his arrest. After a trial that dragged on for years, he was convicted and sentenced in 2016 to forty years imprisonment. Having pleaded not guilty to all the charges, he appealed. In 2019, he lost his appeal and the sentence was increased to life in prison. At last his surviving victims got some sort of closure, though their lives had been destroyed.

Later in 1993, the war between the Serbs and the Bosnians expanded into a "war within a war," between the Bosnians and the Croats in Central Bosnia. For about a year we went in and out of that region, basing ourselves with the British Battalion of UNPROFOR outside the town of Vitez. It was known as BRITBAT. The commander at the time was an outspoken and completely charming man named Colonel Bob Stewart, who allowed the BBC and other news teams to dine in his officers' mess and to go out with him on patrol. We all adored Colonel Bob. BRITBAT was often shot at by snipers, and would immediately shoot back, against UNPROFOR's rules of engagement. We called the battalion SHOOTBACK. Their presence gave isolated villagers some protection and saved civilian lives. Colonel Stewart's public affairs officer gave daily briefings on the situation and was extremely helpful to the press corps. The colonel was also remarkably diplomatic. He would often compliment me on my appearance, when I knew that, after a day in the field, I looked awful. (British officers are probably trained to do this.)

"What a jolly nice sweater you're wearing today, Hilary!" he would say with a boyish smile. This gallantry didn't always filter down to his subordinates. A young press officer once scrutinized my press card and its photo, which had been taken in Israel during the Yom Kippur War in 1973. I liked it so much I'd had about a thousand copies made and had been using it for my press identification ever since. For twenty years, in other words. He looked at me, looked at the card, and said evenly: "You know, Hilary, I don't think you should use this photo anymore."

In the Bosnian-Croat War there were sporadic conflicts and massacres on both sides, but we could show little more than civilians in body bags. Even those images could be considered to be "insensitive" for an American television audience. The charred remains of people burned inside their own village mosque, for example, was impossible to show, even though the only recognizable images were of bones inside boots, and pieces of clothing. The war-within-a-war was confusing for an American audience to follow anyway. A ceasefire was reached in February 1994, which led to the establishment of the Federation of Bosnia and Herzegovina and joint Bosnian-Croat operations against the Serb forces. The Bosnians were no longer so hopelessly outgunned.

So the siege of Sarajevo was the compelling narrative, and I kept going back to the city again and again. Peter Jennings, our anchor, was absolutely committed to the story and on at least one occasion came to the besieged city himself, to the horror of the corporate geniuses. They were terrified that their star would get hurt or even killed. The Serbs had issued a death threat against him. For Peter, that was a badge of honour. He stayed in the Holiday Inn just like the rest of us, 200 yards from the front line. He drove up and down

Snipers' Alley to the TV station and went out to "commit television." He was there when the Serbs shelled a market in Sarajevo in July 1994, killing sixty-eight people and wounding dozens more. He rushed to the scene, in spite of the danger of a second bomb. Serb soldiers would often shell a human target, wait for people to run to the aid of the wounded, then bomb the target again. Peter would stop and talk to people endlessly, driving his producers mad with anxiety, knowing that they were all sitting ducks.

On that trip, Peter chatted up a boy of about thirteen, who had excellent English and who spoke with a wisdom way beyond his years. Because Peter was the anchor, they could let that interview run on *World News Tonight* for two or three minutes. It had quite an impact. On a later assignment to Sarajevo, I looked up this boy, named Eki Foco, and filmed a day in his life: going to the cemetery to visit the grave of his best friend, who had been killed by a Serb shell; going to school, taking a roundabout route to avoid the snipers; collecting firewood; hugging his exhausted, shell-shocked father when he came home from the front line. It was a strong piece. "That was very moving, Hils," Peter said. "*Mabrouk!*" Eki survived the war, and ABC helped him immigrate to the United States.

By this time, ABC was sharing a workspace in the Sarajevo TV Centre with the BBC, and I got to know and admire the BBC reporters who regularly covered that war. There was Kate Adie, who was one hell of an operator though rather bossy. But she was a great raconteuse and a lot of fun. Her position as the BBC's chief foreign correspondent was later taken by the great Lyse Doucet, an extraordinary TV journalist with a distinctive New Brunswick accent who can talk to camera endlessly without autocue, in live broadcasts from anywhere in the world. "I do Lives until I'm Dead," as she once said to me. In spite of her fame and her talent, Lyse has no ego and is probably the nicest person in broadcasting. There was Alan Little, a born storyteller. There was Jeremy Bowen, who could crash a spot in twenty minutes. There was Martin Bell, who could do the same thing. When Jeremy first came to Bosnia to replace Martin after a tour of duty, Martin greeted him with a single sentence: "Welcome to Sarajevo; you'll enjoy it—if you live."[4]

I knew Martin from Washington, when he was romancing my best friend Rebecca Sobel. Martin would look at the video, tell the editor what opening sequence he wanted, and record one or two sentences to cover it. While the editor was cutting that sequence, Martin would pace the room and think up the next couple of sentences. Then he would record that. And on and on. "How else can you produce a report in twenty minutes?" he would say. Like many journalists who routinely risk their lives, Martin was superstitious. He had all sorts of tics and obsessions. Such as walking around a room clockwise after he'd crossed the threshold. Or maybe it was counter-clockwise. He always wore a white suit. He felt it made him stand out . . . as a noncombatant. He came very close to being killed by a shell in Sarajevo, however. It wounded him in the upper inside leg, but he was working again within a few weeks. As he later pointed out in his courtly way: "My manhood remains intact."

Like Vietnam, Bosnia turned some reporters into stars. Notably Christiane Amanpour of CNN. She was already well established after her work in the first Gulf War, but she just took off in Bosnia, anchoring one special after another, live. Apart from her courage and energy and good looks, she could talk about any subject under the sun, live on air, without missing a beat. She later became a mega-star with her own program on CNN and PBS. In Bosnia, she was warm and friendly with almost everybody.

The international press corps in Sarajevo was a kind of club anyway. The same reporters kept coming back, along with the same camera crews. My favourites were Bartley Price and Tim Lambon. Tim formerly served in some crack Special Service in southern Africa and you always felt very safe with him. Bartley, apart from being good at his craft, was also good with people, especially armed and dangerous people, manning checkpoints. Most of us stayed in the gloomy Holiday Inn, which somehow managed to keep going throughout the siege (bribery must have been involved), though the windows were frequently shattered and then taped up by the shelling. There was only sporadic running water and electricity. But the staff produced an evening meal for everyone in a windowless dining room, and the waiters were always dressed in white shirts, trying to maintain some kind of standard.

One of my favourite stories in Bosnia was on the tenth anniversary of the Sarajevo Winter Olympics in 1994. Those Winter Games had been covered by ABC Sports and we had all the archive footage from the glory days in 1984. We cut from the historical sports events to the same venue in wartime, ten years later. We showed the bobsled run, for example, in the hills above Sarajevo in 1984, and then cut to bearded Serb soldiers in 1994, brandishing their automatic rifles, careening down what was left of the course on beaten-up toboggans. The climax was in the arena in Sarajevo, where British figure skaters Jayne Torvill and Christopher Dean performed their famous routine to the music of Ravel's *Boléro*, winning an Olympic gold medal. We showed the last few seconds of their performance, followed by huge applause from the audience in 1984, and then dissolved to the same bombed-out arena in 1994, with the sound of rain coming through the open roof. Then dissolved to me inside the ruined arena, in a stand-up bridge to camera. The report ran for almost four minutes. It's the only piece I've ever done where I actually *stopped talking* for sixty seconds. We brought up the natural sound and just let it run. I say "we." My location producer was Marcus Wilford, and the whole concept of the piece was the brainchild of Rick Kaplan, a senior producer in New York. He didn't change a word of my script, mainly because I did exactly what he told me to do. After all, I'm just a blonde.

40

"YOU DON'T REALLY KNOW ME"

In the fall of 1993, we had a domestic crisis that changed all of our lives. It ended up costing hundreds of thousands of dollars and meant that we were to be separated from our beloved son for more than half of each year until Jonnie was eighteen.

Jonnie was enrolled in an English school in Nicosia run by a Greek Cypriot martinet called Ierides. It taught the British GCSE curriculum and was the best school in Nicosia. Jonnie was quite happy there, among a mix of British and Cypriot kids.

The school had computer classes several times a week. In one of these classes, Jonnie insulted a classmate online. He used language that he would have never heard at home. We can be foul-mouthed, but words like this had never escaped our lips, ever. This obscenity was seen by everyone in the class, and inevitably one of the girls told her mother. Her mother complained to the headmaster, and Jonathan was expelled, immediately. He came home sobbing and shaking, in a state of shock.

His classmates (including the boy he'd insulted) all signed a petition asking that he be re-admitted to the school, but the headmaster was adamant. Jonnie was out, for good. An apology was not accepted. He'd been given thirty minutes to clear his desk and locker.

This happened when I was in London, just back from another assignment in Bosnia. John called me and we talked endlessly about what to do. Send him to the American School in Nicosia? It had different standards, notably multiple-choice exams. Send him to the International School in Paphos, near our cottage? Not an option.

I called David Cornwell, Jonnie's famous godfather, who had once taught at Eton before he became known as John le Carré.

"Look, Hils," he said. "You can't keep fooling around with his education. He needs to go to a good British boarding school, and I mean in Britain. He can go to Millfield, in Somerset. I know the headmaster. I'll arrange it, all right? Get Jonnie over here, come down to Cornwall and stay with us. We'll talk about it, and then you can drive Jonnie up to the school. It's not far from us."

I phoned John in Cyprus and he agreed that David was probably right. He put Jonnie on a plane for London and within a couple of days we were driving down to the Cornwells' spectacular seaside house near Land's End. David was wonderful with Jonnie, who fell completely under his spell. We were both under his spell. If David thought Millfield was a good idea, then we did too. Never mind that it was the most expensive school in England, more expensive than Eton. This was because it developed sports stars, offering big scholarships for promising young athletes. Therefore, it had extraordinary facilities, such as twenty-five tennis courts, an Olympic-size swimming pool, and a half-dozen playing fields. It had a reasonable academic standard too, but sports was what Millfield was known for.

Jonnie had an interview with the headmaster, Christopher Martin, and the matter of his expulsion was discussed. David said there would be no point in lying about what had happened. "They've got a sense of these things," he said. "No one applies for admission in the middle of a school term unless there's been some drama. It's better to come out with it straight away."

Jonnie handled himself well and Martin offered him a place, to start after the midterm break. As a foreign student he needed a British-based guardian, and David offered to sign off on that. He said that Jonnie could always contact him. He could even come down to Cornwall for a weekend or two. Jonnie and I flew back to Cyprus, got his things together, labelled his clothes, and had some close family time with John. Ten days later Jonnie and I flew back to England and I drove him down to Somerset. He was just fourteen, already very tall and very handsome, but still a boy. I tried not to cry when we hugged each other and said goodbye.

It was the same sinking, wrenching, heartbreaking feeling I had when we sent him to boarding school in Canada, though this time he wasn't quite so young and vulnerable. In upper middle-class English families, generations of parents have sent their children away to boarding school. My father and his father before him were sent away to school (known since the eighteenth century as "public schools" because the children were educated in an independent institution, rather than by a tutor at home). Parents would have no contact with their children for weeks, even months, apart from the occasional letter or phone call. But that's what the Best People did. After all, that's how Britain produced young men who were capable of running an Empire, wasn't it? Children could be at the mercy of predatory teachers and sadistic school bullies. And if they were, they would never "tell." That was The Code. If they did tell, they would be bullied and hurt even more. My friend Patrick Macnee, who had survived Eton to become a successful actor, hated this system and wrote about it in his autobiography, *Blind in One Ear*. "Parents abuse their children at home," he once said to me. "They flog them when they misbehave, and then send them away to boarding school, where they allow perfect strangers to flog and abuse them even more."

All of this was going through my mind as I hugged my beautiful son and fought back my tears. Since he was tall, I thought he had a good chance of *not* being picked on. He could always just thump his tormentor . . . John had taught him a few effective manoeuvres, learned in his time with the Royal Marines.

In the four and a half years he spent at Millfield, Jonnie never complained to us about any mistreatment. That was The Code. Twenty-five years later, while talking about a school bullying scandal in Toronto, Jonnie told me what had happened to him when he was fifteen. An older boy, a notorious bully, ordered Jonnie to buy an item from the school tuck shop, giving him some money. When Jonnie returned with the item, the bully claimed that Jonnie had short-changed him. Jonnie hotly denied this. So the bully got another bully, and together they dragged Jonnie up to the top of the stairs and *hung him upside down* over the stairwell, holding him by his heels. To shake out the spare change, you understand. Jonnie was over six feet by then, must have weighed close to 180 pounds, and could have been killed or permanently paralyzed if they'd lost their grip and he'd fallen three storeys to the ground floor, on his head.

Of course, Jonnie didn't report this to his house master, or tell us. Not long after, the older boy was expelled, for bullying someone else. I think if Jonnie had told us this story at the time, we would have pulled him out of Millfield immediately and brought him back to some inferior school in Cyprus. At least he would have been living at home, and we would have known what was happening to him. Ever since, my advice to anyone who will listen is that you should keep your children close. *Don't* send them away to school. So that they can never say, "You don't really know me anymore," as Jonnie once did, in a remark that cut me to the quick. In a way, it was true.

But Millfield was good at developing a child's special talents, and he benefited from this. He became very well spoken, acquiring an attractive transatlantic accent that he has to this day. The British think he's American, and the Americans think he's British. Whatever its drawbacks, boarding school did teach Jonnie to get on with absolutely *anybody*, without being a milquetoast. That is a great social skill, a skill that his own parents could never have taught him.

The other skill perhaps is that of self-sufficiency. To survive the cruelty of your classmates, and possibly the abuse of adults, without ever telling anybody requires inner strength. My father had this quality. He was sent away to school at the age of six, to a spartan prep school. He then went on to Winchester, one of the best public schools in England. In Dad's case, the worst part of being sent away was the fact that he was rarely allowed to come back to his own home during the holidays. Dad's mother, Maisie (who was his father's first cousin), died of tuberculosis when he was four. Dad's father, Dr. William Brown, remarried soon afterwards and his second wife was not interested in Maisie's child, Tony. She didn't want him in *her* home. Her husband, an eminent psychiatrist with a royal clientele (literally), went along with this, and so during most holidays my dad stayed as a paying guest with a spinster in the town of Winchester. Incredibly, if that wasn't possible, Dad was sent to a *mental asylum*, where his father worked as a consultant. Dad was still a boy. But if there was a vacant room in the asylum, he would be put there, alongside the adult mental patients.

Dad didn't reveal this to me until he was eighty-seven years old, over a lakeside dinner one evening in Geneva, after a few glasses of wine. And even then, there was no note of self-pity in his voice, or even any criticism of his father. Was that, too, part of The Code? Honour thy Father, however badly he may have treated you? He'd denied his son a home life but gave him a first-class education. Because Dad had survived the experience, he became stronger.

So I remain grateful to John le Carré, for making us send Jonnie to a British boarding school, in the great British tradition. Jonnie never did go down to the house in Cornwall. David was busy writing best-selling books, and he had children and grandchildren of his own, after all. But he would send his godson beautiful and original pieces of antique silver—an eighteenth-century travelling clock, or a nutmeg grater—bought from his favourite antique dealer. Jonnie has them to this day.

41

TWO GENOCIDES

In the spring of 1994, one of the worst, most shocking stories of the decade came out of Rwanda, in central Africa. In the space of one hundred days, as many as one million Rwandans—members of the Tutsi minority—were butchered by their own people, those of the Hutu majority. Most of the killing was done by the extremist Hutu militia known as the Interahamwe. But ordinary Hutus joined in the bloodbath. Their weapon of choice was the machete.

It started on April 6, when a plane carrying Rwanda's Hutu president, Juvénal Habyarimana, was shot down outside the capital of Kigali, killing everyone on board. The Hutus immediately blamed the Rwanda Patriotic Front (RPF), a Tutsi rebel group based in neighbouring Uganda. Within days Hutu death squads were terrorizing the country, murdering Tutsis and so-called "moderate Hutus," people who were opposed to the killing and thus were killed as "traitors." The holocaust was planned—Rwanda was run by an extremist Hutu elite who believed that their survival depended on the extermination of the Tutsis (about 14 percent of the population). An extremist radio station, Radio Milles Collines, was on the air constantly telling people to "kill the cockroaches," meaning the Tutsis (the term itself was a cruel irony: the Tutsis were tall and slim). In three and a half months, hundreds of thousands of Tutsis and moderate Hutus were massacred. It was a genocide. The killing finally stopped when RPF troops, led by Paul Kagame, invaded Rwanda and put the Hutus to flight. Tens of thousands of Hutus fled across the border into Tanzania and eastern Zaire, near the town of Goma, where they began to die of cholera and other diseases.

Most of the world stood on the sidelines when this horror show was unfolding. The United States didn't want to get involved, after its disaster in Somalia in 1993 (when eighteen American soldiers were killed in a botched raid to capture allies of a powerful Somali warlord). The United Nations peacekeeping force in Rwanda, under the Canadian Commander Roméo Dallaire, was hopelessly ill-equipped and under-manned, in spite of General Dallaire's pleas for reinforcements, which he believed could have stopped the genocide. Human Rights Watch agreed with him. It reported that: "UN peacekeepers could have saved many lives by intervening at an early stage—all the more so if their numbers had been increased." It went on: "Despite repeated warnings by Rwanda and international human rights organizations . . . that a genocide was being prepared, governments, . . . including the United Nations and the Organization of African Unity (now the African Union), dramatically failed to act to prevent the genocide. . . ."[1]

In June 1994, France sent in troops in what it called Operation Turquoise. Some lives were saved. But France had backed the extremist Hutu government and was accused of arming and training the murderous Rwandan militias. Eventually, in July, the UN Security Council authorized the deployment of five thousand additional

UN troops to Rwanda, but by then it was too late. The killing had stopped. The genocide was over.

That was about the time that ABC asked me to help cover the Rwanda story. I flew in with Carlos Mavroleon, a freelance cameraman and producer who'd already been in and out of Rwanda several times and knew the hideous story pretty well. Tall, dark and handsome, Carlos was heir to a Greek shipping empire, educated at Eton and Harvard, and had a posh British accent. As a young man he'd converted to Islam to join the Mujahedeen in Afghanistan and fight against the Russians. He was often described as an "adventurer-turned-journalist" and was known as a "shit-hole specialist." Just the sort of person you would want to have in your bunker.

(Four years later, Carlos was found dead in a hotel room in Pakistan, reportedly from an overdose of heroin. He was on assignment for CBS's *60 Minutes* and was trying to get into Afghanistan, disguised as a local, after U.S. President Clinton's cruise missile attacks on the camps of Osama bin Laden.)

Carlos and I flew to Nairobi and then straight on by prop plane to Goma, in Zaire. Terrified of retribution from the Rwanda Patriotic Front, the Hutus were pouring across the border from Rwanda at the rate of twelve thousand people *a day*. They were camped all over the bare volcanic hills outside the town, in a strange lunar landscape that looked like the end of the world. The camp seemed to stretch for miles, and the conditions were awful. Along the roads, bodies were stacked like cordwood, the victims of disease, starvation, and overexposure.

Various UN relief agencies were already set up in Goma, and in the first few days our job was to show what they were doing to stop the spread of disease, and how they were distributing food and relief supplies. Much of the food was being grabbed by the Interahamwe militia, which had quickly taken control of the huge camp. We talked to the refugees about the hardship they were now facing. Normally when you see people without food or shelter, threatened with cholera and typhoid, you feel compassion. For once, I felt no sympathy at all for these people. As many as a million Tutsis were murdered in Rwanda, at an average rate of ten thousand a day. The military death squads could not have carried out that unspeakable task alone. Ordinary people, tens of thousands of them, had to have helped with the slaughter. As the BBC's Fergal Keane wrote in his memoir, "With so many hundreds of thousands dead, you knew that it had taken a great many hands to do the killing."[2] Like him, I couldn't help thinking that most of those huddled Hutu masses in that chaotic refugee camp had blood on their hands.

Those we interviewed all denied that they'd taken part in the genocide themselves. "Oh no!" they cried. "Our Tutsi neighbours were our friends! We would never hurt them!" Is that so? It was hard to believe.

We found just one Hutu who was planning to leave the camp and take his family back to their home in Rwanda. He was blameless, he said. We followed the man and his family to their village—it was just across the border. His Tutsi neighbours showed no emotion on his return, perhaps because they were still in a state of shock. But they showed no hostility either. We thought that this man must have been one of those moderate Hutus who refrained from what the Irish poet Seamus Heaney once called "neighbourly murder" (though that was in another context; Heaney was referring to the inter-communal killings between Catholics and Protestants in Northern Ireland).

Two years later, in 1996, the Rwandan Patriotic Front, backed by Uganda and supported by a Congolese rebel group, invaded the big refugee camps. Thousands of Hutu refugees were killed, thousands returned to Rwanda, and thousands fled into the forests of Congo, where they were massacred by the Congolese rebels and RPF troops.

Many of those who went back to Rwanda were thrown into an overcrowded jail in Kigali. At its height, it was holding one hundred and thirty thousand prisoners, many of whom died from the prison conditions themselves. In 1998, twenty-two prisoners were executed for crimes against humanity, in public.

The great mass of Hutu refugees went back to their villages, once again to live side by side with the Tutsi survivors of their "neighbourly" killing. The government of Paul Kagame told the traumatized Tutsi population that they had to accept this, and they did. None of the survivors ever received any kind of reparation.

The International Criminal Tribunal for Rwanda (ICTR) was set up in Tanzania to try people who played prominent roles in the genocide, those whom it could track down and bring to justice. Forty-nine men were convicted before the tribunal shut down in 2011. Several suspects who fled to Europe were found and put on trial, including a former Rwandan intelligence chief who was sentenced in France to twenty-five years for genocide and crimes against humanity.

This was the one positive development that emerged from the Rwandan horror. The establishment of the ICTR, along with the International Criminal Tribunal for the Former Yugoslavia (in the Hague), marked an international commitment to make war criminals accountable and bring them to justice.

I continued to go in and out of Bosnia until the first week of July 1995, when the Bosnian Serb Army under General Ratko Mladić surrounded and laid siege to the so-called "safe haven" of Srebrenica, in eastern Bosnia. Tens of thousands of Bosnian civilians and fighters had taken refuge there from previous Serb offensives against Muslims in eastern Bosnia. The UN had set up six Muslim towns in Bosnia as safe havens, each under the supervision of a small number of UN troops—usually a battalion—but with strict orders not to use force. The safe havens weren't safe at all, though Bosnian civilians, already driven from their homes in the Serbs' campaign of ethnic cleansing, believed that they were. It was a cruel, fatal delusion.

The international media knew that something terrible was about to happen in Srebrenica; it was only a matter of time. But it was a completely closed area. The nearest you could get was the town of Tuzla, northeast of Srebrenica, where I had spent my first few weeks in Bosnia in early 1993. We flew in to Split, on the Adriatic Coast, and prepared to drive north. Since it was summer, it would only take about twelve hours to get to the town (unlike those four atrocious days in winter, two years before).

Our camera was being carried in by a freelance editor, Derek Kingsmill, a fussy little Englishman of a certain age who for some reason had checked the camera in as cargo rather than bringing it out as carry-on. The gear did not arrive, along with a lot of other checked baggage. On arrival in Split I found that the competition—NBC and CBS—were already on their way to Tuzla. I thought that at least the correspondent (me) should get into position as soon as possible to stay competitive. In the presence of Kingsmill and the producer—a young American who was based in Moscow and had never been to Bosnia—I called ABC in London to explain the situation.

"The camera hasn't arrived, but both CBS and NBC are already on their way to Tuzla. I could drive up with the editor now and at least do a voice-over piece with a Bosnia sign-off, using the BBC footage [in Bosnia we shared video and sometimes office space with the BBC and had a very good working relationship]. The producer can follow with the camera when it arrives."

The folks in the ABC London bureau considered this but weren't as worried as I was about being beaten by CBS/NBC. They thought it better that we all wait in Split until the camera arrived and go up to Tuzla together as a team. "Okay, it's your call," I said. I arranged to meet my team later for dinner.

As I sit down in the hotel restaurant, the editor, Kingsmill, narrows his eyes and points a shaking finger at me.

"You're trying to get me killed, just to puff yourself up and enhance your reputation!" he shouts.

"What on earth are you talking about, Derek?" I reply, really quite stunned.

"You want me to risk *my* life on that drive up to Tuzla just so *you* can get yourself on the air!"

"Well, if you consider it life-threatening, I'm risking my own life as well. But I don't think it's dangerous, and I happen to think it's important to stay competitive on this story, which is going to be a very big one. You don't, it seems."

Derek sputters something and gulps down his gin and tonic . . . possibly not his first. No one else says anything.

"Anyway, it's not an issue now, is it?" I go on. "We're not hitting the road until the camera arrives and then we'll all go to Tuzla, in convoy, together. Is that safe enough for you?"

In the meantime, I'm wondering what the hell is the matter with this horrid little man. If he's that scared, he shouldn't bloody *be* here.

Fortunately, the camera arrived the next day and we set off in convoy to Tuzla. Since we had more than one armoured car, I didn't have to ride with Derek. I rode with our translator. Derek teamed up with the young producer for the twelve-hour journey. Which was perfectly safe and passed without incident.

Once in Tuzla it was a scramble to get up to speed. By this time the Bosnian Serb Army had entered Srebrenica and the Muslim inhabitants had crowded inside the compound of the Dutch UN Battalion. Those who could get in. General Ratko Mladić had ordered that the men and boys over age twelve and under age seventy-seven be separated from the women and taken away for "interrogation." But everything would be fine, he assured the terrified population, patting the head of a small boy. These sinister images had been fed out to the world by Serb television.

The women, children, and old people—more than twenty thousand of them—had fled to Tuzla and were taking refuge in a UN camp outside town. The UN was restricting access to the camp: each news team was allowed access for two hours only. We were given a UN escort, to ensure we didn't exceed that time. Families were huddled around the small tents that were issued to them. They were completely traumatized. There was a register posted at the camp entrance, listing the names of people who'd already arrived. People kept checking it, to see who was still alive. There were no men on that list.

We filmed the camp conditions, interviewed a few families, and learned their heartbreaking stories. One pretty young woman held her child in her arms as she talked about the last moments she'd spent with her husband before he was taken away. As she talked, her eyes filled with tears and as she wept, her child started kissing her, trying to wipe the tears from his mother's eyes. For me it was a pitiful, moving sight, and I was tearful too. Then our two hours were up. We had just enough time to shoot a piece to camera.

We continued to work this way for the better part of a week, as the number of refugees from Srebrenica continue to grow. But no men between the ages of eighteen and seventy-seven, and no boys over twelve. Given the past conduct of the Serbs in the Balkans, we feared the worst. But I don't think anyone at that time realized that the Bosnian Serb Army under General Ratko Mladić was carrying out a genocide. Only later did the world learn, from survivors, that a total of eight thousand Bosnian men and boys were taken away and shot. Massacred, over a period of five days. Then dumped in mass graves, all over eastern Bosnia. It took years of investigation by prosecutors at the International Criminal Tribunal to establish all the gruesome details. They dug up the graves and brought in relatives for the unbearable task of identifying the remains of their loved ones, mainly by their clothes and jewellery. Then they were called to testify before the international court.

General Ratko Mladić, chief of staff of the Bosnian Serb Army and otherwise known as "the Butcher of Bosnia," was on the run until 2011, when he was finally arrested in northern Serbia by Serb Special Forces and extradited to the war crimes tribunal in the Hague. (By this time, the government of Serbia wanted to end its diplomatic isolation, get sanctions lifted, and join the European Union.) In 2017, Mladić was convicted of genocide, war crimes, and crimes against humanity, and sentenced to life imprisonment. He was seventy-four. He was disruptive during the course of the trial, and once made a cut-throat gesture toward the mother of one of the victims of his massacre at Srebrenica. Before the verdict was read, he stood up and shouted, "This is all lies! I'll fuck your mother!" and was removed from the court. His extremist supporters in Serbia still regard him as a national hero.

Radovan Karadžić, the Bosnian Serb leader, had been convicted of genocide, war crimes, and crimes against humanity a year earlier. The prosecutions of these two contemptible men went on for a total of twelve years and were seen as the most important war crimes trials since the Second World War. They will both be in prison until they die.

I can't say that I "covered" these two genocides, in Rwanda in 1994 and in Bosnia in 1995. Along with many other members of the press, I was merely in the region when it was happening, or just after it had happened. I talked to survivors and saw the stark terror in their eyes. That was in Bosnia. In Africa, I saw shifty-eyed guilt in the faces of the killers. In both places, you felt—though you didn't actually see—the pure, evil enormity of what had happened. Two more examples in the twentieth century of man's inhumanity to man.

42

THE VERY WORST...
AND THE VERY BEST

ABC was pleased with our coverage in Bosnia, and the brass called me from New York to tell me so. I found that a little embarrassing, though it made me feel a bit better about what was happening to me personally, on the ground, at the hands of the producer. He had just a few years' experience in television, having come to ABC from a newspaper. He was young and arrogant and spent a lot of time stalking around, stating the blindingly obvious, such as "We've got to advance this story." He also seemed to think that to assert his authority, he needed to humiliate and insult his female correspondent.

When I walked into the workspace to do a live two-way with *Good Morning America* on my last day in Tuzla, he suddenly started shouting at me, accusing me of "waking him up" for no good reason (I had knocked on his door at 9 a.m. to tell him that I planned to check out some lead or other). He claimed that I "didn't care about facts," that I "upset the translators," that I had "temper tantrums." He was the one having a temper tantrum, it seemed to me. His unwarranted personal attack took place in a crowded workspace, approximately fifteen minutes before I was to do a live two-way with New York for the morning broadcast. I remember thinking, *This jerk is trying to sabotage me. He's trying to make me lose my temper so that I won't be able to go on the air. I can't start shouting back at him.* No one in the room—our translator Maggie, our camerawoman Jane Hartney, and Anderson Cooper (then a freelancer, passing through, and not the mega-star he later became)—said anything. I noticed the editor, Derek Kingsmill, smirking over his tape deck.

I was careful not to raise my voice. "How did I upset the translator? Under what circumstances, exactly?" I said.

"Oh, I don't know exactly, but you did! Many times!" he shouted back, waving his arms.

I looked at Maggie. "Did I upset you about anything? This is a difficult, terrible story. We're all under strain."

Maggie didn't say anything. I turned to the producer, the jerk.

"How dare you say I don't care about the facts? What facts, exactly, do you think I don't care about?"

"Aw, all kinds of things, I can't list them all now!" he shouts.

By this time, it was about ten minutes before my live hit with *Good Morning America*.

"Well, you better be more specific with your insults. I have to go on the air in a few minutes. Or are you trying to upset me so much that I can't perform?"

I went up to the camera position on top of the roof, my heart beating a mile a minute from anger and humiliation. I was shaking. I hoped it didn't show.

I got through the rest of the day and filed my report for *World News Tonight* without exchanging more than a half-dozen words with this miserable excuse of a man. (Fortunately, I was leaving Tuzla the next morning: another correspondent was coming in to replace me.) I knew that if I got into a screaming match with this prize prick, I would be the loser. If a man starts shouting, he's a Tough Guy. When a woman raises her voice, she's a Bitch. That's the way it is. If I allowed him to provoke me into a knock-down, drag-out fight, that's what would get played back to the brass in London and New York. "Hilary is losing her rag. Maybe we can't keep sending her out on tough assignments, et cetera, et cetera." God knows there have been plenty of fights between male journalists on the road. An ABC producer in another theatre of war had recently tried to throw a correspondent out of the window. That just made a good story. This would be different.

At the end of my tour of duty, the executive producer, the manager of TV News, and the president of ABC News all called to congratulate me on my reports. I said thank you, and wasn't it a terrible, shocking story, and how grateful I was to be given this extraordinary assignment.

Now, twenty-five years later, in the age of the feminist #MeToo movement, I think about this episode. In my forty-five years in the broadcasting business, I can honestly say that I was never sexually harassed by a male colleague or boss, ever. But in Bosnia in 1995, I was the victim of a vicious verbal assault by a producer thirty years my junior, who had very little experience in television and had never been to the region. A region that I had covered, again and again, since the conflict itself had started. That attack was every bit as traumatic as a sexual assault. Having once been raped in Mexico, I can say that.

The next morning, before leaving, I went back to the workspace to return a piece of equipment. My abuser was sprawled on the bed (we worked out of hotel room), eating a sandwich, with his mouth open.

"Well, Hilary," he drawled, "we may not like each other, but New York sure loves our work."

I was leaving. I was basically off the clock and there was no one else in the room except Derek, his co-conspirator.

"Why don't you go fuck yourself," I said quietly. "That is, if you haven't done it already." And I walked out. I don't think he heard me, however. He was too busy congratulating himself on the way he handles women.

I don't know how I can mention this jerk on the same page as a prince like Clark Bentson, but I can, and I shall. Clarkie came to work at ABC London about the same time as I returned to ABC, in 1993. He started on "the desk," an entry-level job coordinating foreign coverage. But it wasn't long before he was on the road as a producer. He was an absolute joy to work with: energetic, full of ideas, a fine eye for pictures, terrific under pressure, a great sense of humour, and wonderful to his colleagues. Everybody liked Clark. I first worked with him in Sarajevo, and we hit it off immediately. Though he later told me that he thought I was crazy. I took far too many risks, he said. You too, Clarkie! Then as his stock went up and he began pitching feature stories, he would sometimes ask for me as the correspondent. We became a bit of a conspiracy. Like me, he was a hopeless packrat and picked up beautiful things on all his far-flung assignments. In that sense we were a terrible influence on each other. We would just egg each other on, and buy more, more, *more*.

When I pitched stories, I would always ask for Clark as my producer, if he was available. In the spring of 1995, I submitted a proposal for some stories on the Twentieth Anniversary of the Fall of Saigon. I thought I had a chance since I'd covered the Fall itself in 1975. Vietnam had changed enormously in the two decades since the Communist takeover of South Vietnam. Not just because the North and South were reunified, but because the Communist government had adopted a free market economy. Which is capitalism, by any other name. On April 30, 1995, there would be street celebrations and military parades, led by the decorated veterans of the war. Their economy was booming, private enterprise was flourishing, the country was trading with the west, and former boat people had returned to Saigon to open smart restaurants and bars.

ABC liked the pitch, assigning Clark as my producer. "I have just been anointed," Clark said when he called to say we would be working together again. This story was quite a Big Deal.

We showed the growing prosperity in Saigon, renamed Ho Chi Minh City. Clark found a small factory run by an English-speaking former officer in the South Vietnamese Army, which produced scissors and other kitchen utensils from melted-down arms and armour. He turned swords into ploughshares, literally. It made a pretty good piece. In its intro to our report, ABC ran a clip of me at the Battle of Newport Bridge in April 1975 (lying down to stay out of the crossfire). Our report was followed by a great spot from Mark Litke, ABC's chief Asia correspondent, about the rise of tourism in Vietnam. "It was always Vietnam, the War. Now it's Vietnam, the Country," Mark said in his closing line. New York was really pleased with the coverage that day. I know this because the news director, Bob Murphy, woke me up at 6:30 a.m. to tell me so. I think he might have forgotten about the twelve-hour time difference.

Clark and I celebrated with dinner on the roof of the Rex Hotel. Walking down Tu Do Street, we were waylaid by a curbside masseuse who wanted to apply the ancient practice of "cupping" on our backs. We must have been well into our own cups by then because we both promptly flopped face down onto her wafer-thin mattress, exposed our backs, and let her get on with it. This was on the *sidewalk*. All I remember is looking around to see this tiny Vietnamese girl perched on my back, igniting a blowtorch. Extremely hot glass cups were then applied to my delicate white skin as I yelped in pain. Clarkie was next to me, getting the same treatment from the girl's assistant.

"What are we *doing*, Clarkie?" I cried.

"I think it's supposed to be good for the circulation," he said, laughing uncontrollably.

The next morning, I woke up, looked in the mirror, and saw a line of large, interlocking rings across my back. I looked like a walking advertisement for the Olympic Games. I was horrified. "I'll never be able to wear a backless dress again! Or a bathing suit!" I shouted to my scarred image in the looking glass. I rushed down to the front desk (I had by then become quite friendly with the girl at reception) and blurted out my story. Talk about getting drunk and waking up with a huge tattoo. I know this can happen to people. Really stupid people. She took me into the ladies' room to examine the damage.

"No no, this is nothing!" she said. "My grandmother used to do this for me. It will go away."

"*When* will it go away?"

"It will go away in a few days. Or weeks," she said, without much conviction. Yeah right. Or maybe *months*, or possibly *never*.

Clarkie was still laughing at me as we said goodbye in Saigon: he was re-basing to London. I had decided to explore the north of the country with Edie Lederer of AP, Larry Kramer of *The Wall Street Journal*, and Jurate Kazale, a beautiful woman who had been injured in Vietnam while covering the Tet Offensive in 1968. Our little group became known as "Larry Kramer and the Kramerettes."

We went to Hue, Hanoi, and Halong Bay. This happened to coincide with the demobilization of a quarter of a million troops of the North Vietnamese Army (NVA). There were thousands of young men on the streets of Hanoi, still in uniform, looking for work. Many had found jobs as cyclo-drivers, taking passengers in their rickety pedicabs around the city. Having covered the final days of the Vietnam War in South Vietnam for an American network, it was absolutely surreal to be taken around Hanoi in a pedicab operated by an NVA soldier, *still in uniform*. One of the unforgettable images from that trip was of Jurate in her pedicab, tapping her NVA driver on the back as she extended a long, tanned, elegant arm, pointing to a shop she wanted to visit. To paraphrase Mark Litke: It used to be Vietnam, the War. Now it's Vietnam, the Tourist Destination.

Later that year Clark pitched a couple of feature stories for *World News Tonight with Peter Jennings*: one in Greenland, and the other in Mali, in Sub-Saharan Africa. For some reason we had to do these stories back to back in the space of a week. The temperature change between the two was 100 degrees. Packing for this was quite tricky.

The story in Mali was about national archaeological treasure, and how it was being systematically plundered and sold to collectors in Europe and the United States. Next to Egypt, Mali has the most extensive repository of archaeological artifacts on the African continent. These are relics of the Mali Empire, which thrived between the thirteenth and seventeenth centuries, and those remains lie about one or two feet under the ground. They are very easy to dig up. Which is exactly what had been happening. Peasants would unearth pots and bowls and other ancient objects, selling them to a local middleman for $30 or $40. A fortune, for them. The local middleman would sell them to another middleman in the capital of Bamako, who would sell them to a European agent, who would sell them to a dealer in Paris or London, who would sell them to a collector for tens of thousands of dollars.

The president of Mali at the time, Alpha Oumar Konaré, was interested in archaeology (he was educated at the University of Geneva), and he was trying to stop the hemorrhage of his country's precious heritage. At that time there was no problem getting into Mali or operating inside the country: this was long before the appearance of the Boko Haram Islamic fanatics, whose attacks have now made much of Mali a no-go area.

We first drove to the Bandiagara Escarpment, a huge sandstone cliff more than 1,500 feet high, where the Dogon people lived. They are believed to be of Egyptian descent and their culture goes back thousands of years, to 3200 BC. Their villages were built into the walls of the escarpment itself and could only be reached on foot, along a path that dropped down into a deep gorge. It was said that the Dogon retreated to this region because of their refusal to convert to Islam a thousand years ago. For hundreds of years they had been producing beautiful sculptures and wood carvings, most of which ended up in museums or private collections in Europe and the United States.

There weren't many people in the village when we trekked in, but we talked to a village elder, who described how their art had been taken away by "foreign visitors." They were still making intricate doors and shutters for their dwellings. Naturally, Clarkie and I each bought a wooden shutter, about eighteen inches square, with its distinctive carvings of narrow human forms, standing in rows. We told ourselves that these were not antiquities. Anyway, the villagers needed the money. I did a stand-up on the way out at the top of the escarpment. It was an absolutely stunning location, and our cameraman, Michal Bukojemski, made it look every bit as magnificent as it was. Michal came from Poland and had a lot of experience in feature-length movies.

We drove on to Mopti, a wild, noisy town on the Niger river, full of Tuareg traders. They were selling magnificent handwoven wedding blankets, which they folded and stacked on their heads, on top of their turbans. The Tuareg are already tall. With a half-dozen folded blankets on their heads, they were about eight feet high. As soon as one of these traders spotted a possible customer, he would reach up, whip the top blanket off the pile on his turban, and spread it out on the ground with a flourish. Then he would go through the rest of his stock, flicking the blankets onto the ground, one by one, until he was reduced to his normal height, in turban and flowing robes. The Tuareg got very animated when they spotted us, as you can imagine. Clarkie bought three blankets; I bought two. (I gave one to my friend Jerilyn Ross when she married Ronnie Cohen. They loved it.)

From Mopti we took a ferry across the Bani River to the island village of Djenné, famous for its great mud mosque, one of the most notable landmarks in Africa. The mosque (first built in the thirteenth century and rebuilt in 1906) is now a World Heritage Site. It's surrounded by a lively, open-air market, filled with statuesque women drifting around in colourful caftans called "boo-boos" and with large, twisted gold earrings framing their lovely faces. Djenné is also known for the archaeological artifacts that you can buy from certain dealers. All you have to do is ask around, and someone will lead you down a narrow alley and into a shop full of pots and ancient treasure. I had a hidden camera in my hat, and we showed just how easy it is to acquire an artifact.

"Is this an antique?" I asked, picking up a beautiful pot, "or is it just a copy?"

"No no, this is real. Very old! Very good!" the shopkeeper said.

"How much?"

"Thirty dollars."

Maybe he asked for the equivalent in local currency. I obviously could have bargained with him.

We had the footage we needed. I thanked him, put the pot down, and said we would think about it and come back later. We'd shown how easy it was to buy archaeological objects that were supposed to remain inside Mali as part of its national heritage.

On the way back to the capital I was kicking myself for being so damned honest. That pot was beautiful. I would have loved to take it home.

"No no *no!*" says my honourable inner voice. "We're doing a story about the theft of a nation's archaeological heritage! You can't smuggle a priceless antiquity out of the country!"

What a goody two shoes. Yeah, but not for long. Just out of Mopti we pass a roadside stall, with a few pots for sale.

"*Stop the car!*" I cry. I really wanted one of those lovely artifacts. We had already interviewed an art expert who said there's so much of this treasure, just a few feet under the ground, that it wasn't worth making copies. Anything you pick up was likely to be the real thing.

I rush out and seize one of the pots, pay the man, and jump back into the car. Clarkie gives me a dark look. "Well, nobody's perfect," I tell him as I stuff the pot into my tote bag.

When we get back to our hotel outside Bamako, an overzealous bellhop grabs my bag and swings it over his shoulder. The bag is unzipped. The pot falls out, hits the ground, and cracks.

"Serves you right, *thief!*" my inner voice says as I recover the pot. All the same, I take it home as part of my permanent collection of booty. The crack is a silent reminder of my own shameful double standards.

We left the intense heat of Sub-Saharan Africa and within forty-eight hours we were on the west coast of Greenland, in the Arctic Circle, having flown via Copenhagen to the settlement of Ilulissat, which means "iceberg." Greenland is the world's largest island and an autonomous Danish territory with limited self-government. Clark had discovered that Greenland, in a bid to win recognition as the true home of Santa Claus, was staging the first International Santa Claus Games. About twenty large jolly men in Santa Claus suits were due to converge on the island a few weeks before Christmas, coming from Australia, the United States, Great Britain, and a few other European countries. It was a complete PR stunt—but hey, it would make a great feature piece for the Christmas Eve show when normally there isn't much news. Clarkie sold the idea to the foreign editor of *World News Tonight*.

Having switched from safari suits to padded parkas, there we were, shivering and stamping our feet on top of the Ilulissat Glacier, along with a company of round bearded men in red suits. Ilulissat is the fastest-moving glacier on Earth, advancing at the breakneck speed of 113 feet a *day*. It produced the iceberg that sank the *Titanic*. The organizers of this ludicrous Santa Summit thought it would be a great location for a photo op, and it was. But by god it was cold! My parka—a lined green suede garment, made in Italy for normal winter wear on the streets of Rome—was hopelessly inadequate. I could barely utter my fifteen-second piece to camera before my whole face started to seize up. The camera seized up too, but our crew, the husband-and-wife team of Francesca Neidhardt and Alex Bruckner, managed to get it going again.

The location was spectacular, however. The glacier is not so much white as blue, especially in deep canyons that cut through the great mass of ice. It was accessible only by helicopter, flown by one of those deranged chopper pilots who thought it would be fun to fly *into* the canyons, just to give his passengers a run for their money.

The only other outdoor event was a tour of Disco Bay, in an open boat. We shot a surreal sequence of two dozen Santas standing on deck singing "Jingle Bells." Behind them an enormous iceberg broke away from the frozen white cliff of the glacier, crashed into the ocean, and very nearly swamped the boat.

Incredibly, this ridiculous story actually got on the air, mainly because Clark Bentson can sell anything. We all agreed that we'd never been so cold in our lives—and for me, that's saying something since I grew up in Eastern Canada. As we waited for our flight back to Copenhagen and London, we wandered into a small souvenir shop. At the back was a rack of fur parkas, with one long coat in dark-brown sealskin. I tried it on.

"God, Hils, you should buy that! It looks great on you!" said Clarkie. Francesca and Alex agreed.

My teeth were still chattering from our two days in the Arctic Circle with the international Santa Claus troupe. I looked at the price tag. $1,800. A garment like this would retail in New York for ten times that amount.

"We could give it to you for $1,500," the shop owner said. The fur trade in Greenland had been virtually destroyed by the anti-fur lobby. They weren't making fur coats and jackets anymore because they couldn't sell them.

"Done!" I said. I consider that the livelihood of an Inuit human being is more important than the life of a mature adult seal. Anyway, it was a beautiful coat, and I was still chilled to the bone.

I have had compliments about it ever since, from the most elegant of women, and no anti-fur fanatics have thrown paint at me. That's because I tell them it's fake. If they don't believe me, I tell them to get lost.

43

BHUTAN: THE COUNTRY OF GROSS NATIONAL HAPPINESS

By this time, Clarkie had invented a name for our far-flung feature reports: Four Corners. "We go to the four corners of the earth, in search of stories that will amaze you!" His next Big Idea was almost life-changing, for both of us.

Clark wanted to go to the hidden Himalayan kingdom of Bhutan, south of Tibet, east and north of India. At the time (1996), no American television news network had been allowed into this secretive Shangri-La. In the seventies, the total number of tourists to enter the country was less than three hundred. The only route into Bhutan was by tortuous mountain roads from India and Tibet, until an airport was built in Paro in 1981. Until then, there was no infrastructure at all. There were no roads, no currency, no postal service, no radio. There was no poverty, no famine, and very little crime. Ninety-eight percent of the peasantry owned their own land. Life in Bhutan was centred around Buddhist beliefs and practices, and people still lived pretty much as they'd done since the Middle Ages.

Bhutan had an enlightened king named Jigme Singye Wangchuck, who came to the throne in 1972 at the age of sixteen and who wished to bring his country into the modern world—but without losing the traditions and customs that had been practised by his people for centuries. He said he was less interested in his country's Gross National Product than in its Gross National Happiness. He had four wives, all of them sisters. He was acutely aware that Bhutan, like other Himalayan mountain kingdoms, could be swallowed up by a large aggressive neighbour. Tibet had been invaded by China in 1950; the independent state of Sikkim had been annexed by India in 1975. Bhutan was exquisite, and almost empty. It was as big as Switzerland, with a population of just over five hundred thousand in 1996. Its highest mountain was 24,836 feet. At the time, 60 percent of the land was still covered in virgin forest and two dozen different languages were spoken, since the people were divided physically by huge mountain ranges. In schools, English was the main language of instruction. The white Himalayan peaks towered over the deep green mountain valleys, and all the houses were in the traditional half-timbered design, with such details as flying phalluses carved in wood and attached to every rooftop, to encourage fertility. (I wanted to buy one of these, but for some reason Clarkie stopped me.)

King Wangchuck had decreed that all buildings in Bhutan be in this traditional half-timbered style, adorned with elaborate carvings and paintings of Buddhist signs and symbols. No unsightly concrete boxes. The people themselves should wear national dress. For the women, that was a handwoven, full-length wraparound garment called a *kira*, cinched at the waist with an embroidered cummerbund and clipped at the shoulders with a pair of gilded brooches called *komas*. It was very elegant. For the men, it was a woven dressing gown called a *gho*, with deep white cuffs, and worn with knee socks. The higher the rank, the shorter the dressing gown. I discovered this when interviewing an important government minister. He was seated, with his legs apart in a manly pose. We chose *not* to show him in a wide shot.

Bhutan had started to open up to tourists in the mid-nineties but in a very tentative way, knowing that mass tourism can corrupt a people and become a form of environmental pollution. It had an annual quota of three thousand visitors, and each visitor was required to pay $200 a day on a planned, pre-paid guided tour. This was to eliminate the backpackers, but the fee included a car, a driver, and an English-speaking guide, so it was a pretty good deal. Twenty-five years later, the tourist quota has gone up considerably, and the country has become a favourite destination among the cognoscenti, travelling on high-end tours from the west. But in 1996, Bhutan was still a secret place known to very few people. It had no television network itself and therefore did not especially want foreign TV crews roaming around the country. It had a handful of diplomatic missions abroad, among them Washington and the United Nations (Bhutan joined the UN in 1971). At my own expense, I flew to New York and made an appointment with the ambassador.

Like many Bhutanese, he was soft-spoken and extremely polite and gave me at least half an hour, which is a long time for a diplomat. Short of sitting on his lap, I did everything I could to convince him that it would be in his country's interest to allow an American television crew into his country for the first time, to show what Bhutan was doing to preserve its unique cultural identity. We were extremely sensitive to their values, I said, and we admired the remarkable, enlightened leadership of their king. (We were not interested in the Nepalese Question, I went on, alluding to Bhutan's controversial expulsion of Nepalese settlers in the south of the country, described as ethnic cleansing by the Nepalese themselves.)

I guess that did it because within a few weeks I was informed that we would be welcome that coming November, a month that coincided with one of their major Buddhist festivals. We could visit monasteries and schools, interview officials and anyone else we liked, apart from members of the royal family. We would be assigned a van, a driver, and an English-speaking guide who would accompany us at all times.

Hallelujah! Clarkie booked Doug Vogt, one of the best cameramen in the business and who, apart from me, is the only person at ABC who can claim to have spent part of his childhood in Medicine Hat, Alberta. This made for a unique bond between us. We also had a young and personable soundman named Roydon.

We flew into Bangkok, changing to a Drukair flight to Paro in western Bhutan. At the time I didn't know that the Paro airport is ranked as one of the top ten most dangerous airports in the world. It has a short runway (6,500 feet) tucked in between two towering mountain ranges and approached through a long, winding narrow valley. Strong winds often whip through the valley. The airport had no radar, and pilots had to land manually, operating on visual flight rules only. Very few pilots are willing to attempt this. Our arrival in Bhutan was like landing on an aircraft carrier.

As always in TV news, we were on a tight schedule. We checked in to the Olathang Hotel, set in a pine forest about a mile out of Paro. But early the next morning, we started our trek up to the famous Tiger's Nest, the most venerated site in Bhutan and a place of pilgrimage among Buddhists since the eighth century. Built in 1692, the temple itself clings to a sheer rock cliff, 2,600 feet above the Paro

Valley. Buddhism is deeply meaningful for the people of Bhutan, informing every aspect of their daily lives. It was very important for us to do a stand-up next to this sacred site. Our guide said it was just a two-hour walk up the mountain.

"Two hours? Not a problem!" I cried as I set off at a brisk pace with Clarkie, Doug, and Roydon. "After all, this is not the first mountain I've climbed," I said with a careless laugh. "I've climbed up a mountain eleven thousand feet high, and then skied down it! I've trekked from Tehran to the Caspian Sea over three mountain ranges!" With a smug little smile, I assured everyone that I was *perfectly* fit and couldn't possibly slow us down.

Things went well for about forty-five minutes. Then suddenly I was gasping for breath and could barely put one foot in front of the other. Could this be altitude sickness? Jet lag? Nope, you're just out of shape, honey-bunch. This wouldn't have been so embarrassing if Clarkie, Doug, and Roydon were having the same experience. But oh no, they were sprinting up the trail like mountain goats. Our camera gear had been loaded onto a donkey. Our guide took one look at me and out of nowhere another donkey appeared and I was hoisted onto its tiny back without a word. It was deeply humiliating.

At least I was able to compose myself to perform a good stand-up, with prayer flags in the background, flapping against the bright blue sky, and the Tiger's Nest looming above me, a few hundred yards away. "We really are so close to heaven!" I said to Clarkie. (I was thinking of the title of Barbara Crossette's germinal book, on the vanishing Buddhist kingdoms of the Himalayas. She had given me a signed copy in New York.) Doug framed the shot beautifully, and I like to think that I redeemed myself by trekking back *down* the trail under my own steam. I bought a pair of silver prayer bells from a solitary wayside merchant on the path, and I still use these for my dinner parties, to summon guests to the table. It's just one of the many eclectic touches that makes my style of entertaining so special. Yeah, so special, and *so weird*, some might say.

Our next stop was the capital of Thimphu, where there are cars but no stop lights. Only police officers, in white gloves, directing traffic with slow and graceful arm movements, more commonly seen at the Royal Ballet. At the time there weren't many hotels in the capital, and we checked in to a new four-star establishment that was opening for business that very day. We were their first guests and were immediately invited to their Grand Opening Party that night. I had read a little about Bhutanese manners: you should never touch a person's head because it's considered to be the most sacred part of the body. The feet, on the other hand, are considered the most impure, and I can certainly relate to that. My feet are enormous.

But we had a wardrobe issue. We were travelling in jeans and safari jackets.

"I'm so sorry, we would love to come, but we don't have anything suitable to wear," I say.

"Not a problem!" says a delightful girl on the front desk, in perfect English (I think her family owned the hotel). "We can lend you some of our traditional garments." She takes us into a room with two large carved chests, opening them to reveal dozens of *gho*s for the men and for me an enormous selection of beautiful *kiras*. They are exquisite, elaborately handwoven in cotton and silk and embroidered in rich jewel colours.

"I can't possibly wear anything so precious," I say as I stroke one of the *kira*s, knowing that, as the world's clumsiest woman, I would be certain to spill something all over it.

"No no, don't worry! I have many of these," the girl says. "You are our first guests. I would be honoured to lend you something to wear!"

So I chose the most beautiful *kira* in her collection. Then this delightful Bhutanese girl puts a chiffon blouse over my head, wraps the *kira* around me, clips on the two gilded brooches, and cinches the whole thing with a woven cummerbund. Honestly, I felt transformed. The boys looked terrific in their silk *ghos* and we all had a great time at a very lively party attended by "le tout Thimphu," finishing up with disco-dancing to the music of The Beatles and Elton John. I could have boogied all night. Being invited to dance by a courtly Bhutanese official in a dressing gown, to the amplified sound of "Crocodile Rock," was one of life's unforgettable moments.

The next morning, we all went to the market and outfitted ourselves in national costume. We wore traditional dress for the rest of our assignment. Journalistic Objectivity went right out the window. We fell completely under the spell of this magic mountain kingdom. By the time we left the country, we were laden with *kiras, komas, ghos,* and god knows what else. I also bought a ceremonial scarf, fifteen feet long and worn on special occasions by men only. That's why I bought it. They drape them round and round their shoulders and look incredibly elegant. I later wore mine to a wedding. Since I never got the knack of draping fifteen feet of silk around my torso, I looked like an Egyptian mummy.

It was pretty easy to assemble the elements for our story: we showed the school where young boys learned to paint and carve the traditional Buddhist signs and symbols. We showed the weaving and embroidery that enhanced their national dress, using dyes made from plants and minerals. We interviewed teachers and students. We filmed a noted local journalist, Kenly Dorji, who already saw isolated incidents of crime and blamed it on the cheap action videos from Hong Kong that were now permitted and that, he thought, could slowly corrupt the people. Journalists always see the glass half empty, right?

We talked to the great American expert on Bhutanese textiles, Diana Myers, who happened to be in the country and who became an instant, lifelong friend. We filmed Diana outside our hotel, and as we began, a small van moved silently across the frame. The driver somehow understood that this was a television interview, and that the sound of his engine might be disturbing. So he just *pushed* his vehicle out of the way, turning on the ignition a few hundred feet down the hill, where it wouldn't be heard. The episode was typical of the impeccable manners of these perfect people.

We saw no tourists, and apart from Diana, the only other foreign visitor we met was the famous British actress Joanna Lumley (best known for her starring role as Patsy in the TV series *Absolutely Fabulous*), who was making a film about her adventurous ancestors, who trekked into Bhutan in the nineteenth century. We ran into each other so much over a period of days that we became quite friendly. One morning we found ourselves, quite by chance, at the same beautiful monastery—the "Dzong" at Tongsa. I asked her if she would pose for a picture with me, to send to my husband. "He's one of your greatest fans, Joanna," I said. "My stock would go up enormously if he saw me standing next to you in front of an ancient monument in Bhutan."

Joanna Lumley is what's known in the theatre world as a "lovey." She's warm and affectionate and addresses everyone with a term of endearment. She's also a complete diplomat.

"Of *course*, Hilary!" she said. We arranged ourselves in front of the sensational backdrop of a seventeenth-century monastery. She gazed at me.

"Darling, you look *lovely!*" she said. Though, of course, she was the one who looked spectacular.

When we first pitched our idea of a Four Corners report from Bhutan, ABC's foreign editor, Tom Nagorski, said we had to get a second story to justify the considerable expense of air travel from London to the Far East for a four-person team. This was perfectly reasonable. It was my job to find that second story. What I found was a fascinating medical program, funded by the European Union, to bring Bhutan's system of traditional Oriental medicine up to the standards and practices of the West. It was run by an Italian physician, Dr. Paolo Marisco. He was charming, as only the Italians can be. He showed us around the little laboratory in Thimphu where the traditional medications were made, by hand, from more than five hundred plants and minerals. He showed us a traditional clinic, where treatments consist mainly of diet, special medication, and acupuncture. We showed all that. The diagnosis began with an examination of the pulse, the tongue…. and the urine. We showed only stage one and two of that.

Based on his eight years of study of Bhutanese medicine, Dr. Marisco said that there were certain conditions—such as stress, heart ailments, and diabetes—that can often be better treated in the traditional way, using methods and medications that go back to the seventh century. We went up into the mountains with a team of his students to gather the some of the many herbs and flowers used for medicinal purposes. They were all in national dress, and they fanned out over the high alpine meadow, gathering the plants and singing a song about the beauty of their countryside. It was a wonderful sight, and we opened our piece with this, using the sound of their singing in later sequences. Once again we were spellbound.

For the last element of our major story, we drove to the east of the country, where they were about to celebrate a Fire Festival. In Bhutan, it's always difficult to pin down the precise dates for such important religious events. The time must be "auspicious," depending on the position of the moon and the stars and heaven knows what else, and this is always decided by the holy men, usually at the last minute. But at the last minute we did indeed learn that the Fire Festival would take place in Bumthang, a day and a night from Thimphu, along the one east–west road. We drove past mile upon mile of virgin forest, lying on the landscape like a thick, green pile carpet. We passed cultivated fields and painted half-timbered houses. We stopped often to film one breathtaking medieval scene after the other. It was achingly beautiful, and more so because of the absolute stillness, with only the trilling sound of insects and birds to break the silence.

Bumthang is a general name given to a complex of four valleys, which we reached after crossing over a high mountain pass. We then dropped down into a wide, cultivated valley, quite unlike any other landscape we had seen in Bhutan. The slopes were gentle; there were many small hamlets and a remarkable number of temples and monasteries. It was in one of these temples that the religious festival was to take place, and we knew that it was really going to happen because people from the surrounding countryside began to gather outside its ancient walls. They were coming for the *wang*, a spoken blessing given by a high-ranking monk. In this festival, there was to be a *mewang*, or blessing by fire. People were expected to jump over a fire, to burn away all their sins. We saw a large bonfire being prepared, around an even larger metal arch that I thought might be mistaken for the Gates of Hell.

"Does anyone ever get hurt in these fire festivals?" I asked our guide. "That bonfire looks as though it could turn into quite a blaze."

"No no," he said. "People do run through the fire, but they can run quite quickly. And they gain merit by taking part."

"They run *through* that fire?" I said, shooting a concerned look at Clarkie. We didn't want to be covering some terrible local emergency.

"Yes, yes, you will see," the guide said with a smile. "Don't worry. We've been doing this for hundreds of years."

As the crowd grew larger there was an almost carnival atmosphere, as clowns in fabulous painted masks came out to make risqué jokes and confront the monks in mock defiance. This was all part of the ritual. You could see that the people were dressed in their best clothes, they had brought food and alcoholic drink, and socialized easily with each other.

Then the fire was lit around the metal arch, and in a trice, huge flames leapt into the air. People surged toward it, and Doug and Roydon got into position on the other side of the burning arch to film the people as they came running through. We were all in national dress, by the way: me in my full-length *kira* and the boys in their dressing gowns. Clarkie and I got on either side of Doug and held him steady as, still filming, he moved back and away from what quickly became a solid, moving mass of shrieking people, laughing like children as they leapt through the flames and streaked past into the darkness. It made a wonderful closing sequence for our story. When we felt we had all the images we needed, there was just one more thing to do.

"I don't know about you guys," I said, adjusting my cummerbund, "but speaking personally, I have quite a few sins that I'd like to burn away. I'm going through that flaming arch too."

And I did. We all did. Afterwards we felt as pure as the driven snow on the Himalayan peaks, high above us.

44

IT CAN'T GET BETTER THAN THIS

In the course of our assignment in Bhutan, I managed to make one successful phone call from our hotel to John and Jonnie back home in Cyprus. (Jonnie was on one of his many school breaks.) It seemed extraordinary that I was able to make this kind of contact in a country that had only recently emerged from the Middle Ages. I raved about the beauty of the place and remember promising them that we should all come back together to this Shangri-La.

By then John was working on *Fire in the Night*, a biography of an eccentric British Second World War commander named Orde Wingate. Wingate was a military maverick whose eccentricities enchanted Winston Churchill. He was a fundamentalist Christian (he belonged to the Plymouth Brethren) with a passion for Zionism, a cause that he embraced fully when he was posted to British-ruled Palestine as a military intelligence officer in 1936. He spoke Hebrew and Arabic and believed fervently in the sacred right of the Jews from anywhere in the world to return to their biblical homeland in Palestine, never mind the rights of its indigenous Arab inhabitants who had been living in the region for centuries. He founded and trained the highly effective Special Night Squads, an irregular force who attacked the rebel Arab bands that resisted the Jewish independence movement. The book quotes an American-born Jewish volunteer named Zvi Brenner: "He taught us to go beyond the wire. Not just to defend our settlements, but to go out and confront the enemy in his lair."[1] The working title of the book was "Praise the Lord and Pass the Ammunition."

John co-authored this book with Colin Smith, an award-winning correspondent for the British Sunday paper the *Observer*, who, like John, had retired to Cyprus to write books. As both Colin and John quickly learned, Wingate's remarkable career didn't stop with the Special Night Squads in Palestine. In 1941, he trained and led another special force (the Gideon Force) into Ethiopia, then occupied by the Italians, an Axis power. He put the Italians to flight and helped restore Emperor Haile Selassie to his throne.

But Wingate's greatest achievement was in occupied Burma, between 1943 and 1944. He created special operations units of the British and Indian armies, along with Gurkhas from Nepal and West African servicemen, who went deep behind Japanese enemy lines. Officially named the Long Range Penetration (LRP) groups, Wingate called his men the "Chindits," and their endurance and valour were legendary. They lived for months on end in the jungle, with only the occasional airdrop to keep them resupplied and alive.

Their first campaign, Operation Longcloth, involved three thousand men who marched more than 1,000 miles through the jungle. The second campaign, Operation Thursday, deployed twelve thousand British and Commonwealth soldiers, with U.S. air support. It was the second largest airborne invasion of the war. Wingate never lived to see the success of this campaign, however. He was killed when his plane crashed into a mountain in northeast India twenty minutes after takeoff in March 1944.

John and Colin were a terrific team, though there may have been times when neither of them thought so. Colin is a superb researcher and extremely knowledgeable on military matters, so he wrote mainly about the battles themselves. John was a master of character delineation and was also very good at persuading retired ladies to give him access to their family records. He wrote beautifully, and he was a first-class editor. As Colin himself said seven years later, in his eulogy at John's memorial service in London: "He knew instinctively what was boring and cut it out. Mercilessly."[2]

They produced a book that was compelling and absolutely seamless: you couldn't tell where the work of one writer ended and the other began. I was in awe of the way John worked, in our original one-room stone farmhouse that had now become his study. It had a desktop computer, some filing cabinets, and a couple of bookshelves, but really it was a pretty primitive workspace. I was also impressed at the way John handled Colin when he was editing Colin's copy. This would involve removing great chunks of carefully researched material. John is not a diplomat. But he respected Colin's knowledge and well-stocked mind. He just knew, as an editor, that if you have too much detail, you'll lose your reader. *Fire in the Night* was published by Random House in 1999. It has been optioned and re-optioned as a movie, continuously, to this day.

During this period John also found time to work with his incompetent wife, Hilary. In Burma, as it happened. Burma was a hermit state run by an oppressive military junta aptly named the SLORC (State Law and Order Restoration Council) that until very recently had closed the country to journalists and visitors of almost any kind.

But in an abrupt reversal of policy, the SLORC declared 1995 to be the "Year of the Tourist." Suddenly you could get a visa into the country, as a tourist, without too much difficulty.

I pitched a story idea to ABC's *Nightline*, that I could go into Burma with my husband and a small hand-held camera, posing as an academics on holiday. We could produce an undercover travelogue about what life is really like for people in that repressive, secretive country. Burma's most famous citizen was the beautiful Aung San Suu Kyi, leader of the National League for Democracy, who had been awarded the Nobel Prize in 1991 for her non-violent struggle for democracy and human rights. She had been under house arrest for more than five years, since 1989, cut off from almost everyone except her housekeeper. On occasion, her British husband, Michael Aris, was allowed to visit her. But in 1995, the "Year of the Tourist," it was whispered that the generals were planning to release her. I proposed that *Nightline* could have a pre-packaged documentary from us, ready to broadcast on the day of her release, whenever that might be. To my astonishment, the program's executive producer, Tom Bettag, bought the idea on the spot. ABC would give us an advance, lend us a small camera, and we would make all our travel, visa, and hotel arrangements ourselves. Tom didn't mind that neither of us were professional camera operators. He wanted the documentary to be in the genre of a traveller's home movie.

We flew into Bangkok, checked into the famous Oriental Hotel, and got our visas at the Embassy of Myanmar, the junta's new unlovely name for Burma. I went to the local office of George Soros's Open Society Foundation, whose people gave me some useful contacts in the country. Then John checked out the camera. To our horror, it had completely misted up from the humidity of Bangkok. You couldn't see a damn thing, only vague outlines. Our great undercover documentary in Burma would be in total fog! We would have to pay back our advance and crawl home in disgrace. I called London to see if anyone in the crew room could troubleshoot over the phone. I got the name and coordinates of an American freelance cameraman based in Bangkok (his name was Al, I think) who might *just* be home. We call him. He answers! There is a god! Al says yes, he can have a look at it, but we'd have to bring the camera to him. He lives in some remote suburb of the city. He dictates his address to the concierge at the Oriental, who writes it out in Thai, with a phone number.

Traffic in Bangkok is terrible at all times of the day. It's probably the worst in the world. John takes one look at the gridlock and realizes that he'll never get to Al in time, not in a *car*. With the help of the concierge, he gets a man on a motorbike to take him. Bangkok also has the highest per capita rate of motorcycle fatalities in the world. With my heart in my mouth, I watch my husband disappear on the back of a bike into the sea of trucks and automobiles.

Three hours later John comes back to the hotel. Al found the problem and fixed it. Hallelujah!

Don't ask me what he did, but we got through the next ten days without a technical hitch. We hired a car with a driver and a translator and shot our undercover travelogue of Burma, showing all its strange sights. We filmed the Shwedagon Pagoda in Rangoon, glistening with real gold. We filmed the famous fishermen of Inle Lake, who row their boats in a standing position, one foot wrapped around an oar, leaving the hands free to toss their nets. We filmed the floating markets, where the men wear skirts, and the women smoke cigars, their faces covered in a white cosmetic paste to protect them from the sun.

But we also filmed scenes of child labour—children as young as five working as unpaid road crews. We filmed a former dissident named Raymond Hey Toon, who'd spent more than ten years in Burma's notorious Insein Prison (pronounced "insane"). He told us that a woman had recently been sentenced to fifteen years in Insein, merely for *talking* to a French television network. We were painfully aware that we could endanger people just by exchanging a few words with them on camera.

But some were brave enough to approach us on their own, though there were spies everywhere. While shooting a sequence near a temple, a young monk came up and said, in English: "This is Moscow."

"You mean there's no freedom here? That life is the way it was under Communism in the Soviet Union?" I replied while John continued to film.

"Yes, yes!" he answered. Suddenly we were surrounded by men in dark glasses. The little monk slipped away, and the informers melted back into the crowd. We have no idea what happened to the monk.

People lived in a climate of fear. We understood this when we reached Mandalay, the last royal capital of the Burmese kings, the city of Kipling, where "the dawn comes up like thunder outer China 'crost the Bay."[3] The Soros foundation had given us the name of a woman activist who might talk to us. All we had to do was inquire at the hotel desk on arrival. So we did.

Within hours, our driver and translator announced that they couldn't work for us anymore. We'd told them that we were tourists, but the news that we wanted to contact a well-known dissident was an instant signal that we weren't tourists at all. They disappeared without a word, with the car. At least they didn't take our luggage. We got on a passenger boat the next day and sailed down the Irrawaddy

River to Pagan, with its great field of ancient Buddhist pagodas. Another wondrous sight in Burma. We never did make contact with the woman activist, and maybe it was just as well. She could have ended up in prison too.

We managed to get out of the country with all our material, which I edited in London with Paolo Marenghi, one of *Nightline*'s overseas producers (it ran about eight minutes). A few weeks later, the military junta announced that it was releasing Aung San Suu Kyi from house arrest. The BBC's Fergal Keane got the first interview with her, and shortly after her release on July 10, 1995, *Nightline* ran his interview, along with our undercover travelogue plus a debrief with me. It was a good program and I think that Tom Bettag was pleased. We couldn't know that Suu Kyi would fall from grace almost twenty-five years later when, as Burma's civilian leader, she defended the military against charges of genocide of the Rohingya Muslims in the country.

With all my assignments to Saigon and Mali and Greenland and Bosnia, life in the mid-nineties was a golden period, professionally and personally. I was telling stories with pictures in faraway places for a top American TV news network. This was my heart's desire! John was doing what he loved best: writing another biography. We saw Jonnie every six weeks or so, either in Cyprus when he came home on long school breaks or in London in my new apartment. I had bought a flat on a shaded cul-de-sac in fashionable Knightsbridge, with a Canadian friend named Carla Singer, an independent film producer in Hollywood. We used the little flat a lot, separately and occasionally together. In the intervening periods we let the place out, through a disreputable agent, at an exorbitant rate. Since it was four blocks from Harrods, a London landmark, it was very easy to find tenants. Basically, it paid for itself.

Everything was coming up roses. At fifty-six, I felt that I was still in the prime of my life, professionally and personally. Until I went for a walk along the coastal cliffs of Cyprus.

45

THE BLACK DOG

A fairly rich vein of lunacy runs through my family, on both sides, and I don't exclude myself. My mother, Jocelyn, had her first episode of depression when she was about forty-eight, in London, Ontario. Suddenly, my sweet, energetic, selfless mother, a woman who was busy from morning to night, could not get out of bed. Would not get out of bed, even to eat. The psychiatrist immediately ordered shock treatment known as ECT, or electroconvulsive therapy. Electrodes are applied to the head and the treatment brings about a grand mal seizure, similar to an epileptic fit. In the early, primitive days of ECT, the convulsions were so violent that on rare occasions they could break the patient's back. ECT was the preferred treatment at the time—the late fifties—for psychotic patients. It terrified Mum. I will never forget the frightened look on her face as she was loaded into the ambulance in yet another mental breakdown.

Mum's depression turned into manic depression and the cycle continued, on and off, until the end of her life forty years later. She had more than ninety shock treatments. Fortunately, in the seventies, psychiatrists switched to a chemical cocktail, starting with lithium, the "miracle drug," which came on the market in the early fifties.

Nothing, however, could really stop her regular mood swings, from mild mania to deep depression. Dad looked after her, even as he continued his brilliant career as an entomologist. Our whole extended family thinks of him as a saint. He wasn't quite that, of course, and he would reject that epithet anyway. But he was a true gentleman. It would never occur to him to abandon his wife or to do anything but stay by her side, in sickness and in health.

Mum's mental illness wasn't the only cross he had to bear. In 1967, my sister Kathy, his youngest daughter, literally lost her mind at the age of eighteen while on a school trip to New York. She was diagnosed with schizophrenia, and immediately committed to a mental hospital back home in London for a course of shock treatments. She was in and out of mental hospitals for the next four years until she was suddenly discharged, along with tens of thousands of other mental patients in Canada and the U.S., in a process known as "deinstitutionalization." The theory was that people with mental illness would do much better living outside hospital and "in the community." The problem was that there were no outpatient centres "in the community" to give them the help and support they still needed.

Kathy moved to Switzerland to live with our parents. Dad still did consulting work for the World Health Organization, and he also edited an entomological magazine, turning scientific essays into intelligible English. In her good periods, Mum loved Switzerland and the charming village where they lived, overlooking Lake Geneva. She cultivated the large garden around their hillside chalet, she went hiking with friends, she even drove a motor scooter.

Dad hooked Kathy up with a young people's group called "Club Vagabondes" and miraculously she stabilized. At twenty-two, Kathy was very beautiful—tall, slender, and shapely, with a long mane of thick red hair. Within a year she met and married a young Englishman, Nicolas Quinlan. The service was in a small church, close to a lakeside restaurant, where the wedding supper was held. Gingie flew in from Montreal, and I flew in from Iran. Kathy looked sensational in a cream-coloured silk crepe pantsuit. She and Nick settled down in England, in a resort on the English Channel called Westcliffe. Two years later, she gave birth to a red-haired baby named Emily Louise.

Then the madness descended again. Nick remained as loyal to her as Dad had been to Mum, though no one had warned him about Kathy's medical history. Dad said he thought it was a case of "dementia precox," and that it would not return. Kathy was sent to a clinic called The Priory, in Roehampton outside London, a well-known private detox centre for the rich and famous. It must have cost Nick a fortune. Kathy had long periods of stability, but for the rest of her life she had periodic mental breakdowns that left her in hospital for months at a time. She showed great courage in the face of this disability. "Mental illness is what I have, not who I am," she says.

Where did this mental illness come from? We know that it's hereditary, generally speaking. We also know of its enormous stigma, among previous generations. People simply didn't talk about it. In our family, on Mum's side, it could have been covered up, if it had existed. There was no known case of mental illness among her parents or grandparents or close relatives. Okay, her grandfather died in the arms of his mistress, but that's not so crazy, is it?

On Dad's side, his half-sister Joan was unstable, though she was never hospitalized. She was, however, crazy enough to cash out her entire inheritance and burn it, literally. Dad's father, Dr. William Brown, was an eminent psychiatrist who'd studied in Vienna under Jung and ended up as a don at Oxford University. But he *was* a shrink, and for some people, many shrinks are also . . . slightly nuts. Dad himself had unpredictable and frightening outbursts of temper, suddenly taking offence at some imagined insult.

In all of this, my sister Gingie and I managed to dodge the genetic bullet. Or so I thought. Until I went for a walk on a clear January day along the white limestone cliffs of the west coast of Cyprus. I was with John and an American couple, Chris and Scott Halliday, who were staying with us for the weekend. I had my hands in my pockets, which is never a good idea when on a nature walk. I was looking out at the glorious view, thinking how lucky we all were to be living in a region where you can walk in your shirtsleeves in January.

I opened my mouth to express this trivial thought and suddenly I was pitched forward and landed directly on my head. Since my hands were still in my pockets, I didn't break my fall, which was from my considerable height of five-foot-ten. We were walking on absolutely flat, smooth rocks. I must have tripped over my own enormous feet. I didn't lose consciousness. But I have never, ever, experienced that kind of pain. John and the Hallidays helped me stagger back along the cliffs to the car.

By the time we got to the house, I had a bump the size of an orange on the left side of my forehead, and it was beginning to change colour. In fact, almost every colour in the rainbow. We called the doctor, and he determined that because I was conscious, and still coherent, there was no reason to make a house call, or for me to come into the clinic. Just take a Tylenol, he said.

The next day I tried to be the Perfect Hostess, making dinner and amusing conversation, with the bump on my forehead getting larger and more colourful by the minute. It must have been very embarrassing for the Hallidays.

I was planning to leave the island the following week, to go to the World Economic Forum in Davos, Switzerland. That's the exclusive annual gathering of the Movers and Shakers of the Entire World. I was going to meet Diane Francis, author of ten books and the first female editor of a national newspaper in Canada (the *Financial Post*). Months ago she'd suggested that I get accredited to the Forum as a journalist, share a room with her, and soak up all the lectures and symposiums on offer. I would make some fantastic contacts, she said.

It's a measure of the madness that had already started to set in that I thought I should still fly to Switzerland, with a multicoloured orange growing out of my forehead. It's a measure of John's tolerance that he actually let me go. I guess he knew he couldn't stop me.

And on arrival, it was a measure of the fundamental difference in manners that normally exists between Europeans and Americans. The Europeans would take one look at me and say, in a low voice, "You know, I have a very good ointment that you might like to try on that forehead. Shall I go up to my room and get it for you?" The Americans would take one look at me and shout, "Jesus Christ! What the *hell* happened to your *head*!? I guess the other guy is still in hospital, right?"

It wasn't until the last day of the Forum that I suspected there might be something really wrong with me. By this time the large lump on my head had produced a bruise that was migrating all the way down the left side of my face and onto my throat. It took me more than three hours to pack up my clothes. It was as though my brain was slowly going into neutral. Diane noticed this too but didn't say anything. Not to me, anyway. Diane had packed her bag in about fifteen minutes.

I flew to London to stay for a few days before going back to Cyprus. I didn't check in with the ABC desk, hoping they wouldn't assign me somewhere. I was still functioning, but I knew I couldn't perform. I wasn't even sure I could add one and one and get two. I went to see my cousin Dr. Jonathan Hunt, a highly successful GP who treats the Great and the Good and who was always very kind to his Canadian cousins.

"That's quite a bump you've got on your head, Hilly," he said as he gently poked around my forehead. "Let's do a scan. In the meantime, I'll send you over to Gerry to drain all the fluid." Gerry was a very competent practitioner who lanced the wound and made me look a little less like a prize-fighter who has just lost a round. He and my cousin had been at Oxford together and he refused to charge me. In the meantime, the result of the CAT scan came back and apparently showed no damage to the brain.

I was immensely relieved, thanked Jonnie Hunt profusely, and flew home to Cyprus. All I needed was some rest in our lovely stone cottage, listening to music, swimming laps in the pool, and dining at night on our terrace, watching the moon cast its pale light over the Mediterranean Sea. I just wanted to lie low for a while, with John. Jonnie was at school and I didn't want him to know anything about this.

Within a week, the ABC assignment desk in London phoned, wanting me to go to Israel for two or three weeks to replace the Jerusalem correspondent while she was on holiday. I couldn't say no. I never said no, though I had the kind of contract that allowed me to do so. The bruise on my face and neck had disappeared. I packed my bags, called my regular driver, and kissed John goodbye. He seemed happy that I felt good enough to go on the road again. John liked having me at home with him, but he also liked it when Hurricane Brown blew out of town, leaving him to concentrate on his writing.

In Jerusalem I always stayed at the famous American Colony Hotel, a beautiful converted pasha's palace near the Old City that is used by journalists and diplomats and United Nations types. The Colony was one of the world's great meeting places. You always ran into old friends there, friends whom you were actually glad to see again. An antiques dealer named Munir had a shop within the grounds of the hotel, and whenever he heard that I was coming, he would send a few embroidered *suzanis* and other tribal treasures to be spread out on the bed in my room. Knowing that I would end up buying them. All of them. Beautiful things are, to me, what stray dogs and cats are to some other people: I want to give them a loving home. Munir understood this, all too well.

This time Munir had arranged for some tribal jewellery to be laid out on the bedroom table. For once, I wasn't interested. I didn't even try the pieces on. It was the end of the day. I checked in with the Jerusalem bureau. The bureau chief, Kathy McManus, said that all was quiet and that there was no need for me to come until the following morning. I ordered room service. Normally at the Colony you had only to walk into its lovely courtyard restaurant to spot someone you knew. Someone you might have dinner with. I just didn't feel up to that. I didn't feel that I had anything interesting to say. I tried to read up on the translations from the Israeli press (an invaluable service provided by the Ministry of Information, though the Israeli press itself was often highly critical of government policy). But I couldn't concentrate. I went to bed.

Normally I rise early, especially when on assignment. That morning I slept through the deafening pre-dawn call to prayer, broadcast at full volume from the mosque next to the hotel. I slept through my own alarm. I slept until about 9 a.m. Then I couldn't get up. I could not haul myself out of bed. Every time I attempted to get vertical, an invisible rope pulled me back into a horizontal position. I was in a complete stupor. Eventually I managed to pull on some clothes. I looked terrible. Normally I take trouble with my appearance—one producer once described me as "the best accessorized correspondent at ABC." That's a compliment, isn't it? At about 11:30 a.m., the assignment desk called.

"Ah Hilary, it's Jake. Are you planning to come in to the bureau any time soon?"

I stammered some response. "I . . . I think I have a problem," I found myself saying, in a voice that even I didn't recognize.

There was a long pause, and then Kathy McManus got on the phone. Kathy was a top producer and we had always got along well. She was tall and slim and had a wicked sense of humour. I liked her very much.

"I-I-I'm sorry, Kathy," I stammered. "I think there is something wrong with me. I don't think I can drive myself into the office. I don't think I can actually work."

"I'm coming over to the Colony right now," Kathy said in a firm voice. "Meet me in the garden."

She arrived in fifteen minutes and I managed to put on some makeup and get myself down to the garden to meet her.

For the next half-hour Kathy talked to me as a psychiatrist might talk to her patient. She told me that I should not attempt to work in my present state, that I should not feel guilty or ashamed, that everyone knows I'm normally courageous and hard-working, that everyone loves my work, that I've done a fantastic job for ABC, and on and on and on. Her calm, quiet voice was mesmerizing.

"Now we're going to pack up your room and get you on a plane to go home again, where you've got to get treatment," she said. I didn't attempt to argue with her. I barely uttered a word. I felt like a child who was being sent home from boarding school with some dangerous infectious disease. I could barely look her in the eye.

I phoned John to warn him that I was coming back, twenty-four hours after I'd left for what was supposed to be a three-week assignment. When I got back to the cottage, he folded me in his arms. Kathy must have phoned him to explain the situation.

"Hilly, we're going to find out what's really wrong with you and get you better. This is the best possible place for you to recover. It's quiet, and there will be no pressure at all. I'll look after you. I'm in charge now."

He might not have said that had he known how long this nightmare would last. We started with a local psychiatrist in Paphos, who was hopeless. He declared that I was suffering from SAD, or seasonally adjusted depression (it was early spring, and the sun was shining). He prescribed a massive dose of some antidepressant that was so strong I collapsed while walking across our terrace. I spent most of the days in bed, without eating or even drinking anything. I had no appetite, and no will to get up. It was as though my whole system was shutting down. At the end of the day John would finally make me get up and I would spend the rest of the evening moving around the cottage and grounds, unable to settle anywhere, unable to read, not even able to listen to music. I had no feeling, no emotion, for anyone. Not for John, who was so good to me. Not for my friends. Not even for our beloved son, Jonnie. I had become a zombie. Zombies are the un-dead, the "speechless humans without will," walking corpses brought back from the grave. When you are in a deep depression, you are in a state of despair. This leads very quickly to thoughts of suicide, and those thoughts crossed my mind constantly. But I remembered what my godmother Natalie once said: "The child of a suicide never recovers. He believes that he is somehow responsible, and he can later do the same thing to himself." In my debilitated state, I remembered her words. I could not, should not, do that to Jonnie and to John. Anyway, I didn't have enough sleeping pills.

In the middle of this terrible period we got a call from Dad. "Mum has died. It's a mercy, after all these years. I'd like the funeral to be within a week. Gingie is coming—she was always Mum's favourite. I hope you can come too, with John."

Well of course we had to go. We flew to Geneva the next day. Dad had no idea of the state I was in, but it didn't take long for him to realize what had happened to me. I think we both tried to pretend that I was all right.

I wanted to give a eulogy—at the funerals of friends I'd always been able to find the right words. I started to write something. I couldn't get beyond the first paragraph. It is a matter of everlasting shame to me that I could not honour my own mother at her funeral. She'd given her children everything. She'd spent the last seven years of her life completely bedridden, speechless and partially paralyzed after a series of strokes. It was a terrible, cruel end for this sweet, selfless lady. At the funeral service, in a large, cold, empty crematorium chapel, we all remained silent, listening to a pastor who we didn't know talk in a foreign language. The only personal touch was an enormous bouquet of roses from Dad, and three vases of wildflowers picked from the mountain slopes by Gingie and Karina.

John and I were staying in Dad's house. Gingie and Karina were in a small hotel nearby. Kathy by this time was living in Canada and wasn't well enough to travel. My beloved Aunt Elisabeth flew out from London. John had told Jonnie to stay in England, afraid that he would be upset not by my mum's death but by my own mental state. It was deteriorating by the day. I was starting to have hallucinations. I was convinced that Dad's tenants, in the basement apartment, were stealing from him in the night. I overheard John calling my sister-in-law (the other Hilary Bierman) in London. "She's completely off the rails," he said. At a time when we should all be rallying around Dad, and celebrating the happy times of his life with Mum, the focus had shifted to me. I was mortified.

"This is no good, Hilly," John said. "We've got to go to London to see someone really qualified. I'll call Jonnie Hunt again. He can set up an appointment." Once again, my cousin Jonnie came to my aid.

We saw a Dr. Peter Rowan at The Priory, the very place that Kathy had stayed years before. By this time, I was beginning to think that I hadn't dodged the genetic bullet after all. That I must have inherited my mother's mental illness, late in life. I'm sure that John was afraid of that too, though he didn't utter that dreadful thought. He'd seen my mother in her depressive state, several times. Dr. Rowan was a great bear of a man who inspired confidence, gave me his full attention, and spent a good hour with us. His verdict was that I was suffering from a clinical depression. He didn't talk about heredity or suggest any other cause. He prescribed a different course of psychiatric pills, saying they would take two to three weeks to have an effect.

This coincided with one of Jonnie's multiple school breaks, but this time I think he stayed with my sister-in-law, Hilary. He was very attentive, in a very grown-up way for a seventeen-year-old schoolboy.

He took me out for walks in Hyde Park, put his arm around me, and tried to cheer me up. I remember thinking, *Jonnie shouldn't see me like this. It's damaging for him.* I was actually glad when he had to go back to school.

John and I flew back to Cyprus, armed with my new medication and a prescription for more. Within ten days I started to feel like a normal human being again. I could get out of bed in the morning, my appetite returned (I had lost about twenty-five pounds), I wanted to go out and see friends and live my life again. John was delighted, and hugely relieved.

I was even able to fly back to England for the funeral of my beloved Aunt Elisabeth, who had been struck down suddenly with pancreatic cancer. She had been my idol since childhood, and my lifelong friend. I gave the Eulogy, quoting the lines by William Cory that she loved so much: "I wept as I remembered how often you and I, did tire the sun with talking and send him down the sky."

Around this time Clarkie called and said there was a famine in south Sudan and we should cover it together. Since I felt like my old self, I said yes. We met in Nairobi, hooked up with a terrific one-man-band cameraman David Hands, and flew up to Lokochokio, in northern Kenya, armed with camping gear, mosquito nets, and our own food supplies. From there we hitched a ride on a World Food Program (WFP) flight into southern Sudan. I was feeling absolutely fine. I was shocked by the scenes of starvation among the people, who would walk for miles from their villages in the blistering heat to collect a bag of rice or a gallon of cooking oil or whatever food-aid the WFP was flying in. Then they would hoist the bags of food onto their emaciated backs and walk away into the drought-stricken, wind-blown wasteland, back to their villages. South Sudan was one of the most miserable, godforsaken places I had ever seen, anywhere.

After a couple of days, we flew back to Nairobi with our material and put together our report for *World News Tonight with Peter Jennings*. They had a full show that night, and we were dropped from the lineup. In the meantime, the BBC Nairobi correspondent, Martin Dawes, wandered into our edit suite, saw our pictures, and pounced.

"I say, that's pretty powerful stuff! I can get that on the *Nine O'Clock News!*" Martin cried, picking up the phone to call London. ABC had an agreement with the BBC whereby the two news organizations could share each other's video, with no embargo. This benefited us both, though it could sometimes be pretty galling when you get scooped with your own material. Martin immediately sold a two-minute piece to BBC TV News on the famine in Sudan, using our pictures. Clarkie made a last-ditch attempt to get New York to broadcast our report, saying that the video would be broadcast on the BBC within a couple of hours. Nah, they didn't care. I think our piece was broadcast two days later.

I was perfectly normal through all of this. On my last night in Nairobi, I looked up my friend Scott Griffin, the businessman/philanthropist/pilot/sailor, who was spending two years in Africa working as a volunteer for the Flying Doctors Service. He put the charity on a business footing and often flew its medics to remote parts of Kenya in *Charlie Foxtrot*, his single-engine Cessna. Scott actually flew this Cessna solo across the Atlantic, from Newfoundland to Nairobi, in an extraordinary exploit that he later described in his best-selling memoir, *My Heart is Africa*. Scott happened to be in town though his wife, my close friend Krystyne, was away in Europe at the time.

We went to one of the best restaurants in Nairobi and ran into Martin Dawes.

I opened my mouth to introduce Scott to Martin. I could not remember Martin's name, though he had been very much on my mind the day before. I knew him well, for God's sake. I was starting to get that old, awful brain-dead feeling. I got through dinner mainly because Scott did most of the talking. He's a great raconteur, and he always has stories to tell about his recent adventures, mainly life-threatening. Such as crash-landing *Charlie Foxtrot* onto a beach on South Island, in the middle of Lake Turkana, with Krystyne and a Samburu warrior on board. They all survived, unhurt. *Charlie Foxtrot* required $40,000 in repairs to become airworthy again. "I know it was crazy to try to land, but I'm sure that it was because of the Lariam I was taking," Scott said to me that evening. (Lariam is the malaria drug that often produces hallucinations, delirium, and, in his case, illusions of invincibility.)

Scott drove me to the airport and I flew home to Cyprus. By the time I got off the plane I was a zombie again. John's face fell as I dragged my suitcase across the flagstones, and I went straight to bed. This awful thing, this depression, hits you like a ton of bricks. One minute you're firing on all cylinders, the next minute you're catatonic.

By this time the secret was out about my precarious mental state, and friends and colleagues had started to call and commiserate. Diana Myers (my friend from Bhutan) phoned from Washington, but I could barely manage a coherent response. Another British friend named Juliet rang, saying, "I know you're not well. I had the same thing, but I found a cure." "What was that?" I said, desperate to know what had worked for her. "Well, I can't tell you that," she said and hung up. The woman was very competitive.

Then Carla Singer called from Los Angeles. She was a real friend, and was worried. "You've got to see this psychiatrist I know on Harley Street in London," she said. "He's brilliant." At this stage I was ready to try anyone, and so was John. We ended up going back to London just to see this man, my third shrink in six months. He was very stern, and rather expensive. He asked for the history of my psychiatric problem, and whether there was mental illness in my family. (I won't give his name: incredibly, he is still practising though he must be well into his eighties.)

When I finished, he held up one hand, like an Old Testament prophet.

"*You* have inherited a *tendency* for mental *instability* from your family, probably your mother," he intoned. "But you can live a *normal life*, if you take tricyclics." I had no idea what these were, but if I can go back to my normal happy, busy life, I'll take 'em. He gave me a renewable prescription for two drugs called imipramine and trimipramine. "They will take three weeks to have any effect," he said. In the meantime, I asked, what do I say to my employers, to explain my inability to work? Mental illness still carried a stigma.

"Oh, just tell them you've got hepatitis B," he said with a wave of his hand.

Hepatitis B? What the hell is he talking about? Is depression a possible symptom of hepatitis B? But armed with this latest medication, John took me back to Cyprus.

I stayed in bed for the better part of ten days, but within two weeks I felt myself again. We saw friends, and went swimming in our favourite secret coves. Since the psychiatrist claimed that I could live a "normal life" with these meds, I thought I could signal my availability to the ABC desk. Remarkably, ABC was happy to have me back on the roster again.

Within a week or so I was assigned to Moscow, again, to replace the permanent Moscow correspondent who was on vacation. I was thrilled to be back in harness and planned a number of feature reports. I suggested that John follow me (there are daily direct flights from Cyprus to Moscow) since he'd never been to Russia. Within a day of his arrival, I crashed. My brain went into neutral again. I couldn't write a script. I couldn't write the first line of a script. I think I claimed that I had an overpowering migraine, which seemed more sensible than saying I had hepatitis B. The symptoms of migraine and depression are quite similar. Splitting headache, intolerance of light, inability to concentrate, lack of motivation, and so on.

Clarkie happened to be in Moscow at the time and he covered for me. I was in a catatonic state again and couldn't get out of bed. ABC got a Washington-based correspondent to fly in and replace me. They booked me onto the next flight to Cyprus, with John. I was convinced that my career with ABC was over.

But John was determined that I *shall* get better. He called the London psychiatrist and made yet another appointment. We flew to the U.K. with hand-baggage only and went straight to his consulting rooms on Harley Street. We were his first appointment of the day. I was again in my zombie-like state. He started asking me questions, rapid-fire.

As soon as I opened my mouth to answer, one of his phones rang. He had at least three of them in his office. He answered it and talked for a few minutes. I resumed my answer to his first question, and another phone rang. He answered that call too. This happened for the entire consultation. His appointments secretary has phoned in sick, he said. (It seems he was too cheap to hire a temporary replacement.) After about the third phone call I showed some exasperation, or as much as I was capable of. I think he charged about £500 an hour.

"Oh, are you irritable? Do you have shortness of temper?" he cried as he reached for yet another ringing phone. By this time he was blinking wildly at me, as though he had a piece of soot in his eye.

His phones finally stopped ringing, and he gave me his full attention.

"Well, I really don't know what to do with you! I think you should have shock treatment." In the late nineties, shock treatment was used mainly in the case of suicidal patients or schizophrenia.

"There is no way I will have shock treatment, *ever*," I replied in a firm voice that I didn't think I possessed. John nodded in assent.

This brilliant psychiatrist was obviously annoyed with me. "Well I don't know, you can try this drug," he said, and gave me a prescription for Tegretol, medication mainly used for epileptics. We left his office without a word as he picked up another phone call.

"There is no way we will go back to this guy," I said to John as we walked along Harley Street. "He's as crazy as I am." I think we both managed a laugh.

These mood swings continued, in what the shrinks called "rapid cycling," for at least a year until John and I ended up in Washington, D.C. John was working on another book with Colin Smith, titled *War Without Hate*, about the North African campaign in the Second World War. As they'd done for their previous book, John focused on the character delineation—of the two opposing commanders, General Rommel and Field Marshal Montgomery—while Colin concentrated on the battles themselves. They both had research to do in the United States.

John and I stayed with my psychologist friend Jerilyn Ross and her husband, Ronnie Cohen, in their beautiful house in Potomac. Suddenly I started to feel yet another depression descending on me.

"Hil, this is treatable!" Jerilyn said in her wonderful, optimistic way. "I'm setting you up with a colleague at the National Institute of Health." Jerilyn had contacts everywhere.

This psychiatrist was tops in his field and had a completely different approach from the London shrink. (He was married to Dr. Kay Jamison, author of the best-selling memoir *An Unquiet Mind*, about her own moods and madness.) "Of course you shouldn't have shock treatment. I think you have a simple case of depression. The tricyclics that you were prescribed actually made your condition worse," he said. He suggested that I try lithium, the drug that has been in wide use since the fifties to treat depression and schizophrenia. My mother had been on lithium for years.

The possible side effects of lithium are pretty daunting. You can get hand tremors, diarrhea, lack of coordination, slurred speech, drowsiness, and weight gain. "Good lord, I can't risk those kinds of symptoms. I'll never work again," I said.

"Well, how much are you working now?" he asked pointedly. He told me to think about it, to continue taking the Tegretol (the epilepsy drug), and to keep in touch with him by email. That's an extremely generous offer for a psychiatrist to make to a mental patient.

But this ended up being a lifeline. With Dr. Jonathan Hunt's encouragement, I went back to see Peter Rowan at The Priory. His advice was very simple. "Try the lithium. You may not get any of those side effects. But if you do, you can just stop taking it and we will look for some other medication. But I think the American doctor may be right."

I started on low doses of lithium, which I took along with the Tegretol. I got better. I *stayed* better. The nightmare was finally over. I'm convinced that this awful period of depression was not an inherited mental illness, but the direct result of that fall on the head in 1997. A concussion, in other words. According to current definitions on the Internet (where else?), a concussion is a mild traumatic brain injury, whose symptoms *can often be delayed*. One of the symptoms is depression. A CAT scan does *not* always show concussion, and therefore is not good in diagnosing the injury. Rushing back into activities as soon as the symptoms have disappeared *can often bring them back again*.

Sir Winston Churchill suffered from depression, which he called The Black Dog. Whatever the cause of the great man's condition, *my* Black Dog, I am convinced, was caused by a concussion when I fell on my head on that fateful coastal walk in Cyprus in 1997. It was a mild, traumatic brain injury that had long-term effects, possibly exacerbated by psychiatric drugs. The wrong drugs. I finally got better, after three terrible years, thanks to a low dose of the right drugs. I've been stable ever since.

Stable? *Moi?* Well, up to a point.

46

ALL ROADS LEAD TO ROME

Through those three years of my Black Dog, ABC remained loyal to me. The London bureau chief, Rex Granum, would still assign me to stories that he thought I could handle. "You have a great reputation within ABC News for your strong reporting, resourcefulness and hard work," he wrote to me in a May 19, 1997, memo. "These minor situations are just a tiny blip on the road. Don't worry about them. Just get well, and get back to work."[1] I will never forget his kindness.

And there was Clarkie, constantly dreaming up ideas for us. By the year 2000, he had moved to Rome and was living above a bar in Trastevere. Whenever he went away on assignment, he'd just leave the key to his apartment with the bartender, in an act of great folly, I thought. One day while I was reading by our pool in Cyprus, he called with another Bright Idea.

"Listen, Hils. ABC doesn't have a reporter in Rome anymore, but there's still a bureau here with a manager and a camera team, and a producer, when I'm in town." (He was talking about the bubbly, bilingual Phoebe Natanson and ace camerawoman Jane Hartney.) "There are lots of good feature stories in Italy that we could do together. Not to mention the Pope. You could get an apartment here and become the de facto Rome correspondent. It shouldn't cost that much. I'll help you look for a place."

He touched a nerve with me, and it was fatal. I had never forgotten my great disappointment, seventeen years earlier, when ABC named me as their new Rome correspondent and then cancelled all foreign relocations two weeks before I was due to move to Rome with John and Jonathan. At the time I thought we would buy a villa in Tuscany and live there forever.

But wait! This could be my chance to recover that lost dream! We would keep our Cyprus house, of course. John could find some great Italian subject to write about for his next book! How about a biography of Garibaldi? Sophia Loren? t Anybody Italian! In the meantime, he had some research to do in Italy for *War Without Hate*. He could work on that! Clarkie had talked me into it. I started scheming immediately. I didn't bother to say anything to John.

To my surprise, John was not at all happy to hear about my plan to set up another residence in another country. He was especially cross that I hadn't even consulted him. He was right. It was monstrous, after everything he'd done for me in those awful three years of my Black Dog. Maybe I was still unstable? Throughout our married life John had always cared for me, done everything for me. He had also always let me have my way, even when he thought that what I was doing was crazy. Once again, he let me press on, alone, with my lunatic plan. I began to suspect that secretly he was glad that I'd be out of his hair so he could get on with his current book. He almost always dedicated his books to me. Though he once threatened that the dedication on his next biography should be changed to read: "To Hilary, without whose help this book would have been finished *three years ago.*" I left him in Cyprus, rather grumpy. We promised each other that we would meet in Rome once I was settled in.

A week or two later Clarkie called to say that a friend was giving up her penthouse apartment in Roma Antiqua. This is the heart of Old Rome. "Mamma mia! A miracle!" I viewed the apartment and took it on the spot. It was on the Campo de' Fiori, with a large terrace that looked down on the famous pedestrian piazza. The Campo de' Fiori is a lively market in the morning, a jumble of open-air trattorias and cafés in the daytime, and great place for the *passeggiata* in the evening. The flat was a fifteen-minute walk to the ABC office, past the glorious fountains of the Piazza Navona, past the great looming mass of the Pantheon, and past the Minerva church, where you could stroke its marble statues by Bernini and Michelangelo. I was sure John would change his mind and love it too.

He did love it, up to a point. A penthouse apartment is obviously at the top of the building. This particular building had no elevator. It was built in the seventeenth century, after all. You had to climb five flights of steep stairs to access the beautiful sunlit space. John said he would have a plaque made for the top landing saying, "John Bierman collapsed here in an attempt to visit Hilary Brown."

John never actually moved in to the Campo de' Fiori penthouse, though he came to stay a couple of times and completed his Italian research for *War Without Hate*. His first visit coincided with a visit from Gingie and her Italian American boyfriend, Tony de Vito, and we had a great time together exploring the ancient city and all its trattorias and bars. (Gingie was now divorced from Freddy, who remains one of her best friends.) In the early morning we would wake up to the sound of the fruit-and-vegetable sellers setting up their umbrellas for the morning market. In a complete break with Italian custom, the vendors didn't shout back and forth as most merchants do. They were required *not* to make a noise and disturb the residents of the district. What you heard was a soft, *click-click-clicking* sound as they quietly set up their stalls just before daybreak. It was magic.

Jonnie came out on one of his longer university holidays. He saw the Eternal City and then I took him to Venice and Capri so that he could tell his friends that he'd been to the three most famous, most fabulous spots in Italy.

Apart from John and Jonnie and Gingie, I had a fairly endless stream of visitors, some of them mere acquaintances. It's amazing how many friends you suddenly have when you're living in a penthouse apartment on a pedestrian piazza in one of the greatest cities on earth.

Clark and I did several feature pieces in the country, notably a ridiculous report on the bid by the Italian government to have Pizza declared a National Heritage Site. There is actually a Pizza Academy in Rome, where it takes *four months* to learn how to make a pizza margherita. Inevitably, we did a story on the Italian phenomenon of *mammismo*, which means "slavish mother love." Statistically, most Italian men live at home until they marry, which is usually around age thirty. During this entire time, their mothers continue to wash their clothes, cook their meals, make their beds, and look after them, just as they've always done since they were little boys. That's *mammismo*! After marriage, most Italian men return home at least once a week for the same kind of treatment. And if they divorce, many Italian men move *back* into the family home, for more slavish mother love. We shot the piece in the pretty Tuscan town of Perugia, with an attractive man of about thirty, along with his girlfriend. And his mother. We also featured a divorced senator who'd moved back in with Mama after his marital breakdown, shooting the interview with the senator and his mother sitting side by side. She interrupted him continually, telling him to pull up his socks, straighten his tie, comb away that stray hair, and so on. That's *mammismo*!

Everything was going according to plan. Then on the bright sunny morning of September 11, 2001, two hijacked U.S. airliners (American Airlines Flight 11 and United Airlines Flight 175) flew into the Twin Towers of the World Trade Centre, which collapsed in one hour and forty-two minutes. A third plane (American Airlines Flight 77) flew into the Pentagon. A fourth plane (United Airlines Flight 93) crashed into a field in Pennsylvania after a group of courageous passengers stormed the cockpit and attempted to overpower the hijackers. A total of 2,977 innocent people were killed, of which 200 fell or jumped to their deaths. Thousands were injured. In the rescue effort, 415 first responders lost their lives. Thousands of people suffered permanent respiratory ailments or cancer.

It was the single, deadliest terror attack in human history, and the first organized attack on American soil by foreigners since Pearl Harbor. It was quickly established that the coordinated attacks were carried out by nineteen militants of the terrorist group Al Qaeda. Fifteen of the militants came from Saudi Arabia. Peter Jennings was on the air, live, for almost forty-eight hours.

Within days the administration of U.S. President George W. Bush launched the War on Terror and the invasion of Afghanistan, home of the Saudi Arabian extremist Osama bin Laden, though Bin Laden didn't admit his responsibility for the attack until 2004. A native of Saudi Arabia, he had been living in Afghanistan with the blessing and the protection of the Islamic fundamentalist regime of the Taliban. On October 7, 2001, the war in Afghanistan started with the bombing of Al Qaeda camps and Taliban targets by a U.S.-led international coalition. A few weeks later, American troops recovered a videotape of Bin Laden and his co-conspirators, congratulating each other on the September 11 attacks with hugs and kisses in their mountain hideout. On December 7, 2001, the southern town of Kandahar fell to coalition forces, the government of the Taliban collapsed, and Taliban militants melted away into the mountains. We couldn't know then that the Afghan War would last for twenty years.

By the end of September, the world's press had converged on Pakistan, including me. We were all trying to get into Afghanistan, of course, but for weeks most of us were mainly doing rooftop journalism in the capital of Islamabad. That was with the exception of John Simpson of the BBC, who disguised himself as a woman by putting on a burka and crossing the border with his crew for just enough time to do an on-camera sign-off with an Afghanistan dateline (he obviously removed his burka). Since John is six-foot-four and weighs more than two hundred pounds, that was quite a feat.

I was soon transferred to the western city of Quetta, but not before I'd acquired a matched pair of spectacular Kochi tribal bangles from a local trader. Quetta is close to the border of Afghanistan and a popular rear base for Al Qaeda operatives. Of course we couldn't make direct contact with them. It would have been extremely dangerous to do so. (The story of Daniel Pearl of *The Wall Street Journal* became a cautionary tale. He had made contact with the militants in Karachi, was kidnapped, and then beheaded in February 2002.)

But we could safely meet Hamid Karzai, a former Afghan cabinet minister living in exile who was waiting to make his move into Afghanistan. (Karzai became interim leader of Afghanistan after the Americans put the Taliban to flight. He later became president and remained in office for more than ten years.) And while we couldn't get into Afghanistan, we could do stories about the huge Afghan refugee community in Pakistan, an estimated 2.5 million who'd been living in camps for more than a decade.

I was with one of my favourite cameramen, Doug Vogt, whom I'd last worked with in Bhutan. We pitched a story to *Nightline* on child labour among the Afghan refugee children. Child labour—*bad!* Right? That's what we thought. The children were working for eight hours a day in carpet factories, sitting at benches with no back support, tying woollen knots at the rate of ten knots a minute, with just one ten-minute break for lunch. They were as young as five, and most no older than twelve. They had exquisite faces. They were paid a pittance for this excruciating labour.

Yes, what a scandal. But they were then allowed to go to school for evening classes. For another four hours. All of them said they were very lucky to have this work, and that it made a big difference for them to learn to read and write, and to speak a little English. Because of their meagre earnings, their families could afford to eat meat once a week. It also meant a lot to them personally, the children said. They didn't want to be illiterate, like their parents.

We filmed the children working at their benches, tiny fingers flying non-stop for hours on end. And we followed them to school after their exhausting eight-hour shift and filmed their classwork. Their schoolbooks showed beautiful, careful penmanship, in English as well as in Pashto. The work was back-breaking and hard on their young eyes. But this kind of child labour was defended by an exiled Afghan human rights activist, Dr. Sima Samar. They were getting an education, and a possible future, she told us.

I loved this story, not just because the children were beautiful. I loved it because it was another example of how things aren't always black or white. Sometimes there are shades of grey. At first, we thought our story was going to be an exposé of the abuse of Afghan refugee children as virtual slave labour in Pakistani-owned carpet factories. But it wasn't quite that. The children actually competed for the work, they were paid, their families benefited, and they themselves got a primary education. Dr. Simar later became a cabinet minister in the new post-Taliban Afghan government.

Osama bin Laden remained in hiding in Afghanistan in spite of a U.S. bombing campaign over the Tora Bora mountains and its cave complex in the east of the country. Bin Laden was finally run to ground ten years later, shot dead in his fortified compound in Abbottabad, in Northern Pakistan in 2011, in a meticulously planned operation by the U.S. Navy SEALs Team Six, authorized by President Barack Obama.

I finally got into Afghanistan in January 2002 and for a few weeks was based in Kandahar. We had an Afghan security detail: a team of about eleven young men who were paid more money than they'd ever dreamed of. I wasn't quite sure just how well protected we were, however. One of our cameramen, Bartley Price, took them out to the desert one day for target practice. "They can't shoot straight, Hilly," he said, in his roundabout way. "If we get in a jam, we're fucked."

We lived and worked out of a large villa previously occupied by a relative of Bin Laden. That was the rumour anyway. It was next to a male *hamam*, or bathhouse, and this turned out to be terribly convenient. The women used the two bathrooms in the villa, and the men just used the *hamam* next door for their ablutions. In one of the weirdest arrangements I have ever experienced in the competitive TV news business, we shared this house with the opposition, CBS News. I actually shared a *room* with the CBS correspondent, Liz Palmer, who was another Canadian. It was very strange. I was supposed to share the room with my producer, Tina Babarovic, but we arranged that Tina should share with her own husband, Bartley Price. I'm not quite sure where Bartley's former male roommate slept, but it wasn't with Liz and me.

The ostensibly successful Afghan campaign by the United States in the fall and winter of 2001 meant that western journalists could move around relatively freely and talk to people. I didn't have to wear a headscarf. Some Afghan women were bareheaded too. This was an enormous relief after the oppressive years under the Taliban, where they had to be covered from head to toe. Little boys were flying kites again, a harmless sport that had been banned by the Taliban. People could play folk music, which had been forbidden for years. Men could be clean-shaven. There were no more public stonings or executions or amputations, of people accused of theft or adultery, in accordance with fundamentalist Sharia law. It seemed to be a happy, optimistic period.

Whenever we shot TV pictures on the street, we would instantly attract a mob of people. But it would be a curious mob, not hostile. The only way I could do my stand-ups without being swallowed up by the crowd was to get onto the back of one of our pickup trucks with a radio mic attached to my belt and lapel. Bartley would get onto the back of another pickup truck, and on his signal I would do my stand-up. It worked beautifully. The only problem was getting *onto* the truck, which was high off the ground. None of the males on our Afghan security team were willing to hoist me up (that would mean they would have to *touch a woman*, in public). So the crowd was routinely treated to the spectacle of a five-foot-ten blonde of a certain age hauling herself over the transom of a pickup, and collapsing in a heap on the other side.

We did stories on the opium trade—the opium poppy is an ideal crop in a war-torn country because it's cheap and quick to grow and is easily transported. The Taliban encouraged it and collected taxes on it. We did reports on the medieval conditions of life under the Taliban, on hyper-inflation, on the influence of warlords, on American aid efforts in the countryside, and so on. But my favourite was a report on the Afghan Olympic cycling team. This was an ABC exclusive, you understand. It was an exclusive because I was the only one to spot the five Olympic rings in the window of a run-down building in Kandahar.

"*Stop the car!*" I shout and our truck screeches to a halt. We scramble out and climb two flights of rickety stairs to a dimly lit room with two or three men in *shalwar kameez* hunched over a hot plate and a pot of tea.

"Does this, ah, office have anything to do with the Olympics?" I ask through our translator.

"Oh yes," they said, "we are the Olympic Committee of Kandahar."

"I see. What events are Afghan athletes competing in?"

"Cycling."

"Can we meet some of the cyclists?"

"Yes, there are two of them. One sells vegetables in the market. The other has a bicycle repair shop."

The committee is happy to take us to meet their two Olympic hopefuls, and we shoot great sequences in the market and in the bike shop. Then we go out to a road on the outskirts of town where the cyclists "train." They are riding the most clapped-out, rust-encrusted, ancient bicycles we've ever seen. They have no cycling gear, but at least they don't try to ride in their *shalwar kameez* (they wore jeans). They have a lot of spirit. Bartley spots a train of camels loping along the road and shoots a beautiful closing sequence of the boys pedalling behind, alongside, and past the camels, across a wild desert landscape. Bartley is not only a lot of fun on the road, he's pretty creative.

The piece was aired as a show-closer on *World News Tonight with Peter Jennings* and the reaction was instant. People called in, wanting to send the Afghan boys top-of-the-line cycling gear—jerseys and padded shorts and running shoes and helmets. The maker of competitive titanium road bikes wanted to send them two cycles worth $25,000 each. A Congressman planning a fact-finding trip to Afghanistan offered to hand-deliver all this stuff. The boys were thrilled, as you can imagine. I don't think they made it to the Olympics in Athens in 2004, however, and we didn't follow up. By then Afghanistan was on the back burner, news-wise. All eyes were on the American invasion of Iraq, and I was in Baghdad.

47

THE GREATEST GIFT OF ALL

With the attack on the World Trade Center and the invasion of Afghanistan, my dreams about being the de facto Rome correspondent went right out the window. New York wasn't interested in anything that wasn't related to the War on Terror. I don't think I spent more than a couple of months, in total, in my charming penthouse apartment on the Campo de' Fiori. Eventually I gave it up, with many backward glances.

I also gave it up because John had started to become ill. In all our thirty years of life together, I'd never known John to be sick, ever, except for a case of meningitis that lasted a couple of weeks. He was always a fine figure of a man: tall, straight, broad-shouldered, and with a permanent tan that often made me wonder whether he'd been entirely candid with me about his true ethnic origins. After a few hours in the sun he looked like an Aztec.

The last week in September 2001 was the time we'd planned to fly to Toronto with Jonathan for a twenty-fifth anniversary party that our friends were throwing for us. (Jonnie was at Durham University, happily reading History and Politics.) Gloria Bishop, Lindsay Dale-Harris, Krystyne Griffin, Noelle Grace, and Carla Singer had all got together to arrange it, and people were going to be flying in from the United States as well. But after the 9/11 terrorist attack, a party was out of the question. American airspace was closed to all international flights anyway. The gathering was postponed until spring 2002.

It was a wonderful party, starting with drinks and hors d'oeuvres at the Griffins' eclectic house in Rosedale and moving on to dinner in a cozy downtown restaurant that had been taken over for the occasion. But John wasn't looking well at all. He'd developed kidney failure, and doctors in both Cyprus and London had told him that the only answer was dialysis, three days a week, four hours a session, forever. A dialysis machine does the job of the defective kidneys, removing waste products and excess water from the body. John had a deep-rooted, philosophical objection to dialysis. He felt that this would no longer be living. It would be merely existing. Without telling me or Jonathan, John decided that he wasn't going to be tethered to a machine to stay alive. He'd let nature take its course.

That was before a number of doctors at the anniversary party in Toronto got hold of him. They took one look at him and said he should see a nephrologist in Toronto, immediately. He'd lost more than twenty pounds and was breathless and anemic. Gloria was now public affairs officer for the Toronto Health Network, and she set up a consultation with the director of the leading kidney clinic at Toronto General Hospital, two days after the party. I went with him.

The Canadian nephrologist was extremely cordial and open, not at all like the consultants John had seen in London. Tests showed that John's kidneys were only 15 percent effective, what they called "end stage renal failure." He said that without treatment John would have six months to live.

"Yes, you have kidney failure and dialysis is one way to treat it," the nephrologist said. "But have you ever thought of a living donor transplant, from a close relative?"

"No one ever suggested it, not even the high-priced doctors in Harley Street," John replied. "Anyway, I assume that I'm too old for a transplant." John was seventy-three.

"Absolutely not. You are in good health otherwise. Even at your age, a living donor is the best form of treatment, with a 95 percent success rate," the nephrologist said. "If you have a donor—your son, for example—we can set you up with tests tomorrow. If we have a good match, we would perform the transplant as soon as possible."

For John, the prospect seemed extraordinary, but out of the question. "I couldn't possibly ask my son to do a thing like that," John said. "I don't want to jeopardize his health or his life."

But the nephrologist persisted. He said that if one kidney is taken out of a healthy donor, the donor's second kidney takes over the work. "There is no risk to the donor," he said. "Thousands of people are walking around with just one functional kidney. The only precaution they must take is to avoid contact sports, such as boxing or rugby."

My immediate reaction was, "Oh no, don't take our son's kidney, take mine!" But the nephrologist said that generally the best match is from a blood relative. He suggested that we talk it over and come back and see him the next day.

John and I went to a coffee shop and talked it through. John said it was unfair to ask Jonathan. "He'll feel that he's backed into a corner, and then how could he say no?" John said. In spite of frequent personality clashes with his father, Jonnie had always been a loyal, loving son with a strong moral sense.

In the end, we decided to explain the situation to Jonnie that afternoon, knowing that he would never forgive us if we didn't share this critical moment of decision with him. We were all staying with Rupert Field-Marsham and Lindsay Dale-Harris in their pretty house on Roxborough Avenue. We sat down together in their garden. John repeated what the nephrologist had told him.

Jonnie didn't hesitate. "I'll do it, Dad."

John said he should think about it. But Jonnie was adamant. "I should be the living donor," he said. "They say it's a safe, proven operation. I *want* to give you one of my kidneys. I can save your life!"

He looked at us with his clear blue eyes, and with that direct, earnest expression he always had when he was serious about something. And he was really serious about this. We felt that if we were to try to talk him out of it, he would feel humiliated and put down. He later said that he thought it was the best possible thing he could do for his father, after all the love and support that his father had given him. He was twenty-two years old.

John and Jonnie did the tests and tissue-typing at Toronto General the next day, and they showed a near-perfect match. We made plans to fly back to Toronto from Cyprus in a month's time for the operation. Jonnie would fly direct from the U.K. We put down a deposit—at the time, Ontario hospitals would perform surgery on foreign patients for a fee. (John was British.) In the meantime, I would look for an apartment in Toronto: we would need to stay at least six weeks for his convalescence.

On our return to Cyprus, John decided to contact the Cypriot nephrologist who'd told him that dialysis was the only possible treatment for his condition. "Well, if you *want* to do that, there *is* a clinic in Nicosia that has been doing living donor transplants successfully for twenty years. I didn't tell you about it because I thought you were too old."

Thank you very much. We checked out the clinic, which was the internationally recognized Transplant Centre called the Paraskaveidon, staffed by a team of American-trained Cypriot doctors. It was funded by a private donor, and it had a good reputation. People came from all over the Middle East to be treated. We decided that John would have a much better chance of a good convalescence in his own home in Cyprus, rather than in a cramped rented apartment in Toronto. In a cordial exchange of emails, the Toronto doctors agreed. Jonnie was happy about this arrangement too. He liked our house in Cyprus and could invite his girlfriend to visit us after the transplant.

So it was that on August 2, 2002, the two most important men in my life went under the knife together in a private operating theatre in Nicosia. Dr. George Kyriakides was the lead surgeon. He made an incision into the lower part of John's abdomen and placed one of Jonnie's kidneys (removed by a second surgeon) inside John's body, attaching the blood vessels of the new kidney and connecting the new kidney's ureter to John's bladder. John's own defective kidneys were left inside his body. I think the operation took three hours. That's what it felt like anyway, as I paced up and down in the waiting room. Jonnie said he felt nervous only ten minutes before they were wheeled into the operating theatre. But he took John's hand, and father and son wished each other "good luck!" before they went under the anaesthetic.

Afterwards both patients were wheeled into the intensive care ward together, both of them crying out in pain. I was allowed into the ward, without any protective clothing or mask. I didn't know who to comfort first. I shouldn't really have been allowed to touch either of them.

Soon after they were each given a jab of pethidine in the backside and they both fell asleep, while I went back to the waiting room, wringing my hands. You place such enormous faith in doctors, since you know nothing and they know everything. But you have this awful moment of doubt, and that definitely hit me on that hot August afternoon. I recorded an interview with them the next day, and while John said he felt absolutely fine, Jonnie's wry comment was "I'm not sure I would have done this if I knew it would be so painful." He didn't mean that, of course. But much later he confessed that the pain had been excruciating, the worst he'd ever known. Three months later our friend Christine Doyle, medical correspondent for *The Daily Telegraph*, did a two-page spread on the procedure that she headlined "the greatest gift of all." Living donor kidney transplants were not then widely practised in the United Kingdom. Christine thought they should be. There was a big photo of John and Jonnie, sitting in our communal garden in Holland Park, plus my photo of Jonnie in hospital, pointing to his scar (it went right across his middle). Christine also managed to mention John's upcoming book, *War Without Hate*, and my war reports from Vietnam for ABC. What a star! But my favourite line was a quote from Jonnie, my courageous son, my Beamish Boy:

"I feel lucky to be able to do this," he said. "It's the most meaningful thing I've done in my life so far."[1]

John had a very good convalescence in the home he loved so much, in the company of his beloved son (who recovered in record time), and his incompetent, merciless wife with her Nurse Ratched approach to caregiving. Fortunately, he also had the services of a real nurse, a lovely Welsh woman called Jean Sanford, to whom he became very attached. We had great difficulty getting Sister Jean to submit a bill. Jonnie's pretty girlfriend Hannah Spencer came out from England to see him, which is probably why he recovered so quickly. For two weeks he was doubled over as he walked around the house and garden, but by the time Hannah arrived he was upright and felt fine. He was just upset when the huge scar around his middle began to fade. His friends always made him show off his incision in the pub, and as it faded, he talked wistfully about having it tattooed back on.

John had to take immuno-suppressant drugs for the rest of his life, to keep his immune system from attacking and rejecting his son's kidney. The side effect was that he lost his taste for wine and spirits, completely. This civilized, sophisticated Englishman—who would often take a beer at lunch, a gin and tonic before dinner, half a bottle of wine with his evening meal, and possibly a shot of brandy before bed—would forever more sit down to a frugal glass of Perrier or lemonade with his food. He became as slim as he was the day I met him, with an enormous scar across his torso, oddly enough in the shape of a J. Ten weeks after the transplant, he and Colin Smith went on a book tour across England to promote *War Without Hate*. This included a great double-act at the prestigious Hay-on-Wye Festival. As a veteran BBC broadcaster, John was a very good speaker. So was Colin. They were especially chuffed after a rave review in *The Daily Telegraph* by the military historian John Keegan. "Few historians write as fluently as Bierman or Smith do; few journalists achieve their standards of accuracy," wrote Keegan.[2] I was so proud of them.

Jonnie's gift of life to his father gave John a new lease on life. We were all so grateful to our Canadian friends, and to the Canadian and Cypriot doctors, for making this transplant happen. But what mattered most to John was the great bond that developed with Jonnie. They got on well together, most of the time, but after the operation there was something almost spiritual about his attachment to his youngest child.

"Now there's a piece of him that will go with me to my grave," he said. Jonnie had the same deep feelings. "Dad once told me that gentlemen of his era tend to keep their emotions on the inside," he said. "I'm incredibly grateful that by giving him a kidney, I have not only prolonged his life, but that we're so much more affectionate and loving toward each other."

John was always the Tough Guy, on the surface. Underneath, he was a Softie. By this time, Jonnie had graduated from Durham University and was working in London, but he would visit us in Cyprus as often as he could. Whenever he said goodbye, John would hug him, again and again, and then look away, to hide his tears.

48

IRAQ, AND MY LOVE IS GONE

In spite of the quick victory against the Taliban in Afghanistan in October 2001, a decision was made within the Bush Administration to begin building up for an all-out invasion of Iraq. Having tried to place the blame for the 9/11 attacks on Saddam Hussein (though Saddam's regime was a secular dictatorship and opposed to Al Qaeda), the administration claimed that Saddam posed a threat because he still had weapons of mass destruction. This was a lie. The American bombing of Iraq during the 1991 war destroyed Saddam's nuclear weapons infrastructure, which had not been rebuilt. Subsequent UN inspections found nothing. But never mind, the intelligence was distorted by Bush and the neo-conservatives who seemed to have taken over foreign policy: Vice President Dick Cheney; Deputy Secretary of Defense Paul Wolfowitz; and Defense Policy Board Chairman Richard Perle (a.k.a. the Prince of Darkness). They were supported in this assertion by British Prime Minister Tony Blair, whose government issued a paper (known as the Dodgy Dossier) that claimed Saddam still possessed weapons of mass destruction and had reconstituted his nuclear weapons program. The American public initially supported the invasion—the Administration said basically that to oppose it would be tantamount to treason. Almost no one dared to speak against it, with the notable exception of Senators Bernie Sanders and Barack Obama.

But the British public was overwhelmingly against an invasion and in February 2003 staged one of the largest demonstrations ever seen in London, with an estimated one million people gathered in Hyde Park carrying signs reading, "Not in My Name." British Foreign Secretary Robin Cook resigned, writing in his book, *The Point of Departure*, that Blair supported the invasion because he believed that, above all, you had to stay "in" with the Americans.

The great American investigative reporter Seymour Hersh wrote in his memoir *Reporter* that the U.S. neo-cons wanted to impose a *Pax Americana* on the entire Mid-East region, and that this was the real reason for the invasion of Iraq. In his book, Hersh says that he obtained (from a foreign intelligence source) a copy of a Republican neo-con plan for American dominance of the Middle East. "The document declared that the war to reshape the Middle East had to begin 'with the assault on Iraq. The fundamental reason for this . . . is that the war will start making the U.S. the hegemon of the Middle East.' . . . '*Pax Americana* is on its way.'" Hersh says that he and his source both agreed that America's neo-cons were a "menace to civilization."[1]

Paul Wolfowitz initially claimed that the invasion would pay for itself, though in an interview in 2013 he conceded that the campaign plunged Iraq into a cycle of violence that spiralled out of control. Cheney still insists that the invasion was the right thing to do. According to the think tank Foreign Policy in Focus, the War on Terror cost $5.6 trillion from 2001 to 2018 (the fifteenth anniversary of the invasion of Iraq). That is $24,000 for every taxpayer in America. It led to a vicious civil war between Shia and Sunnis, and the death of at least two hundred thousand Iraqi civilians, according to Iraq Body Count. Other estimates put that death toll at over a million Iraqis. More than forty-four hundred American soldiers died. Three million Iraqi civilians were made homeless.

I didn't have what reporters call a Good War. I was sent to Turkey in late February 2003, where the U.S. expected to deploy its 4th Armored Division to join the attack on Iraq from the West. Turkey wisely refused to allow U.S. troops on its territory. I went in with Patrick Etcheverry (now a cameraman), but we were rebased within a week.

The war went badly anyway and very soon became an Occupation, not a Liberation. Resistance began to grow, and U.S. troops became extremely unpopular. They carried out house raids, seized people's money, harassed people at checkpoints, arrested civilians by the thousands, imprisoned and tortured them. They outlawed the Ba'ath Party and decommissioned every officer in the armed forces, earning the enduring enmity of the officer class. Along with every other major news organization, ABC set up a bureau in Baghdad and covered the story daily. Reporters, camera crews, and producers were rotated in and out, including me. In the first eighteen months, it was possible to move around the city and the countryside with a TV crew, plus an escort of retired British SAS (Special Air Service) soldiers who were making a fortune providing security. I think they were paid something like $500 a day. Most of them were compact, super-fit, super-tough men who were Trained Killers, basically. We called them TKs and we were very happy to have their protection. We did stories on the de-Ba'athification of the Iraqi Army, the sacking of the National Museum of Iraq, the growing despair and destitution of the Iraqi officer corps, who were left without jobs. We did feature stories, such as the Baghdad-to-Basra "Express," which moved so slowly that our cameraman, Doug Vogt, was able to hop on and off the train and follow it in our Land Rover for cutaway shots as it crawled south across the desert. It was one of my favourite pieces—we just interviewed people on the train and asked them why they were travelling, giving a slice-of-life look at ordinary Iraqis, before their country degenerated into civil war.

Within three years, there were daily sectarian killings between Sunnis and Shias, where victims as young as twelve would be dumped in the street, their tortured bodies covered in welts and lacerations and bruises, with a single shot in the head. Often their relatives would be too terrified to take away the corpse, afraid that they too would be captured and killed. And there were kidnappings, of westerners and Iraqis alike. Many westerners were killed in gruesome executions that were videotaped and posted online. ABC put its reporters in a lockdown mode; we lived behind twenty-foot blast walls and concertina wire and only went out when the TKs said it was safe to do so. If we did go out, we couldn't stay in one place for more than fifteen minutes because of the risk of kidnapping. Most of our reports were conducted on the roof of the villa where we lived and worked: the video material was gathered by Iraqi cameramen and producers. I didn't feel good about this at all. Especially after one of our cameramen, a great guy named Aladdin, was ambushed and shot dead with his soundman as they left the bureau one evening, killed because they were working for the Americans.

It was during this period that John's health began to deteriorate again. In the summer of 2004, he had a mild heart attack, caused by a leaking heart valve. It was replaced with a pig's valve. But within a few months the doctors said that he'd have to have a heart bypass.

There was a clinic in Nicosia that specialized in open-heart surgery, with surgeons trained in the United States. Like the transplant clinic, it attracted patients from around the Middle East. Already on a chemical cocktail of pills for the kidney transplant, John accepted the inevitability of another major operation. I remember sitting with him in hospital the night before the surgery, in early winter 2004. He was in a striped dressing gown, his tanned limbs hanging over the side of the bed and he looked almost debonair, like a character in a Noel Coward play. He expected to survive the operation, just as he'd survived the transplant of Jonnie's kidney two years before.

The operation itself went well. Though in subsequent weeks and months, the patient suffered terribly. On Boxing Day 2004, ABC called me to say there had been a huge tsunami across a half-dozen countries in Asia, and could I fly to Sri Lanka with Bartley Price to cover it? I wanted to go, but I felt I couldn't leave John in his fragile state for an open-ended assignment, even though he had Sister Jean for a few hours each day, and our Sri Lankan houseboy called Jayantha. I don't regret missing the huge tsunami story. John needed me. He wasn't given effective medication for the enormous post-operative pain. He developed an infection from the heart bypass. He had to have a pacemaker installed. He had a prostate operation. He was prescribed a dizzying list of drugs, adding to those he already had to take. He said he felt like a walking pharmacy. He developed a mysterious neurological condition that affected his shoulders and arms. If I touched him, he would jump. He lost even more weight. But he still stood tall, and though he used a cane, he never stooped. He kept his tan. People would visit him and say how well he looked, which used to annoy him. "I don't *feel* well *at all*," he would say.

As Shakespeare wrote, "When sorrows come, they come not single spies, but in battalions."[2] And so it was that in the second month of 2005, our *annus horribilis*, I got the news that my father was dying. Since Mum's death in 1997, Dad had been living independently in their house outside Geneva, taking trips to Canada to visit Gingie and Kathy, and to Cyprus to see me. But at the age of ninety, he fell and broke his hip. He survived the hip replacement operation, but his mind—that brilliant, steel-trap mind—suddenly started to deteriorate. Gingie and I had to move him into a Residence. Gingie found a beautiful place with a view of Lake Geneva, but he hated it there. He was now an invalid, completely dependent on others. His long, useful, active life had become a Calvary. Ginge and I would take turns visiting him, flying in from Canada or Cyprus or London. We tried to see him once a month. Then we got a call from the director of the residence saying that Dad was sinking fast. If we wanted to say goodbye to him, we should come quickly.

I flew to Geneva (leaving John with Jay and Sister Jean), met Gingie, and together we went out to Dad's residence to be with him in his final days. The director found rooms for us close to his suite. I'm not sure he even knew we were there. He was conscious, but he was staring into space, speechless. We talked to him and stroked his arm. In the end he was in terrible pain, crying out, "Oh please, oh please!" as the nurse gave him more morphine. On February 17, 2005, my beloved father died. He had given us everything. In early May we organized a memorial service for him in the Parish Church of St. John-at-Hampstead, in Church Row, the very church where he and Mum were married sixty-seven years before. In my eulogy, which was a tribute to both my parents, I recited my favourite lines from Shakespeare, about life . . . and death:

> "Fear no more the heat o' the sun,
> Nor the furious winter's rages;
> Thou thy worldly task hast done,
> Home art gone, and ta'en thy wages:
> Golden lads and girls all must,
> As chimney-sweepers, come to dust."³

Through his last period of illness John was still writing. Writing, as he always said, was his life, and he would do it until his dying day. After the kidney transplant, he'd researched, wrote, and published the Penguin-commissioned biography of Laszlo Almasy, the real English Patient, in less than three years. Almasy was a homosexual Hungarian aristocrat who worked as a geographer and desert explorer in Egypt in the years before the Second World War. When war broke out, he worked for the German Intelligence Service. Initially John didn't want to take on the commission. He didn't want to appear to be riding on the coat-tails of Michael Ondaatje's best-selling novel, *The English Patient*. We knew Michael a little, since he lives in Toronto. John's biography was published in 2004.

After the heart bypass, John felt that he couldn't take on another biography because he was too weak to travel. So he started a novel titled "Guttersnipes," set in the East End of London and loosely based on the life of his mother, Bessie. A kind of Becky Sharp story, as in Thackeray's *Vanity Fair*. He had extraordinary recall of the details of life in the East End of London in the thirties and had an endless repertoire of truly terrible music-hall songs. His first four chapters were lively and picaresque, with well-drawn characters and a good plot line. John was an author who always left you wanting to know what happens next. But then the chapters stopped.

Just after Christmas in 2005, ABC asked if I could do a few weeks of bureau duty in London. John seemed to be getting better: my niece Karina had come from the States to see him in October (she was a favourite). Jonnie had come out from London for a happy family Christmas. John still had Sister Jean and Jayantha, he had his music, and his books. "I'll be fine, darling. You go," he said. Jonnie and I flew to the U.K. together.

Five days later, John's doctor, a compassionate man named Kondozis, called me in London to say that John had suffered a minor stroke and that he was in the clinic in Paphos. He was not incapacitated in any way, he said, but he thought he should be watched for a couple of days. I called John immediately. He sounded exactly the same: his beautiful baritone voice hadn't changed, he was feeling absolutely fine; he said, "You carry on with your assignment in London, darling. I'll just spend the weekend here at the clinic. It's my second home anyway." I was reassured, and we talked for a long time, gossiping happily about this and that. Then as we were about to hang up, I said something that we rarely said to each other on the telephone.

"Goodbye, darling. I do love you."

"I love you too, babe," John replied.

As it turned out, those were the last words that he ever spoke to me.

Twelve hours later, as I was sitting down to a New Year's Eve dinner with Bartley's wife, Tina, I got another call from Dr. Kondozis. "John has had a massive stroke," he said. "He is still alive, but he is paralyzed down one side and can't speak."

ABC put me on the next plane to Cyprus. Sister Jean and her husband, Geoff Sanford, met me at the airport and took me straight to the clinic. For the entire four-hour flight, I was praying, literally praying, that John would wait for me. I knew that in the past year he'd had a strong intimation of his own mortality. "I'm not afraid to die," he had once said as we sat together on our terrace, looking out to sea. "I just don't want to die alone."

I couldn't get those words out of my head. "Please wait for me, John! I'm on my way! You won't die alone!" I repeated this to myself over and over again, right up until the moment that Jean and Geoff led me into John's hospital room.

He was lying on the bed with a dozen tubes coming out of him, but his eyes were open. I bent over him. "I'm here, darling, I'm here!" He knew it was me. I know that because with his good hand he reached up, pulled my face down close to his, and kissed me.

Dr. Kondozis and I both knew that John did not want to be kept alive. "If I ever lose my faculties, Hilly, I want you to put me down!" John had said to me, many times. He'd had a similar discussion with his doctor. Lying there helpless on that hospital bed, with one paralyzed leg slipping off the side, John kept pointing to the floor with his good arm. At first I thought he'd dropped something that he wanted me to pick up. He tried to speak, but only animal noises came out of his mouth. Then I realized that he was saying he wanted to be under the ground, six feet under, in his grave.

I asked him if he wanted his children to come out to Cyprus to see him. He drew his good hand across his body in a gesture he often used when he meant "absolutely not." Did he want to see Jonnie, his youngest child, who had saved his life only three years before? Again, the same negative gesture. I think he didn't want his children to see him in his debilitated state. In the case of Jonnie, he knew it would upset him terribly. It would upset them both.

It is very strange to find yourself wanting the love of your life to be allowed to die. But that's how I felt, knowing that this is what John himself wanted. I stayed with him in that hospital room for three nights and three days, listening to his laboured breathing. His paralyzed leg kept slipping off the bed and I kept getting up to put it back under the covers. I wanted to get into bed with him, but it wasn't big enough for both of us.

On January 4, 2006, my handsome, talented, loving, loyal husband drew his last breath. He was not alone.

My great friend Gilly Rich had come up from her house in Limassol to stay with me through this awful period, helping with the funeral arrangements and sending out the death notice. She manned the phone when the calls started coming in. When you are bereft, you are physically and emotionally drained. I was so grateful to her.

I had called my sister-in-law in London (the other Hilary Bierman), asking her to invite Jonnie to her house for dinner. I would then call him and break the news. I wanted Jonnie to hear the news in the company of someone he knew and loved. With my sister-in-law sitting beside him, Jonnie took my call. I told him his father was gone, that he hadn't wanted his favourite child to see him in such a helpless state. We had a pretty emotional exchange. Jonnie got on a plane for Cyprus the next day.

Apart from calls from friends all over the world, there were calls from *The Times*, *The Guardian*, and *The Daily Telegraph*, all wanting to do major obituaries. Sandra Martin of *The Globe and Mail* also called. The British obits were all written by friends of John, fellow hacks and all beautiful writers: Colin Smith, Robert Chesshyre, and Ronnie Payne. Jonnie emailed pictures to all the papers, and then helped me write and print the order of service for the funeral. It included my favourite picture of John, on the terrace of our house in Persia, reading the reviews of his first book with a glass of wine in his hand, eating caviar and grinning from ear to ear.

The funeral on January 14, 2006, was in an ancient Byzantine church set among Roman ruins in the old section of Paphos. I picked flowers from our garden and placed them on his coffin. Many people came, including a lot of cameramen from Nicosia whom John had worked with when he was making documentaries. Gingie came all the way from Canada. Colin gave a moving eulogy, Jonnie read those lovely lines from Shakespeare ("Fear no more the heat o' the sun"[4]), and I gave a tribute. "John was everything to me," I said, borrowing those great lines from W.H. Auden. "'He was my North, my South, my East and West. My working week, and my Sunday rest.'[5] He was my lover, my teacher, my protector, and my best friend. He will live on in my heart forever, until I, too, am no more."[6]

The reception was at our house, Calypso, with food brought by our friends, and as it was a fine day we all sat outside on the terrace and enjoyed the view. John absolutely loved that house and always said he would only leave it "feet first." He was buried in the cemetery of a Latin church in a nearby village. I didn't tell the priest that John was actually an atheist, and a Jew. Later I found the perfect inscription for his headstone. It came from a poem by Hafez, the fourteenth-century Persian poet, translated by Gertrude Bell. Since John and I had started our long and happy life together in Persia, it seemed just right.

> "Light of mine eyes and harvest of my heart,
> And mine at least in changeless memory,
> Ah, when he found it easy to depart,
> He left the harder pilgrimage to me!"[7]

For me, losing John was like losing a limb. I found it very difficult to live alone in our house. There were too many ghosts. Jonnie flew back to London, and Gingie insisted that we go to Zermatt for a few days of skiing. That did me so much good, and I loved her for that. But when I got back to Calypso, I simply didn't know where to put myself. I couldn't sleep in our room, so I slept in the cot in John's study. But then I would just stare at his empty desk, sobbing. Of course, my friends were all very sympathetic. I even got some long emails from Kayce Freed, Peter Jennings's widow. Peter had died of lung cancer only six months before, in August 2005. (ABC flew me to New York for his memorial service.)

On January 7, three days after John's death, Kayce wrote:

> "I wish there was something more I could do or say. . . . There are moments now, not often, but there are moments when the memories are happy and make me laugh. And when that happens, for those short moments, I'm back with Peter again and there is joy. I wish for you many of those moments."[8]

I wrote back:

> "I find one has this strange defense mechanism that does *not* allow me to think about how he looked and sounded when I was at his bedside at the end of his life, or how he looked and sounded in his prime. Do you experience this? You just tick over, and do all the tiresome administrative things you have to do. Then you find yourself weeping without warning. In the dentist's chair, for example."[9]

Kayce and I carried on this correspondence for several months after John's death. I called it "Widows Anonymous."

What also meant a lot was the memorial service I arranged for John in London in June, at St. James' Church in Holland Park. More friends and relatives came, from all over the U.S., Canada, Britain, even Turkey. Karen Akers sang the Hoagy Carmichael classic "I Get Along Without You Very Well." Jonnie's friend Gwyneth Herbert, a successful jazz singer, sang "Please Don't Talk About Me When I'm Gone." I had an organist and classically trained choir. I had three eulogies, for the three periods in John's professional life. Jonathan and Richard read out loud. Karina read her Ode to a Favourite Uncle. And I gave another tribute. "John always told me he wanted to be buried in a cardboard box, without ceremony," I said. "So true to my custom over thirty years of marriage, I listened very nicely, and then planned to do things . . . my way."[10] John would have been pleased, in spite of himself.

By then I had closed up the cottage in Cyprus and moved into my flat in London. (Carla had sold out her share and it was mine alone.) And by then Clarkie was on my case.

"Hils, you can't mope around. You've just got to get back to work. You should go to Iraq. I'm putting you on the roster."

It wasn't long before I was on my way to Baghdad, in early spring 2006. It's very difficult to feel sorry for yourself when all around you people are getting blown up and kidnapped and tortured and killed every day of the week. Though we were mainly on lockdown, confined to our compound behind twenty-foot blast walls, we were busy all the time, filing to the morning and evening shows, the webcast, radio, and other platforms. Sometimes we would set up an embed with the U.S. military, and occasionally we could venture out to do a story if our ex-SAS bodyguards thought it was safe. For the next few years, I became one of the regular correspondents who ABC rotated in and out of Iraq. I was very chuffed when I received a herogram from the then president of ABC News, David Westin, dated April 16, 2007.

> "You've done again, superb work for us in Iraq. You must know, but should hear, how good it is back here in the States to look up and see such a strong professional reporting for us from the field. Thank you very much, and congratulations."[11]

Okay, I didn't get an *Emmy*. But of course I framed this and placed it in my living room where no one notices it (right next to the other unnoticed herogram of 2011 from Howard Bernstein).

By this time a great number of journalists working for the American networks in Iraq had been killed or severely injured. When the U.S. withdrew all combat forces in 2011, at least one hundred and fifty journalists and fifty-four media support workers had lost their lives covering the conflict. In May 2006, CBS cameraman Paul Douglas was killed by a car bomb along with his soundman, James Brolan. They were on an embed with the U.S. 4th Infantry Division when their convoy stopped at a checkpoint in a middle-class shopping district of Baghdad. Their correspondent, Kimberly Dozier, was critically injured. We heard the blast from our compound, which was less than a kilometre away. Explosions were common in the city, but within minutes we'd learned that this time our colleagues were among the dead. I remember thinking, hoping, that Paul and James were killed instantly (I knew them both), that they didn't survive long enough to suffer the terrible pain of their wounds. I reported the details of the attack from my rooftop position, with the knowledge that "there but for the grace of God go I."

Only four months earlier, in January 2006, an ABC team was hit by a roadside bomb while travelling in an Iraqi tank in Baghdad. The correspondent, Bob Woodruff, and his cameraman, Doug Vogt, had put their heads through the hatch to do a piece to camera. Then the bomb went off. Although both men were wearing helmets and body armour, Bob suffered a traumatic brain injury and Doug a crushed skull. Both had surgery in Iraq and were transferred to the same hospital in the U.S. Bob was put into an induced coma for more than five weeks and took months to recover. Doug, too, took a long time to recuperate. One of the best in the business (he won six Emmys for his work), Doug retired from war coverage and moved with his family to France. Bob and his wife, Lee, were so grateful for the care that Bob received in the Shock-Trauma Unit of the U.S. Air Force hospital in Iraq, and later at the National Naval Medical Center in Bethesda, Maryland, that they set up the Bob Woodruff Foundation. This was to help the tens of thousands of U.S. soldiers who also suffered traumatic brain injuries in Iraq, but who, unlike Bob, had little assistance in adjusting to their terrible disabilities once they were sent home. Bob went on to produce and present many award-winning documentaries for ABC. But I suspect that he regards the Woodruff Foundation as his best work.

49

REGENERATION

I think it was General Douglas MacArthur who once said, "Old soldiers never die, they just fade away." (He was actually quoting a barrack-room ballad.) That was the way I felt when my career as a TV foreign correspondent finally came to an end. My ambition was to keep working until the age of seventy. That might be a record of sorts, wouldn't it? I almost made it. My last story was shot in Australia and Indonesia in September 2009, with cameraman Bartley Price, one of my favourites. It was an anniversary piece, to focus on the survivors of the great tsunami on Boxing Day 2004 (the deadliest in recorded history, which killed more than 227,000 people in fourteen countries) and the terrorist attacks in Bali, Indonesia, on October 2002, which killed 202 people.

First, we went to Banda Aceh, on the island of Sumatra in Indonesia, which had the largest single number of tsunami victims. This included the entire family of a five-year-old girl who had survived but was so traumatized that she lost the power of speech. Bartley had filmed her in 2004, and five years later we found her and filmed her again, telling her story of survival (she had recovered her voice). Then we went to Australia, where the surviving members of the Coogee Dolphins rugby team continued to play and compete in memory of the six teammates they'd lost in the Bali bombings.

The trip was not without its embarrassing moment. Embarrassing to Ms. Brown, I mean. When we checked in for our flight to Sumatra at the Singapore airport, the check-in clerk of Indonesia Airways refused to let me board because I "didn't have enough room in my U.K. passport for a visa" (you can get visas on arrival in Jakarta).

"But there is *one full page* left in my passport!" I cried. "*And* space on the previous page too!" That was not enough, he said impassively. Indonesia requires two complete empty pages. (I obviously had quite a lot of stamps in my passport.) "Okay, what about my Canadian passport? I have dual nationality!" I cried in mounting panic. I always carried both passports on assignment. He examined it. "It expires in five months. It needs to be valid for six full months." Bartley and I looked at each other in horror. We agreed that he should board the flight and start shooting the story in Banda Aceh while I tried to get an emergency passport from the U.K. or Canadian embassies in Singapore. "Don't worry, Hilly," Bartley said. "No one needs to know. Road rules." I got an emergency British passport two days later and caught up with him. So on her last assignment for ABC News, Brown had broken one of the cardinal rules for foreign correspondents: always carry a valid passport with at least four empty pages.

Our story aired on December 26, 2009, on *Good Morning America*. I was in Stowe, Vermont, celebrating Christmas with Gingie, Karina, and Jonathan. Though we were all hung over from Christmas dinner the night before, I made them get up to watch it. They weren't that impressed, especially Gingie, who never watches TV news anyway, preferring to listen to NPR (National Public Radio). But New York liked it, notably the senior producer, Richard Morse (now a vice president at CNN), and that's all that mattered. I had a feeling this was going to be my last hurrah. ABC was on an economy drive and by early 2009 had made deep staff cuts in its large London bureau. They had not renewed my last three-year contract: I was working on an ad hoc basis, though I still had a desk and an ABC mobile phone. I wasn't getting any big assignments, and after a few months the acting bureau chief, Robin Wiener, said I should probably hand in the phone. I was sixty-nine. I was still invited to office parties and included in all-girl lunches or dinners, especially with those I called my daughter substitutes—Lama Hasan, Sonia Gallego, and Zoe Magee—but there was no official farewell and I didn't want one anyway. It's better to fade away than be the guest of honour at an Old Trout's Goodbye Party.

Then Jonnie decided that he wanted to start a new life in Vancouver. He had dual nationality so there was no problem with immigration. Ever since we'd taken him skiing in Whistler as a child he'd fantasized about the Great Canadian West. My cousin Dr. Chris Hunt (twin brother of Dr. Jonathan Hunt), an immensely kind and hospitable man (with a kind and hospitable wife, Lydia), offered to put him up until he found his feet. Jonnie and I had been living under the same roof in London since John's death in 2006, in my garden flat. It was the first time that we'd lived together since he went off to boarding school at age fourteen, and of course I treasured every moment of it, inflicting lashings of *mammismo* on him whenever I was back from a foreign assignment. We even did a foreign assignment together in Argentina, while visiting Gilly and Sebastian Rich and their daughter Sabina (they had recently settled there). ABC gave Jonnie a camera (thanks to Robin Wiener, he'd got a job with ABC London as an associate producer) and we did a few feature stories together: on the tango halls of Buenos Aires (the *milongas*), tourism in Iguazu Falls, and graffiti art in the capital. He was a delightful and protective travel companion, and it was a pleasure to work with him. He was big and strong and good-looking and could shoot straight. He handled people beautifully whenever we got into a tight spot. We edited the pieces together back in London.

So my heart was broken when he packed up his belongings and walked out the door. "I don't want you to come to the airport, Mum," he said. "You'll only burst into tears and then I might cry too. You can come and see me in Vancouver once I'm settled." His great friend Gwyn Herbert (the jazz singer) came by to collect him on that bright November morning in 2009. I gave him a huge hug and then stood by my front gate and watched him stride down the street to her car, a duffle bag on each shoulder, so tall and straight and hopeful. I was shattered.

Friendship is my substitute for religion, along with a certain amount of ancestor worship. For the next two years, I went on a succession of pilgrimages, seeing much-loved friends and relatives in England and abroad. I went sailing in the Mediterranean with Krystyne and Scott Griffin on their beautiful sloop *Thyateira*. They kept inviting me, again and again, and our voyages were unforgettable. We sailed the Aegean Coast of Turkey, the Greek Islands, the Adriatic Coast of Croatia and Montenegro, all places of staggering beauty. Often once we had dropped anchor in a secluded cove, Scott would sit on deck, throw back his head, and recite great chunks of poetry into the starlit sky. (He founded the Griffin Poetry Prize, the most distinguished poetry prize in the world.)

I saw various friends in France: Sue and Ian Cameron in the Dordogne, and my lovely cousin Gilly Richards in her family farmhouse nearby. I stayed with Lydia O'Ryan in her house near St. Tropez. I flew to Rome for my seventieth birthday with Clarkie. He arranged a jolly lunch in a cozy trattoria, and the next day I went to a second birthday feast in Lake Bracciano, at the home of journalists Judith Harris and David Willey. I went to Paris to visit Catherine de Monicault, staying in her big apartment near Place Victor Hugo and going back together to all our favourite haunts. I went to Jonnie and Monika's Elizabethan cottage near Henley, in Buckinghamshire, the great family gathering place where my beloved Aunt Elisabeth, his mother, had lived and died. I spent weekends with the Brooks in their rambling house and four-acre garden near Lymington. I Kept Going.

Though I loved the communal garden in Holland Park, I didn't have any great attachment to the London flat itself. It had flooded in 2007 after a biblical rain caused a drain surge in the whole district, temporarily dispossessing anyone who lived on a ground floor, like me. (It was uninhabitable for six months.) And I was burnt out of the apartment in 2010 after a fire in the brand-new dryer swept right through the flat. It could've burned down the entire building without the quick response of my wonderful neighbour, Ann Johns, who called the fire brigade (I was out shopping at the time). Ann put me up in her spare room for a night and even took me out to dinner. The apartment had to be completely stripped and renovated twice in the space of three years. It must have been jinxed. At least I had Liam Irwin to come to my rescue. He was a successful design/builder who married my great friend Annie Jennings and who always got me out of any scrape. I called him my Knight in Shining Armour. He called me The Pest.

I still used Calypso Cottage in Cyprus. Though I'd abandoned it after John died, in time all the sweet memories came back, just as

Kayce Jennings said they would, and I was able to return and live there from time to time. I had a lot of friends there too. We were all getting a bit long in the tooth: some people were leaving the island for good, or leaving the stage altogether. But I assumed that I would eventually sell the London flat and retire to Cyprus along with all the other ancient Brits, doing sedate daily laps in my pool and talking to the plants. (I generally just say, "Grow, you buggers.") I thought of moving to Vancouver to be near Jonnie, but I didn't want to become the sort of woman who follows her grown child around.

Though I still had a pretty good lifestyle, basically I was a bit lost. In December 2011, I went back to Canada for Christmas, to see all my old friends in Toronto and Jonnie in Vancouver. My pal Ellie Tesher said I seemed cast-down, and she should know. She was now an Agony Aunt for the *Toronto Star*, writing a daily syndicated advice column. "Maybe you could try a hormone regime. Doctor-approved, of course," she said. Yikes, was it that bad?

I also contacted Diane Francis. She was working on her ninth book and had recently married a divine man named John Beck, chairman and CEO of Aecon, the largest publicly traded construction company in Canada. They had moved into a luxurious penthouse apartment downtown, just south of Bloor Street.

"Great, Hilly! We'll have a dinner party for you. Give me a guest list . . . we can seat ten comfortably. I'll have it catered. It'll be fun!" Both Diane and John are very busy people and it was remarkable that they were even in the city together at that time, let alone free to throw a dinner party for Little Me. I gave her a list of my closest friends: Gloria, Noelle and Mori, Lindsay and Rupert, Krystyne and Scott. The usual suspects.

Among the many details in Diane and John's apartment was a lighting system that was entirely on dimmer switches. Lighting is *all*. For this party, Diane made sure that the lighting was *low*. I wore a form-fitting red silk pullover with a sequined sleeveless jacket, a black belt studded with crystals, and my usual twenty pounds of silver tribal jewellery. It was a terrific evening.

Of course, I called Diane the next morning to thank her.

"Delighted to have you, Hilly. You know, John said this morning that you really should meet J.D. He's on the Aecon board, a widower, and a really nice guy."

"Oh really?" I said. "Where does he live?" I was still living in London, of course.

"Edmonton," she said.

"Well in that case I don't see much point," I said dismissively. She might as well have said he lives in Siberia.

"Okay, sweetie, just a thought. He's Alberta Royalty, you know—comes from a big philanthropic family. By the way, I'm giving a speech in Vancouver next week. Why don't we meet again when you're visiting Jonnie?"

I had a lovely time with Jonnie in Vancouver: he was getting established as a digital media producer working for various independent production companies. And he was developing a sideline in electronic music, his true passion. Then I met Diane for lunch.

"You know, you really should meet J.D., even if it's just for practice," Diane said as she toyed with her salad. "He's a sophisticated guy, and he travels to London a lot. You could have a pretty good lifestyle with him."

"Oh all right, give him my email," I replied, thinking that this would go absolutely nowhere. As for "Alberta Royalty," I'm such an

East Coast snob that I think this is a contradiction in terms. What kind of relationship could you have with someone who lives 4,200 miles away? Anyway, I wasn't interested in men anymore. Or so I thought.

A couple of weeks later I get an email from this J.D. person, saying that he was in London and that Diane Francis suggested we "have tea together." I responded, giving him my phone number. He calls.

"I don't know how you feel about it, but I'm not much of a one for tea," he says. "How about a drink, or dinner?"

"Let's meet for dinner," I reply. (*Might as well make an evening of it, I think.*)

J.D. suggests that I choose the restaurant, saying that he's staying with his daughter in Westbourne Grove. I choose a place in Notting Hill Gate, which is relatively close to both of us. It's called The Ledbury. My sailing friends Sandra and Martin Jay told me that they always eat there when staying in their London pied-à-terre so I think this would be a good choice. I have no idea that it's a Michelin Two Star restaurant. I'd forgotten that Sandra and Martin live . . . rather well.

We agree on a day and a time. This is a Date, basically. I am still not that excited about it. What can an engineer from Edmonton actually be like? Probably short, fat, and balding. But it's always nice to meet another Canadian when you're living abroad, isn't it?

I arrive at The Ledbury about five minutes late, wearing exactly what I wore to Diane and John's dinner party, with a short black leather jacket trimmed with fur and covered in twelve hundred and fifty metal studs. That is what the Turkish merchant told me when I bought it. Yeah, I know, a bit extreme.

A man stands up, wearing a black turtleneck sweater, black slacks, and a lightweight check jacket. He is six-foot-two, has an athletic physique, grey-blue eyes, and a million-dollar smile. He's handsome. More out of Jimmy Stewart than Gary Cooper, but handsome. He extends his large hand and gives me a firm but not crushing handshake.

He had me at "hello."

For me, the evening passed in a blur. I think we talked about skiing, mainly. He was a big powder skier, in the backwoods, accessible only by helicopter, as opposed to boring old chairlifts. He was born and bred in Montreal and I liked his Canadian accent, even when he said "anyways." He'd made his fortune in the west, in Edmonton, taking over a family construction business and building it up until it merged with Aecon. He trained as an engineer and wore the engineer's iron ring. He had three homes, including a ranch south of Edmonton with eight quarter-horses, a couple of Clydesdales, and a plane. I didn't bother to list the number of homes I'd owned and occupied. We didn't discuss our careers, our late spouses, or family. We established that we'd both been to the same university, at different times. That we'd both travelled across the subcontinent and Afghanistan and Iran and Turkey, at different times. That we'd both lived in Montreal at the same time, during the great summer of Expo 67, when the whole world came to the city. We talked non-stop for at least two hours, the service was impeccable, and the food was delicious. Of course it was. I still hadn't realized that I'd lured this man into one of the best restaurants in London.

J.D. offers to take me home, but in my besotted state I say, Oh no, I can just take the Number 33 bus. What the hell is the matter with me, anyway? Once inside the door I seize the phone and call Diane. Having airily turned up my nose at the idea of meeting this J.D.

person only a few weeks ago, I am now wildly interested in repeating the experience, many times. Suddenly the fact that he lives 4,200 miles away doesn't seem so impossible.

"Diane! I think J.D. is terrific! I really like him. How can I see him again?"

She tells me he has a board meeting in Toronto in early March. I immediately invent a reason to go to Toronto in early March. In the meantime, I establish a regular email correspondence with J.D. Obviously, he spends quite a lot of time on his iPad. I send him short messages, trying to be witty, and he answers the same day, telling me about his upcoming heli-ski trips to British Columbia, his daughter's destination wedding in Mexico, and so on. After a decent interval, I write and say that it "just so happens" that I'll be in Toronto in early March and would he be there at that time, by any chance? If so, maybe we could meet? Back comes the answer I was hoping for.

"Yeah, I'll be in Toronto on March 8th. I'll make it happen."

I think, *No, maybe this time, I'm the one who is making it happen.*

What I didn't know was that J.D. had looked me up online and found a half-hour TV interview I'd recently done with my old friend Steve Paikin, who has his own nightly program on TVOntario called *The Agenda*. Steve was incredibly flattering about me, describing me as "One of the greatest foreign correspondents this country has ever produced," or something like that. He'd included a few clips of my reports in the broadcast—God knows how he got hold of them.

"You've reported from around the world, Hilary," Steve said. "Have you ever counted the number of countries?"

"Well no, not really. But I think I've reported from every continent, except Antarctica," I replied. "And I'm *not* really interested in Antarctica."[1]

I guess J.D. had watched the whole interview and thought, *Maybe this dame is worth a second look.*

For the next few weeks I'm in a fever of excitement. What will I wear? More important, what jewellery will I wear? What restaurant should I suggest? What's the ostensible reason for my trip to Toronto anyway?

I fly in to Toronto a couple of days early, staying with Gloria. She immediately becomes part of the conspiracy, of course, and the three of us—Diane, Gloria, and me—meet for lunch to choose The Right Restaurant. It has to be central, and have *dim* lighting. We decide on a spot aptly named The One, in Yorkville. At night, the whole place is candlelit. Perfect.

When the day comes, I'm in a torment about what to wear and what tribal jewellery to put on. I decide on a Max Mara suit with a slim silk pullover and Turkoman jewellery. I pile on a silver Turkoman bracelet studded with agates, three large agate rings, a matching agate-and-silver link belt, and thick, hooped silver earrings. I must have looked like a fortune teller.

I'm early. I'm shown to a corner table and then, right on time, *he* walks in. Yup. I'm still a goner. I have that strange sense that I've known this man before, in a previous life. "Twice or thrice had I loved thee, Before I knew thy face or name."[2]

This time, we did talk about our careers, and our late spouses and family. His wife, June, had died suddenly in his arms in the middle of the night while they were at their remote lakeside cottage in Quebec, where they had no electricity. The autopsy said the cause of death was a rare form of cancer that attacks the muscles of the heart, leading to heart failure. He couldn't save her. It wasn't that long ago. He seemed to be still traumatized by her death: his eyes filled with tears when he talked of her, and my heart went out to him. I told him about John and our last days together. John also died in my arms, just as June died in his. In that lively, candlelit restaurant, I was filled with feelings of tenderness for this handsome, emotional man. Tenderness, and lust. We talked and talked for at least two hours, interrupted by the waitress, who kept asking if she could see my jewellery . . . again. I floated out onto the street with him and took his arm, thinking, *Well, at least we could have a stroll through Yorkville before I have to say goodnight.*

J.D. looked down at me. "Well, Hilary, why don't you come up to my suite and let me show you photos of my family?" He's staying at the Four Seasons Hotel, across the street.

I say demurely that I would be delighted. My inner voice is shouting, "Yes, yes, *yes!*"

In his hotel suite, which is bigger than Gloria's entire apartment, we do actually look at dozens of family photos on his iPad for an hour or so before he finally takes me in his arms and gazes into my eyes.

"You have very little muscle mass in your shoulders," he says. So romantic!

50

THE FOUNTAIN OF YOUTH IS LOVE

I slept very little that night. Oh yes, there was *that*. But afterwards I kept waking up with excruciating cramps in my calves and ankles. I get them from time to time, and of course they *would* strike when I'm lying next to a sexy, six-foot-two-inch hunk of a man. The only way to relieve the unbearable pain was to get up and pace the room, which inevitably woke up my Stranger in the Night. We spent a lot of time trying possible treatments, ransacking the mini-bar for electrolyte drinks. The treatment would work, we'd go back to bed, and in an hour or so the cramps would strike again. I was up and down like a bucket in a well. "This is so embarrassing," I muttered to myself. "How can he possibly want to see me again?"

In the morning, J.D. reminded me that I should call Gloria, my hostess, to reassure her that I hadn't been mugged and left for dead in the street. As if Gloria would worry that I hadn't come home that night. On the contrary, she would've already called Diane to break the news that Hils finally got lucky.

After breakfast, we took a taxi to Gloria's apartment building in Rosedale. On a crisp, bright winter morning, J.D. walked me to the door, kissed me goodbye, and took the cab on to Pearson airport. I floated up to Gloria's in a daze.

She flung open the door. "*Well?* How was it?"

"Divine, divine, divine. I have no idea if I will ever see him again." I flung myself onto her spare bed and promptly fell asleep.

I flew back to London a few days later, but not before I signed a lease on a centrally located one-bedroom apartment in Toronto overlooking a park and ravine, available for occupancy on May 1. Diane and Gloria talked me into this. "You really should come back to Canada anyway. This is where your son, your sisters, and most of your friends are," they said, as of one voice. "You can't stay in Europe forever. If you want to see this man again, you should at least be living in the same country." Diane offered to lend me a complete set of furniture that she happened to have in her storeroom. It didn't take much to convince me. This was my last chance, I thought. This was my *only* chance.

I had written to my heart-throb, of course, thanking him for a wonderful evening and saying how special it was. Silence. But then, oh joy!, he wrote back and we resumed our email correspondence. Very quickly our letters became more frequent, more personal. We wrote to each other almost every day. Within a few weeks I was crazy in love with a man I had met exactly twice. I lost twenty pounds and looked ten years younger. That's what my friends said anyway, and I still cling to that. People I hadn't seen for a few months would say, "Christ, Hils, what happened to *you?* You look... ten years younger!"

Sometime in early April, J.D. wrote to say that he was planning to come to London: "I want to spend some serious time with you," he said. Suddenly I'm in a panic. I called Diane. "He's says he wants to spend some Serious Time with me! That means he's going to see me in *daylight!*" I cried. "What am I gonna do? We can't spend the entire time in candlelit restaurants!"

Diane just laughed at me. "I don't think you have to worry, sweetie."

The day came—it was mid-May and coincided with the memorial service for Marie Colvin, the famous American journalist who was killed by a Syrian government rocket while covering the siege of Homs from a rebel stronghold. Her reports in *The Sunday Times* about the murder and mayhem visited on ordinary Syrian people were having enormous effect, and she was also giving interviews live from the war zone to major news networks. Some think she had been targeted by Syrian forces. Marie was unmistakable because of the black patch over her left eye, destroyed in an ambush by Tamil Tigers in Sri Lanka. I knew Marie, having met her on the road in various Mid-East locations, and I wanted to go. It was in St. Martin-in-the-Fields on Trafalgar Square, and it was a very moving service. The great Lyse Doucet gave the eulogy. I went with the BBC reporter and author Humphrey Hawksley, an old friend, who invited me to lunch at his club on Pall Mall afterwards. J.D. was going to arrive at my apartment in the late afternoon. Humphrey is great company, but this time I couldn't get out of that elegant club dining room fast enough. Life is full of irony, cruel irony! There was brave, beautiful Marie, not yet cold in her grave after taking one chance too many in her brilliant career. And here was Hilary, who had somehow survived whatever risks she'd taken in her professional life, now beside herself with excitement about a new romance.

J.D. came to my door at the appointed time, bearing an enormous bouquet of flowers. Yup. He's the One. Those eyes, that smile, that physique . . . I still had *that* feeling. We embraced, many times, then walked around the communal garden. Round and round the garden until it was early evening and dim enough for Ms. Brown to remove her clothes and jump into bed. We had dinner with friends and agreed to meet again the next evening. J.D. was staying with his recently married daughter. The next evening, we went to the theatre and a late supper at The Wolseley, and this time he stayed with me, all night. I thought it would be charming if we walked to my local grocer the following morning to buy its famous croissants, which were delivered daily by some French bakery. Then we would have breakfast with hot croissants on my patio, looking out onto the communal garden, one of the loveliest in London. Wouldn't *that* be romantic?

Of course, in my love-struck state I managed to burn the croissants while heating them up. I gave a little nervous laugh and sent the Man of My Dreams out to buy four more. He went without a murmur. I burnt those too. I was so determined to serve those frigging hot croissants that I actually asked him to go out a third time. He said something like: "Okay, Hilary, that's three times and you're out. Got any eggs?"

But J.D.'s visit went swimmingly, and he surprised me by renting a car and taking me down to Devon, in the west country, near Salcombe Harbour, an area of Outstanding Natural Beauty. By a miracle the weather was perfect, and we stayed in a boutique hotel right on the sea, tucked into its own cove and set against the famous cliffs. We could walk up onto the coastal footpaths straight from the hotel. In spite of my fiasco with the croissants, I suggested we have a picnic. "We can buy some bread and cheese and wine in the village, and then walk straight onto the trails," I said. I had cleverly brought a knapsack.

It was a sunny day and the view out to sea was spectacular. We walked a few kilometres and then settled down at a lookout point for my picnic.

"So tell me, Hilary, what's left on your bucket list?" J.D. said as he opened the wine. "You've travelled the world. Where would you like to go?"

"Gosh, I don't know, there are so many beautiful places," I said, afraid to mention a spot that he might hate. "What's on *your* bucket list?"

"Well, I've always wanted to go to Antarctica," J.D. said as he stared out to sea, mentioning the one place he *knew* (from my TVO interview with Steve Paikin) that I had no interest in whatsoever. But I didn't know . . . that he knew.

I didn't miss a beat. "Oh, so have I!" I cried. "I think Antarctica would be *fascinating!*"

"Gotcha!" he murmured.

At this point I was confident enough to tell him that I didn't much like addressing him by his initials. "When I call you J.D., I feel that we're walk-on characters in an episode of *Dallas*. Or that you're my boss."

He explained that all the male children in his huge extended family were called either Jim, Bill, Bob, or Harry. He'd assumed the J.D. moniker to distinguish himself from all the other Jims. "My favourite sister calls me Jimmy," he said. From that moment on, I called him Jimmy too.

Jimmy and I spent the rest of his time in England visiting friends. His friends the Lees (Fenella and David) happened to live within a mile of my friends Ian and Frances Brook, in Lymington, near the New Forest. Later we drove up to Gloucestershire to see Judith Hahn and John Exelby in their extraordinary house and garden in Gloucestershire. Ju was a famous science reporter and author, and one of the warmest, most sympathetic women I have ever known. I wanted Jimmy to meet all my pals, though I still had absolutely no idea how long this romance was going to last.

After a little more than a week, our Serious Time together was over. Jimmy took me home and we walked through the communal garden one last time before we said goodbye.

"Hilary, it's been great," Jimmy said as he gave me another devastating smile and folded me in his arms. Then he strode through the garden gate onto Holland Park Avenue and up toward Westbourne Grove. Nothing about when we might meet again. Which probably meant Never. I called Diane.

"Don't *worry!*" Diane said. "He hasn't been a widower for that long. Your romance has been very quick. He's not a player, he's got no one else. Concentrate on moving yourself to Toronto. That way you'll be only two thousand miles away from him instead of four."

So I did. I packed up my clothes, personal effects, and a few carpets, paintings, and ethnic Stuff and shipped them off to Toronto, arranging to rent out my London apartment for a year starting in July. "Nothing ventured, nothing gained," I said to myself, without much conviction. This was early June.

To my astonishment, Jimmy wrote a few days later saying he wanted me to stay with him at his lakeside cottage in the Laurentian Mountains, near Mont Tremblant in Quebec. For the whole summer. "The cottage means a lot to me, and I'd like to share it with you." I was ecstatic. He wanted to *share* his summer home with me! I had lunch at the Chelsea Arts Club with my chum Sue Arnold (the journalist who wrote about me in *The Observer* forty years ago). She immediately weighed in on this.

"Now *don't* commit yourself to more than ten days, two weeks at the most. You can't just make yourself completely available to a man.

I'm right, you know. Listen to Auntie Sue." She had taken to referring to Jimmy as "your cowboy."

"But I *want* to be completely available. Anyway, where would I go after two weeks? Sit and stew in a one-bedroom apartment in Toronto? If it doesn't work out, he'll just take me to the airport. He's a gentleman. But if it does, we'll have a wonderful summer together, won't we?"

"Oh all *right*. Are cowboys actually gentlemen? What clothes are you going to take? Describe, please." Sue had become clinically blind from a genetic condition called retinitis pigmentosa (RP) and always demanded a detailed account of things she could no longer see. "Are you going to wear a bikini, and if so what are you going to cover it up with? How about a burka?" Sue is half Burmese, has produced six children by two husbands, and still has a perfect, permanently tanned, size 6 figure. Unlike most of her friends, including me.

I got my friend Maggie Tyler to help me pack. Maggie worked for the Duke of Edinburgh Awards and was an absolute fashion plate, which she had to be for all the events she organized at Buckingham Palace. She called it Buckpal. She went through my wardrobe with military precision. "Chuck this. Chuck that. You can't still be wearing *this*, can you?" Et cetera, et cetera. But at least she allowed that my weight loss was a big plus. "Take these tight black jeans. Wear this scarf for colour. Have you got any more skinny trousers? Buy some. You look terrific in them and they're in fashion. Now let's see your belts." I happen to have one of the largest collections of belts of anyone I know outside the fashion industry. Silver tribal, gold filigree, leather studded with crystals: you name it, I've got it. Maggie was pleased with that. "Take them all," she said. "You still have a waist and I hate you."

For my flight back to Canada I naturally hand-carried my collection of tribal jewellery, filling an entire carry-on bag. The check-in clerk at Air Transat put the bag on the scales. "This bag weighs more than *twenty kilos*, madam. There is a five-kilo limit on hand-carry," she said dispassionately. "You'll have to transfer some of these things to your checked bag."

What?? I absolutely *must* carry my tribal jewellery by hand! I can't put it in with my checked bag, that's too risky! I thanked the clerk, took my carry-on bag into a nearby ladies' room, removed the heaviest pieces of jewellery, and put them on my own dear body. All of them. That was about four metal belts, a half-dozen necklaces, and three matched pairs of tribal bangles. What remained in the bag was just under the airline's impossible limit of five kilos. I threw on a raincoat and checked in. Then I clanked across the departure lounge into security, where I removed all the tribal pieces around my waist, wrist, and neck and dropped them, one by one, into a bin. I crossed through the metal detector to the other side.

Three female security officers had already gathered round to inspect my collection as my bin came along the conveyor belt. I expected a hassle, which shows how wrong you can be. "Oh my *God*! Where did you get *that*? Is that real silver? How much does that necklace actually *weigh*? Are these bangles antique?" And so on. I think I could have dropped an AK-47 into the bin and they wouldn't have noticed.

I moved into my little rental apartment in Toronto, installed Diane's furniture, and within a few days flew to Montreal. Jimmy collected me in his enormous Ford pickup truck, and we drove into the Laurentian Mountains.

"The cottage is seventy miles from Montreal but a thousand miles from nowhere," Jimmy said as we turned onto a narrow private road at Lac-de-Seize-Îles. The road wound its way through thick woods for several miles before Jimmy turned left up a steep hill and down onto his property. His cottage was in a clearing in the woods, on high ground overlooking a beautiful lake about a mile long. It was unlike any cottage I'd ever seen. It was a barn, basically, three storeys high, with a deep wraparound deck and a very long wooden staircase leading down to the dock. There were two Adirondack chairs on the dock, and a canoe tied up alongside. You couldn't see any other cottages on the lake, though they were there, tucked into the woods along the shore. You felt that the lake was yours and yours alone. It was like a sheet of tinted glass, reflecting every detail of the shoreline and the shifting clouds in the sky. It was completely quiet, except for the occasional call of the loon, a beautiful, unearthly sound that I'd last heard as a child.

"Well, this is it," Jimmy said, smiling down at me. "Do you like it?"

"Everything that a summer cottage should be," I said. "So when can we jump in the lake?" I realized that I hadn't had a freshwater swim since I'd left Canada for Cyprus more than twenty years before.

Jimmy's lake, with the rather pedestrian name of Proctor, was shared among an original group of six cottagers, including Jimmy's late father, who had jointly agreed that there would be no electricity and no jet-skis or motorboats of any kind. Just canoes, rowboats, and paddleboards. There was complete, unadulterated, glorious silence. Though he was off the grid, Jimmy had all the creature comforts. Thank God. Ms. Brown does *not* like roughing it. He had a generator that pumped water up from the lake into a storage tank to supply the cottage with running water. He had solar panels that powered a Sirius satellite radio system, and charged up his iPhone, iPad, and laptop. He had a propane tank for his stove, refrigerator, and outdoor barbecue. There was a huge wood-burning fireplace in the living room, and a pot-bellied stove in the kitchen-dining area that could warm up the room in a trice. At night, he lit the cottage with candles and a vast collection of antique oil lamps. My kind of lighting.

Jimmy described his cottage as a family house, but as far as I was concerned it was suitable for just two people. That was because there was no privacy whatsoever. Being a barn, it was a vast open space with a tongue-and-groove cedar ceiling three storeys high, and forty-foot exposed beams of Douglas fir. The two bedrooms were basically balconies, stacked on two floors, overlooking the huge living room below. They had only three walls, and a parapet. If you wanted to change your clothes without being spotted by someone on the living room couch, for example, you had to flatten yourself against the far wall. The only room with four walls was the bathroom, which didn't have a ceiling. The faintest sound, *any* sound, would reverberate from one end of the house to the other.

All the building materials, including the forty-foot beams, came in on the back of a power wagon, and the workmen had to set up a tented camp to live in while the cottage was built. In the corner of the living room was a glass solarium looking up at the sky, out to the lake, and onto to a semi-wild garden filled with spirea and digitalis. A deep divan was piled high with cushions, and we spent many intimate moments there. I called it the Bower of Bliss. Yes, the cottage was really quite eccentric. But Jimmy loved it, and with just the two of us staying there, I did too.

Of course, at the outset there was the unspoken issue of our sleeping arrangements, a question that Sue Arnold had raised. "Is your cowboy going to install you in the matrimonial bedroom? That's a bit tricky, isn't it?" she said. I had no answer to that. But when the time came, Jimmy simply took my bags up to one of the spare bedrooms. "This is your room," he said. "You have lots of space for your clothes here. But at night I hope you'll come down to my room and keep me company." That felt right, and that is exactly what we did.

The first morning Jimmy dictated that we should always start our day with a dip in the lake. Whatever the weather. We'd descend the fifty-two steps to the dock, check the lake temperature (being an engineer, Jimmy monitored both air and water temperature at *all* times), count to five and plunge in, in a synchronized dive. I pretended that I loved this. On occasion, the temperature got as low as 55° Fahrenheit. But after the initial shock to the system, the water felt absolutely fabulous. I called this exercise the Compulsory Daily Pre-Breakfast Swim and we never missed a morning, not even when it was raining or the wind was whipping across the lake. Afterwards there was the reward of freshly percolated coffee and a big breakfast, either on the deck or, if it was cold, in the dining room with the pot-bellied stove fired up.

Then there was the Compulsory Gourmet Dinner that I was expected to cook for Jimmy's Québécois neighbours, Alain Lanoue and Marie-France Bouchard. They had a log cottage at the southern end of the lake and Jimmy was devoted to them. They were foodies. The dinner took place one day after my arrival. "You can cook whatever you want," said my Beloved, making it clear that Alain and Marie-France, being French, had very high standards. I had an overambitious recipe up my sleeve involving three types of fish and a wine-and-cream sauce. Lindsay Dale-Harris had given it to me. We bought all the ingredients in Saint-Sauveur and got back to the cottage in time for me to do all the scullery, set the table, pick some wildflowers for an attractive table arrangement, get dressed in a casual-but-elegant sarong, do my hair, apply my makeup, and put on two pounds of tribal jewellery. This was a Test, I *knew* it was a Test.

The trouble with my fancy fish recipe was that it had to be put together at the last minute (never overcook fish). In other words, after one's guests have arrived and, in this case, as night was falling. Even when the candles and oil lamps were lit, I could barely make out the faces of Alain and Marie-France, let alone the simple, thirty-nine-step procedure for the damned fish recipe. Of course, I had yet to learn my way around Jimmy's kitchen: I couldn't find a thing. I thought I might at least impress with my fluent French, but I was having trouble understanding the Québécois accent. Yup. This whole thing was a Test and I was *not* doing well. Somehow in the pitch-darkness I was able to pull the whole wretched dish together, hurling some chopped dill over it to disguise the imperfections. But in my moment of triumph I managed to set fire to an oven mitt as I took it off the stove. I could have burned the whole cottage down.

This was only the first of many accidents that befell Ms. Calamity Brown in those first few days. I was crazy in love with this man and wanted to make myself useful. This could be fatal. While attempting to help him at the barbecue, I closed the steel plate on the side burner, over an invisible flame that was still burning. The plastic control buttons basically melted away. I had various minor accidents at the wheel of his giant Ford pickup truck. On one occasion, I swear that a rock just jumped out from the side of the road and sliced through the rear tire.

But Jimmy forgave me all this. In the daytime, we swam and ate and talked and laughed. At night, we ate and talked and laughed and loved. He talked about his late wife, June, all the time, and he often wept as he spoke of her. June had been an athlete, a woman who could run Iron Man half-marathons at the age of sixty. Everyone loved her. Her spirit was everywhere. Friends and relatives would come to the cottage and talk about her. I could see that Jimmy was still in mourning for June, and I so much wanted to help him. Though I felt that I was somehow competing with a ghost.

After a week or so his favourite sister, Jeannie, came to stay with her husband, Bernie. From the moment we met, they embraced me and seemed to accept me. Then his older son, David, came with his lovely wife, Denise, and their three beautiful children. They lived in Jimmy's second cottage across the bay, known as Springs. They often came to dinner with us, or we went over to dinner with them, and in the daytime we spent hours jumping in and out of the lake with the kids. I fell in love with them, all of them. Especially after Denise (whom I now call Diesel) pulled me aside one evening. "I just want you to know that we're thrilled that Papa has met you," she said. "You're making him so happy." I could have kissed her. I probably did kiss her. Three years later, Diesel flew herself from Edmonton to Toronto to design the renovation of my new apartment. She refused to charge me. "This is to thank you for everything you've done for us," she said. You can see why I love them so much.

In all this I kept my feelings, my true feelings, to myself. "I can*not* tell him I love him," I repeated to myself, over and over again. "I have no idea how he feels about me. He just needs a woman to help him through his grief." Jimmy would often come up behind me, kiss my neck, and say, "I'm so glad that you're here." But this wasn't enough to convince me that I was anything more than a summer romance. I just thought of Noel Coward's dictum: "Grab every scrap of happiness you can."

Then one evening, after another long, candlelit dinner, Jimmy suddenly brought the conversation around to the night we first met. "So . . . what was your first impression of me?" he said.

I paused for a few seconds. Oh what the hell, I can't keep up the pretense any longer. I'm gonna tell him the truth. I looked into his grey-blue eyes.

"From the moment I first met you in that London restaurant, when your eyes met mine and you gave me that million-dollar smile, I thought you were . . . absolutely fantastic." There. I finally said it. I've screwed up—again.

Jimmy said nothing but got up, retrieved his iPad, tapped into it, and pulled up a Draft email on the screen. Written by him to me but Unsent. Still standing, he held it up to me.

"MEETING YOU WAS FATE. BECOMING YOUR FRIEND WAS A CHOICE. FALLING IN LOVE WITH YOU WAS BEYOND MY CONTROL."

At first I couldn't believe what I was reading. I was barely coherent. "You mean? . . . you . . . you actually . . ." I babbled, then drifted off, unable to finish my sentence.

"Yes," he said, smiling down at me in the soft light of a dozen burning candles. "I love you, Hils."

"But but but but . . . that's how I feel too! I have loved you from the moment I first clapped eyes on you!" I blurted out, and then threw myself into his arms. We went to bed early that night, though we didn't sleep that much.

The rest of the summer was like an idyll. We were living under a spell. As it happened, it was one of the finest summers ever recorded in Quebec, day after sunny day and only occasional bouts of rain or cold. The lake was exquisite. We continued our now-familiar delicious routine: we swam, we ate, we laughed, and we loved. Gingie came to visit, dying to have a look at Hilly's new beau. Jimmy took us on a 30-mile cycling trip along the Rouge River up to Mont Tremblant, the only time I've ever outpaced Ginge in any sport. "He's pretty hyperactive, isn't he?" she said. "Obviously, he has to keep moving or he'll die. Like a shark." She also allowed that he was pretty damn attractive. "He's gorgeous, Hil!"

One by one my girlfriends wrote to ask how Hilary's affair with her Canadian cowboy was going. "I'm the happiest, luckiest woman alive" was my answer, basically. When Sue Arnold called, I was a bit more specific.

"I always thought that at this stage in my life, I would be a Working Granny, doing everything for my children's children. I didn't think I would end up as a 'Grande Horizontale.'" (The *grandes horizontales* were the courtesans of Parisian society in the nineteenth century, who spent most of their time on their backs.)

"That's very funny," Sue said. "Can I put that in my next column about Senior Sex?"

The summer of 2012 was without question the most wonderful summer I'd had since the time Jonnie was born in England, thirty-three years before. I was in a beautiful place with a beautiful man and was so infatuated I could only think of that old song "The Nearness of You" by Hoagy Carmichael: "It's not the pale moon that excites me, That thrills and delights me, oh no! It's just the nearness of you."[1]

Jonnie himself was secretly pleased that his mum had fallen in love again, though he found it hard to believe the amount of texting and emailing and phoning that went on between Jimmy and me. "You're like a couple of teenagers," he would say, with a withering look. (Fortunately he and Jimmy seem to like each other. We later had a lovely white Christmas in Alberta with Jimmy's family.)

When that summer finally came to an end, Jimmy had a thousand plans for us. Plans for pseudo-extreme sports for which I had no experience or aptitude whatsover. Helicopters and small planes were often involved. We cycled across northern Sicily, a region that has almost no flat surfaces. "How are you doing, Hils?" Jimmy would shout as he overtook me, toiling up yet another hill. "Just trying to get up this frigging mountain," I would reply through clenched teeth. We pedalled 30 miles a day, for eight days, and I used to have a phobia about cycling. How did I do this? Love is a performance-enhancing drug, that's how.

He made me go white-water rafting down the Zambezi River in Zambia, through hair-raising rapids with names like "The Terminator" and "Suicide." He made me go cat-skiing in the southern Rockies, asserting that because I was a good skier on piste, I would be good in deep snow. To cat-ski, you climb into a tracked vehicle that looks like an armoured personnel carrier, go straight up a mountain, get out, and ski down through four feet of powder snow. I felt as though I was going to my own execution. Which I was, since after two turns my left ski came off and went hurtling down the hill, leaving me to traverse across the slope on one leg, clinging to Jimmy with my left boot on his right ski, weeping with fear. "*Stop* hyperventilating!" was his single piece of advice.

He took me to the jungles of Costa Rica, which began with a terrifying trip down the raging Pacuare River, through so-called "class IV" rapids. The kind that boil up into the raft and all over everyone inside it. Afterwards we zip-lined through the tropical canopy, hurtling through the air like aging orangutans, from one precarious tree platform to the next. Then it was a "walk through the jungle." This was actually a commando-type slog through dense underbrush to a heart-stoppingly beautiful waterfall rising 100 feet straight above us. Great fun standing under that shower. Until we learned that we had to *rappel* down the next vertical section of the falls, a sheer drop of a mere 70 feet. "This is *not dangerous!*" Jimmy said. "I'll go first, just follow me!" and he disappeared over the sheer rockface. I followed him. I had no choice.

He made me ski out of a helicopter in the coastal mountains of British Columbia. He took me to a famous lodge on a ledge in the Monashee Mountains of south-central B.C. called Mustang Powder, where he's been back-country skiing for thirty years. He considered that I could handle this too. Fortunately, the owner of the lodge thought otherwise and assigned a couple of guides to look after me in what became known as the "Hilary Sandwich"—one guide in front of me, and one behind, Hils in the middle. On my first day, we skied through a virgin forest, a thing that seasoned powder skiers just love to do. Tree-holes five feet deep yawn open at every turn. "You're doing *great—just breathe!*" said my guides, trying to give me positive reinforcement as I gasped and whimpered my way down this impossibly steep mountain slope, through impossibly deep snow. "How long is this run anyway?" I cried. Jimmy was bopping down the mountain in front of me in perfect form, like a wild stag, until he stopped, turned, and said, "Just shut up and ski." So I did.

He took me for a road trip through the Rocky Mountains on his Harley-Davidson. Getting onto the thing was like mounting a very large, dangerous stallion. The only attraction for me was dressing up in black leather. Though after a hundred miles or so I kind of liked it, especially when we finally thundered up to the four-star Jasper Park Lodge and strode into the bar with our helmets under our arms. "Gimme a beer, and make it snappy," I snarled, in a passable imitation of a Hell's Angel.

He took me riding over his thousand-acre ranch in the Battle River Valley. I hadn't been on a horse in almost forty years. He took me up in his tiny single-engine plane, called a Husky. "Any landing is a good landing if you can walk away from it," he said. "What happens if you have a heart attack?" I asked. "Don't worry," he said. "You'll have one too."

He took me back to Italy, three times—to Tuscany and Puglia and southern Sicily—always with the requirement that we cycle straight up and straight down for a minimum of 30 miles a day. When we weren't cycling, we were hiking, on the spectacular "Path of the Gods," for example, along the Amalfi Coast. One false step and you would hurtle down the cliff into the Mediterranean 1,600 feet below.

He took me to Turkey to sail along the Aegean Coast. He took me to Laos and Cambodia, cycling along the banks of the Mekong River, then switching to elephants in Thailand. He took me deep-sea fishing off the Pacific Coast of Mexico. He took me to Colombia, long a no-go area because of the violence of the drug cartels, but beautiful, with a boutique hotel on an offshore island accessible only by catamaran. Our room was 116 steps up the mountainside, no elevator. He took me to Ethiopia, to visit rural schools that he supported through his work with a small Canadian charity called the Cosco Foundation.

This involved driving over dust-covered, bone-rattling roads for hours. I told him I didn't *want* to go to Ethiopia: I wanted to go to Italy again and stay in four-star palazzos. But when we finally arrived at the remote Ethiopian village, we were met by a mounted escort of men in tribal livery, and children singing in close harmony. We were treated like *gods*. That's when I said to Jimmy, "You know, I kind of like it here after all."

He took me ski-touring in the remote Purcell Mountains of B.C., kitting me out with his old equipment and expecting me to trudge straight up the mountain, and then ski down it in boots that were two sizes too big for me. I had no control over his skis, *at all*. This didn't concern him. Half the time I was convinced he was trying to get rid of me. For the rest of the time, I loved it.

Don't think that he's indifferent to any real suffering that might befall me, however. While on a solo trip to a colonial town in Mexico in 2018, I was attacked by a mugger, who threw me to the ground with such force that it broke my hip. (That was because I fought back when he grabbed my cellphone, thinking that I was Wonder Woman.) Jimmy flew through the night from Alberta with $9,000 in cash to pay for the hip replacement, in Mexico, a day later. He looked after me for two weeks until I was fit enough to fly home with him. This involved two changes of plane and five changes of wheelchair.

I see Jimmy for about six months of the year, but we do *not* live together. That's probably why it's such a good relationship. He is so hyperactive that I need the separations, just to *rest up*.

I eventually sold my London flat and bought an apartment for myself in Toronto and a townhouse for Jonnie in Vancouver. I sold Calypso Cottage in Cyprus to John's grandson Ben, who has loved it since childhood and asked to buy it. I have an open invitation to visit. I know John would be pleased, looking down from the Great Newsroom in the Sky.

I never expected that, at this stage in my life, I would be running around with an attractive, adventurous, generous man; practising sports for which I have almost no ability; and feeling twenty years younger than I actually am.

I consider that my generation is the luckiest that ever lived, and ever will live. We had no world wars, but instead post-war prosperity. We had education, jet travel, job opportunities, and women's liberation. We had the Internet, and cellphones and email and FaceTime and all the other wonders of the technological revolution. We were young and mainly single in the golden age of sex—post-pill and pre-AIDS.

I had more lucky breaks, by far, than I ever deserved. I misplayed my hand routinely. But somehow I ended up with a completely charmed life. I had the luxury of first being loved by a handsome, intelligent, accomplished, loyal husband who gave me a beautiful, affectionate son. More than anyone, he turned me into a reporter and helped me do what I always wanted to do but never thought I could.

My only real regret in life is that I couldn't have a second child. And that, so far, I have no grandchildren, the only kind of immortality that I can believe in.

I've been called a trailblazer and a role model (apart from all the insults, of course). I might have been the former, but I couldn't possibly be a model for anyone in today's world. The women reporting on TV and radio now are phenomenal. Up against them, I wouldn't last a day.

Now at the end of my career, and fifteen years a widow, I have fallen in love with a man who enhances my life beyond measure. Jimmy is showing me the world—not the war zones, but all the beauty spots, as wild and remote and as dangerous as possible. Recently he asked if I would like to go hang-gliding in Columbia. I actually said that I'd love to. So as you can see, he is still keeping me in a constant state of excitement and fear.

Which is just like being a foreign correspondent, all over again.

Acknowledgements

I would like to thank my editor, Heather Sangster, for putting her professional hand to my manuscript, checking my facts and quotes, and telling me what's boring, in the nicest possible way. Because of the coronavirus pandemic, I have yet to meet her face to face, but I look forward to that.

I would like to thank Krystyne Griffin for digitizing my photographs and helping me choose them in the first place. That is apart from everything else she has done for me in fifty years of friendship.

I would also like to thank ABC News for granting me permission to reproduce stills from some of my reports, and to the gallant Anthony Perrone for making them available to me with such dispatch. ABC News made my dreams come true when it hired me as its first female foreign correspondent, and gave me the best professional years of my life.

I would also like to thank the following friends and family who either ploughed through my various drafts, helped me source material, told me where I should pull my punches, or nagged me into writing this memoir in the first place.

They are: Sally Armstrong, Tina Babarovic, Leith Bishop, Vian Ewart, Diane Francis, Douglas Gibson, Jane Gibson, Lorraine Greey, Lama Hasan, Sir Max Hastings, Virginia Huber, Diane King, Steve Paikin, Anna Porter, Julian Porter, Colin Smith, Susan Swan, and Ellie Tesher.

Endnotes

PROLOGUE

1. Robert Chesshyre, "John Bierman" (obituary), theguardian.com, January 17, 2006. https://www.theguardian.com/media/2006/jan/17/broadcasting.pressandpublishing.

CHAPTER 2

1. John Kenneth Galbraith, *The Scotch* (Toronto: Penguin Books, 1966), 28.

CHAPTER 7

1. Recorded as "Suzanne," *Songs of Leonard Cohen*, Columbia Studio E, New York City, 1967.
2. J. Kelly Nestruck, "Back in the Game: Leonard Cohen Makes His Return to Working Life." *The National Post*/Canada.com. February 7, 2006. https://web.archive.org/web/20150813033152/http://www.canada.com/nationalpost/artslife/story.html?id=a20d2c96-796a-4d38-a3bf-01b163d19f82&k=23941.
3. Andrea Warner, "Leonard Cohen, the Women He Loved, and the Women who Loved Him." cbc.ca. November 11, 2016. https://www.cbc.ca/music/read/leonard-cohen-the-women-he-loved-and-the-women-who-loved-him-1.4998473.

CHAPTER 8

1. Thomas S. Axworthy, "General De Gaulle and 'Vive le Québec libre,'" thecanadianencyclopedia.ca, July 23, 2013; revised July 19, 2016. https://www.thecanadianencyclopedia.ca/en/article/de-gaulle-and-vive-le-quebec-libre-feature.
2. Joan Capreol, "Counterparts Tough on Her: Female TV Announcer Began Career in Paris," *The Globe and Mail*, October 19, 1967.

CHAPTER 10

1. https://cape2rio2020.com/past_races/1971-cape-to-rio/ and https://cape2rio2020.com/past_races/1973-cape-to-rio/.

CHAPTER 11

1. Peter Bregg, "Trudeau: 'Just Watch Me.'" theglobeandmail.com, October 5, 2010; updated May 1, 2018. https://www.theglobeandmail.com/news/national/trudeau-just-watch-me/article4327998.

CHAPTER 12

1. http://onenewsbox.com/2017/09/09/2500-year-celebration-of-the-persian-empire/16/.
2. Farah Pahlavi, *An Enduring Love: My Life with the Shah* (New York City: Miramax Books, 2005), 217.

CHAPTER 13

1. Philip Hensher, "The War Bangladesh Can Never Forget," independent.co.uk, February 19, 2013. https://www.independent.co.uk/news/world/asia/the-war-bangladesh-can-never-forget-8501636.html.
2. Personal archives, n.d.

CHAPTER 14

1. Editorial, "Storing Up Trouble: Pakistan's Nuclear Bombs," theguardian.com, February 3, 2011. https://www.theguardian.com/commentisfree/2011/feb/03/pakistan-nuclear-bombs-editorial.

CHAPTER 15

1. Sue Arnold, "Pendennis Column," *The Observer*, January 9, 1972.
2. Personal archives, various dates.
3. Personal archives, various dates.
4. Martin Melaugh and Fionnuala Mckenna, "'Bloody Sunday,' 30 January 1972—A Chronology of Events," CAIN Web Service, n.d. https://cain.ulster.ac.uk/events/bsunday/chron.htm.
5. Transcript from BBC News at Six, BBC TV News, January 30, 1972.
6. Personal archives, February 1, 1972.
7. W.B. Yeats, "The Stare's Nest by My Window," The Collected Works of W.B. Yeats, Vol. 1, ed. Richard J. Finneran (New York: Macmillan Publishing Company, 1989).

8. https://cain.ulster.ac.uk/victims/memorials/static/photos/1029.html.
9. Paddy McGuigan, "The Men Behind the Wire," recorded in Belfast by the Barleycorn (Dublin: Release Records, 1971). https://alphahistory.com/northernireland/the-men-behind-the-wire-barleycorn-1971/ and https://en.wikipedia.org/wiki/The_Men_Behind_the_Wire.

CHAPTER 16

1. Amnesty International Publications, *Amnesty International Annual Report 1974/75* (London: Amnesty International Publications, 1975).
2. Ryszard Kapuściński, Shah of Shahs, trans. William R. Brand and Katarzyna Mroczkowska-Brand (London & New York: Picador Books, 1986), 45.
3. Marvin Zonis, Majestic Failure: The Fall of the Shah (Chicago: University of Chicago Press, 1991), 65.

CHAPTER 18

1. Abraham Rabinovich, "Golda's Meltdown," *The Jerusalem Post*, October 7, 2008. https://www.jpost.com/features/in-thespotlight/goldas-meltdown. *The Jerusalem Post* featured excerpts from Rabinovich's book *The Yom Kippur War* (New York: Schocken Books, 2004).
2. Nicholas Tomalin, "Stop the Press, I Want to Get On," Sunday Times Magazine, October 26, 1969.

CHAPTER 19

1. Personal archives, n.d.

CHAPTER 21

1. Personal archives, June 1974.

CHAPTER 22

1. Philip Caputo, *Means of Escape: A War Correspondent's Memoir of Life and Death in Afghanistan, the Middle East, and Vietnam* (New York: Holt Paperbacks, 2009), 244.
2. https://www.imdb.com/title/tt0077416/characters/nm0113712.

CHAPTER 26

1. Personal archives, February 14, 1977.
2. Personal recollection.

CHAPTER 27

1. Personal archives, n.d.

CHAPTER 28

1. "Home from Home, John Bierman in Toronto," *The Daily Telegraph Weekend Magazine*, 1991.
2. Tanja Schult, A Hero's Many Faces: Raoul Wallenberg in Contemporary Monuments (London: Palgrave Macmillan, 2009), 339.
3. Personal recollection.

CHAPTER 29

1. John Bierman, *Righteous Gentile: The Story of Raoul Wallenberg, Missing Hero of the Holocaust* (London, U.K.: Viking, 1981), n.p.

CHAPTER 30

1. John Bierman, "Notes on Sources," *Odyssey* (New York: Simon & Schuster, 1984; London: Severn House Publishers, 1985), 254.

CHAPTER 31

1. "British Journalist Slain by Sniper," *The New York Times*, November 18, 1989, section 1 page 5, quoting *Newsweek* photographer Bill Gentile, who was with Blundy when he was struck.

CHAPTER 32

1. Ze'ev Schiff and Ehud Ya'ari, *Israel's Lebanon War* (New York: Simon & Schuster, 1984), 283–284.
2. Personal recollection, June 1982.

CHAPTER 33

1. John Bierman, "Notes on Sources," *Odyssey* (New York: Simon & Schuster, 1984; London: Severn House Publishers, 1985), 254.

CHAPTER 34

1. Personal archives, December 30, 2011.
2. Personal archives, May 1985.
3. Personal archives, August 1988.

CHAPTER 35

1. Ellie Tesher, "A 'Powerhouse' Gets High Pay," *Toronto Star*, March 3, 1985.
2. John Haslett Cuff, "Shades of Brown," The Globe and Mail, August 16, 1986.
3. George Frajkor, quoted in John Haslett Cuff, "Shades of Brown," The Globe and Mail, August 16, 1986.
4. Personal archives, August 1968.
5. John Haslett Cuff, "From Hard-Hitters to Cheerleaders, Toronto Newscasts Cover the Dome," The Globe and Mail, June 1, 1989.
6. John Bierman, Dark Safari: The Life Behind the Legend of Henry Morton Stanley (New York: Alfred A. Knopf, 1990), 3.
7. Ibid., n.p.
8. CBC at Six, "Searching the Past," CBC News, April 1990.
9. Reg Rymer, World Relief Canada, interviewed in CBC at Six, "Searching the Past," CBC News, April 1990.
10. CBC at Six, "Searching the Past," CBC News, April 1990.

CHAPTER 36

1. Greg Quill, "CBC News Veteran Ups Anchor," *The Globe and Mail*, March 1, 1991.
2. Personal correspondence, May 21, 1991.
3. Personal correspondence, March 5, 1991.

CHAPTER 38

1. John F. Burns, "Racing Through Snipers' Alley on Ride to Sarajevo," *The New York Times*, September 26, 1992. https://www.nytimes.com/1992/09/26/world/racing-through-snipers-alley-on-ride-to-sarajevo.html.
2. Otto von Bismarck, Speech to the Reichstag, December 5, 1876. https://www.oxfordreference.com/view/10.1093/acref/9780191826719.001.0001/q-oro-ed4-00001699.
3. Ian Traynor, "Trying the Tyrant We Helped to Create," The Guardian, January 16, 2002. https://www.theguardian.com/world/2002/jan/16/milosevictrial.
4. World News Tonight with Peter Jennings, ABC News, January 23, 1994.
5. Personal archives, n.d.

CHAPTER 39

1. David Rieff, *Slaughterhouse: Bosnia and the Failure of the West* (New York: Touchstone/Simon & Schuster, 1995), 257.
2. Jeremy Bowen, War Stories (London: Simon & Schuster, 2006), c. 5.
3. Personal recollection.

4. Jeremy Bowen, *War Stories* (London: Simon & Schuster, 2006), 129.

CHAPTER 41

1. Human Rights Watch, "Rwanda: Justice After Genocide—20 Years Later," March 28, 2014. https://www.hrw.org/news/2014/03/28/rwanda-justice-after-genocide-20-years.
2. Fergal Keane, *All of These People* (New York: HarperCollins Publishers, 2005), 306.

CHAPTER 44

1. John Bierman and Colin Smith, *Fire in the Night: Wingate of Burma, Ethiopia and Zion* (New York: Random House, 1999), 93.
2. Personal recollection, St. James's Church, in St. James's Gardens, London, June 13, 2006.
3. Rudyard Kipling, "Mandalay," *Barrack-Room Ballads and Other Verses* (London: Methuen Publishing, [1892] 1989).

CHAPTER 46

1. Personal archives, May 19, 1997.

CHAPTER 47

1. Christine Doyle, "The Greatest Gift of All," *The Daily Telegraph*, October 22, 2002.
2. John Keegan, "Keen on Heroes: John Keegan Reviews *Alamein* by John Bierman and Colin Smith," *The Daily Telegraph*, October 5, 2002. https://www.telegraph.co.uk/culture/4728909/Keen-on-heroes.html.

CHAPTER 48

1. Seymour M. Hersh, *Reporter: A Memoir* (New York: Vintage Books, 2018), 306.
2. William Shakespeare, Hamlet, Act IV, Scene V, circa 1602.
3. William Shakespeare, "Fear no more the heat o' the sun," song from Cymbeline, circa 1609. http://shakespeare.mit.edu/cymbeline/full.html.
4. Ibid.
5. W. H. Auden, "Funeral Blues." https://allpoetry.com/Funeral-Blues.
6. Personal recollection.
7. Hafiz, "The Poem: XIV," The Garden of Heaven, tr. Gertrude Bell (Mineola, New York: Dover Publications, Inc.), 44.
8. Personal correspondence, January 2006.
9. Personal correspondence, January 2006.
10. Personal recollection.

11. Personal correspondence, April 16, 2007.

CHAPTER 49

1. The Agenda with Steve Paikin, "Who Is Canada's Best Ever Female Foreign Correspondent," TVO, January 23, 2012. https://www.tvo.org/article/who-is-canadas-best-ever-female-foreign-correspondent.
1. John Donne, "Air and Angels," *The Complete English Poems*, ed. A.J. Smith (London: Penguin Books Ltd., 1986).

CHAPTER 50

1. Hoagy Carmichael and Ned Washington, "The Nearness of You," written in 1938, released in 1940 © Sony/ATV Music Publishing LLC.

Author Bio

Hilary Brown has filed television reports from every continent except Antarctica. She was once profiled on TVO's 'The Agenda' as **'Canada's best-ever female foreign correspondent.'**

This embarrasses her.

She was one of the last journalists to **be lifted by helicopter from the roof of the American Embassy in Saigon in 1975,** during the Communist takeover of South Vietnam. One of her ABC reports later appeared in the motion picture **'The Deer Hunter'** in what Brown calls her 'fifteen seconds of fame.'

During the 1980's she was an Anchor for the **Canadian Broadcasting Corporation** in Toronto, an experience she describes as 'death by hairspray.' She later returned to ABC News for another 18 years to do the work she loved best: foreign news reporting.

She was married to the British biographer and BBC correspondent **John Bierman,** who she met in Pakistan during the Indo-Pak war of 1971. He became her mentor, best friend, and father of her only child. Their life together, in half a dozen countries over three decades, is a **great love story** that only ended with his death in 2006. As a widow, Brown continued to work at what she calls **'the best job in the world'** before she finally hung up her trench coat. Two years later she fell in love with a Canadian businessman who, until the global pandemic, flew her around the world in the relentless pursuit of **pseudo-extreme sport**s for which she was totally unqualified. She says he keeps her in a constant state of excitement and fear, which is just like being a foreign correspondent, all over again.

'**Foreign correspondents are like war tourists in flak jackets,' she writes. 'They document human misery, and then move on.**' But many are left with the emotional baggage of guilt, and a search for atonement. This is one of the many themes in Brown's lively memoir, and it's quite a ride.

To readers of all ages, but especially her own, her message is that life is never over… until it's over.

Photo: **Krystyne Griffin**

Hilary Brown has lived and worked out of 10 cities in **eight countries** in the course of her career. She now lives in **Toronto**.

Jacket Design: **Jonathan Bierman**

Index

Note the italicized "*n*" after certain page numbers refers to the endnote number.

A

Aaron, Betsy,	166
The Abandoned Woman (Condon),	172
ABC Evening News,	144, 194
ABC Radio News,	135, 144
ABC Sports,	303
ABC Television Network,	90
London, UK office,	43
ABC World News Tonight,	289
Absolutely Fabulous (TV series),	341
Achilleas, Nicolas,	153–154
Adagio in G Minor (Albinoni),	292
Adie, Kate,	301
Afghanistan, 1971,	80–81
Afghanistan, 1972,	111
Afghan war (2001–present),	377–384
child refugee labour,	379–380
invasion by U.S. 2001,	377–378
opium trade,	382
U.S. victory over Taliban, 2001,	392
African Union (prev. Organization of African Unity),	312
Agence France Presse,	207
The Agenda (TV Ontario program),	416
AIDS epidemic,	256
Akers, Karen,	218, 404

Albinoni, Tomaso,	292
Alexander the Great,	113
Alfonsin, Raúl,	224
Alice's Adventures in Wonderland (Carroll),	100
All of These People (Keane),	314n2
Almasy, Laszlo,	398
Al Qaeda,	377, 378, 392
AM America, ABC,	172, 175
Amanpour, Christiane,	302
American Broadcasting Company (ABC),	164, 169, 171, 172, 173
London bureau,	324
American Broadcasting Company (ABC) News,	44, 130–131, 135–136, 140, 143, 151, 155, 175, 176, 204, 215, 220–221, 227, 228, 230, 233, 234–236, 275, 276, 295–296, 323, 342, 359, 373
Baghdad bureau,	394–395, 404–406
London, UK correspondent base,	131, 132–133, 134, 135, 140, 142–144, 159, 409
Paris bureau,	192–195, 199–201, 205
Saigon bureau,	161
Amnesty International,	101n1, 176
Amnesty International Annual Report 1974/1975,	101n1
Anderson, Alexandra,	136, 137–138
Anderson, David,	19, 20, 60, 61
Angleton, James Jesus,	185
animism,	114
Annan, Kofi,	152
Annels, Dickie,	63, 104
Arabian Gulf War (1990–1991),	392
Arafat, Yasser,	232
Archer, Nick,	136–137, 140
Argov, Shlomo,	230
Aris, Michael,	349
Arledge, Roone,	204, 205, 235
Army of Republika Srpska (Serbian army),	285
Army of the Republic of Vietnam (ARVN),	160, 162, 165, 170
Arnold, Sue,	90, 90n1, 424–425, 429

Arrowsmith, John,	275
assassination of Martin Luther King Jr. (1968),	38
assassination of Robert Kennedy (1968),	38
Associated Press (AP),	6, 189, 326
Auden, W.H.,	402, 402*n*5
Austin, Chuck,	12
Automation (Diebold),	40
The Avengers (TV series),	249
Aviation Week,	215
Axworthy, Thomas S.,	38*n*1
Azores archipelago,	51–53

B

Babarovic, Tina,	381
"Back in the Game: Leonard Cohen Makes His Return to Working Life" (Nestruck),	37*n*2
Bakhash, Shaul,	117
Bangladesh,	84
Bartley, Tina,	399
Baybea (yacht),	64
BBC News at Six,	92*n*5
Beatty, Warren,	35
Beck, John,	412–413
Beck, Phineaus,	100
Begin, Menachem,	128, 206
Beirut, Lebanon,	40
Bell, Gertrude,	402, 402*n*7
Bell, Martin,	302
Bennett, Jim,	160, 161
Bentson, Clark, 324, 325–326, 328, 329, 330, 331, 332, 334, 337, 365, 369, 373, 374–375, 376, 404, 411	
Ben-Yishai, Ron,	150
Berlin Philharmonic Orchestra,	40
Bermuda Race (1970),	46–49
Bernini, Gian Lorenzo,	375
Bernstein, Carl,	217

Bernstein, Howard,	237, 238, 239, 244–245, 257
Bernstein, Joel,	209–210
Bettag, Tom,	349, 352
Bhutan, 1996,	334–345
Buddhism in,	335–336, 337–338
fire festival,	343–344
traditional Oriental medicine,	342–343
Bhutto, Zulfiqar Ali,	77, 78, 79, 84
Bierman, Dick,	108, 117

Bierman, John, 2, 76–77, 78, 79, 80, 82, 85, 88, 90, 91, 92, 93, 95, 96, 97–110, 128–129, 133–134, 138, 140, 147, 148, 152, 153, 173, 178, 179, 180, 187–188, 192, 204, 205, 208, 216–217, 216n1, 220–223, 235, 236, 237–238, 239, 248, 249–251, 252, 258–259, 259n6, 259n7, 346–347, 348, 352, 357, 369–371, 374–375, 384, 385–386, 387, 388–391, 395–396, 398–403

Bierman, Jonathan ("Jonnie") Anthony David, 212, 218, 237–238, 252, 271, 273, 305–310, 346–347, 347n1, 352, 364–365, 374–375, 387, 388–391, 403, 409

birth of, 1979,	212–213
Bingham, Charlotte,	22, 23
bin Laden, Osama,	313, 377, 378, 380
Birtley, Tony,	290
Bishop, Gloria,	35, 384, 385
Bitter Lemons (Durrell),	141
Blackburn, Marjorie,	270
Blair, Tony,	392, 393
Blakemore, Bill,	225, 234
Blanch, Lesley,	117–118
Bleier, Ed,	44, 216
Blind in One Ear (Macnee),	308
Blobel, Dr. Günter,	36
Bloody Sunday, Londonderry, Northern Ireland,	92–93
"Bloody Sunday, 30 January 1972—A Chronology of Events" (Melaugh & Mckenna),	92n4
Bloom, Dan,	151
Blundy, David,	226, 226n1
Boldini, Giovanni,	31
Bolero (Ravel),	303

Boras, Igor, 293–294
Bosnia and Herzegovina war, 1992–1995, 285–295
   1994 Olympics compared to 10 years later, 303–304
   Dayton Peace Accord, 297
   death of journalists in, 290–291
   ethnic cleansing by Serbs of eastern Bosnia, 286
   excitement and fear as reporter covering, 297–298
   international press corps in Sarajevo, 302–303
   Sarajevo's Romeo and Juliet, 294
   siege of Sarajevo, 285–286, 290–295, 298, 300–301
   sporadic conflicts and massacres after peace accord, 300
Bosnian Serb army, 315–316, 318
The Boston Globe, 208, 235, 236
Bottin Mondain, 28
Bouchard, Marie-France, 429–430
Bowen, Jeremy, 294, 297, 297*n*2, 302, 302*n*4
Bradley, Ed, 161
Brckić, Boško, 294
Bregg, Peter, 59*n*1
Brenner, Zvi, 347
British Broadcasting Corporation (BBC), 2, 21, 77, 78, 80, 81, 82, 85, 90, 110, 128, 179, 180, 186, 192, 205, 223, 301–302
   Panorama documentary on Iran, 117
   Persian Service, 116
British Broadcasting Corporation (BBC) TV News, 91, 92*n*5, 135, 142, 147, 366
"British Journalist Slain by Sniper" (*The New York Times*), 226*n*1
British Special Air Service (SAS), 394, 405
Broinowski, Alison, 99
Broinowski, Richard, 99
Brolan, James, 405
Brook, Frances, 99, 105, 190–191, 192
Brook, Ian, 99, 105
Brown, Jocelyn, 7, 8, 10, 12, 61, 88, 138, 191, 212, 354–355, 356, 363, 397
Brown, Kathy, 7, 10, 12, 355–356, 364, 397
Brown, Ray, 27

Brown, Tony,	7–8, 10, 12, 31, 61, 88, 138, 191, 212, 355, 356, 363, 397
Brown, Virginia (Gingie),	7, 10, 12, 95, 96, 190, 192, 276, 356, 357, 363–364, 375, 397, 402, 403, 433
Brown, William,	356
Browne, Diana,	99
Browne, Harold,	297
Browne, Nick,	99, 117
Bruynzeel, C.B.,	50
Buddha statues, Bamiyan, Afghanistan,	112
Buenos Aires, 1982,	224
Bukojemski, Michal,	329
Burke, Stanley,	27
Burma, 1999,	348–352
child labour in,	351
Burns, John F.,	58, 291n1
Bush, George W.,	377, 392

C

Cable News Network (CNN),	241, 302–303, 409
Caine, Michael,	113
CAIN Web Service,	92n4
Calendar (CBC Montreal TV show),	32–33
Calvert, Brian,	4, 6
Cameron, Sue,	410
Cameron, Ian,	410
Camp David Accord, September, 1978,	128, 206, 217, 230
Canadian Broadcasting Corporation (CBC),	22, 81, 82, 94, 194, 237, 239–272
London, UK bureau,	22–23, 26
Montreal,	32–37, 38
Paris, France office,	27–28, 32–33
Canadian Broadcasting Corporation (CBC) Radio,	129, 130, 132
Canadian Press,	18
Cape Town to Rio yacht race,	50–51, 53–56
Capreol, Joan,	39n2
Caputo, Philip,	164, 164n1

Carlin, Vince,	240
Carmichael, Hoagy,	404, 434
Carroll, Lewis,	100
Carter, Jimmy,	2, 128
Cash, Johnny,	35
"CBC News Veteran Ups Anchor" (Quill),	271n1
CBC Radio,	273
CBM Magazine (CBC radio show),	35, 39
Central Intelligence Agency (CIA),	184
Chamberlain, Neville,	223
Champ, Henry,	169
Champagne, Edith,	241, 245, 256, 257
Charalambous, Joseph,	141
Chariots of Fire (movie),	257
chastity is outmoded debate, Brock Hall, UBC,	17–19
Cheatham, Tom,	209–210, 212
Cheney, Dick,	392
Chesshyre, Robert,	401
Child, Julia,	39, 100
Chrétien, Jean,	19
Churchill, Winston,	7, 346, 372
Cioffi, Lou,	130, 192
CJOH-TV, Ottawa,	51, 53, 56, 60, 63, 65, 67, 89, 93, 135
Clementine in the Kitchen (Beck),	100
Clery, Val,	22
Clifton, Tony,	191
Clinton, Bill,	313
Cohen, Leonard,	36–37, 37n1, 130
Cohen, Ronnie,	371
Cole, Neil,	36
collapse of communism in Eastern Europe, 1989,	270
The Collected Works of W.B. Yeats (ed. Finneran),	93n7
Columbia Broadcasting System (CBS),	139, 151, 161, 197, 209, 210, 215
Columbia Broadcasting System (CBS) News,	101–102, 116, 129, 381
Colvin, Marie,	421

Condon, Richard,	172, 173
Connery, Sean,	113
Cook, Robin,	393
Cooper, Anderson,	322
Coronet Among the Weeds (Bingham),	23
Cory, William,	365
"Counterparts Tough on Her: Female TV Announcer Began Career in Paris" (Capreol),	39n2
Coward, Noel,	396, 432
Cowes yacht regatta, Isle of Wight,	64
Cross, James,	58, 59
Crossette, Barbara,	339
CTV News,	169
The Current (CBC),	272
Cymbeline (Shakespeare),	398n3, 402n4
Cyprus,	
Annan Plan referendum in 2004,	152
coup d'éta in 1974,	147–148, 151–152
disaster for Greek Cypriots of coup d'éta,	151–152
Green Line in,	150
independence from UK in 1960,	147
Turkish invasion of,	140, 149–152, 179, 180
UN peacekeeping force in 1964,	148
Cyprus, 1973,	141–142
Cyprus, 1974,	153–157
Cyprus, 1975,	173–175
Cyprus, 1976,	190–192
Cyprus, 1991,	272–273

D

The Daily Telegraph,	389n1, 390, 390n2, 401
The Daily Telegraph Weekend Magazine,	208
Dale-Harris, Lindsay,	247, 384, 387, 430
Dallaire, Roméo,	312
Damascus,	40

Damascus, 1968,	72
Dark Safari: The Life Behind the Legend of Henry Morton Stanley (Bierman),	259–260, 259n6, 259n7
Dawes, Martin,	366, 367
Day of the Jackal (Forsyth),	110
Dean, Christopher,	303
Debenham, Liz,	148
Debrett's Peerage,	28
The Deer Hunter (movie),	170
Defense Attachés Office (DAO), Saigon,	166–167
de Gaulle, Charles,	38
de Kooning, Willem,	42
Delaney, Kevin,	164–165, 169, 171
de la Presle, Catherine,	25, 26, 28, 30, 32, 194
del Campo, Frederico,	223
de Monicault, Catherine,	211, 411
de Monicault, Olivier,	194
Denktash, Rauf,	149
depression,	354–357
genetics and,	354, 357, 368–370
treatments for,	354–355, 356, 371–372
de Saint-Exupéry, Antoine,	28
Los Desaparecidos ("The Disappeared"), Argentina,	224
Descartes, René,	29
de Soto, Álvaro,	152
de Vito, Tony,	375
Diebold, John,	40, 41, 43–44
Dietrich, Marlene,	35
Dior, Christine,	199–200
Donaldson, Joan,	239, 240
Dorji, Kenly,	340
Dorozynski, Alexandre,	26, 27
Doucet, Lyse,	301, 421
Douglas, Paul,	405
Dowbiggin, Bruce,	241

Doyle, Christine,	389, 389n1
Dozier, James,	225
Dozier, Kimberly,	405
Drumm, Máire,	93–94
Dubrovnik, Croatia,	1969
Durrell, Lawrence,	141

E

Editions des Deux Coqs d'Or (Two Golden Cockerels),	25–26, 27
Egypt,	
Camp David Accord,	128
involvement in Yom Kippur War,	127–128
Eichmann, Adolf,	208
electroconvulsive therapy (ECT),	354
Elizabeth II, Queen, Silver Jubilee celebrations,	203–204
El Salvador civil war (1979–1992),	224, 226–229
dangers for journalists of covering urban civil war,	226–227
risks in countryside in,	226–228
An Enduring Love: My Life with the Shah (Pahlavi),	69n2
The English Patient (Ondaatje),	398
entomology,	7
Ephron, Nora,	217, 218
Erikson, Arthur,	248
Erikson, Christopher,	248
Esfandiari, Haleh,	117
Estrade, Bernard,	207
Etcheverry, Patrick,	143, 176, 177, 193, 196, 200, 201, 394
ethnic cleansing, eastern Bosnia, 1993,	286
Ethniki Organosis Kyprion Agoniston (EOKA),	149
Evening News, ABC,	139
Evill, Gerda,	24
Exelby, John,	424
Expo 67, Montreal,	35, 248

F

Falklands War, 1982,	222–224
fall of Berlin Wall, 1989,	270
famine, south Sudan,	365–366
Farsi language,	5, 99, 116
Fear and Loathing in Las Vegas (Thompson),	223
Fecan, Ivan,	274
Field-Marsham, Rupert,	247, 387
Financial Post,	358
Financial Times,	99
Finneran, Richard J.,	93n7
Fire in the Night: Wingate of Burma, Ethiopia and Zion (Bierman & Smith),	346–347, 347n1, 348–349
Firenze (yawl),	65
Fisk, Robert,	4
Fitzgerald, Ella,	27
Foco, Eki,	301
Forces Armées Zaïroises (FAZ),	195, 197
Ford, Gerald,	166
Forsyth, Freddy,	110
Fox, Barry,	161, 165, 166, 168, 169
Fox, Peter,	161, 165, 168, 169
Frajkor, George,	255n3
Francis, Diane,	271, 273, 358, 412–413, 414, 415–416, 424
Franklin, Aretha,	218
Freed, Kayce,	403, 404
"From Hard-Hitters to Cheerleaders, Toronto Newscasts Cover the Dome" (Haslett Cuff),	256n5
Front de Libération du Québec (FLQ),	58
Front de Libération Nationale Congolaise (FLNC),	195
Frum, Barbara,	255
"Funeral Blues" (Auden),	402n5

G

Gabor, Zsa Zsa,	214

Galbraith, John Kenneth,	9, 9n1
Gallego, Sonia,	409
Galtieri, Leopoldo,	222
The Gambia, 1977,	201–203
Gandhi, Indira,	75–76, 81
The Garden of Heaven: Poems of Hafez (Hafez, trans. by Bell),	402n7
Garibaldi, Giuseppe,	374
Garrels, Annie,	251
Gedrinsky, Nicolas,	193, 196, 200, 203
"General De Gaulle and 'Vive le Québec libre,'" (Axworthy),	38n1
genetics,	7
Geneva, Switzerland,	10–11
Gentile, Bill,	226n1
Georgiou, Stavros,	154
germ warfare,	7
Giap, Vo Nguyen,	160
Global Nuclear Club,	84
The Globe and Mail,	39, 39n2, 58, 253–256, 254n2, 255n3, 256n5, 269, 271n1, 401
Godfrey, Jim,	134, 143, 145
"Golda's Meltdown" (Rabinovich),	127n1
Goldman, Bob,	156
Good Morning America (ABC),	298, 321–322, 408
Gozlan, Renate,	193
Grace, Noelle,	10, 248, 384
Granum, Rex,	373
"The Greatest Gift of All" (Doyle),	389n1
Greece, military junta overthrown in July, 1974,	151
Greek Cypriot National Guard,	150
Green, Robin,	41, 42, 51
Greenberg, Yossi,	209
Greene, Graham,	110
Greenland, 1995,	331–333
Grego, Meir,	155–156, 157
Grenada, U.S. invasion of,	222
Griffin, Krystyne,	248, 310, 366, 367, 384, 385

Griffin, Scott,	248, 366, 367, 410
Griffiths, Stuart,	51
The Guardian newspaper,	180, 192, 292n3, 401
Guggenheim, Peggy,	42
Guggenheim Museum, New York,	41, 51, 136

H

Habib, Philip,	232
Habyarimana, Juvénal,	311
Hafez (or Hafiz),	402, 402n7
Hahn, Judith,	423–424
Haley, Alex,	201, 202, 203
Halliday, Chris,	357
Halliday, Scott,	357
Halton, David,	39, 41
Hamlet (Shakespeare),	397n2
Hampstead, London, UK,	8
Hands, David,	365
Harper's Bazaar,	23, 26
Harrington, Beth,	240, 271
Harris, Judith,	411
Hartney, Jane,	322, 373
Hasan, Lama,	409
Haslett Cuff, John,	254, 254n2, 255n3, 256, 256n5
Hastings, Max,	223
Hawkes, Cheryl,	241
Hawksley, Humphrey,	421
Hayes, Bill,	146
head covering (in Iran),	5
Heaney, Seamus,	314
Heartburn (movie),	218
The Heart's Grown Brutal (Bierman),	93, 110
Heath, Edward, Prime Minister,	64, 65, 184
Heikal, Mohammed,	102
Hemingway, Ernest,	90

Hensher, Philip,	75n1
Herbert, Gwyneth,	404, 410
A Hero's Many Faces: Raoul Wallenberg in Contemporary Monuments (Schult),	209n2
Hersh, Seymour, M.,	393, 393n1
Hezbollah,	233, 275
Hill, David,	30
Hillary, Edmund,	70
Hillier, Scott,	275
Hirashiki, Yasutsune "Tony",	161, 163
Hitler, Adolf,	236
Ho Chi Minh City (prev. Saigon), 1985,	325–326
Hoffman, Fred,	216
Holbrooke, Richard,	297
"Home from Home, John Bierman in Toronto" (*The Daily Telegraph Weekend Magazine*),	208n1
Hong Kong,	20, 261–264
hostage-taking at U.S. Embassy, Tehran (November 4, 1979),	2
as big news story in U.S.,	4
Housego, David,	99, 117
Housego, Jenny,	99, 117
Hoveyda, Amir-Abbas,	100
Howard, Harriet,	250
Howard, Leslie,	247
Hubbard, Robert,	145, 147
Huber, Freddy,	95, 96
Huber, Karina,	96, 276, 363–364
Human Rights Watch,	176, 312, 312n1
Hunt, Chris,	4009
Hunt, Elisabeth,	24
Hunt, Jonathan,	359, 371, 409
Hunter, Paul,	241
Hunt Saboteurs Association,	182–183
Hurd, Douglas,	292
Hussein, Saddam,	392
Hyslop, Tom,	61

I

"I Get Along Without You Very Well" (Carmichael),	404
independence referendum, Quebec, 1980,	60
Indian nuclear test, 1974,	84
Indo-Pak War of 1971,	75, 80–82, 84, 90
International Criminal Court, The Hague,	299, 315
International Criminal Tribunal for Former Yugoslavia,	315, 319
International Criminal Tribunal for Rwanda (ICTR),	315
International Monetary Fund,	198
International Santa Claus Games,	331
International School of Geneva (Ecolint),	10
Iran (Persia until 1935), 1971,	72
expulsion from,	116–118
Iran (Persia until 1935), 1972–1973,	91–110, 116–118
caviar in,	105–106
Nixon's visit to,	102
as police state,	99–101
Iran (Persia until 1935), 1975,	176–179
Iran (Persia until 1935), 1979,	1–6
Iran (Persia until 1935), 1980,	216
Iranian secret police (SAVAK),	99–101
Iraq War (2003–2011),	392
casualties of,	393–394
journalists killed or injured during,	405–406
kidnappings during,	395
Sunnis *vs.* Shias in,	393, 395
weapons of mass destruction claim for,	392–393
Irish Northern Aid Committee (NORAID),	184, 185
Irish Republican Army (IRA),	93, 184
Islamabad, Pakistan, 1971,	74–81
Islamic fundamentalism,	2, 79
alcohol ban,	3
Ismić, Admira,	294
Israel,	129–132
expulsion of Gaza Strip fundamentalists to Lebanon, 1992,	274–275

invasion of Lebanon, 1982,	229–233
Israeli Defense Forces (IDF),	131, 230–231, 233
Israel's Lebanon War (Schiff & Yáari),	232n1
Israel-Syria disengagement agreement, June, 1974,	155
return of POWs provision,	155–157
Istanbul, 1973,	140–141, 142

J

Jamison, Kay,	371
Jan, Tahir, Air Commodore,	79, 113
Jay, Margaret,	217, 414
Jay, Peter,	217
Jay, Sandra,	414
Jeal, Tim,	259–260
Jeffery, Mike,	20, 21
Jennings, Annie,	411
Jennings, Kayce,	412
Jennings, Peter,	44, 139, 159, 175, 203, 204–205, 255–256, 289, 293n4, 300–301, 403
Jerusalem,	360–362
The Jerusalem Post,	127n1
Johns, Ann,	411
The Journal (CBC),	255
Jung, Carl,	356
Juno Awards,	37
"Justice After Genocide—20 Years Later" (Human Rights Watch),	312n1

K

Kabul, Afghanistan, 1971,	81, 84–88
Kabul, Afghanistan, 1972,	111–112
Kafiristan, Pakistan, 1972,	113–116
Kagame, Paul,	312, 315
Kaplan, Bernard,	32, 161, 194
Kaplan, David,	290
Kaplan, Rick,	304

Kapuściński, Ryszard,	101, 101*n*2
Karadžić, Radovan,	298, 299, 320
Karzai, Hamid,	378–379
Kashiwahara, Ken,	160
Kathmandu, Nepal, 1971,	70–74
Kazale, Jurate,	327
Kazem Shariatmadari, Sayyid Mohammad,	4
Keane, Fergal,	314, 314*n*2, 352
Keegan, John,	390n2, 390
"Keen on Heroes: John Keegan Reviews *Alamein* by John Bierman and Colin Smith" (Keegan),	390*n*2
Keith, Vicki,	256–257
Kelley, Brian,	231
Kennedy, Jackie,	42
Kennedy, Robert,	38
Kerr, Douglas,	211
Khan, Abdul Qadeer,	84
Khan, Gengis,	112
Khan, Reza,	69
Khan, Yahya,	75
Khmer Rouge,	161
Khomeini, Ayatollah,	2, 67, 99
kidney dialysis,	385–386, 387, 388
kidney transplant,	388–389, 396, 398
Kinch, Cynthia,	237
King, Jerry,	143
King, Martin Luther, Jr.,	38
Kingsmill, Derek,	316, 317, 322
Kinsey Reports,	18
Kipling, Rudyard,	82, 113, 351, 351*n*3
Kissinger, Henry,	155
Knox-Johnston, Robin,	45
Konaré, Alpha Oumar,	328
Koufax, Sandy,	34
Kramer, Larry,	326

Kyriakides, George, 388

L

Lambon, Tim, 303
Lambrides, Theo, 174
Lanoue, Alain, 429–430
Laporte, Pierre, 58, 59
Laurie, Jim, 161
Lebanon,
   first Israeli invasion of, 206
   invasion of by Israel, 1982, 229–233
   refusal of to let in expelled Palestinians, 1992, 275
Lebanon, 1992, 275–276
le Carré, John (a.k.a. David Cornwell), 186–187, 207, 212, 249, 259, 306, 310
Lech, Austria, 10
Lederer, Edie, 326
Lee, Joe, 161, 171
Leibner, Richard, 205, 214–215, 218, 238
"Leonard Cohen, the Women He Loved, and the Women Who Loved Him" (Warner), 37n3
Leopold II, King, 258
Leroy, Catherine, 150–151, 207
Leshem, Avraham, 207
Leshem, Ziona, 207
Lévesque, René, 60
Lewis, George, 161
Lichtenstein, Roy, 42
Lieberman, Natalie, 252
Litke, Mark, 325, 327
Little, Alan, 302
The Little Drummer Girl (le Carré), 207
Livingstone, David, 258
Logan, Matt, 286
Loiselle, Gilles, 38
Lomas, Oggie, 81

London, Ontario,	7, 12–16, 19
puritanical, self-righteous, conformist atmosphere in fifties in,	9
London, UK,	21–24, 90
London, UK, 1973,	132–135
London, UK, 1974,	143–144, 147, 157–158
London, UK, 1975,	159–160, 175, 181–189, 192
London, UK, 1977,	203–204
London, UK, 1979,	211–212
Loomis, Gloria,	222, 236, 251
Lord, Bill,	231–232
Loren, Sophia,	374
Lower, Elmer,	143
Ludington, Nick,	189
Lumley, Joanna,	341–342

M

MacArthur, Douglas,	407
MacIntyr, Peter,	143, 159
Maclean's magazine,	249–250, 270
Maclear, Michael,	67, 265
Macnee, Patrick,	249, 307
Magee, Zoe,	409
Majestic Failure: The Fall of the Shah (Zonis),	102n3
Makarios III, Archbishop,	147–148
Malcolm, John,	103
Mali, 1995,	327–331
Man Alive (BBC documentary series),	208, 217
The Manchurian Candidate (Condon),	172
"Mandalay," *Barrack-Room Ballads and Other Verses* (Kipling),	351n3
Mann, Jonathan,	241
"The Man Who Would Be King" (Kipling),	113
Marchand, Paul,	291
Marenghi, Paolo,	352
Marisco, Paolo,	342
marriage in Cyprus, 1976,	188–191

Martin, Christopher,	306–307
Martin, Graham,	164
Martin, Sandra,	401
Mastering the Art of French Cooking (Child),	39, 100
maternity leave,	210–211, 213
Matthau, Walter,	42
Mavroleon, Carlos,	313
McCluskey, Peter,	241
McDaniel, Joanne,	145, 146–147
McDougall, Pat,	35
McGuigan, Paddy,	94n9
Mckenna, Fionbuala,	92n4
McLaren, Norman,	42
McManus, Kathy,	360, 361–362
McWethy, Jack,	215, 216
Means of Escape: A War Correspondent's Memoir of Life and Death in Afghanistan, the Middle East, and Vietnam (Caputo),	164n1
Medicine Hat, Alberta,	7
Melaugh, Martin,	92n4
Member of the Most Excellent Order of the British Empire (MBE),	7
"The Men Behind the Wire" (McGuigan),	94, 94n9
mental illness,	245, 309–310, 354, 355–356, 364, 367–368, 371–372
Messer, Thomas,	42
Me Too movement,	323
Michelangelo,	375
Michener, Roland,	66
Midnight Express (movie),	146
Mikuliç, Planinka,	293
Millard, Niki,	286
Milldyke, Bill,	157
Miller, John,	187
Millfield school, Street, Somerset,	306, 308–309
Mills, David,	286, 288, 289
Milne, Mary,	213
Mladić, Ratko,	315, 319

Mobutu Sese Seko,	196, 197–198
Montgomery, Bernard, Field Marshal,	370
Montreal,	32–39
Montreal Press Club,	34
The Montreal Star,	64, 65, 67, 69, 116
Morning Cloud (yacht),	64
Morrison, Keith,	269
Morse, Richard,	408
Moscow,	369
Moth, Margaret,	291
The Mothers of Invention,	35
Mothers of the Plaza de Mayo, Argentina,	224
The Mountain Fund to Save the Vietnamese Boat People,	260–261
Moussus, Fabrice,	230
Mowat, Farley,	35
Munir, Metin,	146
Murphy, Bob,	220, 234
Myers, Diana,	341, 367
My Heart is Africa (Griffin),	366

N

Nagorski, Tom,	342
Napoleon, Bonaparte,	250
Napoleon, Louis,	250–251
Napoleon III and His Carnival Empire (Bierman),	251, 258
Natanson, Phoebe,	373
The National (CBC network news show),	253, 273
National Broadcasting Company (NBC),	2, 139, 151, 161
Pentagon correspondent, Washington D.C.,	215–219
National Broadcasting Company (NBC) News,	205
Tel Aviv bureau,	205–211
National Film Board (NFB) of Canada,	36, 113–114
National Institute of Health, Washington, D.C.,	371
nationalism, Quebec,	33
National League for Democracy, Burma,	349

The National Post,	37n2, 273
National Public Radio (NPR),	251, 273, 408
NBC Nightly News,	215
near-death experience (Dubrovnik),	10–11
near-death experience (Iran),	5, 6
"The Nearness of You" (Carmichael),	433–434
Negin, Mark,	36
Nestruck, J. Kelly,	37n2
Newington, Mike,	207
Newington, Nina,	207
Newshour (CBC),	255
News of the World,	213
Newsweek,	226n1
New York,	41–46, 51
New York, 1973,	135–140
New York, 1975,	171–173
New York, 1981,	219–221
The New York Review of Books,	259–260
The New York Times,	58, 73, 198, 216, 226n1, 291n1
The New York Times Book Review,	217
Nicolson, Marjorie,	60
Nightline (ABC),	144, 221, 232, 275, 349, 352, 379
Nixon, Richard,	102, 160
non-governmental organizations (NGOs),	227
Norgay, Tenzing,	70
Northern Ireland Troubles,	91–94, 314
North Korea,	84
North Vietnamese Army (NVA),	160, 162, 164, 165, 166
demobilization of,	327
"Notes on Sources" (Bierman),	222n1
Novo, Estado,	143

O

Obama, Barak,	380, 393
Obama, Michelle,	271

The Observer,	90, 90n1, 91, 347
October Crisis, Quebec (1970–1971),	58–60
Odyssey (Bierman),	221, 235, 236
Old Chelsea, Quebec,	61, 64, 93, 94–96
Olivier, Sir Laurence,	35
Ondaatje, Michael,	398
Open Society Foundation,	349, 351
The Oprah Winfrey Show,	218
Organization of the Petroleum Exporting Companies (OPEC),	98, 176
Ormiston, Susan,	241
O'Ryan, Lydia,	411
Ottawa, 1970–1971,	51, 53, 56, 58–65
Owen, David,	292

P

Pachter, Charles,	271
Pahlavi, Farah,	69n2
Paikin, Steve,	241, 244, 271, 416
Pakistan, 1971,	74–81
Pakistan, 1972,	113–116
Palestine,	
as biblical Jewish homeland,	346–347
British-ruled,	346
Palestinian Liberation Organization (PLO),	230, 232
Palmer, Liz,	381
Papp, Susan,	271
Pappas, Ike,	215, 216
Paris, France,	25–31, 32–33
Paris, France, 1976–1977,	192–195, 199–201
Paris Peace Accords, 1973,	160
Payne, Ronnie,	401
Pearl, Daniel,	378
Pearson, Lester,	38
"Pendennis Column" (Arnold),	90n1
Pentcho (boat),	222, 223

Perle, Richard (a.k.a. the Prince of Darkness),	392
Persepolis, Shiraz, Iran,	67–69
Persia. *See* Iran (Persia until 1935)	
Peterson, Oscar,	27
Le Petit Prince (de Saint-Exupéry),	28
Petra, Jordan,	40
Phalange,	232
Phillips, Mark,	134, 135
Plaskett, Joe,	30, 31
"Please Don't Talk About Me When I'm Gone" (Herbert),	404
Plummer, Christopher,	35
The Point of Departure (Cook),	393
Poitier, Sidney,	35
Pompidou, Georges,	29
Portuguese Revolution, 1974,	140, 143–144, 174
"A 'Powerhouse' Gets High Pay" (Tesher),	253*n*1
The Prague Spring, 1968,	38
pregnancy,	210–211
Press Gallery Dinner, Ottawa, 1971,	62–63, 104
Price, Bartley,	275, 303, 380, 381, 396, 407, 408
Prizzi's Honor (Condon),	172
Public Broadcasting System (PBS),	45, 217, 303
Pulitzer Prizes,	58

Q

Quill, Greg,	271*n*1
Quinlan, Nicolas,	356

R

Rabin, Yitzhak,	274
Rabinovich, Abraham,	127*n*1
"Racing Through Snipers' Alley on Ride to Sarajevo" (Burns),	291*n*1
Radio-Canada,	38
Radio Milles Collines, Rwanda,	311–312

Rahman, Mujibur,	75
Ralfe, Tim,	59
Ramsbotham, Peter,	116, 117
Ramsing, Thor,	47
Ravel, Maurice,	303
Reasoner, Harry,	139–140
Red Brigades, Italy,	225–226
Reilly, Peter,	60
Reporter: A Memoir (Hersh),	393, 393*n*1
"A Reporter's Atonement" (H. Brown documentary),	263–266
retinis pigmentosa (RP),	90, 425
Reuters,	180, 192
Rich, Gilly,	401, 409
Rich, Sebastian,	409
Richards, Gilly,	410
Rieff, David,	297*n*1
Righteous Gentile: The Story of Raoul Wallenberg, Missing Hero of the Holocaust (Bierman), 208, 216, 216*n*1, 222	
Riley, Jean,	251
Riley, Jeremy,	251
Romanian revolution, 1989,	270
Rome, 2001,	375–376
Rommel, Erwin,	370
Roots (Haley),	201
Roots (TV miniseries),	201
Rose, Paul,	60
Ross, Jerilyn,	218, 371
Rowan, Peter,	364, 371
Rubinstein, Arthur,	35
A Rumor of War (Caputo),	164
Rwanda genocide, 1994,	311–315, 320
refugee camps,	313–315
United Nations peacekeeping force and,	312–313
Rwanda Patriotic Front (RPF),	311, 312, 313, 314, 315
Rymer, Reg,	264*n*9

S

Sadat, Anwar,	127, 205, 206
Safire, Bill,	216
Saigon, Vietnam, 1975,	160–169
20th anniversary of fall of,	324–325
escape from,	169–170
fall of,	164, 169–170, 172, 173, 260, 263
U.S. Embassy in,	164, 167–168
Salazar, António de Oliveira,	143
Samaranch, Julio Antonio,	293
Sampson, Nikos,	149
Sanders, Bernie,	393
Sanders, George,	214
Sanford, Geoff,	399
Sanford, Ted,	50, 51, 53, 54, 57, 64, 65
Sarajevo String Quartet,	292
Sayle, Murray,	85, 86
Schiff, Zéev,	232n1
schizophrenia,	355
Schlesinger, James,	165
Schork, Kurt,	294
Schult, Tanja,	209n2
The Scotch (Galbraith),	9, 9n1
Scully, John,	263, 264, 265
"Searching the Past" (CBC News),	263n8, 264n9, 265n10
seasonally adjusted depression (SAD),	362
Second World War, children evacuated from London,	108
Selassie, Haile,	68, 347
September 11, 2001 attacks,	377, 378, 392
"Shades of Brown" (Haslett Cuff),	254n2, 255n3
Shah, Mohammed Zahir,	111
Shah of Iran (a.k.a. Mohammad Reza Pahlavi) (1941–1979),	3, 65–66, 67, 69, 98, 99, 101, 102, 116–117, 176–178
Shah of Shahs (Kapuściński),	101, 101n2
Shakespeare, William,	397–398, 397n2, 398n3, 402, 402n4

Shakespeare Festival, Stratford, Ontario,	13
Sharon, Ariel,	230, 232
Sheehan, Bill,	157, 158, 175, 205
Shelley, Percy Bysshe,	20
Shohet, Mori,	248
Simon, Bob,	161, 209, 276
Simpson, John,	185, 378
Singer, Carla,	352, 368, 384
Sinn Féin (political wing of IRA),	93
Six-Day War of 1967 (a.k.a. 1967 Arab-Israeli War),	75, 127
60 Minutes, CBS,	177, 313
Slaughterhouse: Bosnia and the Failure of the West 297(Rieff),	n1
Smailoviç, Vedran,	292
Smith, Colin,	208, 347, 347n1, 348, 370, 390, 401
Smith, Howard K.,	194, 204
Smith, Jack,	194, 238–239
Smith, John,	261
Smith, Judy,	261
Sobel, Rebecca,	302
Solution (yacht),	47
Somalian botched raid by U.S., 1993,	312
Soros, George,	349, 351
Soviet invasion of Czechoslovakia, 1968,	38
Soviet Union, 1967,	39
Springate, Robin,	134, 143, 145, 159
Srebrenica genocide, 1995,	315–320
Bosnian Serb army enters,	318
International Criminal Tribunal investigated,	319
UN safe havens,	316, 318–319
Stahl, Lesley,	210
Stanley, Henry Morton,	258, 259, 260
"The Stare's Nest by My Window" (Yeats),	93n7
Stark, Freya,	105
State Law and Order Restoration Council (SLORC), Burma,	348–349
Stewart, Bob, Colonel,	299–300

"Stop the Press, I Want to Get On" (Tomalin),	131*n*2
"Storing Up Trouble: Pakistan's Nuclear Bombs" (*theguardian.com*),	84*n*1
Stormy (yacht),	50, 51, 52, 53, 56
Stuart, Eleanor,	36
Suckling, Ken,	286, 287, 288
Sullivan, Mike,	149
Sunday Correspondent,	226
The Sunday Times,	85, 421
The Sunday Times Magazine,	131*n*2
Suu Kyi, Aung San,	349, 352
"Suzanne" (*Songs of Leonard Cohen*),	37*n*1
"Suzanne by the River" (Cohen),	37
Svengali character,	13–14, 15
Switzerland,	88–89

T

Taliban,	112, 377, 378, 381, 392
Tehran, Iran, 1972–1973,	97–110, 128–129
unmarried status in,	116
Tel Aviv,	129–132
Sadat meets with Begin,	207
Tel Aviv, 1977–1979,	205–211
terror attacks, Bali, Indonesia, 2002,	407–408
Tesher, Ellie,	253, 253*n*1, 271, 412
Thackeray, William,	398
Thatcher, Margaret, Prime Minister,	222–223
the Holocaust,	221, 222, 311
Thigpen, Ed,	27
Thompson, Hunter S.,	222
Threlkeld, Dick,	161
Tibet, invaded by China, 1950,	335
The Times,	401
Today show, NBC,	215, 217
Tomalin, Nicholas,	131, 131*n*2
Topolski, Feliks,	147

Topolski, Marion,	147
Toronto, 1984–1991,	239–272
Toronto General Hospital,	385, 387
Toronto Health Network,	385
Toronto Star,	245, 251, 252, 253, 253n1, 269
Toronto the Dark Side (CBC series),	258
Torvill, Jane,	303
Townsend, Peter,	130
Trans-Canada Matinee (CBC radio program),	22, 26
Traynor, Ian,	292n3
Trudeau, Pierre Elliott,	58, 59, 63–64, 251
"Trudeau:'Just Watch Me'" (Bregg),	59n1
Truscott, Michael,	187
"Trying the Tyrant We Helped to Create" (Traynor),	292n3
tsunami, Indian Ocean, 2004,	407
Turkey, 1973–1974,	140–141
drug smuggling in,	145–147
Tuzi, Chuck,	257
TVOntario,	241, 416
two solitudes,	38
Tyler, Maggie,	425–426

U

United Nations Educational, Scientific and Cultural Organization (UNESCO) World Heritage Sites,	112
United Nations Protection Force (UNPROFOR),	299
United Press International (UPI),	209
University of British Columbia (UBC),	14, 17–19, 20–21
University of Michigan,	138
An Unquiet Mind (Jamison),	371
USS *Hancock,*	169, 170

V

The Valley of the Assassins and Other Persian Travels (Stark),	105

Vancouver Province,	18
Vancouver Sun,	18
Van de Stadt, E.G.,	50
The Vanishing Buddhist Kingdoms of the Himalayas (Crossette),	339
Vanity Fair (Thackeray),	398
Van Thieu, Nguyen,	160
Velvet Revolution, Czechoslovakia, 1989,	270
Viet Cong (VC),	160, 161, 166, 194
Vietnam, 1995,	325–327
Vietnamese boat people,	260–267
Vietnam War (1955–1975),	
20th anniversary of fall of Saigon,	325–326
Convoy of Tears,	162
death toll,	161
fall of Phnom Penh,	168
fall of Saigon, April, 1975,	140, 169–170, 172
Ford's evacuation order,	166–167
Spring Offensive, August 1974,	160, 162–167
Tet Offensive, 1968,	166
U.S. embassy in Saigon surrounded,	167–168
Vogt, Doug,	337, 338, 379, 395, 406
Vogue magazine,	41
Voltaire,	29
von Bismarck, Otto,	292, 292n2
von Karajan, Herbert,	40
Vosimorukian, Rupen,	148, 150

W

Wallace, Mike,	177
Wallenberg, Raoul,	208, 216, 221
The Wall Street Journal,	326, 378
Wangchuck, Jigme Singye,	334
"The War Bangladesh Can Never Forget" (Hensher),	75n1
Warhol, Andy,	170
War Measures Act (Quebec),	59

Warner, Andrea,	37n3
Warner Brothers,	44
War Stories (Bowen),	297n2, 302n4
Warwick, Ned,	295
War Without Hate (Bierman & Smith),	370, 374, 389
Washington, D.C.,	370–371
Washington, D.C., 1980,	215–219
Washington Journalism Review,	225
Watson, Ellen,	238
Watson, George,	132, 134, 135, 142–143, 238
Western University,	7, 12
Westin, David,	405
When Harry Met Sally … (movie),	217
Widnell, Katherine,	190
Widnell, Sally,	190
Wiener, Robin,	409
The Wilder Shores of Love (Blanch),	117
Wilford, Marcus,	286, 288, 304
Willey, David,	411
Wilson, Harold,	184, 185
Wingate, Orde, General,	346–348
Wolfe, Thomas,	247
Wolfowitz, Paul,	392, 393
Women's Liberation Movement,	130
Women's Wear Daily,	43
Woodruff, Bob,	406
World Bank,	198
World Economic Forum, Davos, Switzerland,	358
World Food Program (WFP),	365, 366
World Health Organization (WHO),	10, 355
World News Tonight (ABC),	301, 322–323, 331
World News Tonight with Peter Jennings (ABC News),	293n4, 327, 366, 383
World Service, British Broadcasting Corporation (BBC),	89, 132, 135, 147
Tehran office,	97, 99, 116
Wright, Robin,	197

Y

Yáari, Ehud,	232n1
Yazdanpanah, Kambiz,	178–179
Yeats, W.B.,	93, 93n7
Yom Kippur War, 1973,	118, 127–132, 300
casualties in,	131
Egyptian and Syrian retreats during,	131–132
journalists as casualties in,	131
United Nations-brokered ceasefire in October,	132
The Yom Kippur War (Rabinovich),	127n1
Yugoslav People's Army (JNA),	285
Yurt Islam (a.k.a. Cat Stevens),	154

Z

Zaire rebellion, 1977,	195–198
Zappa, Frank,	35
Zaritsky, John,	36, 294
Zenz, Katherine,	145, 146–147
Zetlin, Arnold,	76
Zia-uil-Haq, Muhammad,	79
Zim, Peter,	263
Zonis, Marvin,	102n3

CPSIA information can be obtained
at www.ICGtesting.com
Printed in the USA
LVHW021004240323
742475LV00001B/1